The Harcourt Brace Guide to

WRITING IN THE DISCIPLINES

The Harcourt Brace Guide to

WRITING IN
THE DISCIPLINES

ROBERT W. JONES
Arizona State University West

PATRICK BIZZARO
East Carolina University

CYNTHIA L. SELFE
Michigan Technological University

HARCOURT BRACE COLLEGE PUBLISHERS

Fort Worth   Philadelphia   San Diego   New York   Orlando   Austin   San Antonio
Toronto   Montreal   London   Sydney   Tokyo

PUBLISHER Christopher P. Klein
EXECUTIVE EDITOR Michael Rosenberg
PRODUCT MANAGER Ilse Wolfe West
DEVELOPMENTAL EDITOR Michell Phifer
PROJECT EDITOR Dee W. Salisbury
PRODUCTION MANAGER Annette Dudley Wiggins
ART DIRECTOR Brian Salisbury

Cover photography by Karl Thibodeaux

ISBN: 0-15-501991-0

Library of Congress Catalog Card Number: 96-75658

Harcourt Brace & Company may provide complimentary instructional aids and supplements or supplement packages to those adopters qualified under our adoption policy. Please contact your sales representative for more information. If as an adopter or potential user you receive supplements you do not need, please return them to your sales representative or send them to: Attn: Returns Department, Troy Warehouse, 465 South Lincoln Drive, Troy, MO 63379.

Address for Editorial Correspondence: Harcourt Brace College Publishers, 301 Commerce Street, Suite 3700, Fort Worth, TX 76102.

Address for Orders: Harcourt Brace & Company, 6277 Sea Harbor Drive, Orlando, FL 32887-6777; 1-800-782-4479.

(Copyright acknowledgments follow the Appendix and constitute a continuation of this copyright page.)

Printed in the United States of America

6 7 8 9 0 1 2 3 4 5   039   10 9 8 7 6 5 4 3 2 1

TO THE INSTRUCTOR

Although *The Harcourt Brace Guide to Writing in the Disciplines* is not the first textbook to advertise itself as a guide to writing in the disciplines, we believe that its publication signals the beginning of a new generation of writing texts. Some textbooks offer essays from a variety of academic fields, while others provide readings arranged by theme (most often essays by academics or documents by professional writers) and then follow those professional essays with questions or writing assignments primarily confined to those essays. *The Harcourt Brace Guide to Writing in the Disciplines* uses the writing, reading, and research of students and professionals to prepare students for writing in college and beyond. It is, we think, the first textbook to offer both students and instructors a comprehensive and accessible approach to writing in the disciplines.

Purpose of the Book

The purpose of the textbook is three-fold:

- To introduce students to the critical acts of writing, reading, and researching and to the connections among these three acts;
- To explore the forms, functions, and implications of writing in disciplinary cultures and to observe the shared characteristics and differences among writing in various disciplines; and
- To prepare students to write in various disciplines through writing in a variety of formats, to a variety of audiences, and for a variety of purposes.

Organization and Content

The Harcourt Brace Guide to Writing in the Disciplines is innovative in many important ways, providing a solid foundation for all composition students. The two major parts of the book are organized so that teachers, program directors, and departmental committees can adapt it to suit the specific needs of individual courses or sequences of courses. The first four chapters focus on writing, reading, and researching in the disciplines and on the relationship of computers to composing. The remaining seven chapters examine writing in academic areas that interest the majority of today's students.

Connecting Writing, Reading, and Researching

Chapters One through Three provide essential instruction in writing, reading, and researching and serve as a foundation for the more sophisticated tasks in later chapters where discipline-specific writing is introduced, explored, and practiced. These chapters treat writing, reading, and researching as acts related to learning, communicating, and building a knowledge base in any subject area, thus extending the application of these critical acts beyond the composition classroom. Presenting them as crucial features of disciplinary cultures situates these acts within the students' majors, prepares for material presented in Chapters Five through Eleven, and, thus, motivates students to value the acts.

Chapter Four, "Written Communication and Computer Technology," provides a foundation for using computers in the writing process, for producing written documents, and for understanding key issues related to informational technologies. This chapter probes such critically related questions as privacy and surveillance, access, and reading and writing problems.

Chapters Five through Eleven introduce students to writing in seven disciplinary areas through readings and writings from undergraduate courses and from a range of professionals in those disciplines. These seven chapters dramatically distinguish this text from other writing in the disciplines texts by following up on the exploration of writing and disciplinary culture discussed in Chapters One through Three and presenting writing as a cultural act.

Chapters Five through Seven focus on the traditional areas of instruction in research writing classes—the humanities, social sciences, and natural sciences. Chapters Eight through Eleven consider writing from mathematics and informational technology programs, business and management, health sciences, and engineering. These disciplines are rarely treated in first-year writing textbooks, yet they enroll almost 50 percent of all undergraduate students. These chapters do not present writing as merely a communication medium which transmits information, but rather they present writing as critical to learning in the disciplines thus enabling students to enter their chosen fields as thoroughly prepared professionals.

Distinguishing Features

The distinguishing features of this textbook are as follows:

- Writing is presented as both a process within the larger cognitive structure and as a medium of learning and communicating framed by disciplinary boundaries.
- Paired and small group assignments promote the benefits and values of collaborative writing.
- Writing assignments range from annotating reading and research, to exploratory notebook and journal entries, to formal research essays and report projects.
- Writing and reading are treated as symbiotic acts. Students are taught to analyze cues from various kinds of texts and then to take this knowledge into their own writing assignments as they learn how to anticipate readers' needs.
- Researching is established as an active process that engages students with various texts and sources. Building on a core of common research skills,

Chapter Three establishes that research skills differ from one discipline to another, thus preparing the student for materials presented in Chapters Five through Eleven.

- Writing-with-computers exercises are included in every chapter; and guides to electronic citation, sources for Universal Resource Locators (URLs), and home page examples provide students with up-to-date information on electronic sources.
- Discipline-specific chapters span from humanities to engineering, with extensive attention paid to all disciplines.
- Discipline-specific chapters include both brief and extended writing assignments, which promote the benefits and values of the writing process and prepare students for major assignments in their disciplines.
- Discipline-specific adaptations of advance-level assignments and examples of workplace writing inform students on such issues as purpose, audience, form, style, and interplay of written and visual language.
- Discipline-specific assignments encourage students from many majors to become contributors during the course.
- The Appendix provides guides to documenting in American Psychological Association (APA), Chicago Manual of Style (CMS), Council of Biological Editors (CBE), and Modern Language Association (MLA) styles.

Acknowledgments

While the project which culminates in the publication of *The Harcourt Brace Guide to Writing in the Disciplines* began less than three years ago, the origin of this book stems from the late 1970s when we began developing writing in the disciplines programs at our respective universities. The commitment each of us felt then to the initial principles of the writing across the curriculum movement and feel today as writing in the disciplines becomes a critical part of American education is unwavering. Our professional and personal lives have been enriched by hundreds of colleagues from our own institutions and from dozens of schools across the country and abroad. Together we have maintained a belief that writing is a crucial part of education in every discipline. Although working with so many colleagues has sustained us over the years, acknowledging all of them in this small space is impossible. We regret that the brief list that follows leaves out some whom we regard as contributing to this book.

First, we would like to thank the following reviewers for their careful, honest, and insightful criticism. During the several stages of the project, their voices have helped determine the final shape and scope of *The Harcourt Brace Guide to Writing in the Disciplines*: Paige Byam, Northern Kentucky University; Allene Cooper, Boise State University; Bill Gholson, Southern Oregon State College; Doug Hesse, Illinois State University; Keith Hjortshoj, Cornell University; Adriane LaPointe, Troy State University; Jack Miller, Normandale Community College; Joan Mullin, University of Toledo; Richard Profozich, Prince George's Community College; and Sam Watson, University of North Carolina–Charlotte.

Next, we wish to thank the many colleagues at Arizona State University West, East Carolina University, and Michigan Technological University whose commitment to integrating writing into their own courses and divisions and whose work with us in developing writing in the disciplines programs have been central to any success we have enjoyed. Though some of these colleagues have moved on to other schools, we want to identify them here with the university where we worked with them—from Arizona State University West: Candace Bredbenner, Dorothy Broaddus, Joseph Comprone, Leslie Di Mare, John Greenhut, Roger Hutt, Ali Malekzadeh, Carol Mueller, Afsaneh Nahavandi, Ramsey Eric Ramsey, Jonathan Silberman, Gordon Schuett, David Schwalm, and Sheldon Zola; from East Carolina University: Jo Allen, Bob Christian, Resa Crane, Collett Dilworth, Frank Farmer, James Kirkland, Nancy Mayberry, Bob Morrison, Dorothy Muller, Rita Reaves, and David White; and from Michigan Technological University: Linda Belot, Ted Bornhorst, Alan Brokaw, Richard Brown, Peck Cho, Randall Freisinger, Toby Fulwiler, Ron Gratz, Neal Hutzler, David Nelson, and the late Bruce Peterson.

Also, we wish to acknowledge colleagues at high schools, colleges, universities, and companies who have influenced our thinking about writing in the disciplines and writing in the workplace. This group includes Charles Bazerman, Susan Bizzaro, Carolyn Cooke, Joan Francioni, Don Gallehr, Tom Hackley, Cindy Hagen, Carol Holder, Tom Knighton, Wilkie Leith, Ted LeRud, Richard Millman, Dick Nowland, Mike Sherdl, Kathy Simpson, Chris Thaiss, Art Young, Steven Youra, Sam Watson, and Angela Williams.

To the countless faculty at places where we have discussed writing in the disciplines, we extend our appreciation; we have learned from each opportunity they afforded us. And to the following colleagues and students who contributed either their work or their advice, in some cases both, and who made the writing of this book much easier than it might have been otherwise, we thank Susan Angelo, Carol Brown, Earnest Boyce, Susan Capps, Jim Curtis, Carrie Deglow, Kayse Fields, Maria Greene, Dan Hopper, Richard Hauser, David Johnson, Vanessa Jones, Brian Kincaid, Tim Mayberry, Christine McGuinness, Tamara Palomino, Jan Philips, Wendy Rountree, Brian Taylor, Nancy Shires, Ron Snell, Gilbert Stevenson, Patrice Stewart, Rob Stryker, Bari Vinson, and James Wilde. Without the inspiration of these students and teachers, there would be no reason to write this book.

We wish also to acknowledge those who assisted us at various places in the process of completing this book; they include Betty Campbell, Robin Mc–Kinnon-Wilkins, Georgia Tanner, Amy Willoughby, and Kristin White. Special thanks go to Lillian Chappelle who is largely responsible for helping us meet deadlines as well as we did and to Diane Gruber whose intelligent critiques, boundless energy, and good humor did, in fact, allow us to finish this book.

Naturally, we want to thank those administrators and staff who supported writing in the disciplines at our universities. Among those to whom we owe a debt are the late Bertie Fearing, Donald Palumbo, Pat Spakes, Keats Sparrow, Dale Stein, and Michael Wirt.

Finally, we thank the editors at Harcourt Brace College Publishers for their belief in the project and for their support over the time it took to finish it. Particularly, we thank Michael Rosenberg, Executive Editor for English, and Michell Phifer, our Developmental Editor, for teaching us about the world of publishing.

Robert W. Jones
Patrick Bizzaro
Cynthia L. Selfe

TO THE STUDENT

The Importance of Writing in College and beyond

One question often asked by students in a composition class is, "How will a writing class prepare me for what I'll do when I graduate?" Since less than 10 percent of current college graduates plan careers as writers or as English teachers, some think the answer is, "Not very well." However, college graduates in all fields who face complex thinking assignments and critical communication tasks know that sound writing and reading skills form the basis of success in almost every profession. We believe that the approach to writing and learning offered in *The Harcourt Brace Guide to Writing in the Disciplines* can contribute significantly to your success both in college and after graduation.

Guiding Principles of *The Harcourt Brace Guide to Writing in the Disciplines*

Because we believe that your success as a writer will be affected by how well you understand the importance of writing in various disciplines, the types of writing valued in the disciplines, and the relationship among writing, learning, and communication in various disciplines, we have organized the book around several key principles:

- To understand the relationship between the cultural values held by disciplines and writing in those disciplines;
- To view writing and learning as processes that increase your potential to create, respond to, and manage critical thinking and writing assignments in all disciplines;
- To use writing as a means of learning subjects and of communicating what you have learned; and
- To connect the writing you will do as a college student to the writing you will do as a college graduate who will enter a profession.

Throughout the book we integrate writing assignments which benefit from these connections and which occur within specific disciplines. We believe you will write better after using this textbook because you will better understand the purposes and requirements of your writing assignments.

Organization of the Book
This textbook is divided into two fundamental sections. Chapters One through Four explore writing, reading, researching, written communication, and computer technology. In these chapters you will read about and practice the critical basics that prepare you for Chapters Five through Eleven—the discipline-

specific chapters in the second section. While the subject matter of the early chapters comprises an important part of many writing texts, we explore those subjects as they relate to a wide variety of disciplines, not from just the narrow range of disciplines often represented in writing texts. When you reach Chapters Five through Eleven, the discipline-specific chapters, you are prepared to examine and practice writing in seven specific areas: humanities, social sciences, natural sciences, mathematics and informational technologies, business and management, health sciences, and engineering and technology programs.

Discipline-specific Assignments

Many of the writing assignments in the discipline-specific chapters are unusual in first-year composition classes. Rather than using assignments from previous composition classes, we drew assignments from both lower division and advanced courses from many majors. In fact, most assignments are recommended by professors from the discipline discussed in that chapter. Some assignments are given here exactly as they were in the undergraduate classes from across the disciplines, while some have been modified to make them accessible for writers and who have not taken advanced courses. In either case, the assignments represent the breadth of assignments, both in form and in intellectual task, valued by diverse disciplines. Finally, to connect the writing and learning you do as a college student to the careers you may enter after graduation, we have included many examples of writing authored by college graduates from a variety of professions.

Writing as a Skill, Writing as Learning

We believe that writing courses are among the most important and valuable courses you take in college. Because writing is an activity that demands inquisitiveness, discipline, reflection, general understanding, and specific knowledge, it engages you in a rich variety of interesting and rigorous ways. We hope this book will prepare you to apply the skills and knowledge you gain as a writer to almost every area of your education and your chosen profession. Ultimately, we hope this book proves a valuable part of your educational experience and paves the way for the learning you will do throughout your lifetime.

CONTENTS

To the Instructor   v
To the Student   x

CHAPTER ONE Writing in the Disciplines   1

Guiding Assumptions for Writing in the Disciplines   2
The Cultural Values of Disciplines and Writing in the Disciplines: An
  Overview   3
The Value of Writing after College   5
A Report Is Not a Report Is Not a Report   5
Defining Disciplinary Culture: Relating Culture and Writing   6
Writing as a Process: An Overview   6
Critical Thinking and Writing in the Disciplines   10
Applying the Writing Process to Writing in the Disciplines   15
The Fundamentals of the Writing Process   16
    Planning   17
    From Planning to Drafting: Exploratory Writing to Formal Writing   22
    Drafting: An Overview   24
A Major Writing Assignment and the Process of Writing   25
    Project Overview   25
    Project Requirements   25
    Step by Step: Connecting the Parts of the Project   26
    Guides to Revision   31
    Guides to Editing   31
    Universal Guiding Question   32
    Moving Forward   32

CHAPTER TWO Reading in the Disciplines   39

Reading in the Disciplines: An Overview   40
Reading with a Purpose   42
Understanding What You Read   45
    Skimming   48
    Annotating for Understanding and Recall   56
Reading Critically: Analyzing, Evaluating, and Responding   59
    Analyzing a Text   59
    Evaluating a Text   67
    Responding to a Text   69

CHAPTER THREE Researching in the Disciplines   81

Researching in College: An Overview   83
    Skills Required to Perform Research in the Humanities   83
    Skills Required to Perform Research in the Social Sciences   85
    Skills Required to Perform Research in the Natural Sciences   87

Research in the Disciplines: Using the Library   89
Using the Reference Area   89
Locating Books and Articles Using Computers   91
Locating Articles in Serials   92
Using Other Technologies   93
Research in the Humanities   94
Appropriate Evidence in the Humanities   94
Questions Asked in the Humanities   96
Research in the Social Sciences   101
Appropriate Evidence in the Social Sciences   103
Questions Asked in the Social Sciences   105
Research in the Natural Sciences   109
Appropriate Evidence in the Natural Sciences   111
Questions Asked in the Natural Sciences   112
Universal Resource Locators (URLs)   116
Cautions and Reminders about Electronic Material on the
World Wide Web   116
URLs for Researching in the Disciplines   117

CHAPTER FOUR   Written Communication and Computer
Technology   119

Fluency, Organization, Invention, and Revision Aids   121
Support for Collaboration and Group Exchanges   121
Information and Research Aids   123
Problems and Challenges Associated with Computers   124
Flaming   124
Surveillance   125
Writing and Reading   126
Access and Distribution   128
Some Computer-Supported Writers' Tools   129
Word-Processing Packages   129
Hypertext and Hypermedia Environments for Writing and Composing   130
E-Mail, Listservs, Bulletin Boards, and Newsgroups   132
Synchronous Conferencing Software   133
Wide Area Information Service (WAIS), Gopher, and Mosaic   135
The World Wide Web   136
URLs for Written Communication and Computer Technology   139

CHAPTER FIVE   Writing in the Humanities   141

Reflective and Interpretive Writing   142
Responsibilities of Humanists   144
Importance of Communications to the Humanist   146
Writing in the Undergraduate Humanities   149
Planning   149
Preparing to Draft   151

Moving from Exploratory Writing to Finished Drafts   152
Writing a Reflective and Reconstructive Essay   154
Writing a Critical Interpretation Essay   162
URLs for the Humanities   179

CHAPTER SIX   Writing in the Social Sciences   181

Inquiring in the Social Sciences: Three Methods   182
Responsibilities of Social Scientists   185
Importance of Communications to the Social Scientist   188
Writing in the Undergraduate Social Sciences   188
Writing a Library Research Report   188
Writing a Personal Observation Report   195
Writing an Application of Theory Report   199
URLs for the Social Sciences   212

CHAPTER SEVEN   Writing in the Natural Sciences   213

Divisions between the Humanities and the Sciences   214
Responsibilities of Natural Scientists   215
Importance of Communications to the Natural Scientist   217
Connecting Writing in Liberal Arts and Social Sciences to Writing in the
Natural Sciences   219
The Writing of a Professional Scientist   219
Writing in the Community   220
Writing to Expert Audiences   222
Formatting Scientific Writing   229
Writing in the Workplace   232
Writing in the Undergraduate Natural Sciences   235
Laboratory Summary Assignment   236
Laboratory Notebooks   238
The Microtheme   240
The Journal Critique Paper   242
The Laboratory Report   249
URLs for the Natural Sciences   255

CHAPTER EIGHT   Writing in Mathematics and Information
Technology   257

Responsibilities of Mathematicians and Information Technologists   258
Importance of Communications to the Mathematician and Information
Technology Professional   261
Writing in Undergraduate Mathematics and Information Technology
Programs   263
Writing in Mathematics Courses   264
Writing in Information Technology Programs   270

Writing in Computer Science and the Decision Sciences   272
   Writing in Computer Science   273
   Writing in Decision Sciences   280
URLs for Mathematics and Information Technology   295

CHAPTER NINE   Writing in Business and
Management   297

Responsibilities of Business and Management Professionals   298
Individual and Collaborative Writing   300
Importance of Communications to the Business and Management
   Professional   305
   Writing Memorandums and E-Mail   305
   Writing Letters   313
   Writing Informal and Formal Reports   321
URLs for Business and Management   340

CHAPTER TEN   Writing in the Health Sciences   343

Responsibilities of Health Sciences Professionals   345
Importance of Communications to the Health Sciences Professional   355
Writing in the Undergraduate Health Sciences   356
   Review of Current Literature   357
   Writing an Observational Analysis   366
   Writing about Ethical Issues   370
URLs for the Health Sciences   381

CHAPTER ELEVEN   Writing in Engineering and
Technology   383

Responsibilities of Engineers and Technical Professionals   384
Importance of Communications to the Engineering and Technical
   Professional   385
Writing from the Professional's Viewpoint   387
Writing in Undergraduate Technical Curricula and Preparing to Write in
   Engineering and Technology   388
   The Diversity of Engineering Writing   391
   The Memo: A Critical Writing Activity   395
   The Formal Engineering Report   400
URLs for Engineering and Technology   420

APPENDIX   A Brief Guide to Documentation Style   421

Credits   435
Index   439

CHAPTER ONE

Writing in the Disciplines

Guiding Assumptions for Writing in the Disciplines

The Cultural Values of Disciplines and Writing in the Disciplines: An Overview

The Value of Writing after College

A Report Is Not a Report Is Not a Report

Defining Disciplinary Culture: Relating Culture and Writing

Writing as a Process: An Overview

Critical Thinking and Writing in the Disciplines

Applying the Writing Process to Writing in the Disciplines

The Fundamentals of the Writing Process

A Major Writing Assignment and the Process of Writing

The first three chapters of *The Harcourt Brace Guide to Writing in the Disciplines* will provide you with an overview of strategies and techniques you can use as you approach and fulfill writing assignments in disciplines throughout your college career. As you work with the material in these introductory chapters on writing, reading, and researching, you will learn that each of these activities is intricately connected to the others and that gaining skills in each will support the skills needed to become skillful in the others. You should also keep in mind that these introductory chapters form a continuum, so that information you gain and exercises you do will help you build a broad platform from which to write, read, and conduct research in various disciplines. The assignments and material in the chapters are designed to guide you through this progression.

In this first chapter, we will introduce four major ideas which will be elaborated on in succeeding chapters.

1. understanding the relationship between the **cultural values held by disciplines** and the **writing** in those disciplines
2. viewing writing and learning as **processes** which increase your potential to create, respond to, and manage critical thinking and writing assignments throughout the disciplines
3. using writing as a means of both **learning** subjects and **communicating** what you have learned.
4. connecting the writing you do as **college students** to the writing you will do as **college graduates** who enter professions from various academic majors.

The first two ideas form the basic structure of the chapter, while the third and fourth are integrated throughout the chapter.

So that you have a sound idea of our approach to writing in the disciplines, we offer the following set of assumptions.

Guiding Assumptions for Writing in the Disciplines

- Writing is inseparable from learning.
- Writing is both a skill which can be acquired and practiced and an important means of communicating information, understanding, and knowledge.
- Writers and communities of writers create meaning.
- College-educated people write for a variety of purposes and to a variety of audiences.

We ask not that you accept these assumptions without question, rather we ask that you keep them in mind as you work through this book. We shall try to demonstrate that writing is a manageable process, as well as a critical part of college work and of the professional lives of college graduates. Further, we hope to show that writing is affected significantly by various social, political, and professional forces and that competent writers understand and respond to those forces. In other words, we hope to demonstrate that developing sound writing skills occurs best within a specific context and that acquiring these skills will be a valuable asset for you both during and after college. At all times, however, we encourage you to be critical of these assumptions and to engage your teacher and peers in constructive debate about these assumptions.

Having established a foundation for the subject matter and the assumptions employed in the book, let us now consider our first purpose, the cultural values of disciplines and their relationship to writing in the disciplines.

The Cultural Values of Disciplines and Writing in the Disciplines: An Overview

One key to understanding groups of people, business and government organizations, and, yes, colleges, is to understand the cultural traits of the people who constitute those groups. For example, while Americans of Italian, French, African, English, and Chinese descent share certain values, each group may be characterized by unique cultural traits. Thus, understanding those specific traits helps us understand the people within the group. Additionally, such understanding helps us see that a culture reflects the values of the group. For example, if we know that a specific group highly values close contact between grandparents and grandchildren, we better understand why members of that group might tend to live in the same community rather than dispersing over a wide area.

We believe very strongly that academic institutions are "cultures" and that understanding the types of thinking and writing practiced in various disciplines enables us to better understand the "culture" of those disciplines and, thus, what those disciplines value. For example, most mathematics departments in American colleges offer a course in the history of mathematics. While those of us who will never take advanced mathematics courses might not understand why anyone would take such a course, mathematicians understand clearly that knowing the history of mathematics provides valuable context and background for the work they do. We will contend that increasing your understanding of how disciplines function and what they value will better enable you to succeed in any discipline, for you will understand much more than the surface-level requirements of a class. You will, in fact, understand the class in a different way, a deeper way, for you will understand why the discipline values certain approaches to learning, strategies for learning, and formats for presenting information and knowledge.

As we work through the next few pages, think about your definition of the term *culture*. Begin by responding to the following exercises.

Exercises

1. Write out your definition of the term *culture*. You might define by listing characteristics or providing brief examples. As you think about the definition, note how your definition is informed by personal experience and

knowledge gained in courses you have taken in various disciplines. We will ask that you use your response a bit later; for now, keep in mind your personal definition as we consider the material in the next section.

2. Take a few minutes to record your initial impressions about our claim that understanding the culture of a discipline will help you understand better how to write in that discipline. Does what we have presented seem plausible to you? That is, do you believe, for example, that knowing what scientists value and the ways in which they think about science will help you understand what roles writing plays in science?

Let's now test our belief about writing and disciplinary culture by looking at some typical writing assignments. Consider the following list of writing tasks:

summaries	proposals
memos	essay tests
critiques	letters
reports	abstracts
classifications	analyses

You may have been introduced to some of these assignments in high school classes or perhaps as a job requirement. For example, you may have written essay answers in a history class; you may have used classifications in a biology class; or you may have written a summary for a government class. However, you may have had little or no experience writing memos, abstracts, and proposals. If you are familiar with some of these types, often called *formats,* you will know that some formats are more likely to be assigned in certain disciplines than in others. The memo is more frequently assigned in business and management classes than it is in either science or humanities classes. Both science and engineering instructors often assign laboratory reports, whereas art instructors almost never ask for such writing. Do these choices tell us anything about the values of these disciplines? Why does the scientist prefer that laboratory findings be put in a report format which, as you will see in later chapters, often demands specific parts and a specific order of presentation? Why would a literature professor ask that students write essay answers and persuasive papers, while seldom, if ever, asking for a memo on a student's response to a short story? In subsequent chapters, you will cover the types of writing listed above, especially as they are used in specific disciplines. Take a few minutes now to consider the following exercises.

Exercises

1. Discuss with a partner the following and then write a shared response to the question: Discuss the various types of writing you have done in different

disciplines. You might consider English, history, biology, or mathematics, for example. Try for a variety of courses. What characterizes the writing assigned in these classes and what do the formats and types of writing suggest to you about the values of those disciplines?

2. Divide the class into teams of writers, with each team being responsible for writing a consensus statement about the writing and the suggested values of a specific discipline. You should have at least three members per team and not more than five. Each group should then present its statement to the class.

The Value of Writing after College

The preceding exercises ask that you consider the differences and similarities in writing among disciplines. By engaging in such activities, you will inform yourself about the preferences of disciplines and prepare yourself to complete assignments in college as well as ready yourself for the writing you will do beyond college. Over the past twenty years, studies demonstrate very clearly that writing is a valued skill for people in many fields and at various levels.

As you might expect, your college professors—from virtually all disciplines—devote considerable time to writing. In fact, most colleges nowadays require that professors publish their scholarship and research in journals which are read by the members of specific academic disciplines. What you may not realize is that college graduates who enter such areas as accounting, manufacturing, banking, nursing, and marketing all spend about 20% of their time writing. In other words, almost all occupations place a high value on competent written, as well as oral, communication. Even though you may not have chosen a major and even though many of you will change majors (perhaps more than once) before you graduate, gaining a wide range of writing skills can assist you no matter what field you enter. Let's consider a critical factor in understanding the place of writing in various disciplines.

A Report Is Not a Report Is Not a Report

Many students believe that figuring out what the teacher wants on a writing assignment is the key to getting a good grade. Others might argue that if you write well enough, you can make a good grade on any assignment, regardless of what the professor wants. Let's test this argument by citing an example from the list of assignments on page 4.

Consider the following uses of the word *report:*

1. From a high school English class: "Write a book *report* on Aldous Huxley's novel *Brave New World.*"
2. From a Civil Engineering class: "Your laboratory *report* on stress capacity of the tested aggregate mixtures is due on Wednesday."

3. From a Business class: "Your group's final *report* on research should follow the guidelines provided in Persing's *Business Communication Dynamics.*"

Would you imagine that the English and engineering professors use *report* in the same way? Would their expectations be the same if they assigned a report in their classes?

In an exercise earlier in the chapter, you discussed and wrote about differences among writing in the various disciplines. Most of you would probably agree that because engineering relies heavily on mathematics and science to solve problems, the professor will expect students to submit papers which bear some resemblance to science reports. If you are taking a science course now or have taken one recently, you know that science laboratory reports have required sections on methods, materials, and conclusions. Engineering requires similar sections but often includes others entitled "Executive Summary," "Recommendations," and "Equipment." These latter sections are similar to ones included in many business reports. Could we suppose, then, that engineering is a profession based on science and mathematics but which conducts itself in a "businesslike" way? Regardless of what your response to that question may be, you will probably agree that an English literature professor will not require the same type of reports as an engineering professor. In Chapters Five through Eleven we shall cover representative assignments from many disciplines and explore and practice the forms of writing preferred in those fields.

To summarize this section, we contend that professors from different disciplines will define the term "report" in very different ways. In such technically based majors as engineering, "report" connotes a document containing specific sections arranged in a specific order and accompanied by appropriate uses of charts, tables, graphs, and drawings. In the field of literature, a book report might follow a specific format but probably would not include charts, graphs, and tables. These different expectations tell us a great deal about the communications values of these disciplines.

Defining Disciplinary Culture: Relating Culture and Writing

In an earlier exercise, we asked that you write your own definition of culture and keep it in mind as we went through this chapter. Let us offer the following definition of culture and compare the two. We may define a culture as *a group or organization which shares attitudes, goals, customs, and practices.* Using that definition, the academic disciplines in which you will enroll are, in fact, *subcultures* within a culture. While all professors function within the academic culture of a college or university, they also operate within very carefully established subcultures. They share a generally agreed upon body of knowledge, operate according to established principles in their research, and use specialized languages and forms of communication. Although they share certain cultural assumptions, a marketing professor and a professor of mechanical engineering are members of very different subcultures. While an engineering professor's work and research are based very much on using mathematics and science to understand and solve problems, a marketing professor's work and research explore consumer demand for products and strategies for placing products before the public.

For all their dramatic differences, however, both professors rely on written language to convey information and to construct complex explanations. In fact, while we might say that people in different disciplines "see" the world differently, we might also say that they express that vision through the specialized use of a common medium—language. Yet, as our world becomes increasingly more complex and specialized, the tendency for disciplines to develop these highly specialized subcultures increases. An important feature of virtually all subcultures is that specialized languages often separate them from other parts of the larger culture. Thus, in academic disciplines and in professions, we run the danger of being separated from others by our highly specialized languages. The result is, of course, that we run the risk of being able to communicate with only those inside our discipline. As educated people, one of our tasks should be to find ways of communicating with those inside and outside our field. While it is important for us to develop expertise within our chosen field, it is also critical that we possess the ability to function within organizations comprised of persons from a broad range of fields and from diverse cultural groups.

Of what importance is this to you as a writer? Think about the range of disciplines within which you will take courses, then think of the different types of writing you will be assigned. Now, think about the kind of work you will do as a college graduate. Let's say that you are a business major, focusing on accounting. You will do much of your work with other accountants with whom you share values—including a common specialized language. However, your work may very likely require you to interact with buyers, salespeople, perhaps even manufacturing engineers—all from within your own company. And most likely you will also communicate with customers, media representatives, and employees of other companies, many of whom will know considerably less than you do about accounting. Therefore, developing a range of writing skills in order to meet these situations would certainly be an advantage. For example, accountants often write proposals to prospective clients and communicate regularly with current ones, all of whom know less accounting than the person they hire to look after their financial records. As a writer, you might consider these two goals:

1. acquiring the skills to *communicate with those within your discipline* by using the particular forms and languages of that discipline;
2. learning to *communicate with those diverse audiences outside your discipline* by adapting what you know to the *needs of the audience* and their relationship to you and the group you represent.

Further, in order to become a skillful writer, one who understands writing tasks and who can adapt to a broad range of writing experiences, it is important to know two points:

1. Most academic and professional writing emphasizes such characteristics as sound organization, appropriate diction, and coherent structure. Writing which is intended to present information clearly, argue a point effectively, or provide an in-depth analysis must possess these traits.

2. However, college graduates write for a variety of audiences and use a variety of forms—from brief notes to project reports which may reach hundreds of pages. Knowing your audience and the culture from which the audience comes are crucial to writing successfully; developing a repertoire of forms and styles will enable you to write for many audiences and purposes.

Exercises

1. Select a topic of interest to you and think of how you would explain that interest to the following audiences: yourself and a trusted friend—perhaps a relative, a former teacher, a coach, a former supervisor. Write a brief statement exploring that interest. After you've written the statement, examine it to determine the following: the assumptions behind your statement (Did you reveal the same points and concerns in both statements?); the style of the writing (Is one more formal than the other?).

2. Divide the class into groups of four to five to discuss the following point, and then write a consensus paragraph summarizing your discussion: Specialized languages often separate subcultures from the larger culture. Select a contemporary subculture which has a specialized language; discuss that language—for example, its vocabulary, how it reflects social relationships in the subculture. You might also consider whether features of the language have migrated into the larger culture's language.

3. *If you have access to a stand-alone computer,* create a word-processing file and write exercise two by yourself on the computer. *If you have access to e-mail,* write your statements as e-mail messages and actually send them— one to a close friend and one to a highly regarded acquaintance. Ask the people to respond.

4. If some people in your writing group or class write their messages off-line and some write their statements on-line, compare the tone used in each. Does e-mail have its own distinctive style? Tone? Conventions? Make a list of these and discuss them with your class.

Writing as a Process: An Overview

This section will introduce specific aspects of writing as a process and provide an overview of the basic writing principles and techniques which will be covered in detail in Chapters Five through Eleven. Remember, a central tenet of this book is that *learning writing strategies and techniques is best done within a discipline-specific context.* Also, remember that the next two chapters on reading and researching will provide interesting and valuable connections to your work on the processes of writing and that you should look for ways in which process aids you in learning the material of any course.

Consider the following scheme, which draws a basic connection between the processes of reading and writing.

The Reading Process	The Writing Process
Before reading	Prewriting
During reading	Writing
After reading	Revising and editing

As we proceed in our work on writing in the disciplines, we will develop these broad classifications. While this comparison between reading and writing processes does not take into account the many differences among disciplines nor the subtle differences which exist between reading and writing, it does provide a valuable starting place from which to approach writing assignments in all disciplines. In this section, we offer three reasons why we believe you will benefit from practicing writing as a process.

- First, using a process enables writers to manage their work. Too often, beginning writers believe that writing well depends on receiving an inspiration from some hidden source. The result of such thinking frequently leaves them feeling very much like the following character from a "Shoe" cartoon:

If we wait for the writing to "flow" onto the page, most us will, indeed, be waiting a long time, if that point ever arrives. Thinking of writing as a process which is comprised of stages helps students to manage writing assignments and enables professionals to complete writing tasks. If you think of writing as 95% perspiration and 5% inspiration, you will be much more likely to succeed.

- Second, thinking of writing as a process can help make you a more critical thinker, as well as a more effective writer in your college courses. Professors across the disciplines expect their students to demonstrate a sound understanding of the course material. For example, college teachers will expect you to acquire not just the facts associated with the material, but also to understand the concepts related to the material. Chemistry professors will insist that in addition to being able to state the gas laws, you be able to apply those laws to solving problems and provide examples of how those laws affect the environment in which they function. In an anthropology class studying Samoans, the professor would expect you to know that telecommunications technology has increased the population's access to Western ideas, but that professor would also expect you to evaluate the influence of those ideas on institutions, family structures, and individuals and to speculate on the continued effects of technology. In short, professors in all disciplines expect more than simply memorizing the material in their courses. They expect you to work with that material, to use different approaches, techniques, and strategies to form opinions, arguments, and analysis.

- Third, understanding that reading, writing, and thinking are processes that can be learned and managed will prove vital to your chances for success well beyond your college years, for they form the substance of activities engaged in by college-educated people. In fact, we might argue that the most important accomplishment of your college career will be learning how to learn, for most professionals now understand that learning and working form a lifelong partnership. Another way of thinking about this issue is to understand that change is constant and that those equipped to change and adjust will be much better suited to the future than those who believe that they have learned all they will ever need to know while in college. A second implication here is that writing on the job is often a *collaborative* endeavor which depends on process to work effectively. In later chapters you will find numerous examples of collaborative writing assignments; to prepare you for those discipline-specific activities, we integrate short collaborative exercises throughout the book. We also include collaborative activities because we believe that they play an important part in the culture of university life.

Critical Thinking and Writing in the Disciplines

One useful way of approaching any writing task is to understand the thinking required to fulfill the task. Study the following two writing assignments, for example, and complete the exercises devoted to them.

1. In an introductory business class you are asked to summarize the section on the rise of multinational corporations.
2. In the same class, you are asked to choose one of the two economic theories and state why it is the most reasonable solution to current international financial problems.

Briefly respond to the following: Which of these two assignments would you find the most difficult? What kind of thinking must you do in order to complete the first assignment? What about the second? Describe how you would fulfill each assignment. After everyone has completed the exercise, use the individual responses as the basis for a class listing on each point. Were there frequently mentioned opinions, preferences, strategies, and techniques? If so, you might try to form a consensus response while remembering that there are many effective problem-solving techniques and methods.

On a very basic level, the previous exercise addresses one of the central concerns of today's educators, as well as employers of high-school and college graduates: Students and employees often have difficulty effectively responding to requests that they summarize, argue, analyze, synthesize, and evaluate—intellectual tasks sometimes referred to as critical thinking tasks. These difficulties are especially present in writing assigned on the college level. One of the four purposes of this chapter is to prepare you to view writing and learning as processes which increase your potential to create, respond to, and manage critical thinking and writing assignments throughout the disciplines. We believe that these critical thinking and writing skills can be taught and that most students will respond best if the skills are tied to discipline-specific subject matter, as they will be in Chapters Five through Eleven.

Following is an adaptation of a scheme proposed by Benjamin Bloom, an educational psychologist, which offers a model for understanding thinking, from the least complex to most complex level. There are other schemes which provide models of the thinking process, and we encourage you to consult other sources for different perspectives. We have chosen this model because it is a generally accepted explanation for the thinking process and because the terms Bloom uses are ones frequently used to describe writing assignments throughout the disciplines.

LOWEST LEVEL
Basic Knowledge: Learning specific facts, theorems, theories; having information
Comprehension: Showing understanding of basic knowledge
Application: Using previously gained information in a new situation
Analysis: Classifying or breaking materials into components and recognizing the principle that organizes the system
Synthesis: Putting something together from disparate pieces
Evaluation: Creating standards of judgment and examining issues, problems, etc.
HIGHEST LEVEL

TABLE 1.1	Teaching/Learning/Writing Objectives	

COGNITIVE AREA	INTELLECTUAL ACTIVITY	SAMPLE WRITING TASK
Knowledge	Having information, remembering	List, define, tell: who, what, where.
Understanding	Translating, demonstrating what something means	Put this in your own words.
Application	Using previously learned information in a new situation	Use this rule to solve this problem.
Analysis	Breaking down problem into components	Describe the parts. Explain what you find.
Synthesis	Putting something together from disparate pieces	Explain how these components fit together. Account for unexpected results.
Evaluation	Judging, weighing, evaluating	Argue which method is better. Assess x in terms of y.

SOURCE: Bloom, B. S., et al., *Taxonomy of Educational Objectives: Cognitive Domain,* Adapted by Steven Youra. New York: David McKay, 1956. From R. Smith, "Two Ways of Approaching Cognitive and Ethical Development." Unpub. ms., 1991.

An important consideration: While many of your college writing assignments will fit into the analysis, synthesis, or evaluation categories, we believe that the earlier stages are very important ones as well. Even though you may be able to provide strong analysis of calculus problems, you may not be equally as advanced with analyzing anthropological studies or physics problems. In short, acquiring basic knowledge and then expressing your comprehension and demonstrating your ability to apply that knowledge are important and probably essential acts in the process of learning. As you do the exercises in this book, look for ones which not only ask for synthesis, for example, but also ones aimed at developing knowledge and expressing comprehension.

This taxonomy (a classification for purposes of understanding the relationships among parts) proposes that thinking moves from acquiring information and facts to carefully considering and judging evidence, issues, and principles. We use the scheme here because we feel it shows a movement, a progression from the earliest exploration of an idea to the more complex activities. Similarly, when the writing process works to a writer's best advantage, it moves from developing and exploring initial ideas and fact-gathering, to analyzing those initial impressions and facts, to constructing carefully structured statements. You might think of this process as one which moves from private thoughts about a subject to more public statements about that subject. You should also be aware that disciplines use different terms for these advanced writing assignments. Some disciplines refer to such assignments as *critical inquiry;* some prefer *critique;* others use some variation of *research report.* No matter which term a discipline uses, all fields value the critical thinking that underlies such assignments.

Table 1.1 shows how Bloom's scheme has been adapted by a group of college teachers who work with engineering and science students.

Notice that the writing tasks move from "listing" to "arguing." This is very often the path which you will take in working on a writing assignment that uses a process approach. Note also that this adaptation acknowledges the value of expressing ideas in your own words. Now that you have studied the material on Bloom and the adaptation of Bloom's taxonomy, let's engage in a little process work. Close your textbook and work through the following exercises.

Exercises

1. Divide the class into groups of three students each; if necessary, some groups may have two students. Each student should individually complete the following writing exercise:
   a. Using the six stages of Bloom's taxonomy as a source, state briefly your understanding of why the taxonomy was included in this text.
   b. How might the first three stages of the taxonomy be applied to writing a formal essay on the following topic: College Degree: Necessity or Waste of Time?
2. After each of you has completed the writing exercises, work together in your groups to discuss your written responses and to prepare for a class discussion of the responses. In addition to discussing whatever points your group decides on, address the following:
   a. What similarities and differences did you note in the responses to *a* in exercise 1?
   b. What sorts of applications were mentioned in *b* in exercise 1?
   c. What are the implications of similarities or differences among the group members' responses?
   d. What are the implications of your class's responses to Bloom's taxonomy?

To further explore different stages of thinking, let's now look to a college-level writing assignment which might be given in a business class.

As a solution to the problems faced by the Detroit Shipping Company, recommend one of the three leadership theories we've studied. Why is this theory the appropriate choice?

Once you have been given this assignment, of course, you'll have to do it! So the next step might be to ask, "What questions do I need to ask in order to complete the assignment?" We would suggest the following list:

- What must I know in order to complete this assignment?
- What tasks should I work on first?
- How should I organize the paper?
- What levels of thinking is the professor asking for?

As in any assignment, key words can guide you as you respond to the professor's request. In this case, "recommend" implies that you must go through several levels of thinking in order to fulfill the assignment, and "why" indicates you will have to support your choice with careful reasoning. Here are some possible points you might address:

- You must know the specific points of each leadership theory.
- You might determine the problems faced by the Detroit Shipping Company and how those problems relate to the strengths of the three theories.
- You might compare the strengths of the theories and select the one that you believe best fits the needs of the Detroit Shipping Company.

This assignment, like many others you will face, requires you to gather information and then move through a process to argue for one choice and to propose a solution to a problem. Understanding that writing and critical thinking are inseparable will help prepare you for such assignments.

In the next section, we will present some typical writing assignments from across the disciplines, assignments which provide a glimpse at the range of writing tasks encountered by college students. These examples will demonstrate how control of the writing process and knowledge of disciplinary practices can make you a more skilled writer.

Exercises

1. Think about the various tasks you have performed in the jobs you have held. Write down the ways in which one or two of these tasks have involved processes.
2. Select a part of the writing process which gives you some trouble; for example, introductions prove difficult for some writers. Briefly explain the difficulties you have encountered, then exchange your explanation with a partner.

3. *If your class has a stand-alone computer,* create a word-processing file on a disk, one that the class can use in common to hold a group disk conference. Have everyone place on the disk a writing problem they have had and a solution they have found for the problem. By the time everyone contributes, the class will have a rich resource of the ways writers deal with common writing problems.
4. Form a small group of four or five and discuss the points you've made about process, both related to writing and to working. How do the writing processes of the group members differ? What common points do they share?

Applying the Writing Process to Writing in the Disciplines

A well-known writer named Malcolm Cowley once said, "I hate to write; I like to revise. And the amount of revision I do is terrific. I like to get the first draft out of my system. That's the hardest thing for me" (*The Writer's Quotation Book* 49). Well, many of us who write a great deal would agree with Cowley: Getting that first draft done is often very difficult work. We also agree that substantial time spent revising is generally time well spent, particularly for the professional writer. Yet most of us are not professional writers, so should we spend "terrific" amounts of time revising our writing? Many of us would also ask where we might find the time for such revision. Before you think we are suggesting that you shouldn't revise your writing, let's step back for a moment. We think considering some of the assignments you will write as a college student will help answer questions about process and revision.

Earlier in this chapter, we provided the following list of a few typical writing assignments you would encounter in your college career:

summaries	proposals
memos	essay tests
critiques	letters
reports	descriptions
classifications	analyses

This list presents quite an interesting variety of assignments. Even so, it does not exhaust the possibilities of assignments you can expect in your college career. For example, we didn't mention interpretative essays—which will be the subject of a major section in Chapter Five, "Writing in the Humanities"— nor did we mention the following list of verbs which describe common writing assignments:

compare/contrast	interpret
abstract	evaluate
create	formulate
judge	explain
differentiate	select
relate	recommend

So where does this daunting task leave you when you think about preparing to be a skillful writer who will author papers for, perhaps, ten to fifteen disciplines during a college career, especially after the authors of this book have argued that writing is different from discipline to discipline? Fortunately, we will also argue that you can prepare for such work by understanding the *process approach* to writing. Although we will not suggest that the strategies, techniques, and methods we present in this book are the only ones which will help you produce good writing, we will argue that all writers can approach, plan, and write efficiently and skillfully in two ways: first, by understanding that disciplines value and assign specific types of writing; second, by applying process to your writing assignments in all disicplines.

The Fundamentals of the Writing Process

To get us started in our discussion of the writing process, on page 9 of this chapter we suggested that the writing process was comprised of three stages: pre-writing, writing, and revising and editing; we also suggested that this was a very basic view of writing. Let's now look at a somewhat more detailed version of the process. If they are trying to write for a public audience, most experienced writers move through a process which contains some variation of the following stages:

- Planning
- Early Drafting
- Researching
- Major Drafting
- Critiquing
- Revising
- Editing

Carefully study the points of this model, for they are the principles which guide our definition of writing as a process:

1. This model applies to what is sometimes called "public writing," writing we use to communicate, to persuade, to inform, to describe, to suggest. Almost all the writing we present from the various disciplines will be writing of this type. We are not suggesting that creative writers—authors of novels, plays, poems, and screenplays—use such a model, though we could argue that many of them do.
2. It is a just a model, not an absolute. If you are writing a short essay for a sociology class, you will do less researching for material than if you were writing a senior thesis for your undergraduate degree in sociology. So we are not suggesting that all parts of the model are emphasized equally on every writing occasion.
3. In many respects writing is a singular act. That is, there are a myriad of techniques, strategies, and practices employed by writers to accomplish their tasks. Therefore, we won't give you a list of strategies and say that they will apply with equal success for everyone on every occasion. As a writer, you will have to try different strategies, techniques, and practices, then select the ones which work best for you.
4. We believe that using such a model places writers in a position to do their best work. A central tenet of this book is that writing is a manageable pro-

cess; the better writers *manage,* the better writing they produce. If you plan and research well, you are less likely to encounter certain problems late in the process. If you allow yourself to plan and research, rather than trying to draft before you've done so, you will be a more successful writer. Be aware, however, that writing is not a rigidly linear process; some writers do a little editing as they are drafting early versions of their work. At times you will find that you have to return to researching after you have started drafting. The process of returning to earlier stages again and again is known as a *recursive* process—and we will return to it in later chapters.

5. The model emphasizes the importance of writing to learn and values each stage of thinking processes. While most college-level writing assignments are intended to produce documents for a public audience, the act of composing those documents offers significant opportunities for learning. Writing is not merely an act of transmitting what you already know; it is an act which helps *develop* knowledge and understanding.

6. The model reflects the belief that writing possesses both private and public dimensions. Writing that begins as a personal issue often moves into a public arena. Most of the writing we consider in this text occurs within that public context.

With these guidelines established, in the remainder of this chapter we will briefly consider the various stages of the writing process and how they may be used to understand and respond to writing assignments. Remember, the first four chapters—writing, reading, and researching in the disciplines and written communication and computer technology—provide an overview and guidelines which will be fully developed in Chapters Five through Eleven, which place assignments in a discipline-specific context. Now, let's first sketch the early stages of the writing process—planning and early drafting—through reviewing some representative techniques and examples from several disciplines; then we will model all the stages with selections from a complete writing project.

Planning

When you are given a writing assignment, you should first ask yourself several questions:

- **What is the topic or subject I'm writing about?**
  Was it assigned?
  Am I to choose?
  Will my group or team decide?
- **What is the purpose of the writing?**
  To report? To inform? To persuade? To speculate?
- **Who is my audience?**
  My teacher? Peers? Community member? Multiple readers?
  How much do they know about the subject?
  How much do they want to know?

- **How and where does this assignment fit into the course?**
  Is the paper connected to other parts of the course? To tests? To individual or group presentations?
  How much does it count?
- **What are my sources for information?**
  Library? Media? Interviews? Field Observations? Lab Work? Questionnaires? Class readings? Lectures?
- **What kind of writing is assigned? How long should it be? When is it due?**
  Format or Genre: Essay? Report? Letter? Term Paper?
  Length: Assigned or Chosen?
  Date Due: How much time do I have to plan and complete the assignment?

You might think that questions like these wouldn't matter as much in chemistry, engineering, or business because you would always be given a specific subject to write about, whereas in English you are sometimes free to choose. As we shall see in later chapters, this is not necessarily the case. More and more professors are requiring students to make these decisions for themselves because decision-making can foster critical thinking and responsibility. For example, even though the format or genre of writing might be assigned, students must frequently choose a subject from within a range of possibilities. Some of the above questions will be answered by the professor's requirements, but some will be matters for you to determine.

Planning through exploration

There are a number of very effective ways to explore the subject of your assignment. Listing, clustering, branching, discussing in groups, interviewing, writing in journals, outlining your ideas—all are valuable techniques for exploring your potential subjects. Let's review the use of some of these techniques to show what planning can do in the early stages of the writing process.

Listing and branching

Let's say your first-year biology teacher makes the following assignment: "Select one of the subjects from the first month of classes and write a three-page paper on why you found that subject interesting." You might appeal to "listing" as a first step in the process of writing the paper. For example, you found the subject of viruses interesting, so you draw up a list, which might look something like this one:

Interesting Things about Viruses

discovery of viruses--discovered before being observed

origins

tiny, tiny, tiny!!!! a million could fit on the head of a pin

how they spread

different types and cycles

effects on animals and plants

connection to cancer

viral and bacterial

Notice that this list isn't sophisticated; it isn't even consistent in form from one point to the next. It is just an early attempt to get down on paper some very early thinking about the assignment.

If you were writing a paper which expressed what you found interesting about viruses, you could choose to include everything on your list in your paper. After all, it's a first-year course; it's a three-page paper. You could write eight paragraphs of about 80 words each and there's your paper! On the other hand, you could use this list to intelligently narrow your subject. Let's say you decide you are very interested in the effects of viruses on mammals. You might then convert your listing to a branching which might look like this:

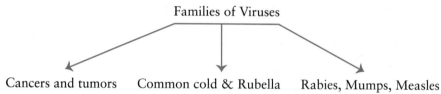

Families of Viruses

Cancers and tumors   Common cold & Rubella   Rabies, Mumps, Measles

You could then take this branching and further develop it through one of the other exploratory techniques, perhaps by writing in a journal about why you found the effects of viruses on animals so interesting. The next section will demonstrate some uses of journals in various classes and provide an idea of how various disciplines adapt the student journal to their field.

Exploring through journal writing

One of the most important means of getting started on a writing assignment is by using exploratory writing, sometimes called journal or speculative writing. Whichever term a professor chooses, this type of writing possesses common characteristics that differentiate it from such assignments as term papers and the traditional essay examination answer. Look at the following example of a journal entry written by a student in a nursing class. The students in this class were asked to write anonymously about how they would respond to working with a twenty-one-year-old patient who had been diagnosed with terminal metastatic melanoma. Here is one student's response:

> It would be very difficult to respond to Susan because she is so young and so much like me. I am twenty-two and I could not imagine knowing I have only a few weeks left to live. It would be so hard working with Susan because we have so much in common. . . . I anticipate nervousness and awkwardness. I would be experiencing so many emotions. I would be terribly sorry for Susan. . . . I would handle my feelings by realizing it's OK to be scared. . . .

Notice the informal prose style which characterizes this entry. The word choice, or diction, is very close to conversational tone; the sentences are short and lack complex structures. Most of us would agree that this type of writing reveals a good deal about how this student feels when faced with a very sensitive situation. Thus, most of us would probably agree that such a topic is suitable for a journal entry because journals are good places to explore our feelings. Many teachers in various subjects do use journals for this very reason. They want to know how a student feels about a topic, whether it is about a problem like this one or an issue in a sociology class—say, the federal government's role in providing day care. Some teachers believe that for students to grapple honestly and intensely with issues they must understand their own beliefs and feelings about those issues, rather than just repeating back to the teacher what's printed in the textbook or presented in a lecture. Having once examined those feelings, the students can then integrate their personal beliefs and knowledge with newly acquired information. Thus, such assignments are common in classes where journals are required. There are, however, other uses of exploratory writing which enable students to establish positions which are not so much based on feelings but are instead based on observations, considerations, and reasoned interpretations.

While writing has been regularly included in courses in the history of mathematics, many mathematics professors are now using journals and observation notebooks, as well as essay examinations and argumentative papers, to assist in the learning of mathematics material from the elementary grades to college. These activities are particularly interesting because such efforts really require the integration of two languages—mathematical and natural. In fact, The Mathematical Association of America recently published a book entitled *Using Writing to Teach Mathematics,* in which mathematicians reported on thirty-one projects using writing to teach mathematics. Several of these projects focused on the use of journals.

One calculus professor requires his students to include weekly journal entries on the following:

- summary of the material covered
- report on work done outside class
- analysis of understanding gained
- analysis of a solution to a problem not covered in class

First, the importance this teacher places on these writing activities is demonstrated by the fact that the journal entries count as one-third of the total semester grade.

Second, note that this professor is assigning three types of writing, ranging from low- to midlevel on Bloom's scheme. A summary asks simply that the writer recall what has been studied, while an analysis requires extended explanations and detailed reasoning. Both assignments are well suited for a class notebook or journal because they show the wide range of application for exploratory writing. In a mathematics course, the professor might focus the entries on summarizing, reporting, and analyzing, while in a nursing course the focus might be on exploring a student's reactions to situations.

Journals are used not only in English, mathematics, and nursing classes, but across the curriculum as well. In fact, many science and engineering professors use journals as a way of preparing their students for an important professional responsibility in those fields. Engineers and scientists almost always keep logbooks or journals which contain thoughts, impressions, possibilities, lists, calculations, and reminders about their projects. These notebooks, which must be signed by the writer, are regarded as legal documents and can be subpoenaed into court. Moreover, they serve as records of technical and scientific work and provide the basis for important decisions on projects and often figure prominently in patent applications and decisions. Later chapters will include examples of these records, and we will include additional examples from professional and academic notebooks.

All planning activities can be thought of as *discovery techniques* which allow writers to explore issues, test out what they know, and often discover a route to the next stage of writing. Once writers are able to write extended journal entries or compose an outline, they may be ready to move from planning to drafting.

Exercises

1. Most of us have been in a situation where we had to witness the illness of someone our own age or who had been injured badly in an accident. Compose a journal entry in which you respond to a situation about which you have had feelings similar to the nursing student's.
2. If you have written journal entries for classes either in high school or college, what is your response to this activity? Did you find it helpful? Were you able to make any connections from the journal writing to formal papers? Respond to these points and discuss your response with a partner.
3. Think about the usefulness of using writing as a tool for exploration—try to remember a time when you have used writing in this manner (for example, a journal, a log, a notebook) on the job, in an internship situation, or in a course associated with your major. Write about this experience on the class's disk conference or on-line conference. See what other students say about their own experiences in using writing as a tool for exploration. Don't be afraid to respond to other people's entries as well—tell them where your difficulties in writing differ from, or are similar to, their own.
4. *If you have access to a computer network and synchronous (real-time) conferencing software,* hold a ten minute in-class, on-line discussion about experiences you have had using writing as a tool for exploration. At the conclusion of the synchronous discussion, jot down what you consider to be the three most important goals for you to work on in connection with writing to learn. Use these goals to continue the discussion in a traditional face-to-face format with the class.

5. *If you have access to electronic mail (e-mail),* write an e-mail message to a friend at another school or to your parents at home (also consider writing to a friend in another country, or to a high-school student back home) that explains some new and interesting information you have learned in one of your classes at college. If you don't know whether or not a particular friend has an e-mail address, call or write to them and ask. Or, if your college has access to Gopher or Mosaic software, use those tools to seek out the address.

6. *If you have access to a stand-alone computer,* write a letter to your friend or your parents on the same topic. Print it out and send it by post.

From Planning to Drafting: Exploratory Writing to Formal Writing

Once you have done some planning, you are well on the way to overcoming one of the major hurdles in accomplishing any task: getting started on that task. Fortunately, the more we know about our task, the better we approach problem-solving related to that task. In other words, once we discover what we already know about a topic, the better we understand how to reconsider that knowledge and identify what new information we need to acquire and what new knowledge we need to develop in order to complete the assignment. Oftentimes, that discovery will take place when you use exploratory writing strategies. In order to begin drafting a formal paper, report, or essay, however, you will need to move beyond the exploratory writing found in journals and notebooks and develop ideas in greater detail. Further, your teachers will expect that you develop those ideas within the context of the specific discipline of the class. Such assignments might ask you to describe, analyze, compare, argue, or evaluate. The following assignment from a sociology class offers a good example of one which requires both the discovery process and presentation of formal writing.

Description and Seriousness of Social Problems
INSTRUCTIONS

The General Idea

In this paper, you will describe the problem that concerns you and explain how serious it is in terms of official statistics. That is, you are in the position of a spokesperson for a group or organization that wants to bring public attention to a problem. To make your case, you will need to convince the public that the problem concerning you and your group should be of concern to more people. You become an advocate or a claimsmaker for your problem.

In this paper, you will first describe the problem. Describe the kind of harm it causes. Does it affect just a few people or does it affect many? In this part of the paper, you may want to use a few case studies like you will find in the first book on the homeless by Jonathan Kozol. You will need to indicate how people's lives are affected by the problem.

Second, you will need to indicate how serious the problem is in terms of whether the incidence or rate (like deaths each year in automobile accidents due to alcohol or deaths each year due to lung cancer caused by smoking) is increasing or decreasing. That is, is the problem getting worse? Is it nearing a crisis? Is it tolerable now but soon going to get much worse? Why should the general public be concerned about it? You will collect statistics over a twenty-year period (1973–1993) to determine how serious the social problem is. This part of the paper is closer to the type of analysis in the book by Rossi.

Deadlines

August 30	Turn in one page description of problem. Must be typed.
September 13	Have your official statistics available for computer workshop.
September 20	Turn in graph on official statistics.
October 4	Turn in paper on seriousness of social problem.
October 4–6	Panels of class presentations on social problems.
October 11	Midterm exam will include a question from class presentations.

Approaching this assignment is quite obviously a more complex task than, say, writing a journal entry about your high-school friends. First, the assignment requires the writers both to select a problem that concerns them and then to describe that problem using statistical evidence. Thus, their task involves both reflecting (or discovering) and developing a formal position, using a form of mathematical language, statistics. All of us describe objects, issues, and terms every day. We make meaning by describing and sharing those descriptions with others in our lives. However, remember our earlier section on the culture of disciplines. Since this is a sociology class, the term *describe* will carry specific meaning within the sociological context, as well as general, or shared, meaning with other academic disciplines. Students writing a paper in response to this assignment must operate within both contexts. This professor's assignment has given the students some very direct hints about what she expects in the paper. Note that the paragraphs in the assignment contain instructions, questions, time-frames, and sources. Clearly, responding to this assignment without covering these points would be a mistake. As the students draft their papers, they should address these points. Additionally, they should know the specific ways terms are applied in this discipline. Were this an assignment for a chemistry class, these terms would, no doubt, either be inappropriate or used somewhat differently.

In part, your success as a college student will be determined by how accurately you understand not only what's required but also what's suggested. While this teacher isn't requiring students to visit the Writing Center, in class she strongly encouraged students to use that service. Note also that this is a "staged assignment," one submitted in parts, rather than as a finished draft only. Thus, this teacher is demonstrating a belief in process, peer review, and other techniques which generally enable writers to better manage a writing task. Note also that the professor has extended the application of the assignment by linking it to oral presentations and the midterm exam.

Finally, these papers, assigned in such areas as literature, social science, history, and business, might require the writer to define, analyze, or evaluate. Frequently, you will be asked to research the topics of these papers, using such sources as your college library, interviews, and information from film, broadcast and print media. We will present an extensive section on researching in the disciplines in Chapter Three.

Exercises

1. What strategies and techniques have you used to complete such assignments as this one from the sociology class? Make a brief list of these and write a short explanation of one such strategy or technique.
2. Share your conclusions with a partner. Given the past assignments you considered in arriving at your conclusions, which strategies and techniques seem to be discipline-specific and which seem to be applicable to more than one discipline?
3. *If you have access to a stand-alone computer,* write a letter to a friend at another school, your parents at home, a friend in another country, or a high school student in your hometown, describing the processes and strategies you use to adjust to and assimilate new information in a particular academic area—math, English, computer science, history, engineering, for example.

Drafting: An Overview

The term "drafting" reveals something very significant about this stage of the writing process and the process as a whole. Drafting carries the meaning of work; it's an active form, showing that the making of an essay, a report, or a documentation section involves a movement from preliminary thoughts to polished expression or statement. The American novelist William Faulkner once said that whenever he wrote he reached into his "toolbox" and found what he needed to complete the job. As with other parts of the process, drafting is improved by knowing your options, your resources, and your plan.

Once you arrive at the drafting stage, you should be working toward the following:

1. **Thesis:** An effective statement of the central point or objective in the draft
2. **Unity:** A strong sense that what's in the writing belongs there
3. **Organization:** An effective and appropriate plan for presentation of information, ideas, arguments

4. **Coherence:** The smooth movement from point to point in the writing
5. **Style:** A clear, effective, and appropriate method of writing

Note that we have not used such terms as *paragraphs, detailed explanations,* or *development.* Because this text covers writing in many disciplines, you will find, for example, that disciplines define *development* in different ways, especially in certain types of writing. If we were presenting precepts related only to argumentative essays in the humanities, we might be able to make more general statements. Again, in this chapter many of our comments are meant to offer advice on the fundamental agreements among disciplines. All disciplines agree that formal writing should be characterized by "clear, effective, and appropriate style," though you will find that "appropriate style" varies from discipline to discipline.

A Major Writing Assignment and the Process of Writing

To demonstrate the writing process at work, let's now consider a major writing project from a literature class. We use this particular project for several reasons:

1. The writing project was divided into several clearly defined stages so that it serves as a sound example of how individual stages of the process work.
2. The parts of this project show a clear progression from beginning to completion, thus modeling the benefits of a coherent assignment.
3. The project required close collaboration among the writer, the professor, the Writing Center, and the writer's peers.

As we move from stage to stage in the process, we shall refer to specific pages from the student's paper. We have left in many of the original comments on the parts, so don't expect clean copy! Among other things, we want to demonstrate that the writing process is just that—an active system at work solving a problem.

Project Overview

This project counted as 40% of the credit in an American literature course. It was the only major, formal writing assignment in the course, and the amount of credit assigned to it made doing well on the assignment imperative for students who wanted to do well in the course.

Project Requirements

The following requirements were attached to this project:

1. A proposal stating the topic of the paper and establishing that the student had done a reasonable job of thinking about and researching the topic. The

proposal had to be approved by the professor before the student could begin writing the preliminary draft.

2. A preliminary draft demonstrating that the student had done all she or he could do without the critiques of the professor and the Writing Center tutor.

3. A critique from the professor with notations on the draft and a written recommendation for revisions.

4. A critique from a Writing Center tutor who had read both the assignment and the paper before talking with the writer.

5. A conference with the professor for which the student would prepare by carefully reading the professor's comments on the preliminary draft; during the conference, the student and professor would agree on the next steps in the revision process.

6. A final draft of the paper, turned in with all other materials relative to the paper.

As you can see, the assignment was structured so that the students would have to do the project in stages. Thus, the temptation to write the paper at the last possible moment was eliminated. Right? Additionally, the professor in this class thought of this project as a collaborative effort among the student, himself, and the Writing Center staff, so ample opportunity for success was built into the assignment.

Let's now trace the development of the paper through the steps the writer took to move from brief notation to formal draft.

Step by Step: Connecting the Parts of the Project

Below is an outline of the progression of the project from the earliest to the final stage:

Planning: class reading, class meetings, class lectures, guided discussions, individual conference with professor, journal entries, response paper, proposal

Drafting: write, write, write, talk with classmates, talk with friend, conference with professor, write

Researching: secondary sources from University library, suggestions from Writing Center tutor, short conference (five minutes) with professor

Critiquing: self-critique, Writing Center tutor critique (resistance to critique) professor's critique (written and conference), informal peer critique

Revising: three revisions after critiques for large-scale issues (for example, paragraph structure, supporting evidence)

Editing: sentence level work and lots of it

As you review this progression, keep in mind that the process is not entirely linear. This student, for example, reviewed her secondary sources throughout the process of writing the paper; she said that she needed to do so to do a complete job. Nor was the process always a smooth one. In the critique stage the student resisted the idea of going to the Writing Center because she wasn't confident that the paper was suitable for review at that point. She later admitted that she probably would never have thought it was suitable!

This section includes parts of the student's work on the project, a paper on Henry David Thoreau's *Walden*. We have included several parts of the project, from a journal entry to several pages from the final draft. Scan the entries from pages 27 to 38 to familiarize yourself with the parts we have included. We think you will find that much of the material is self-explanatory, so we won't belabor obvious points. We will guide you through a reading of this section by asking questions which should engage you in the study of the student's paper.

We will not offer any comments on reading and researching in this section for two reasons. First, those subjects are covered in great detail in Chapters Two and Three. Second, we use this paper for very specific reasons, one of which is that this student does a wonderful job of leading from the early to final stages of the process. We are not implying that her project worked perfectly from beginning to end. We mean that she used the process to its full potential as she moved through the project. In that sense, her paper models how the process can work. Let's now look to her work to see how her project benefited from the process.

Earlier in this chapter we provided some examples of exploratory writing in several courses. We indicated then that such writing could serve as the inception for ideas which could be elaborated later. This student first showed her interest in the topic of her paper in a journal entry the second week of class. In most ways, this entry is typical. The writer covers a couple of points and moves quickly from the first to the second. Her class had only been working with Thoreau's *Walden* for one week, so she hadn't really developed any solid positions. However, she begins this entry with a point that she will later develop into the topic of her major paper.

Date: January 31, 1995

I am going to lay out some of the foundation on which I believe Thoreau may base his position on art so later I can come back and either substantiate or unsubstantiate my theory. The basic ground work is this: Thoreau's position on art is much like that of Shakespeare's in his tragic comedy, *A Winter's Tale.* In this play, Shakespeare posits the belief that the true art is that created by Nature; therefore, Nature is art and art is nature. The artifacts and relics which humans create, even though once a part of nature, cannot truly be pure art. I believe William borrowed his philosophy from a French man—I will have to do a bit of research in my Shakespeare to find his name—however, I believe I may be on to something here. I have paid closer attention to how Thoreau discusses the subject of art, particularly in "Reading" but I am not even close to substantiating my theory.

I wanted to comment again on the purpose of *Walden* again, or what I think Thoreau's purpose is. I keep reworking this in my mind as I read through his work and this time I think I have a firmer grasp on what the "wake up call" might be. Thoreau is very monotonous in his descriptions throughout "Economy" as well as his other chapters because he is trying to show his neighbors how they are caught up in the necessity of necessities instead of experiencing life. There is a clear distinction, for Thoreau, between being alive and living, and I think this is his message to his fellow neighbors, although I am not quite sure I appreciate the way he is going about it—I get caught up in his judgmental tone.

As you read the first paragraph, do you see the beginning stages of what will eventually become her thesis for the final paper? This paragraph raises the questions of Thoreau's "position on art" and mentions Shakespeare's theory of art. The topic quickly shifts, however, to Thoreau's purpose for writing *Walden.*

If we now turn to the student's proposal, we can illustrate several points. First, the connection between the journal entry and the proposal seems clear. She has developed her position over a period of about two months, during which time she read most of Thoreau's *Walden.* She is now able to take a position and defend it, rather than "not being close to substantiating [her] theory."

TO: Dr. Tahini
FROM: Samantha Delacroix
RE: Proposal for Paper (Eng. 345)
DATE: April 8, 1995

   Henry David Thoreau's *Walden* encompasses many tones, arguments, and ambiguities in his contemplation of the world around him, which also includes the subject of Nature. In *Friends on the Shelf,* published in 1906, Bradford Torrey states, "He [Thoreau] loved the society of trees and all manner of growing things. He found a fellowship in them, they were of his kin; which is not at all the same as to say that he enjoyed looking at them as objects of beauty" (92). I agree with Torrey that Thoreau has a kinship with Nature; ~~yet,~~ I also believe Thoreau admires the beauty Nature possesses, and expresses an aesthetic philosophy of Nature in *Walden.* In my paper, I will explore Thoreau's descriptive prose and his reverence for the aesthetic beauty of Nature, his view that Nature, as opposed to civilization, possesses the purest forms of art, and finally, his attempt as a naturalist and a poet, to connect Nature with literature.

Are these mutually exclusive?

Goals— very ambitious

   I am considering the following source materials as I explore the above-related themes:

1. *Walden*, by Henry David Thoreau
2. *Thoreau as Romantic Naturalist*, by James McIntosh
3. "Coming Down the Pages of Nature," by Walter Hesford
4. *Nature's Nation*, by Perry Miller
5. *Modern Critical Interpretations of Walden*, ed. Harold Bloom

 Sound

 *

It is my assertion <u>that there is evidence of an aesthetic philosophy in Walden and that Thoreau's appreciation of the intricate beauty in Nature and his love of writing leads him to seek a parallel between his two loves, Nature and Literature.</u> However, Thoreau also alludes to Nature as the purest form of art, especially in his comparison of things created by Nature and things created by civilization, which could prove difficult in an attempt to bridge Nature with the written word.

 ⟶ *over*

I have few sources which confirm my assertion that Thoreau does, at times, apply an aesthetic philosophy to Nature or that Thoreau views Nature as the purest form of art, yet I am confident, through an exploratory essay, that I will find answers to my claims.

Nothing like confidence?!

Second, the value of the proposal to the process is shown. In his comments to the student, the professor has approved her proposal, but has offered some advice and some caution. Note the comments in the margins of the proposal and read the professor's written comment, which we provide here.

Samantha, This seems very promising. Go ahead. I'd suggest the following cautions: 1. Hold aside the possibility that the three goals may be more than you can manage in the paper. Do one at a time & see what happens. Might result in a less ambitious but more detailed development of a revised thesis. 2. You often state points as oppositional—"but," "yet"—seems to me you may be working with an extension of ideas, not an opposition.

At this stage of planning, students often tend to commit themselves to a larger project than they should. Though judging the scope of your commitment is sometimes difficult early in the process, writing proposals, outlines, and practice paragraphs will help you make such decisions. Remember, try to match your writing goals with the value of the project in the course.

Next let's consider the professor's written critique of the student's preliminary draft. Although this critique represents only one phase of the critique stage, it is one upon which students depend to help guide them to the revision stage. We have included the text of the critique below; please read it now and then answer the questions in the Exercises below.

To: Samantha Delacroix
From: Dr. Tahini
Re: Critique of Formal Paper
Date: May 5, 1995

So, Samantha, what a nice start you've made here. You tackle an interesting and intricate topic in a lively and persuasive manner and develop your argument with a sound gallery of details.

So what can I do to help you fashion this into an expository gem? Here's what I'd suggest we look at:

1. The definition of aesthetic forms is central to the paper; therefore, establishing a precise definition of it becomes crucial. I'd submit that there are points at which the definition becomes cloudy. Are you taking the implications of art out of your consideration of aesthetics? If so, why? Do you regard aesthetics as embracing, at least in this paper, only that which falls within the philosphical and the rhetorical?

2. The structure of the paper, while seemingly simple, confuses me a bit (no smart remarks here, please!). Let's talk about your rationale for the structure. I think you miss some chances to strengthen and add depth to the paper because structural elements are not as delineated as they might be.

3. I've made several sentence-level suggestions/revisions that might serve as models to tighten the prose while adding specificity and range.
OK, let's revise!!!!!!!

Exercises

1. If you had gotten this critique from the professor, how do you think you would have reacted? What are the strengths of the critique? What are the weaknesses?
2. Working in a small group, discuss the kind of critiques you think are most helpful. Once you have discussed a number of points, classify them. Did your group find any consistencies in their preferences?

If you have ever served as a peer critic, you know that advising writers is not an easy task. As a critic, you want to both support and challenge the writer, to point out the strengths of the writing and to constructively criticize the weaknesses. The answers to the questions in the above exercise should indicate how you and your classmates perceive the role of a critic, whether that person is your teacher or one of your classmates. Very few professionals who write regularly turn down advice on their writing. Some writing teachers talk of a "culture of writing" on their campuses, a culture characterized by supportive but critical advice for writers, both student and faculty. Part of that culture would be a strong critic for every writer.

We have held drafting, revising, and editing until the end because we believe they can be efficiently and profitably covered together by referring to the preliminary and final drafts of the paper and by engaging you in several exercises related to the drafts.

In our statement on drafting (pages 24–25) we said that once you got to this stage you were concerned with five goals:

1. A clear and effective thesis
2. Unity
3. Organization
4. Coherence
5. A clear, effective, and appropriate style

Referring to the sections from the preliminary and final drafts on pages 33–38, we find radical differences in the two drafts in all these areas. In the four pages from each draft, for example, we see very little similarity in paragraph structure in the two drafts. What do we learn if we scan the sections from the two drafts?

Use the following questions as guides for answering the questions in the exercise below. While these guides do not extensively cover revision and editing, they will provide you with working strategies and techniques to use as you revise your own writing and serve as a peer critic.

Guides to Revision

1. Is there a strong focusing sentence early in the essay which guides the reader throughout the presentation of the argument or position taken by the writer?
2. Does each paragraph or paragraph section have a central purpose?
3. Is the organization of the material clear? Can the reader follow the presentation of ideas?
4. Does the writer provide and develop details to support her position?
5. Are the paragraphs balanced? That is, are the ideas developed equally or are some clearly underdeveloped?

Guides to Editing

1. Is the paper free of such mechanical errors as typos, misnumbered pages, sentences without punctuation?
2. Are sentences tightly constructed or are they rambling and convoluted?
3. Do sentences present ideas through cohesive, varied constructions, or are they constructed using monotonous sentence patterns?
4. Is diction precise and imaginative or is it mundane and lacking precision?
5. Has the writer cleared up glaring grammatical problems?

Universal Guiding Question

Is the paper appropriate for the audience?

To prepare for these questions, take a few minutes to read the pages from each draft.

1. What similarities do you see in the paragraphs of the two drafts? If there are changes, has the writer actually changed the structure of the paper or merely shifted around the same material so it looks different?
2. Compare pages one and two of the two drafts. What changes has the writer made in the final draft and how have those changes affected the section?
3. Working with a partner, answer the following questions:
   a. Select any two paragraphs (not the introductory paragraph) from the final draft and locate the guiding topic sentence in each. How well does the writer support the topic sentences?
   b. In those same two paragraphs, does the writer depend too much on outside sources, or does she use them to support her main points?
4. Where is the best writing in the section from the final draft? Where is the weakest writing?
5. Choose a section from the preliminary draft which is redrafted in the final version. What sentence-level changes has the writer made? How would you classify those changes?

This brief look at a major writing project has provided a means to see what is possible when writers understand the assignment, manage the project well, and operate within a supportive writing environment. Will all of your writing experiences be like this one? Probably not. We hope, of course, that most will. Yet we are confident that as you gain skills in critical thinking and writing you will become more and more your own critic. Additionally, we encourage you to form writing groups with your peers. Students frequently form study groups to work on mathematics, chemistry, and other technical subjects. Why not carry that practice over to your writing classes and writing assignments in other classes?

Moving Forward

Writing in the academic disciplines, using writing to both learn course material and develop writing skills, and connecting writing with other forms of literacy—verbal, visual, mathematical, informational—will empower you as you strive to become part of a community of learners and to prepare for a career in a profession. The more you know about the basic principles of sound writing and the more you appreciate the differences among writing in the various disciplines, the more skillful and effective you become as a writer. We hope that this brief introduction has been interesting and helpful and that it has provided you with a glimpse of the richness and diversity of writing across the disciplines. While some of you may be firmly committed to a specific academic major, many of you are probably exploring the numerous opportunities available. Experiencing, practicing, and valuing the role of writing in various disciplines may very well help you make more informed decisions.

Exercises

1. In your on-line reading log, identify the most important points within this chapter. You can do this either as you read the material or after you read the material. Save the file every time you add material. By the time you finish this book, you should have a useful set of notes/guidelines to consult about writing.

2. In your reading-response conference (on a disk or on a network), respond to the four assumptions that we used to begin this chapter:
   • Writing is inseparable from learning.
   • Writing is both a skill which can be acquired and practiced and an important means of communicating information, understanding and knowledge.
   • Writers and communities of writers create meaning.
   • College-educated people write for a variety of purposes and to a variety of audiences.
   In your experience, are these assumptions true? To what degree or extent? If not, what experiences have you had that convinced you otherwise? Do you think your teachers believe these assumptions? Why or why not?

3. *If you have access to a computer network* (for example, a campus network or the Internet), join a network discussion group or subscribe to an on-line news group related to your career interest (ask the central campus computing folks for help). Ask the discussion question ("What writing strategies have worked particularly well for you? Why?") on-line, and see what kinds of learning strategies others use. Make a list of all the strategies people relate and bring them to class to contribute to the face-to-face discussion.

Dr. Tahani
English 345
April 24, 1995

The Natural Aesthetic?
The Aesthetics of Nature?

The ⟨Aesthetic Nature⟩ in Thoreau's *Walden*

Henry David Thoreau published his autobiographical essay, *Walden*, in 1854, at the peak of the American romantic literary movement, and although

continued

Novel

poem

okay

Do you plan to explore "movement"?

in essay form, Thoreau's *Walden* embodies many ideals of the romantic genre. Romanticism, both in European and American literature, "is an aesthetic movement of various literary distinctions (Harding 1). William Wordsworth, in "Preface to Lyrical Ballads," characterizes the romantic aesthetic as:

> The spontaneous overflow of powerful feelings: it takes its origin from emotion recollected in tranquility: the emotion is contemplated till by a species of reaction the tranquility gradually disappears, and an emotion, kindred to that which was before the subject of contemplation, is gradually produced, and does itself actually exist in the mind. In this mood . . . the emotion, of whatever kind and in whatever degree from various causes is qualified by various pleasure, so that in describing any passions whatso- ever, . . . the mind will upon the whole be in a state of enjoyment. (151)

Don't you just love this ?!

Not artistic?

Do you shift points here?

The aesthetic qualities of romanticism are both philosophical and psychological in that they address the individual's aesthetic preference and the individual's perceptions, recognition, and enjoyment of a specific object— namely nature, art, and literature. Thoreau's autobiographical essay, *Walden*, is, by definition, a rebellion against traditional societal norms and is based in nature. Thoreau is subjective in his writing, and provides many candid, even profound, arguments in his account of a two-year experiment in simple living. Thoreau's style, in recounting his deliberate excursion into the woods, is intentionally polemic as he addresses his audience: "I do not speak to those who are well employed in whatever circumstances, and they know whether they are well employed or not;—but mainly to the mass of men who are discontented, and idly complaining of the hardness of their lot or of their times" (10). He is exacting in his rhetorical style and combines philosophical ideals of simplicity in life with his naturalist views to espouse a direct philosophy of intentionally experiencing life. Thoreau's tone is often judgmental, ambiguous and even stoic in his deliberateness "to brag as lustily as chanticleer in the morning, standing on his roost, if only to wake [his] neighbors up" (1); however, *Walden,* displays another facet of Thoreau— a descriptive prose writer who, between polemical arguments for deliberateness and simplicity, expresses an affection and tenderness for nature. It is in these transitory moments in *Walden* that the reader realizes Thoreau's emotionally intense perception and enjoyment of the diverse aesthetic qualities in Nature. In the romantic sense, Thoreau's essay cannot be considered an aesthetic whole. However, by exploring the text, the reader can appreciate Thoreau's emotional transformation of Nature's objects and passionate illustrations, through descriptive prose images and passionate illustrations.

What's the focus of this section?

Connect to "subjective" above

How could you make this more precise?

Careful here: You're moving quickly through complex ideas

Note all of above is part of ¶ 1

"Economy" is the longest, and perhaps most difficult chapters in *Walden,* because of its conspicuous, subjective style. Yet, it is a good base from which to begin a survey of the aesthetic qualities within *Walden,* because Thoreau's authoritative style in this chapter is, for the most part, in contrast with the splendid images and intense emotions he later shares with his reader. Thoreau begins "Economy" boastfully, while setting the foundation for his socially dissenting theories for deliberately experiencing life. He speaks directly to his audience, criticizing "the mass of men [who] lead lives of quiet desperation. . . . From the desperate city you go into the desperate country, and have to console yourself with the bravery of minks and muskrats" (5). In the midst of his aggressive narrative in "Economy;" however, Thoreau does grant the reader a few impressions of his affection toward nature:

Is there a connection between these?

> So many autumn, ay, and winter days, spent outside the town, trying to hear what was in the wind, to hear and carry it express! . . . At other times watching from the observatory of some cliff or tree, to telegraph any new arrival; or waiting at evening on the hilltop for the sky to fall, that I might catch something, though I never caught much, and that, manna-wise would dissolve again in the sun. (11)

How's that?

Thoreau, in an affectionate, tone, briefly recounts his personal experience as an observer of Nature—a nature that is always in transition and cannot be savored completely. James McIntosh notes, in this passage, that Thoreau allows his reader to perceive "[his] pronounced sense that moments of reverence in nature are transient . . . and one cannot grasp nature all at once or permanently, but must catch what-little-manna he can at the moment" (266). Thoreau's also illustrates his affection for Nature in the midst of his criticisms of ornate social dwellings.

Thoreau relates to the reader that Nature, for him, is where beauty is most enhanced:

> Before we can adorn our houses with beautiful objects the walls must be stripped, and our lives must be stripped, and beautiful housekeeping and beautiful living be laid for a foundation: now, a taste for the beautiful is most cultivated out of doors, where there is no house and no house-keeper. (26).

Thus, in "Economy," the reader is fully informed, in a critical style, of the author's philosophical views of living intentionally and is also introduced to his aesthetic affection for Nature.

A good chance to embody art & artistic concern?

In "Where I Lived, and What I Lived For," Thoreau's stance on simplicity of life gives way to scattered moments of calm, affectionate imagery of Nature. In describing the house he built at Walden Pond, although simplicity and . . .

Dr. Tahini
English 345
May 14, 1995

The Romantic Aesthetics of Thoreau's *Walden*

Henry David Thoreau is a child of the romantic era and one of America's most prominent romantic literary figures. He is often distinguished as a poet, an essayist, and romantic naturalist; and his artistic literary contributions, in many respects, embody the ideals of romantic theory (Herzberg 1133). Romanticism, both in European and American literature, "is an aesthetic movement," a movement that places the individual author at the center of life and experience (Harding 1). "It is an artistic emphasis on the imaginative and emotional—an appeal to the heart rather than the head" (Shaw 327). The artistic literary qualities of romantic aestheticism are philosophical and psychological in that they address the individual artist's preference as well as the artist's perception, recognition, and enjoyment of things beautiful—namely nature, art, or literature.

Poetry and the essay are two prominent artistic literary expressions in the romantic movement and both expressions emphasize the individual artist's personal and subjective preferences and perceptions of beauty. William Wordsworth, in "Preface to Lyrical Ballads," describes the romantic aesthetic in poetry as:

> The spontaneous overflow of powerful feelings: it takes the origin from emotion recollected in tranquility: the emotion is contemplated till by a species of reaction the tranquility gradually disappears, and an emotion, kindred to that which was before the subject of contemplation, is gradually produced, and does itself actually exist in the mind. In this mood . . . the emotion, of whatever kind and in whatever degree from various causes is qualified by various pleasure, so that in describing any passions whatsoever, . . . the mind will upon the whole be in a state of enjoyment. (151)

Henry David Thoreau, too, describes his perception of romantic poetry as the "very private history which unostentatiously lets us into the secret of a man's life" (Unger 168). Poetry, therefore, in the romantic endeavor, is the individual artist's emotional reaction to pleasing species or objects as well as an unassuming record of the artist's nature.

The romantic essay is often "candidly autobiographical, reminiscent, (and) self-analytical; and when writers treat other matters than themselves, they tend to do so impressionistically, so that material is reflected in the temperament of the essayist" (Abrams 14). Thoreau's *Walden* is characteristically an autobiographical essay. It is a history of his deliberate two-year excursion into the woods. In his essay, Thoreau rebels against social norms and he is subjective in his views of life and Nature. He treats his subject matter seriously and addresses his audience with clear intentions: "I do not propose to write an ode to dejection, but to brag as lustily as Chanticleer in the morning, standing on his roost, if only to wake my neighbors up" (1). Thoreau also establishes himself as a naturalist and combines his naturalist philosophies with economic simplicity to espouse a conviction of intentionally experiencing life. *Walden* is largely Thoreau's record of confronting life, unconfined and in natural surroundings. In this respect, *Walden* can also be characterized as a record of Thoreau's aesthetic understanding of Nature's beauty. Throughout *Walden,* Thoreau describes various experiences of pleasures in his observations and interactions with Nature. In moments of repose, Thoreau advances beyond the confines of the essayist style and combines the romantic ideas of poetry, as well as his personal ideas of aestheticism, to communicate an affectionate reverence for Nature's objects. In *Walden,* to appreciate and enjoy Thoreau's personal preference for beauty and his displays of affection and reverence, one must explore Thoreau's transitory and progressively artistic transformations of the images he acknowledges and enjoys.

The individual artist's personal perception of beauty is the fundamental basis in romantic aestheticism, and in *Walden,* Thoreau wastes no time revealing his preference. In his first chapter, "Economy," Thoreau illustrates his inclination of beauty in the midst of his criticisms of ornate social dwellings. He relates to the reader that Nature, for him, is where beauty is most enhanced:

> Before we can adorn our houses with beautiful objects the walls must be stripped, and our lives must be stripped, and beautiful housekeeping and beautiful living be laid for a foundation: now, a taste for the beautiful is most cultivated out of doors, where there is no house and no housekeeper. (26)

Thoreau directly informs the reader of where his aesthetic preference lies and then moves on in his philosophical views of simple living. In "Where I Lived, and What I Lived For," Thoreau's supposition on simple living gives way to scattered moments of tranquil, beautiful images of Nature. Thoreau introduces to the reader the home he built at Walden Pond, a home that is part of the natural, beautiful landscape of the pond:

> When first I took up my abode in the woods . . . my house was not finished for winter, but was merely a defense against the rain. . . .

continued

The upright white hew studs and freshly planed door and window casings gave it a clean and airy look, especially in the morning, when its timbers were saturated with dew, so that I fancied that by noon some sweet gum would exude from them. To my imagination it retained throughout the day more or less of this auroral character. . . . The winds which passed over my dwelling were such as sweep over the ridges of mountains, bearing the broken strains, or celestial parts only, of terrestrial music. The morning wind forever blows, the poem of creation is uninterrupted; but few are the ears that hear it. (57)

Thoreau embodies his home with natural images and "over his house he lets flow a musical and correspondent breeze that links Walden with mountains and with human myths of spirit in nature" (McIntosh 265). Thoreau gradually elevates his artistic prose style as he illuminates the beauty in the natural objects around him, and the reader understands his pleasure in these natural surroundings.

Thoreau begins the "The Bean-Field" in a somewhat yielding manner, with a confession: "I came to love my rows, my beans . . ." (104). He then completely shifts his prose toward peaceful images of beauty. Thoreau transforms, in captivating prose images, the objects of natural beauty he so loves. In magnificent artistic detail, he proclaims an enjoyment and pleasure in observing the minute creatures and objects that . . .

CHAPTER TWO

Reading in the Disciplines

Reading in the Disciplines: An Overview

Reading with a Purpose

Understanding What You Read

Reading Critically: Analyzing, Evaluating, and Responding

In Chapter One you gained valuable information about the writing process that should help you succeed in your college courses. You learned that writing is not only inseparable from learning, but that writing is an important means of communicating what you know. You also learned that writers create meaning and that educated persons write for a variety of purposes and to a variety of audiences. In short, you already have a foundation as a writer which should serve you well in your efforts to succeed in college writing classes.

Yet an understanding of the writing process by itself is not enough if your goal is to succeed in courses across campus. While it is true that *many* of those courses will require that you write, it is equally true that *all* of those courses will require that you read.

We believe that if you want to succeed in college and on the job, you will undoubtedly benefit from any efforts you make to become a better writer. Like many teachers, we also believe that those efforts will prove more satisfactory if you make an effort to improve as a reader as well.

Please read over the following assumptions that serve as the basis in this chapter for helping you become an improved reader.

- Reading is a process.
- Reading involves active engagement with a text.
- Like writers, readers construct meaning in texts.
- Reading is uniquely related to understanding.
- Writers read as they write.
- Improved reading will result in improved writing.
- Reading often serves as the basis for writing.

Keep these assumptions in mind as we explore the reading process in the remainder of this chapter.

Reading in the Disciplines: An Overview

Let us begin, then, with a basic understanding of what happens when someone reads. The first thing we need to understand is that reading, like writing, is an activity that occurs in various cultures. As a result, it is true that people read better in cultures they are familiar with and that people familiar with a topic will be able to read better than those who are not familiar with that topic.

So fundamental is this notion of reading-as-understanding that we can extend it into our daily lives where we busily interpret the words and actions of others, making what we will call in this chapter "life readings." One of many excellent examples of varying reading abilities might be found in the well-publicized range of readings made of the 1994 World Cup of Soccer, played for the first time in the United States where *football* refers to something quite different than the game Europeans call by that name.

Sports analysts were quick to point out that while visitors from other countries could read (and, thereby, understand) the sport excellently because they had had years of experience watching soccer in their countries, Americans often complained about how difficult the game was to watch. Though visitors could read action all over the playing field, many Americans described the game as "slow" and "boring."

Naturally, a second thing we need to understand about reading is that some people do it better than others. Nonetheless, by the final match of the World Cup, many Americans were better able to read and understand movement on the soccer field than they were during the first game they saw.

Your improvement as a reader will likewise depend to a certain extent upon your understanding of the following:

- Reading occurs in certain settings or cultures.
- Reading is uniquely related to understanding.
- Past experiences in a culture contribute to the ability to read in that culture.
- Most people belong to more than one culture and move comfortably from one reading context to another.

This broad definition—that when you actively observe and understand events, people, and places around you, you are reading—demonstrates this last fact, that you belong to more than one culture and, thus, spend most of your time reading. In fact, you probably observe and read a wide range of messages sent in your direction, many of them non-print. You might wonder, for instance, how to read the student who, late for class, walks into the room right in front of the instructor, smiling the whole way. Is he embarrassed? Rude? Crazy?

You might even read such messages while you are listening closely to the teacher, reading in her instructions about an upcoming assignment not only what you are supposed to do, but how your assignment will be graded. As you can see, you spend a great deal of time reading and making meaning of what you read, trying to determine your place among the people, events, and places you typically encounter.

From this perspective, you already know a great deal about certain kinds of readings. After all, you cannot avoid reading as we have defined it here. It should be clear that you will improve upon such "life readings" as the ones above simply by building a reservoir of experience from which you might draw in future situations. Your experience as a student also tells you that you must be taught to make "academic" or "school" readings.

One of these academic endeavors, discipline-specific reading, will be the subject of your coursework in various departments in your college or university. For instance, your accounting teacher will teach you how to read financial figures in light of state and federal laws, your psychology teacher will show you how to read behaviors from certain theoretical perspectives, and your art history teacher will instruct you in how to read the "text" of famous paintings.

But there is a third type of reading that you will find useful throughout college and will employ in all reading you do in all departments. We call it "reading in the disciplines," and it is a set of skills which allows you to read critically in courses throughout the curriculum.

1. Think back over the past twenty-four hours and, in your class notebook, make a list of life readings you can recall having made in that time.
2. Choose one reading from the list made in response to Exercise 1 above and answer the following questions about it in your class notebook.
   a. Fully describe the reading you made.
   b. How did you learn to make that reading?
   c. Cite specific past experiences that prepared you to make that reading.
3. Have you ever done anything that was misread or misinterpreted by others? Describe that occurrence. Why do you suppose you were misunderstood?

4. Readings of people and situations in electronic environments (for example, through on-line conversations, through e-mail exchanges, through home pages on the World Wide Web) often differ from those that occur in face-to-face environments because we are able to observe different things in each environment. *If you have access to a stand-alone computer and to e-mail* create a word-processing file and make two lists. In the first list, jot down those things that help you "read" a person or a situation that you are encountering in a face-to-face manner. In the second list, jot down the things that help you read a person or a situation that you encounter on-line.

   Share your two lists with a friend or with an electronic discussion group and get their responses to the items. Ask your correspondents to add additional items to your lists as well.
5. If you have had experience trying to read people and situations in electronic environments (for example, e-mail conversations, electronic conferences), write about a situation in which you misread someone or some situation on-line. Describe the occurrence. Speculate on the possible reasons underlying your electronic misreading.

Reading with a Purpose

Like writing, reading is a process. In fact, like writing, which involves prewriting, writing, and rewriting, reading involves you in working through stages, not necessarily in a straight line, but in the order you need to draw upon certain skills in making sense of a text. We might call these interdependent stages in the reading process **prereading** (for example, reviewing and skimming), **reading** (for example, annotating), and **postreading** (for example, summarizing, paraphrasing, synthesizing, and critiquing). The emphasis you place on any one phase of the reading process is apt to be determined by your purpose for reading.

As a college student engaged in numerous life readings, many of which need to be revised from day to day, you already know that reasons for reading are not only dictated by the situation you find yourself in but often themselves dictate how you read. In figuring out people and events around you, you probably begin the process of understanding by following a method something like the following:

- **Hypothesizing why something happens:** For instance, why does your classmate walk into the classroom late? Does he have a class immediately before this one in a distant building and find it impossible to traverse campus quickly enough to be on time to this class? If so, will he continue to be late to class throughout the semester?
- **Testing your hypothesis:** To do this, you might pay attention to whether the student continues to be tardy. You might even ask him if he has a class across campus.
- **Reaching an understanding:** If your hypothesis holds true for all elements of your encounter, you will likely be able to predict with some certainty that this guy will continue to be late for class or maybe, after you get to know your teacher, that your teacher just might ask him to drop the class until he can better fit it into his schedule.

The same holds true for all other kinds of reading you might do. In attempting to reach an understanding, you hypothesize what something means, test your hypothesis, and, if your hypothesis holds true, feel satisfied that you have reached an understanding of what you have read.

In both situations, if you test your hypothesis and it does *not* hold true, you return to a prereading strategy and try a new hypothesis. Like the writing process, the reading process does not work in a straight line. Reading and writing processes are recursive.

Let us take this notion of process in relation to purpose a step further. It is unlikely that you are reading this book for enjoyment. We fear, if truth be told, that your purpose for reading this chapter may be simply to get it out of the way before going down the hall and guiltlessly playing cards with your friends. If your purpose is just to get it done, reading will be a linear process, and if you are in a hurry, you probably will not return to the beginning to revise a hypothesis proved wrong.

If your purpose for reading is simply to finish an assignment, you will certainly develop a strategy to do just that. However, we want to begin this chapter in the belief that there are higher purposes for reading than simply getting an assignment out of the way. We also want to begin in the belief that once students learn what to do to satisfy a reading assignment, they will read with these higher purposes foremost in mind.

What are these higher purposes? The most basic is understanding. You no doubt read for understanding in situations where you believe your teacher is likely to give you a pop test, or where you need to find information for something you plan on writing.

Some purposes are more demanding of time and energy than others, however. Though all reading begins with (and from a certain perspective on reading *is*) understanding, most of your teachers will expect you to think more deeply than you do when you read only to **comprehend** a text—that is, when you read to find out what the assignment means. Most of your teachers will require you to read a text **critically**—that is, not only to understand it, but to analyze, evaluate, and respond personally and analytically to it.

Oftentimes, when students don't know how to perform these critical reading tasks, they give up on a reading assignment more quickly than they should. In the remainder of this chapter, our goal is to give you skills that will keep you reading, beginning with skills that will help you better comprehend what you are reading and then moving on to those that will enable you to analyze, evaluate, and respond personally to any text you are apt to encounter as a student in any department.

Keep in mind that in addition to reading to get an assignment out of the way, students read for the following purposes discussed more fully below:

- to understand what is written
- to analyze the author's purpose and how it is achieved
- to evaluate the information received from a text and determine its usefulness in light of the assignment
- to respond personally and analytically to the text's contents

Exercises

1. Return to the list of life readings you have made over the past 24 hours (see page 42). In your class notebook, analyze one of those readings by hypothesizing why the reading occurred, testing your hypothesis against subsequent occurrences, and determining if your initial hypothesis was correct.

2. To see for yourself how the readings of texts require many of the same skills as you use in the reading of life experiences, read through the following passage that is arranged to enable you to hypothesize what the passage is about.

We All Want Life to Make Sense

a. *On the basis of this title, what do you anticipate this passage will be about?*

by Paula Blakey

b. *If you know anything about this author, what do you predict this passage will be about?*

> The year is 1920. On the grassy fertile slopes lining the interior of the island of New Guinea live about one million farmers. These aboriginal highlanders have lived for generations within the isolation of the surrounding mountains, unbeknownst to anyone in the outside world. For years they have planted and harvested and eaten and fought in the day, and have worshipped their dead ancestors and relatives at night. Life in these fertile valleys has been generally uncomplicated.

c. *Based on this first paragraph, what do you predict the passage will be about? What do you believe will come next?*

> Rumors arise—a long chain of people has been seen traveling down into the valleys toward the farmlands. The Blacks wonder as they watch the far-off outsiders pick their way carefully down the precarious mountainside. They watch in mixed excitement and fear as the party of outsiders approaches. Finally, the ancient Blacks behold a sight they had never even conceived of before: three strangely dressed men leading the string of Black outsiders have no color in their faces—their skin is *white.*

d. *What do you predict will happen, based on what you have read thus far?*

> To the farmers who know of no world outside their own valleys, these people—these *white* people—are inexplicable. Faced with such an incredible new situation, the Blacks jump to the first conclusion that makes sense to them. Since these strange-looking men have no color in their skin, they must have no life in them either. Also, since none of the farmers has ever seen the sacred ancestors, whom the Blacks faithfully thank each day, then *these* white men must be the ghosts of the revered dead ancestors. It is decided and passed along to others—the ancestors have come.

3. *If you have access to a computer and e-mail,* monitor an on-line discussion list or conversation to observe the ways in which people enhance their electronic messages with graphic or language devices designed to help readers more accurately comprehend what is going on. Look specifically, for example, at the **emotions** that are used—the symbols used to express emotion: :) to indicate a smile or a joke, ;) to indicate a wink. Look also at signature-block art that people include with their messages to give some indication of their values, lifestyles, occupations, sense of humor, and so on. In writing, describe how these items can help readers of e-mail and e-discourse. Discuss, as well, why these items seem to be necessary for life readings—on-line and popular.

Understanding What You Read

Most people are so accustomed to reading to understand that they do so without any need to acknowledge that they are reading with any particular purpose in mind at all. When they hold a book, article, or chapter in front of them, most are driven quite naturally to understand what they read. Now that you are in college, you will have even greater motivation to read for understanding since many of your teachers will specify chapters you must read to prepare for tests.

Under what circumstances will you read for understanding? On one end of the spectrum of reading situations are informal communications. For instance, if your teacher assigns a chapter for you to read and report on in your next class meeting, you will benefit from taking time to anticipate what the assignment is about and to preview the assignment before interpreting what it means. You should analyze the author's purpose, evaluate the usefulness of the material, and respond personally to what you have read.

These skills are useful in most reading you will do in college. Consider the requirements of the following assignment from an introductory philosphy course.

> Students must do all the reading assignments listed in the syllabus. These reading assignments must be completed for each Monday class.
>
> Students will be given a minor test on their reading each Monday. In that test, they will be expected to state in one sentence the main point the author makes. Once they have done that, students must, in no more than a paragraph, explain their views on the topic.

This task is typical of reading assignments made in courses across the disciplines. Whether you are reading an assignment to prepare for a major test such as a midterm or final examination or, as in the above assignment, to perform well on a minor test intended chiefly to determine if you have actually done more than read to get the assignment out of the way, your purpose is pretty basic: to understand the material.

One useful strategy for preparing to read is **reviewing.** It should be clear that most life reading is done on the basis of past experience. Maybe you understand a glance or stare because others have glanced or stared at you before. This prior experience enables you to read more effectively the glances or stares of others. Reviewing is a strategy that makes use of your prior experiences and knowledge, provided you have had some sort of experience with a topic.

Place yourself in an introductory biology class. Your teacher has just required you to read a chapter on viruses, assuming, of course, that everyone has caught a virus of some kind during their lives. If you were to review your prior experiences with viruses, you might end up with something similar to what a student wrote in the following example.

> I remember catching a cold when I was in high school. My mother said I probably caught it by going outside with wet hair on cold mornings. I usually treat these kinds of viruses by eating chicken soup and taking aspirins.

This student has done something we hope you will learn to do. He has reviewed what he knows as a way of preparing himself for correcting incorrect assumptions he has about the subject—that a cold, for instance, might be something you get from walking around in the cold immediately after washing your hair—and for adding new information onto what he already knows, the kind of learning situation that is apt to occur for you most often in college. Among

other things that might happen if you review prior information before reading—including understanding that writing might be used to help you learn—
you will remind yourself of what you know to be true and you will find out
what you will need to learn if you hope to understand the chapter when you
read it.

What happens if you find out that you really don't know much about a
subject? You might learn to approach reviewing, as the student does below, in
an effort to determine what you need to know to be thoroughly knowledgeable
about a subject. This student was preparing to read about Christopher Colum-
bus in her introductory history course. Notice that this journal entry sounds
like a conversation between the writer and her inner voice.

> I learned in high school that Christopher Columbus isn't viewed by everyone
> as a hero. He invaded the Caribbean islands and made slaves of the people
> he found there. In South America, I can't remember where exactly, he not only
> enslaved people, but he exploited mineral and natural resources. There were
> a few other things he did that really put me off. I'll need to check on them.

You just might find out that you don't know as much about a subject as you
think you do or, like the student above, that you don't remember everything
you learned in high school. The result is likely to be that you will read more
closely in an effort to fill those gaps in information that you have discovered
by reviewing material prior to reading.

Though reviewing is a useful activity, it does not engage you in making sense
of the reading assignment—and it might not serve you at all in the unlikely
event that you know absolutely nothing about the material to be read. In that
case, you might make sense of the material by employing two other strategies
that engage you directly with the reading assignment: skimming and annotating.

Exercises

1. The next section of this chapter is entitled "Skimming." On the basis of that
   title and your past experience as a reader, write down what you think that
   section will be about.
2. In your class notebook, describe what you routinely do when you read, from
   the time you pick up the text to the time you feel you have finished reading.
3. In your class notebook, describe how you were taught to read.
   a. Did you read words phonetically?
   b. What kinds of stories do you recall having read to you?
   c. What of the first stories you read to yourself can you recall?
   d. Did you have a favorite? What was it?
   e. Why was it your favorite?
      Discuss this assignment with a partner or in a small group.

4. *If you have access to the World Wide Web,* access several of the commercial home pages that have been posted there—home pages designed by businesses to describe their products and what they do. Take notes about how you read these pages: what you routinely do when you look at them from the time they appear on the screen to the time you exit them.

   In your journal, describe how your reading of these home pages differs from or is similar to the readings you do of more conventional print texts.

5. *If you have access to e-mail,* read a day's worth of your e-mail and write a reflective journal entry on the processes you use to read e-mail. How do you choose which messages to read first, second, third? What do you do routinely when you open up an e-mail message? Where do you look? What information do you consider important?

Skimming

Skimming, or what some people might call **previewing,** a book, a chapter, or an article is a way of bracing yourself for what's ahead. This isn't really a strategy you are totally unfamiliar with. If you read with the intention of just getting the assignment out of the way, you are likely to settle on skimming as an adequate substitute for the entire reading process. Or, if you tend to see how many pages you have to read, you will probably employ some of the skills related to skimming.

More than just counting the number of pages you have to read and determining based on that number how long your reading assignment will take, skimming helps you discover the main ideas of the reading assignment, the details or examples the author uses for support, the difficulty of the assignment, its usefulness, and the author's purpose.

Here are some guidelines we recommend that you follow in skimming a reading assignment.

1. Look over external clues.
2. Look over internal clues.
3. Study context clues.
4. Read the introduction and conclusion.
5. Read topic sentences.
6. Look over figures, graphs, and other optional textual features.
7. Examine context clues.

External clues

Skimming a reading assignment inevitably begins with the external context for the assignment. If you have ever looked at the last page of an assignment to find out how long it is, you know how important external clues can be. Think over the following questions related to the external context.

- Are you reading a full-length book or a shorter assignment, such as a chapter or an article?
- What is your purpose for reading? To pass a test? To find information for a paper or oral report?

You begin the engagement called reading as soon as you identify the kind of text you must read. As you know quite well, a poem is different in some basic ways from a memo or report or essay precisely because it sets you up to expect different kinds of information in a relatively more difficult format than other kinds of texts.

You also know by now that you will read for understanding differently than you will read for critical purposes, as we describe them below: the kind of thinking that begins with understanding and then moves into analysis, evaluation, and response.

Internal clues

Skimming the text's internal clues begins with noting certain clues that point you toward the text's key points. Finding key points in a reading assignment is easier to do if you pay attention to the title, author, chapter headings of books, abstracts or preliminary information of articles, and all other optional features of the text, including illustrations, tables, and graphs.

Context clues

By skimming, you can also determine how much the author relies on **jargon,** the technical language of a discipline, helpful chiefly in enabling a specialist to write to an audience of other specialists. If you note a high use of jargon when you skim an article, you can anticipate that the article will be difficult to read unless you are familiar with that jargon.

One way to determine the meaning of words with special meanings or special uses is by understanding the context in which the words occur. The context itself is a kind of clue.

"The Smurfette Principle" (pages 50–53), written for a general audience of college-educated men and women (readers of *The New York Times Magazine*), relies less on jargon than does the more specialized writing of Ronald Wishart of Union Carbide Corporation in his statement concerning the Bhopal incident (pages 71–73). See if, by reading the address in context, you can figure out what words fit into the blank spaces.

> Since my responsibilities are _____ , I am not intimate with our international operations. Therefore, in the interest of _____ in responding to your questions, I believe that it will be necessary to _____ to them at a later time, when I have been able to collect the _____ .

(Note that you can check to see if you were correct in using the context to determine meaning by checking paragraph three of Wishart's address on page 71.)

Exercises

If you glance at pages 50–53, you will find a sample reading assignment, "The Smurfette Principle." Answer the following questions about this essay by focusing on internal clues.

1. **Title:** On the basis of this title, what do you suppose this essay is about? To what does the title of the essay refer? On the basis of this reference, what do you think the "smurfette principle" is?
2. **Author:** Do you recognize the author's name? If so, what prior experience have you had as a reader with this author? On the basis of that experience, what do you expect to encounter, in terms of subject and difficulty in this essay?
3. **Preliminary Information:** What information do you receive by reading the summary and introductory material? Under what circumstances, since this summary material indicates the major point of the essay, would a person continue to read?
4. **Other Features of the Text:** What do you conclude about the article when, as you might have already noticed, you see that it first appeared in *The New York Times Magazine?* Do you reach a certain understanding about the essay based on the fact that it does *not* have any tables, graphs, or other highlighted features? Does the author rely on jargon? If so, pick out several examples.

As you can see, skimming the internal features can provide you with an abundance of material that will make the task of reading an assignment much more manageable.

Introduction and conclusion

What can you find out by reading the introduction and conclusion of a text? First, you may discover the author's main point. Second, you will be able to determine the author's purpose. Third, you will gain some insight into the relative difficulty and usefulness of the assignment.

THE SMURFETTE PRINCIPLE

Katha Pollitt

This Christmas, I finally caved in: I gave my three-year-old daughter, Sophie, her very own cassette of *The Little Mermaid.* Now, she too, can sit transfixed by Ariel, the perky teenager with the curvy tail who trades her voice for a pair of shapely legs and a shot at marriage to a prince. ("On land it's much preferred for ladies not to say a word," sings the cynical sea witch, "and she who holds her tongue will get her man." Since she's the villain, we're not meant to notice that events prove her correct.)

Usually when parents give a child some item they find repellant, they plead helplessness before a juvenile filibuster. But *The Little Mermaid* was my idea. Ariel may look a lot like Barbie, and her adventure may be limited to romance and over with the wedding bells, but unlike, say, Cinderella or Sleeping Beauty, she's active, brave and determined, the heroine of her own life. She even rescues the prince. And that makes her a rare fish, indeed, in the world of preschool culture.

Take a look at the kids' section of your local video store. You'll find that features starring boys, and usually aimed at them, account for nine out of ten offerings. Clicking the television dial one recent week—admittedly not an encyclopedic study—I came across not a single network cartoon or puppet show starring a female. (Nickelodeon, the children's cable channel, has one of each.) Except for the crudity of the animation and the general air of witlessness and hype, I might as well have been back in my own 1950's childhood, nibbling Frosted Flakes in front of Daffy Duck, Bugs Bunny, Porky Pig and the rest of the all-male Warner Brothers lineup.

Contemporary shows are either essentially all-male, like *Garfield,* or are organized on what I call the Smurfette principle: a group of male buddies will be accented by a lone female, stereotypically defined. In the worst cartoons— the ones that blend seamlessly into the animated cereal commercials—the female is usually a little-sister type, a bunny in a pink dress and hair ribbons who tags along with the adventurous bears and badgers. But the Smurfette principle rules the more carefully made shows, too. Thus, Kanga, the only female in *Winnie-the-Pooh,* is a mother. Piggy, of *Muppet Babies,* is a pint-size version of Miss Piggy, the camp glamour queen of the Muppet movies. April, of the wildly popular *Teen-Age Mutant Ninja Turtles,* functions as a girl Friday to a quartet of male superheroes. The message is clear. Boys are the norm, girls the variation; boys are central, girls peripheral; boys are individuals, girls types. Boys define the group, its story and its code of values. Girls exist only in relation to boys.

Well, commercial television—what did I expect? The surprise is that public television, for all its superior intelligence, charm and commitment to worthy values, shortchanges preschool girls, too. Mister Rogers lives in a neighborhood populated mostly by middle-aged men like himself. *Shining Time Station* features a cartoon in which the male characters are train engines and the female characters are passenger cars. And then there's *Sesame Street.* True, the human characters are neatly divided between the genders (and among the races, too, which is another rarity). The film clips, moreover, are just about the only place on television in which you regularly see girls having fun together: practicing double Dutch, having a sleep-over. But the Muppets are the real stars of *Sesame Street,* and the important ones—the ones with real personalities, who sing on the musical videos, whom kids identify with and cherish in dozens of licensed products—are *all* male. I know one little girl who was so outraged and heartbroken when she realized that even Big Bird—her last hope—was a boy that she hasn't watched the show since.

Well, there's always the library. Some of the best children's books ever written have been about girls—Madeline, Frances the badger. It's even possible to find stories with funny, feminist messages, like *The Paperbag Princess.* (She rescues the prince from a dragon, but he's so ungrateful that she decides not to marry him, after all.) But books about girls are a subset in a field that includes a much larger subset of books about boys (twelve of the fourteen storybooks singled out for praise in last year's Christmas roundup in *Newsweek,* for instance) and books in which the sex of the child is theoretically unimportant—in which case it usually "happens to be" male. Dr. Seuss's books are less about individual characters than about language and imaginative freedom—but, somehow or other, only boys get to go beyond Zebra or see marvels on Mulberry Street. Frog and Toad, Lowly Worm, Lyle the Crococile, all *could* have been female. But they're not.

Do kids pick up on the sexism in children's culture? You bet. Preschoolers are like medieval philosophers: the text—a book, a movie, a TV show—is more authoritative than the evidence of their own eyes. "Let's play weddings," says my little niece. We grownups roll our eyes, but face it: It's still the one scenario in which the girl is the central figure. "Women are *nurses,*" my friend Anna, a doctor, was informed by her then four-year-old, Molly. Even my Sophie is beginning to notice the back-seat role played by girls in some of her favorite books. "Who's that?" she asks every time we reread *The Cat in the Hat.* It's Sally, the timid little sister of the resourceful boy narrator. She wants Sally to matter, I think, and since Sally is really just a name and a hair ribbon, we have to say her name again and again.

The sexism in preschool culture deforms both boys and girls. Little girls learn to split their consciousness, filtering their dreams and ambitions through boy characters while admiring the clothes of the princess. The more privileged and daring can dream of becoming exceptional women in a man's world—Smurfettes. The others are being taught to accept the more usual fate, which is to be a passenger car drawn through life by a masculine train engine. Boys, who are rarely confronted with stories in which males play only minor roles, learn a simpler lesson: girls just don't matter much.

How can it be that twenty-five years of feminist social change have made so little impression on preschool culture? Molly, now six and well aware that women can be doctors, has one theory: children's entertainment is mostly made by men. That's true, as it happens, and I'm sure it explains a lot. It's also true that, as a society, we don't seem to care much what goes on with kids, as long as they are reasonably quiet. Marshmallow cereal, junky toys, endless hours in front of the tube—a society that accepts all that is not going to get in a lather about a little gender stereotyping. It's easier to focus on the bright side. I had *Cinderella,* Sophie has *The Little Mermaid*—that's progress, isn't it?

"We're working on it," Dulcy Singer, the executive producer of *Sesame Street,* told me when I raised the sensitive question of those all-male Muppets.

After all, the show has only been on the air for a quarter of a century; these things take time. The trouble is, our preschoolers don't have time. My funny, clever, bold, adventurous daughter is forming her gender ideas right now. I do what I can to counteract the messages she gets from her entertainment, and so does her father—Sophie watches very little television. But I can see we have our work cut out for us. It sure would help if the bunnies took off their hair ribbons, and if half the monsters were fuzzy, blue—and female.

1. Consider "The Smurfette Principle" by looking over the first and the last two paragraphs of the essay.

   Paragraph 1: This Christmas, I finally caved in: I gave my three-year-old daughter, Sophie, her very own cassette of *The Little Mermaid.* Now, she too, can sit transfixed by Ariel the perky teenager with the curvy tail who trades her voice for a pair of shapely legs and a shot at marriage to a prince. ("On land it's much preferred for ladies not to say a word," sings the cynical sea witch, "and she who holds her tongue will get her man." Since she's the villain, we're not meant to notice that events prove her correct.)

   Paragraphs 9 and 10: How can it be that twenty-five years of feminist social change have made so little impression on preschool culture? Molly, now six and well aware that women can be doctors, has one theory: children's entertainment is mostly made by men. That's true, as it happens, and I'm sure it explains a lot. It's also true that, as a society, we don't seem to care much what goes on with kids, as long as they are reasonably quiet. Marshmallow cereal, junky toys, endless hours in front of the tube—a society that accepts all that is not going to get in a lather about a little gender stereotyping. It's easier to focus on the bright side. I had *Cinderella,* Sophie has *The Little Mermaid*—that's progress, isn't it?

   "We're working on it," Dulcy Singer, the executive producer of *Sesame Street,* told me when I raised the sensitive question of those all-male Muppets. After all, the show has only been on the air for a quarter of a century; these things take time. The trouble is, our preschoolers don't have time. My funny, clever, bold, adventurous daughter is forming her gender ideas right now. I do what I can to counteract the messages she gets from her entertainment, and so does her father—Sophie watches very little television. But I can see we have our work cut out for us. It sure would help if the bunnies took off their hair ribbons and if half of the monsters were fuzzy, blue—and female.

2. Answer the following questions about these paragraphs in your class notebook.

- **Main point:**
  a. What is the subject of "The Smurfette Principle"?
  b. What impression do you get of the author? Is this someone you are apt to agree with? Someone you may disagree with?
  c. Who does she seem to address in this essay? Do you envision yourself as part of her intended audience?
- **Purpose:**
  a. What is the author's purpose for writing on this subject?
  b. What effect do you suppose she wants to have on her audience?
- **Difficulty and usefulness:**
  a. How might you use information from these paragraphs? Is it the kind of information you would use only in academic settings?
  b. Does the level of information seem appropriate to your purposes?
  c. Does the language used fit comfortably into your vocabulary?

3. *If you have access to the World Wide Web,* access three personal home pages that people have posted there. In your reading journal, answer the following questions: What kinds of text serve as an introduction to a home page? What characteristics do the introductions to these three home pages have in common? What impressions do these introductions give you of the people represented by these home pages?

4. Now, look at the conclusions of these three home pages. What characteristics do these have in common? What constitutes the conclusion of a home page? What characteristics do such conclusions have? What impressions do these conclusions give you of the people represented by these home pages?

5. *If you have access to a computer and e-mail,* use the next e-mail message you receive to answer the following questions in your reading journal:

Subject line: What is the subject line of this message? On the basis of the subject line, what do you suppose the e-mail message is going to be about?

Author: Whose name appears in the "From" line of the message? Do you recognize the sender's name? If so, what prior experience do you have with the author? On the basis of that experience, what do you expect to encounter in this e-mail message?

Other features of the text: What can you conclude about this message by virtue of the fact that it was sent in an electronic environment rather than a hard-copy environment? Is it more or less urgent or important? More or less timely? Is it of a more or less personal nature? Is it going to be longer or shorter than print texts?

Topic sentences

In many of the kinds of essays you will read for college, paragraphs have topic sentences that lend support to the author's main point. These sentences are usually the first ones in their paragraphs (though they might be found elsewhere from time to time). Basically, since these sentences summarize what the entire paragraph will be about, readers use them to prepare for what follows in a paragraph.

1. The sentences that follow are topic sentences from "The Smurfette Principle." Read them and see if you can predict by writing your predictions in your class notebook what the paragraphs they introduce will be about.

   Paragraph 2: Usually when parents give a child some item they find repellent, they plead helplessness before a juvenile filibuster.

   a. *What do you believe Paragraph 2 will be about?*

   Paragraph 3: Take a look at the kids' section of your local video store.

   b. *What do you believe Paragraph 3 will be about?*

   Paragraph 4: Contemporary shows are either essentially all-male, like *Garfield,* or are organized on what I call the Smurfette principle: a group of male buddies will be accented by a lone female, stereotypically defined.

   c. *What do you believe Paragraph 4 will be about?*

   As the above exercise shows, by reading the introduction and conclusion as well as the topic sentences of each paragraph in between, you will be able to determine the subject of the essay, the key supporting points, the organizational strategy, and the writer's attitude toward the subject.

2. *If you have access to the World Wide Web,* access one personal home page that someone has posted there. Look at the links that the person has identified on this home page, but do not go to these links or activate them. Instead, in your reading journal, write down predictions of what you would find should you choose to activate each link.

   When you are done, go to each of the links and compare your predictions to the information you find there. In each case, answer the following questions in your reading journal: What is the difference between what you predicted for the linked information and what was actually there? What factors either misled you or informed you in your prediction?

Other textual features

Many of the kinds of texts you will read in college, including textbooks such as this one, rely heavily on other textual features such as figures, graphs, and charts. For instance, in longer works, such as textbooks or research studies, you might want to review the table of contents or the index to determine what you should expect to find between the covers. In shorter works, you might look at abstracts or figures for the same purpose: to enable yourself to predict what the essay will be about.

Certain kinds of texts will invite certain kinds of previews. For instance, a chapter might begin with an abstract, highlight portions in the margins, and offer exercises at the end. Your job, as a reader who is not in a rush to get to a card game, is to learn how to look at a reading assignment and bring to any text you must read prior information that will enable you to read successfully. Previewing is just one of those useful skills. Annotating is another.

1. Using the advice offered in this section, skim the Preface to *Cultural Literacy* by E. D. Hirsch (pages 64–67).

Annotating for Understanding and Recall

Annotation provides you with the opportunity to use your pencil or pen to mark parts of your reading assignment that you think are important enough to return to later. One way to think of annotating is that it is a process of entering into a dialogue with the author. Another way to think about annotating is that it is a process of recording what you have read so that you can return to the text later and recall its main points without having to reread the entire thing.

You will probably find yourself entering such dialogues with a desire not only to highlight main points and to record in summary fashion major points in the author's argument or explanation, but, like any other dialogue you might enter, with a desire to question, object, explain your objections, and evaluate the author's treatment of the topic. This type of annotation, as discussed below, will enable you to more easily read with critical purposes in mind.

Let us look first at annotating for understanding. Since you make annotations with the intention of returning to them, your annotations ought to be done systematically. If you annotate to understand, for instance, you might be satisfied with those marks on the page itself which will assist you later when you want to quickly recall information. Good annotations will make it possible for you to review your marks on the page and understand the text later without having to reread the entire document.

Annotating a text, though, can be as complex an activity as you want it to be. If you are annotating for simple recall, try to keep in mind the various technical elements or clues in the document that will remind you of the author's subject, purpose, and organizational strategy.

In annotating a document for simple recall, keep these basic questions in mind:

- What is the thesis statement (if the document, indeed, has one)?
- How is the text organized?
- What are the central divisions in the text?

- How does the author support these ideas?
- What does the author use as evidence?

Keeping these questions in mind as you mark up the text will enable you to annotate so that you will recall the reading assignment later without having to reread the entire thing. While this procedure might seem laborious at first, the more you practice reading with these questions in mind, the better you will get at annotating.

What's more, the more you practice, the more apt you will be to develop your own methods for annotating, perhaps using some variation on the above questions (though to meet the demands of certain specific instructors, you may develop questions of your own). In any case, the following practical guidelines for annotating should prove helpful.

Annotating for recall: some guidelines

- Always read with a pen or pencil in hand.
- Underline clues to the document's meaning: statements of purpose, definitions, thesis statement, topic sentences.
- Circle context clues (that is, key words and phrases) that indicate a sequence of information (for example, first, second) or relationships among the parts of the text (for example, because, although) or conclusions (for example, thus, therefore, as a result).

Notice the way the following annotation serves to answer the questions listed above.

An important research tool in protecting wildlife involves tracking the journey of a species from its birthplace to its mating site. In the case of the green turtle, which does not start breeding until the age of thirty, this has proven to be a difficult challenge. Researchers have tried to monitor its meanderings by tagging it with metal disks of wires, but the turtle's dramatic growth over the decades—from four inches at infancy to four feet in adulthood—has stymied efforts to keep the tags in place.

Seeking an alternative tracking method, Brian W. Bowen, an evolutionary geneticist, turned instead to natural markings. Bowen analyzed mitochondrial DNA from eggs and hatchlings at four green-turtle breeding sites in the Atlantic and the Caribbean. He and his coworkers report that turtles from the four breeding sites tended to differ slightly in genetic sequence. The existence of variations in DNA among geographically distinct groups has helped scientists sway the balance between different theories of the mating habits of the green turtle.

Annotating with the intention of recalling enough of the document so that you do not have to reread it requires finding the most essential clues to the text's meaning and underlining, highlighting, circling, and/or numbering parts, as in the above passage.

1. Annotate the following passage.
   a. Underline, highlight, and circle key words, ideas, and sentences with the intention of using these markings as a way of recalling the passage later without having to reread it.
   b. When you have finished, discuss with a partner the kinds of marks you have made. Why did you make the marks you made? How does your annotation for understanding differ from your partner's?

> In Roman times, defeated enemies were generally put to death as criminals for having offended the emperor of Rome. In the Middle Ages, however, the practice of ransoming, or returning prisoners in exchange for money, became common. Though some saw this custom as a step towards a more humane society, the primary reasons behind it were economic rather than humanitarian.
>
> In those times, rulers had only a limited ability to raise taxes. They could neither force their subjects to fight nor pay them to do so. The promise of material compensations in the form of goods and ransom was therefore the only way of inducing combatants to participate in a war.
>
> In the Middle Ages, the predominant incentive for the individual soldier to participate in a war was the expectation of spoils. Although collecting ransom clearly brought financial gain, keeping a prisoner and arranging for his exchange had its costs. Consequently, several procedures were devised to reduce transaction costs.
>
> One such device was a rule asserting that the prisoner had to assess his own value. This compelled the prisoner to establish a value without much distortion; indicating too low a value would increase the captive's chances of being killed, while indicating too high a value would either ruin him financially or create a prohibitively expensive ransom that would also result in death.

2. *If you have access to the World Wide Web,* access one informational home page that has been posted there—not a personal home page or a commercial home page, but a home page that some organization or a group has set up primarily to convey information to the public. Although you cannot annotate this home page on-line, you can write an accompanying document in which you annotate the home page elements.
   a. In your reading journal annotate the first screen only of the home page. Identify key words, sentences, and phrases that you think are important for you as a critical reader of this home page. Choose a partner for this exercise who will agree to annotate the same home page independently.
   b. When you are both done, share the notes you have made with your partner. Discuss why you made the annotations you did. Discuss why your partner made the annotations he/she did. Focus on the differences in your annotations and try to speculate on why they exist.

Reading Critically: Analyzing, Evaluating, and Responding

During your college career, you will undoubtedly be asked to begin with what you understand about a text and then move into the kind of advanced thinking people call **critical thinking.** While there are many definitions of critical thinking, most people agree that it begins with understanding and moves on to analysis, evaluation, and response or interpretation.

On some occasions, your college teachers will require you to employ critical thinking strategies to reinforce learning. On other occasions, you may be asked to analyze a text, focusing on the author's purpose, the document's organization, the audience addressed as well as the author's assumptions about the audience, and the author's use of evidence. When a teacher asks you to evaluate and respond to a text, the teacher is asking you to build upon your ability to read for understanding and to analyze what you have read.

Analyzing a Text

Analysis begins with what is on the page, but eventually requires you to make judgments about what you have read, offering observations based on prior information and past experiences in the process. In addition to helping you better understand and recall what you have read, annotation provides you with a tool for entering the kind of conversation that makes analysis possible.

Annotations that foster analysis and lead to critical thinking tend to answer questions such as the following:

- How might this information be connected to other things you have read, seen or done?
- Does the author's rendering of the subject seem correct?
- If the author's rendering of the subject does not seem correct, on what issues does your view differ from the author's?
- Would other authors you have read disagree with this author's view of the subject?
- Will other authors you plan on reading agree with this author?
- Would your classmates agree with this author?
- Would your instructor agree with this author?

Obviously, these questions cannot be answered by underlining, highlighting, circling, or numbering. Rather, these questions require you to enter into a dialogue with the author, making use of the space around the text where you can write your part of the conversation.

To enter a conversation of this kind, you should first annotate the document to make certain you understand it, using the three guidelines listed in "Annotating for Recall" (page 57). Then follow the suggestions offered below in "Annotating for Critical Reading: Some Guidelines." Remember that your goal in annotating the text for purposes of analysis is not only to understand what the author has said, but to contribute something to what the author has said on the basis of your own information and experience—that is, to begin the process of analysis.

Annotating for critical reading: some guidelines
- Summarize the topic of the document in the margins.
- Note the topic of each paragraph in the margins.
- Ask questions in the margins.
- Make notes in the margins that you might return to later as reminders of what you plan to say about this document.
- Mark passages you might want to quote.
- Keep track of where you (or others you have read on the topic) disagree with the author.

Annotations done in an effort to analyze your reading assignment provide a foundation for other critical tasks you will have to perform in college, including the kind of writing—summarizing, paraphrasing, critiquing, and synthesizing—you must do in analyzing, evaluating, and responding to a reading assignment.

Note how annotations based on the above questions and employing guidelines for annotating critically are made in the margins of the same text as the one annotated on page 57. Remember that when you read critically, rather than just for understanding, you annotate with different purposes in mind and, therefore, use different skills.

Subj: tool to protect wildlife—see Johnson's essay on this subject

How does this differ from other animals?

Bowen's Alternative Bowen's Analysis

Does Bowen's method apply to other animals as well?

An important research tool in protecting wildlife involves tracking the journey of a species from its birthplace to its mating site. In the case of the green turtle, which does not start breeding until the age of thirty, this has proven to be a difficult challenge. Researchers have tried to monitor its meanderings by tagging it with metal disks of wires, but the turtle's dramatic growth over the decades—from four inches at infancy to four feet in adulthood—has stymied efforts to keep the tags in place.

Seeking an alternative tracking method, Brian W. Bowen, an evolutionary geneticist, turned instead to natural markings. Bowen analyzed mitochondrial DNA from eggs and hatchlings at four green-turtle breeding sites in the Atlantic and the Caribbean. He and his co-workers report that turtles from the four breeding sites tended to differ slightly in genetic sequence. The existence of variations in DNA among geographically distinct groups has helped scientists sway the balance between different theories of the mating habits of the green turtle.

Though you may find it convenient to make both kinds of annotations in the same reading session, you will probably find it useful to read for understanding before reading critically since reading is a process. In fact, you will find it very difficult to read critically if you have not taken time to understand what you have read. When you annotate a text in preparation for reading critically—that is, to analyze, evaluate, or respond—you are engaged in the reading assignment differently than you are when you read to understand.

In reading to understand, your goal is to determine what the author intended, an effort accomplished most easily when you find and indicate *on the text* the clues that will help you recall later what the document was about.

In reading to analyze, evaluate, and/or respond, your goal is to move beyond understanding, annotating *in the margins* by summarizing the topic of both the document and each individual paragraph, asking questions, making notes, agreeing and disagreeing with the author, and indicating why you believe what you do. This effort is made most often in preparation for using what you have read in some way in addition to simple recall. In short, when you annotate a text for purposes of analysis, you read the way a writer does in preparing for writing.

Exercises

1. Annotate the following passage in preparation for critical understanding.

    In Roman times, defeated enemies were generally put to death as criminals for having offended the emperor of Rome. In the Middle Ages, however, the practice of ransoming, or returning prisoners in exchange for money, became common. Though some saw this custom as a step toward a more humane society, the primary reasons behind it were economic rather than humanitarian.

    In those times, rulers had only a limited ability to raise taxes. They could neither force their subjects to fight nor pay them to do so. The promise of material compensations in the form of goods and ransom was therefore the only way of inducing combatants to participate in a war.

    In the Middle Ages, the predominant incentive for the individual soldier was the expectation of spoils. Although collecting ransom clearly brought financial gain, keeping a prisoner and arranging for his exchange had its costs. Consequently, several procedures were devised to reduce transaction costs.

    One such device was a rule asserting that the prisoner had to assess his own value. This compelled the prisoner to establish a value without much distortion; indicating too low a value would increase the captive's chances of being killed, while indicating too high a value would either ruin him financially or create a prohibitively expensive ransom that would also result in death.

2. *If you have access to a computer and e-mail,* select the next substantial e-mail message that you receive and print it out. Choose a message that is relatively long, that contains several parts or paragraphs, or that is relatively complex in its subject matter.

Using the guidelines we have provided, analyze the message in preparation for critical understanding.

Analyzing a text using a journal

In completing critical reading tasks, since many are linked to writing, annotating is just the start. Besides skimming and annotating, you might help yourself prepare to use what you have read by taking notes in a journal or on notecards.

As you make your way through your reading assignment, you might use your journal or notecard to satisfy the demand that you fully analyze a text before evaluating and responding personally to it.

Analysis is a natural consequence of having to understand the details of what you have read. In short, when you analyze a text, you are asking, "How is this text constructed?"

We recommend that you begin your analysis by reading over the text carefully with several key questions in mind. These questions will focus on different aspects of what you have read—purpose, organization, audience, and evidence.

Let us take these matters one at a time in analyzing "The Smurfette Principle" which appears on pages 50–53.

What is the writer's purpose?   Pollitt intends to describe what she sees as sex-role stereotyping as it is taught to children by the society they are brought up in. She frames her analysis with personal experiences as a woman and as a mother. She is especially mindful of the fact that children learn about sex roles before they even begin school.

How is the material organized?   Pollitt organizes her material around her concern that her daughter will accept the stereotype she sees in the world around her, especially in the media. She begins by noting that children demand toys, games, and other items that actually reinforce sex role stereotypes. She moves on in paragraph three to describe videos that might be found in the kids' section of a video store. Then in paragraph four, she moves on to discuss television, in paragraph six, children's books, and paragraph seven, the culture at large.

To whom does the author write and what assumptions does the author make about her audience?   Pollitt writes to an audience of readers who might be receptive to her argument. Many are, no doubt, women, and many of those women, young mothers. By citing her husband's efforts to help their children avoid sex-role stereotypes, Pollitt seems to enlist other open-minded men as well.

What does the author use for evidence?   Though sex-role stereotyping is an emotional issue for many people, Pollitt avoids the common pitfalls of emotion that might serve to alienate some portion of her audience. Instead, she provides evidence from the culture at large, citing toys, games, videos, television shows, and children's books that readers are familiar with. She also uses her experience as a mother as support for many of her observations.

FIGURE 2.1   Double-entry Journal: "A Father's Eyes"

<u>Author's Assumptions</u>

* The author takes the view that children are taught early in their lives certain gender roles that influence behavior during their adult lives.

* The author identifies various cultural artifacts that serve to instruct children in sex roles.

* Adult stereotyping is based on childhood learning.

<u>My Reaction</u>

* Some of what we learn about ourselves as men and women is taught subtly. This kind of analysis in interesting.

* I don't think I'd want my daughter to be influenced in this way — before she has a chance to understand what's being done to her.

* How can these sex-role stereotypes be eliminated? Should they be?

You may find it useful, as an alternative to the kind of journal entry used above, to employ a **double-entry journal**. To employ a double-entry journal, divide the page from top to bottom roughly in the middle of the page. On the left side of the line, write what the document is about. On the right side of the line, write your personal response to the material, as in Figure 2.1.

By answering questions such as these or by responding to the essay using the double-entry journal format, you have taken the essay apart and seen how its components contribute to the way it works. Such analysis by itself will, of course, be helpful in certain circumstances (for example, interpreting a literary work, writing a book review, and so forth), but, more importantly, analytical skills can be used in a range of activities and enable you to move beyond comprehension and analysis and into evaluation of and response to a piece of writing.

Exercises

1. Read the Preface to *Cultural Literacy* by E. D. Hirsch on pages 64–67, and analyze that essay by answering the following questions.
   • What is the writer's purpose?
   • How is the material organized?

- To whom does the author write, and what assumptions does the author make about the audience?
- What does the author use for evidence?

In doing this analysis, you may choose to annotate the text before answering the questions.

2. Now respond to the same essay employing a double-entry journal.

3. *If you have access to the World Wide Web,* access one informational home page that has been posted there—not a personal home page or a commercial home page, but a home page that some organization or group has set up primarily to convey information to the public.

   In your reading journal, answer the following analysis questions about this home page:

- What is the writer's purpose?
- How is the material organized?
- To whom does the author/home-page designer write and what assumptions does the author make about the audience?
- What information does the author/home-page designer provide and why?

PREFACE (TO *CULTURAL LITERACY*)

E. D. Hirsch

Rousseau points out the facility with which children lend themselves to our false methods: . . . "The apparent ease with which children learn is their ruin."
—*JOHN DEWEY*

There is no matter what children should learn first, any more than what leg you should put into your breeches first. Sir, you may stand disputing which is best to put in first, but in the meantime your backside is bare. Sir, while you stand considering which of two things you should teach your child first, another boy has learn't 'em both.
—*SAMUEL JOHNSON*

To be culturally literate is to possess the basic information needed to thrive in the modern world. The breadth of that information is great, extending over the major domains of human activity from sports to science. It is by no means confined to "culture" narrowly understood as an acquaintance with the arts. Nor is it confined to one social class. Quite the contrary. Cultural literacy constitutes the only sure avenue of opportunity for disadvantaged children, the only reliable way of combating the social determinism that now condemns them to remain in the same social and educational condition as their parents. That children from poor and illiterate homes tend to remain poor and illiterate is an unacceptable failure of our schools, one which has occurred not because our teachers are inept but chiefly because they are compelled to teach a fragmented curriculum based on faulty educational theories. Some say that our schools by themselves are powerless to change the cycle of poverty and illiteracy. I do not agree. They *can* break the cycle, but only if they themselves break fundamentally with some of the theories and practices that education professors and school administrators have followed over the past fifty years.

Although the chief beneficiaries of the educational reforms advocated in this book will be disadvantaged children, these same reforms will also enhance the literacy of children from middle-class homes. The educational goal advocated is that of mature literacy for *all* our citizens.

The connection between mature literacy and cultural literacy may already be familiar to those who have closely followed recent discussions of education. Shortly after the publication of my essay "Cultural Literacy," Dr. William Bennett, then chairman of the National Endowment for the Humanities and subsequently Secretary of Education in President Ronald Reagan's second administration, championed its ideas. This endorsement from an influential person of conservative views gave my ideas some currency, but such an endorsement was not likely to recommend the concept to liberal thinkers, and in fact the idea of cultural literacy has been attacked by some liberals on the assumption that I must be advocating a list of great books that every child in the land should be forced to read.

But those who examine the Appendix to this book will be able to judge for themselves how thoroughly mistaken such an assumption is. Very few specific titles appear on the list, and they usually appear as words, not works, because they represent writings that culturally literate people have read about but haven't read. *Das Kapital* is a good example. Cultural literacy is represented not by a *prescriptive* list of books but rather by a *descriptive* list of the information actually possessed by literate Americans. My aim in this book is to contribute to making that information the possession of all Americans.

The importance of such widely shared information can best be understood if I explain briefly how the idea of cultural literacy relates to currently prevailing theories of education. The theories that have dominated American education for the past fifty years stem ultimately from Jean Jacques Rousseau, who believed that we should encourage the natural development of young children and not impose adult ideas upon them before they can truly understand them. Rousseau's conception of education as a process of natural development was an abstract generalization meant to apply to all children in any time or place: to French children of the eighteenth century or to Japanese or American children of the twentieth century. He thought that a child's intellectual and social skills would develop naturally without regard to the specific content of education. His content-neutral conception of educational development has long been triumphant in American schools of education and has long dominated the "developmental," content-neutral curricula of our elementary schools.

In the first decades of this century, Rousseau's ideas powerfully influenced the educational conceptions of John Dewey, the writer who has most deeply affected modern American educational theory and practice. Dewey's clearest and, in his time, most widely read book on education, *Schools of To-morrow*, acknowledges Rousseau as the chief source of his educational principles. The first chapter of Dewey's book carries the telling title "Education as Natural Development" and is sprinkled with quotations from Rousseau. In it Dewey strongly seconds Rousseau's opposition to the mere accumulation of information.

> Development emphasizes the need of intimate and extensive personal acquaintance with a small number of typical situations with a view to mastering the way of dealing with the problems of experience, not the piling up of information.

Believing that a few direct experiences would suffice to develop the skills that children require, Dewey assumed that early education need not be tied to specific content. He mistook a half-truth for the whole. He placed too much faith in children's ability to learn general skills from a few typical experiences and too hastily rejected "the piling up of information." Only by piling up specific, communally shared information can children learn to participate in complex cooperative activities with other members of their community.

This old truth, recently rediscovered, requires a countervailing theory of education that once again stresses the importance of specific information in early and late schooling. The corrective theory might be described as an anthropological theory of education, because it is based on the anthropological observation that all human communities are founded upon specific shared information. Americans are different from Germans, who in turn are different from Japanese, because each group possesses specifically different cultural knowledge. In an anthropological perspective, the basic goal of education in a human community is acculturation, the transmission to children of the specific information shared by the adults of the group or polis.

Plato, that other great educational theorist, believed that the specific contents transmitted to children are by far the most important elements of education. In *The Republic* he makes Socrates ask rhetorically, "Shall we carelessly allow children to hear any casual tales which may be devised by casual persons, and to receive into their minds ideas for the most part the very opposite of those which we shall wish them to have when they are grown up?" Plato offered good reasons for being concerned with the specific contents of schooling, one of them ethical: "For great is the issue at stake, greater than appears—whether a person is to be good or bad."

Time has shown that there is much truth in the durable educational theories of both Rousseau and Plato. But even the greatest thinkers, being human, see mainly in one direction at a time, and no thinkers, however profound, can foresee the future implications of their ideas when they are translated into social policy. The great test of social ideas is the crucible of history, which, after a time, usually discloses a one-sidedness in the best of human generalizations. History, not superior wisdom, shows us that neither the content-neutral curriculum of Rousseau and Dewey nor the narrowly specified curriculum of Plato is adequate to the needs of a modern nation.

Plato rightly believed that it is natural for children to learn an adult culture, but too confidently assumed that philosophy could devise the one best culture.

(Nonetheless, we should concede to Plato that within our culture we have an obligation to choose and promote our best traditions.) On the other side, Rousseau and Dewey wrongly believed that adult culture is "unnatural" to young children. Rousseau, Dewey, and their present-day disciples have not shown an adequate appreciation of the need for transmission of specific cultural information.

In contrast to the theories of Plato and Rousseau, an anthropological theory of education accepts the naturalness as well as the relativity of human cultures. It deems it neither wrong nor unnatural to teach young children adult information before they fully understand it. The anthropological view stresses the universal fact that a human group must have effective communications to function effectively, that effective communications require shared culture, and that shared culture requires transmission of specific information to children. Literacy, an essential aim of education in the modern world, is no autonomous, empty skill but depends upon literate culture. Like any other aspect of acculturation, literacy requires the early and continued transmission of specific information. Dewey was deeply mistaken to disdain "accumulating information in the form of symbols." Only by accumulating shared symbols, and the shared information that the symbols represent, can we learn to communicate effectively with one another in our national community.

Evaluating a Text

Since most people spend the bulk of their time making judgments, it is probably fair to say that some of their judgments are about things they read. If you were to read actively, annotating and analyzing as we suggest you should, you would have to strictly discipline and severely restrict yourself to avoid making judgments about the subject of the document and the way the document is written.

These judgments range from relatively informal evaluations—that is, grunts or groans or chuckles or sighs—to the formal judgments you will be asked to make about material read for class. The following questions will help you reach judgments about what you have read.

- Does the author succeed in his/her purpose?
- Is the essay organized in an effective manner?
- Has the author accurately assessed the audience? Has the author provided an appropriate amount of information for the audience? Has the author written in a tone and style the audience will appreciate?
- Is the evidence used by the author sufficient to support her/his view of the subject?

These are the kinds of questions you will need to be able to answer if you plan on evaluating a text in one of the two ways students typically evaluate what they read in college. Students usually evaluate a text either to go on record as reacting to it in some personal way or to determine the usefulness of what they have read in light of a specific assignment, such as writing a research paper, preparing an oral report, or studying for an examination. Consider the following evaluation of "The Smurfette Principle," based on answers to the questions cited above. For further reference, look over the earlier analysis of the essay.

Does the author succeed in her purpose?   Pollitt does an excellent job of pointing out that sex-role stereotyping exists in society and that it is nearly impossible to protect children from encounters with those stereotypes. She is not only well informed about the many ways stereotypes are presented to children, but she makes a powerful appeal as a mother protecting her daughter that something be done about sex stereotypes.

Is the essay organized in an effective manner?   Organizing this essay within the framework of her concerns as a mother works effectively for Pollitt. The reader is able to see her reason for concern, follow her through toy stores and video stores, sit with her in front of her TV and in the library or bookstore, and see that the problem of sex stereotyping is just about everywhere in our culture.

Has the author accurately assessed her audience?   A reader would have to assume that Pollitt's strategy is to write not only to young mothers to encourage them to do something about sex stereotyping, but also to other open-minded persons who are willing to take an objective look at what society offers children as models for the sex roles they will play. In a sense, she is writing to just about anyone who has eyes and ears. Her examples of sex-role stereotypes come not from some distant land, but from our toy stores, video stores, televisions, and libraries.

Is the evidence used by the author sufficient to support her view of the topic?
Pollitt's strong suit in her essay is her evidence. She shapes her method of support around the fact that she is a mother concerned about her daughter's well-being. Only a brute could criticize her for that concern. But her strategy is to use her role as mother—ironically, making use of the same sex-role stereotyping she argues against—as a way of justifying her critique of the kind of media and entertainment available to preschool children. By organizing her argument in this manner, Pollitt has it both ways—as a woman accepting and manipulating her culturally given sex role and as a mother protecting her daughter.

Exercises

1. Evaluate the Preface to *Cultural Literacy* by answering the following questions:
   - Does the author succeed in his purpose?
   - Is the essay organized in an effective way?
   - Has the author accurately assessed his audience?

- Is the evidence used by the author sufficient to support his view of the topic?

To help yourself in this evaluation—and to prove to yourself that evaluation is an outgrowth of analysis—you might look over your analysis of the Preface to *Cultural Literacy* from the exercises on pages 63–64.

2. Using the same informational home page as you did in the last exercise, answer the following evaluation questions in your reading journal:

- Does the author succeed in her/his purpose? Why or why not?
- Is the information arranged in an effective way? Why or why not?
- Has the author/home-page designer accurately assessed her/his audience? Explain your answer and give evidence.

Responding to a Text

As you probably have already guessed, the more work you do to understand, analyze, and evaluate a text, the easier it will be for you to respond to it. Material you read, once properly digested by following strategies we have suggested thus far in this chapter, can be responded to in two ways: (1) in an evaluation or interpretation in which you either take issue with something the author has said or offer insight into what the author has said, or (2) in a paraphrase, summary, critique, or synthesis of the material you read.

The first of these two ways in which you might respond to what you have read is the subject of Chapter One and later chapters in this book devoted to writing in specific disciplines. In the remainder of this chapter, we want to show you how to use material for the second purpose—as a writer relying on what others have written. This is a final stage in the process of reading.

You may refer to the writing of another author in one of the following ways:

- direct quotation
- summary
- paraphrase
- critique
- synthesis

Since the use of direct quotations is taken up elsewhere in this book (see Chapter Three), let us begin with summary. A **summary** is a brief restatement, in your own words (rather than in the author's) of the content of something you have read. When you write a summary, you should focus on the text's central idea. Summaries require you to carefully avoid exact quotations from the text as well as the inclusion of your opinions or conclusions.

Note how the following passage from Ian Harris's "Media Myths and the Reality of Men's Work" is summarized. First, read the passage.

The dominant image of the American male portrayed on television, in film and in magazines depicts a white-collar gentleman living in the suburbs in affluent circumstances. These individuals own American Express cards and buy the latest model cars. From Ozzie and Harriet to Bill Cosby, these images occupy a powerful place in the American psyche and set standards for male behavior. They run the media and the large corporations. They speak to us through radios and television. They teach our children. They are not only standard bearers but also the image makers who provide a model for male expectations.

After reading the passage, you should summarize it by picking out the main point the author is trying to make and restating it briefly in your own words, as the student did in the following summary.

> According to Harris, traditional views of male gender identity dominate the media, providing a model for male behavior and expectations.

In some instances, though, a summary may not satisfy your purposes. Sometimes because the author's style is very appealing or because you need to provide more information than you can adequately provide in a summary, you should use paraphrase.

Like a summary, a **paraphrase** requires that you state in your own words the central idea of what you have read, but you must also provide the main points of support for those ideas. Unlike a summary, which is a shortened version of the main source, a paraphrase is roughly as long as the source itself, each sentence in the paraphrase corresponding to a sentence in the original.

Note the following paraphrase of the above passage from Ian Harris.

> Men in America are rendered through the media as well-to-do gentlemen who have managed to accumulate better-than-adequate wealth. They can afford luxuries most would want to own and, if they cannot pay cash, they can use a credit card. This image is portrayed successfully on television, setting high standards for men to measure themselves by. Such images dominate the mirrors media place before us. Our children are subject to the influence of these images. The male in society has a difficult image to live up to.

Summary and paraphrase are both useful methods for incorporating ideas you have read into papers you are writing.

Exercise

Using the same informational home page as you did in the last exercise, complete the following task:

Write a four- to six-paragraph summary of the information that is contained in this home page. Write this summary as if you were writing to a friend of yours who has asked what information the home page contains.

Critique

A **critique,** in many instances, is the starting point for academic and scholarly writing. Briefly, a critique is an organized critical evaluation of a text. As a result, to write a critique, you must react to something in the text.

Critique, then, requires the use of several skills already discussed in Chapters One and Two. First, you should take time to annotate the text and write comments in the margins. This skill will make the second task manageable. Once annotations and notes in the margins are written, you should write a summary, making certain to identify specific points with which you disagree. Now you are ready to write your critique.

The writing of a critique is usually a five-step procedure:

Step one: Write an introduction that states the author's main point and the points you want to make about the text.

Step two: Write a summary that indicates how the main point is supported.

Step three: Write an anlaysis that indicates the author's argument.

Step four: Write an evaluation, noting which portions of the text you agree with and which you disagree with.

Step five: Write a conclusion in which you summarize your overall position in relation to the critiqued text.

Oftentimes in college, you will be asked to write in response to an assignment such as the following:

> Read the following excerpt from the *Hearing before the Subcommittee on Asian and Pacific Affairs* . . . on "The Implications of the Industrial Disaster in Bhopal, India." Critique Wishart's address, paying particular attention to those elements of his speech that are most apt to be attacked by careful listeners and readers.

Statement of Ronald Wishart, Vice President for Government Relations, Union Carbide Corp., Accompanied by Joseph J. Martyak, and James Gustave Speth, President, World Resources Institute

Mr. Solarz, thank you. I am Ronald Wishart, vice president of Federal Government Relations for the Union Carbide Corp., in Washington, D.C.

I will read a brief statement, following which I will be pleased to receive questions.

Since my responsibilities are domestic, I am not intimate with our international operations. Therefore, in the interests of accuracy in responding to your questions, I believe that it will be necessary to respond to many of them at a later time, when I have been able to collect the information.

Mr. Anderson is indeed sorry he couldn't make it. He arrived, as you know, from India early or late Sunday night, and has been very busy since then in communicating to people.

Here is my statement:

No words can describe the sorrow felt by all employees of Union Carbide Corp., for the people of Bhopal.

Union Carbide is making every effort to work with United States and Indian Government officials to assist in providing quick response and immediate relief to those who need help.

Warren M. Anderson, the corporation's chief executive officer, went to Bhopal to personally convey his and the company's sympathy to the appropriate authorities. A technical team of engineers, scientists, and medical personnel is now working in Bhopal to aid the suffering and to investigate the accident.

Union Carbide India Limited today is an Indian company in which Union Carbide Corp., owns 50.9% of the stock. The remaining 49% is widely held by the Indian public and the stock of Union Carbide India is traded on the Indian Stock Exchange.

Union Carbide India began operations as the Eveready Co.–Indian-Limited on June 20, 1934, fifty years ago, producing dry cell batteries.

As it has grown to its present size, it has experienced several name changes, and is now called Union Carbide India Limited, with its head office in Bombay.

There are fourteen plant locations, three R&D centers, approximately seventeen sales offices and fifty warehouses located throughout India.

Employees number about 9,000. Sales in 1983 were $202 million at the currency rate prevailing then, net income was $8.8 million, and net current assets were $87 million.

There are four principal lines of business: Eveready batteries and raw material processing facilities supporting that business; agricultural products; graphite and carbon products; and two facilities doing metal fabrication. The chemical business in Bombay was sold in 1984.

Since 1934, Union Carbide India has made a significant number of investments in production facilities and has maintained good relationships with the Indian Government.

The management structure of Union Carbide India, Ltd., is entirely Indian and the operating forces in the plants are entirely Indian. This policy has been facilitated by the ready availability of a large pool of technically trained personnel educated both in India and in the United States. This policy has helped to create good working relationships between the company and the people of India.

Union Carbide Corp. will continue to be as cooperative and helpful as possible with Government agencies who have an interest in the situation in Bhopal. When the company's investigation of the accident is completed, relevant information will be made available to the appropriate Federal, State, and local authorities.

At that time, Union Carbide will also be in a better position to provide appropriate and detailed answers to questions raised by committees of the U.S. Congress. Union Carbide intends to cooperate fully to help ensure that what happened at Bhopal cannot happen again.

Look over the following critique of Wishart's address and the way each of the five steps above are completed.

Introduction

Ronald Wishart, as Vice President for Government Relations, Union Carbide, spoke to the Committee on Foreign Affairs of the House of Representatives' Subcommittee on Asian and Pacific Affairs. While Wishart's official statement indicates Union Carbide's sorrow over the Bhopal disaster, Wishart is careful, by providing the history of the company, to detach Union Carbide India from Union Carbide United States.

This introduction satisfies the requirement that the author's main point and the student's attitude toward that point are stated.

Summary

Wishart detaches Union Carbide United States from Union Carbide India by making two points. First, he makes it clear that Union Carbide regrets the Bhopal disaster and will assist in providing help to the people of India. And, second, Wishart makes it clear that Union Carbide India Limited is an Indian company, owned in part by the Indian public and traded on the Indian Stock Exchange.

This summary indicates how the main point is supported.

Analysis

By making these two points, Wishart makes it clear that though connected by name and interest, Union Carbide United States and Union Carbide India are, fundamentally, independent corporations. Wishart seems interested in deflecting from Union Carbide United States any responsibility for errors in judgment that might have resulted in the Bhopal incident. While Union Carbide United States willingly aids victims of the disaster and promises to investigate further the possible causes of the incident, Union Carbide United States is clearly not responsible for the disaster or any subsequent problems caused by the incident.

This analysis explains the author's argument.

Evaluation

This effective use of detachment enables Wishart, as a result, to position himself as a helpful and knowledgeable assistant to any federal, state, or local authority, while effectively deflecting responsibility for the disaster. So positioned, Wishart is able to appear concerned, helpful, and sorrowful without accepting responsibility.

With this paragraph, the student notes the way Wishart has manipulated the situation so that Union Carbide United States now seems charitable.

Conclusion

Much can be learned from Wishart's statement to the Subcommittee on Asian and Pacific Affairs. Not only does a reader learn how to deflect responsibility, but a reader learns how to use historical information to do so. Among other accomplishments, Wishart succeeds at educating those on the Committee who no doubt are uninformed about Union Carbide's world affairs and who, once informed, will clearly see that Union Carbide India is solely responsible for this accident and any problems that might ensue from it.

This conclusion nicely summarizes the student's overall position in relation to the article.

Exercises

1. *If you have access to a computer and to the World Wide Web,* choose and access a home page that you have not yet analyzed for this chapter. Choose a home page that might be of interest to a larger number of people, a general computer-using audience of your choosing.
2. Write a review (a critique) of the home page that would be appropriate to publish as an article in a magazine such as *Home Computing, Internet,* or *Wired.* You might want to get a copy of one of these magazines before you start writing. Look in your campus library or on the magazine shelf of local book stores or grocery stores. Follow each of the steps listed below in writing your review:

a. Write an introduction for your review that states the author's/page designer's main points and the points you want to make about the text.
b. Write a summary of the home page that indicates how the designer's main points are supported.
c. Write an analysis of the home page that examines the information provided.
d. Write a conclusion for your review in which you summarize your evaluation of the home page.

Synthesis

When you write in response to two or more texts, you are likely to be asked to do one of two things: write a brief paper in which you group texts as similar or dissimilar in their approach to a subject or use such groupings in a longer paper, such as a research paper, to highlight various views writers have taken on a particular subject. Grouping texts in this way in order to write in response to readings makes synthesis writing possible.

A **synthesis** is a discussion of a topic that draws upon two or more sources. You would need to employ synthesis to satisfy the demands of the following assignment from an introductory psychology course.

> Select a minimum of two and a maximum of four essays that address the topic of how brand names affect evaluations by consumers of new products marketed by companies with established brand names. Compare and/or contrast views presented in the essays you select.

To complete this assignment, you should first locate sources, selecting only those portions that will aid you in fulfilling the purpose dictated by the assignment. Notice that the assignment requires not only that you find sources, but that they in some way be related to each other so that you can compare and/or contrast the views presented in the essays. Clearly, if a relationship between two sources cannot be determined, you should probably look for another source or two. Synthesis cannot occur where relationships cannot be determined.

As you have already seen with regard to writing a critique, writing a synthesis requires the use of skills already discussed in this chapter: annotating, analyzing, evaluating, and responding.

Synthesis, then, requires you to take several predictable steps:

Step one: Understand the assignment.

Step two: Annotate sources to satisfy the requirements of your assignment.

Step three: Group the sources so that texts with similar approaches to the subject are in the same group.

Step four: Write a summary of each source.

Step five: Write one sentence that summarizes the way that the texts you have read are grouped. This will be your thesis statement.

Step six: Plan to present your summaries of the texts in a way that the reader is prepared for based on your thesis statement.

Step seven: Write your draft, revising as your ideas evolve.

You should keep in mind that some assignments may require that you do nothing more than synthesize or critique texts while longer assignments, such as research papers, may require that you employ synthesis and critique in the process of setting up your own argument on a subject.

Exercises

1. Refer once again to the Preface to *Cultural Literacy* by E. D. Hirsch (pages 64–67).
   a. Write a summary of Hirsch's article.
   b. Choose any paragraph of three or more sentences and summarize it.
2. Read "The Sincerest Flattery" by Gregg Easterbrook on pages 77–79 and, following the earlier suggested procedure, write a critique of the article.
3. Choose one of the topics addressed in essays found in this chapter: sex stereotyping (pages 50–53), cultural liteacy (pages 64–67), the Bhopal incident (pages 71–73), or plagiarism (pages 77–79). Go to the library and find at least two more essays on the chosen topic. Write a synthesis of the three articles you have read about the subject.

4. *If you have access to a computer network and e-mail,* monitor three days of conversation from a fairly active, public, on-line discussion list or listserv. Save all of the messages published during this period. Think about choosing a listserv or discussion in the career path you have chosen or one that deals with a subject you know quite a bit about.

   Using these messages, write a synthesis of the information exchanged during these three days. Use the steps provided on pages 75–76 to accomplish the task of writing this synthesis.
5. *If you have access to a stand-alone computer,* choose a partner with whom you are willing to work. Each of you will need a disk copy of a paper that you have already turned in and had graded for another class. Exchange disks and write a critique of your partner's paper using the steps outlined on page 71 of this chapter.
6. *If you have access to a computer and the World Wide Web,* use a browser like Mosaic or Netscape to find a web site connected to your chosen profession or major discipline in college. Particularly, see if you can find the home page associated with the national professional organization to which you hope some day to belong (e.g., the home page for the American Academy of Child and Adolescent Psychiatry, the American Association of Pe-

troleum Geologists, American Philosphical Association, National Council of Teachers of English, the Society for Technical Communication, American Society of Agricultural Engineers).

Write a review of this web site that is appropriate for publication in the campus newspaper or in a departmental newsletter for students and alumni in your department.

7. *If you have access to a computer network and e-mail,* find and join an on-line discussion list that involves people in a career option that you have identified as of interest to you. After listening in on the conversation for a few days, send a note to the list identifying yourself and asking people to answer a relatively short series of questions about the kinds of reading tasks and challenges they face in their daily professional work (e.g., What kinds of reading do you do in your work? What kinds of reading tasks are the hardest for you and why? What kinds of professional materials do you most hate to read and why? What reading strategies do you find most useful within your profession and why?).

Summarize your findings in a newspaper article about professionals' reading practices that is suitable for publication in your campus newsletter.

THE SINCEREST FLATTERY

Thanks, But I'd Rather You Not Plagiarize My Work

Gregg Easterbrook

It was the best of times, and pretty much the worst of times. I felt borne back ceaselessly to the past. Maybe that's because days on the calendar creep along in a petty pace, and all our yesterdays but light fools the road to dusty death.

OK, the above words are not really mine. But hey, I changed them slightly. I thought nobody would notice.

Some kind of harmonic convergence of plagiarism seems to be in process. A Boston University dean, H. Joachim Maitre, was caught swiping much of a commencement address from an essay by the film critic Michael Medved. Fox Butterfield of *The New York Times* then cribbed from a *Boston Globe* story about the swipe. The *Globe*, in turn, admitted that one of its reporters was disciplined for stealing words from the Georgia politician Julian Bond. Laura Parker of *The Washington Post* (which owns *Newsweek*) was found poaching from *The Miami Herald*'s John Donnelly. And the president of Japan's largest news service, Shinji Sakai, announced his resignation, taking public responsibility for 51 plagiarized articles that were discovered last May.

I personally entered the arena last week when the *Post* reported that a Stanford University business-school lecturer plagiarized me in a recent book, *Managing on the Edge*. Chapters about the Ford Motor Co. contain approximately three pages nearly identical in wording to an article on Ford that I wrote five years ago for *The Washington Monthly* magazine.

What's it like to discover someone has stolen your words? My initial reaction was to feel strangely flattered that another author had liked my writing well enough to pass it off as his own.

OK, I plagiarized that last sentence. It comes from the writer James Fallows, who last week in a National Public Radio commentary described the two times he has been plagiarized. In one case a San Jose State professor published a textbook in which an entire chapter was nearly identical to an article Fallows had written. For good measure, another chapter was nearly identical to an article by the economic analyst Robert Reich. The professor claimed this happened because of computer error. The publisher sent Fallows a letter saying that, since we disseminated your copyrighted work without permission, could we have permission now?

Plagiarism is the world's dumbest crime. If you are caught there is absolutely nothing you can say in your own defense. (Computer error?) And it's easy to commit the underlying sin—presenting as your own someone else's work—without running the risk of sanction, merely by making the effort to reword.

Yet figures as distinguished as Alex Haley, John Hersey, Martin Luther King Jr., and D. M. Thomas have been charged with borrowing excessively from the work of others. One factor is sloth. Another is ego: there are writers who cannot bear even tacit admission that someone else has said something better than they could. The line between being influenced by what others have written, and cribbing from it outright, is one nearly every writer walks up to at some point.

About that last sentence. The *Post* quoted me as saying that: does that mean I just plagiarized myself? It can happen. Conor Cruise O'Brien was accused of self-plagiarism when he sold, to *The Atlantic*, an article hauntingly similar to one previously run under his byline in *Harper's*.

Perhaps word rustlers tell themselves they will never be caught, and indeed, unlikely combinations of events may be necessary for a theft to be exposed. Some no doubt further tell themselves that if they are caught no one will sue. Most writers don't make serious money and so are uninviting targets for litigation.

I might never have learned about *Managing on the Edge* if an alert reader named Robert Levering had not been researching Ford Motor Co. Shortly after reading my article, he saw a *Managing* excerpt from the Stanford business-school magazine. He not only realized he was reading the same words, but more important, remembered where he encountered them first. Levering wrote to Stanford. I heard about his letter, got a copy of the book, and my jaw dropped. Particularly galling, on the book's facing page, was the phrase "Copyright 1990 by Richard Tanner Pascale." The author was asserting ownership of words I composed.

Elegantly crafted: Unlike the Boston University incident, where the dean stole words for an unpaid speech, in this case there was money involved. *Managing* is a commercial book published by Simon & Schuster, a reasonable seller with 35,000 copies in print and another run pending. It's been well received by critics: mainly, I suspect, because of three particularly elegantly crafted pages.

Another person was not only presenting my words as his own, but doing so for gain.

The author of *Managing* apologized for what happened but contended it was not plagiarism, because my name is in the book's footnotes. Footnotes my foot. Footnotes mean the place a fact can be found; they do not confer the right to present someone else's words as your own work. Any Stanford undergraduate who attempted that defense would not get far.

My case dragged on inconclusively for a while. But the moment a reporter for *The Washington Post* called Simon & Schuster, the pace of cooperation accelerated dramatically. Simon & Schuster is now preparing corrections for future editions of *Managing*. Stanford has an academic committee investigating its end of the incident.

The wave of plagiarism disclosures poses an obvious question: are dozens of authors now quaking in their shoes, worried about whether some alert reader will stumble across the resemblance between those pages in their book and, say, that article in some obscure little journal no one ever reads?

Frankly, Scarlet, I don't give a damn.

CHAPTER THREE

Researching in the Disciplines

Researching in College: An Overview

Research in the Disciplines: Using the Library

Research in the Humanities

Research in the Social Sciences

Research in the Natural Sciences

Universal Resource Locators (URLs)

In research, as with the law, what constitutes convincing evidence is the reflection of what the individual making a judgment considers important. When you perform research and write research reports for professors in different departments across campus, you must make certain to use evidence that is appropriate to that discipline. Like evidence used in court, convincing details and examples are necessary as support in research papers in all disciplines.

Evidence reflects values; as a result, evidence in one department on campus does not always serve convincingly as evidence in another. Predictably, one method for gathering evidence in one system or culture is not always an acceptable method in another.

As you can see from what we have suggested thus far in Chapters One and Two, arguing for any cause is a problem-solving activity. By this we mean that both academic and professional writings are generally produced as solutions to problems. And these various problems arise from circumstances unique to the situation you find yourself in, whether in the classroom or on the job.

No matter where the writing is done or under what circumstances, one perspective on writing holds true from one discipline to another: Your argument must employ—for support, exemplification, or proof—evidence that is acceptable to members of the community you are trying to convince.

At all times, you must endeavor to know your audience, its values, and its notion of what constitutes evidence. In this chapter, we will introduce you to the kinds of demands that will be made on you as you perform and report on research from discipline to discipline.

Let us begin, then, with three assumptions that serve as the basis for our discussion of research and research-report writing in courses across the disciplines:

- Like writing and reading, research is a process.
- Research involves active engagement with various texts for the purpose of systematically inquiring into a question worthy of attention.
- Skills required to successfully perform research differ from one discipline to another.

Exercises

1. Interview three people, one humanities major, one social sciences major, and one natural sciences major. Find out why they have chosen their majors. What special qualities of mind and interest do they believe they possess that predispose them to their chosen field?
2. Write a brief report to your teacher highlighting your interviews. Be certain to focus on why these students have chosen their major fields.

3. *If you have access to a computer network with e-mail,* write three friends attending other universities or colleges and ask them to identify the advice they have about how best to undertake a research project that has a written report attached to its conclusion. In writing, summarize their advice.

Researching in College: An Overview

You will encounter various academic problems when you perform research across the disciplines. In this chapter, in an effort to help you remedy at least one of these problems, we will consider what kinds of evidence or data are acceptable in different disciplines. To do so, let us begin by considering descriptions of three typical academic writing assignments given in introductory courses in the humanities, the social sciences, and the natural sciences.

In reading these assignments, keep in mind the following:

- Performing and reporting on research requires you to use writing and reading skills that apply generally to all disciplines.
- Each discipline requires that support for general observations come from details, examples, or other evidence appropriate in those disciplines.
- Each discipline has its own acceptable methods for gathering appropriate details, examples, or evidence to support or "prove" those observations.

Skills Required to Perform Research in the Humanities

In performing research in the humanities, you must

- use evidence appropriate to the discipline.
- read and understand primary and secondary sources from various critical perspectives.
- ask about and understand the implications of research questions in the humanities.
- use the library, including the reference area, computer software, and other technologies.

If you do not already possess the above four skills, you can acquire them by studying the remainder of this chapter. Whether you are writing for courses in English, history, philosophy, communication, or classical and modern languages—which have as their overriding goal the exploration and explanation of the human experience—or for courses in music, art, dance, or drama—which reflect expressions of human experience—the four skills listed above will be very important for you to master. Writing in the humanities, as in response to the assignment below, requires skills unique to the discipline as well as those that are adaptable to all research (for example, reading skills discussed in Chapter Two).

Sample humanities assignment

The following assignment was given in an introductory philosophy course.

> Students must fill out summary sheets in response to all assigned articles as listed in the course packet.
>
> The best summary sheet of those you turn in will serve as the basis for your research paper.
>
> Topics must be approved in advance by the instructor which is why it is imperative that I see your summary sheets on time. Overdone topics like abortion, capital punishment, the drinking age, etc., will not be approved because the temptation to plagiarize is too great.
>
> This paper must be ten to fifteen pages, typed and double-spaced. Students are encouraged to show the instructor rough drafts and to discuss them prior to handing in the final copy.

If you were given this assignment in your introductory philosphy course, you would find it necessary to perform two interrelated tasks. In one, you would read the assignment employing skills discussed in Chapter Two, including annotation and, perhaps, note-taking. In the other, you would fill out summary sheets for each reading assignment since the syllabus states, "The best summary sheet will serve as the basis for your research paper." This procedure would provide you with an opportunity to use your best summary—and, we must assume, a source you understand well—as the basis for your paper. This preparatory task would also give you the opportunity to work confidently, knowing that once successfully completed, this summary will be the basis for a paper on a topic already approved by your instructor.

The professor clearly does *not* want students to write on "overworked" subjects, not only because such topics allow writers to rely upon clichés in establishing their positions, but also because plagiarism is often a product of working with such topics.

This assignment, then, would involve you in three tasks that carry over from discipline to discipline:

- reading a primary or secondary source, as defined below,
- determining the most salient points from that article and reporting them on a summary sheet,
- devising a thesis statement to be defended by reference to that article.

Since the professor wants to see drafts of the research paper, we can assume that he will provide advice about how to use primary and secondary sources to support general observations in the humanities, as we discuss them on pages 83–84 and in "Writing in the Humanities" (Chapter Five).

Writing this paper, then, would require you to argue logically, basing your argument on specific assigned readings. To do so, you would need to employ skills discussed in Chapter Two—paraphrasing, critiquing, and synthesizing in addition to summarizing. You must also learn how to use these sources without **plagiarizing**—that is, without using the ideas of another as if they are your own since plagiarism is not only unethical, but illegal as well.

A cautionary word about plagiarism is in order here. You are entitled to use the words and ideas of others only if you state explicitly whose words and ideas you have used and where they come from. To do otherwise is to plagiarize.

Few students desire to plagiarize. Most of the time, plagiarism is inadvertent. In any case, plagiarism occurs under circumstances that you should be careful to avoid. The circumstance that results in plagiarism and that you should be most conscious of is when you try to put the author's ideas into your own words. Oftentimes, try as you may, the language you settled on will be very close to the language of the original source. Whether you intended it or not, the use of another person's ideas and words is nonetheless illegal, and a teacher who discovers it will no doubt point out the plagiarized material to you. Remember that paraphrase as well as close summary and exact quotations must be carefully documented. (See the Appendix to this textbook.) Give credit where the credit is due.

In any event, the above skills are among those you have already learned by reading Chapter Two and among those that will apply equally to all disciplines.

Skills Required to Perform Research in the Social Sciences

To satisfactorily perform research in the social sciences, you must

- understand evidence appropriate to the discipline.
- observe and record human behavior.
- systematically interpret human behavior.
- employ appropriate research methodology.

These skills will be especially useful when you perform and report on research in courses in sociology, psychology, education, and criminal justice (see Chapter Six), and nursing, occupational therapy, and physical therapy (see Chapter Ten).

Sample social science assignment
The following assignment is taken from a sophomore-level course entitled Introduction to Social Work.

The purpose of this assignment is to identify and state a researchable question in some area relevant to social work. The description of the problem must be anchored in the literature of the field. As an introduction to the kinds of problems explored in social work, this assignment will result in identification of a research question a student might pursue in more advanced courses in social work.

The only limitation on the choice of topic for this paper is that it have demonstrable relevance to social work. The study proposal may be ideal and elaborate or pragmatic and feasible.

The assignment will be graded on the identification and statement of a researchable question or hypothesis and the appropriate and critical use of prior research and theory in the literature review. The paper must be *well-written, typed* (double-spaced), six to eight pages in length (no more or less), and include a *minimum* of five relevant references. APA style must be used throughout. Students are to work in groups (about five students per group), but each student is to write a paper (no group papers).

Be sure to include introduction, literature review, problem formulation, and references, as described in your textbook.

This assignment may at first seem quite foreign to you. On the one hand, it is probably clear to you that many of the writing skills needed for successful completion of the philosophy assignment above are ones encountered most often in high-school writing courses. The skills needed to complete the assignment from social work, on the other hand, at first may seem to be different in kind. Upon closer examination, however, you can probably see for yourself that many of the skills required to complete the social work assignment above are the same as those needed to complete the philosophy assignment. They include:

- finding a topic in the discipline;
- reading primary or secondary sources;
- summarizing, synthesizing, and critiquing sources directly related to the topic; and
- devising a thesis statement—in this case, one that can be restated as a research question for later exploration.

The task of writing a paper following the directives provided in the previous assignment description likewise involves skills you have already encountered in Chapter One or, at least, adaptations of those skills.

This assignment, then, since it comes from an introductory course in the social sciences, is intended to force you to extend your skills so that they may be used in another discipline to solve problems different in kind from those you are apt to encounter in the humanities. Further skills needed for researching and writing in the social sciences are provided here and in "Writing in the Social Sciences" (Chapter Six).

Skills Required to Perform Research in the Natural Sciences

To perform research in the natural sciences, you must

- understand and record observed evidence.
- ask research questions that, once answered, can be answered similarly in future studies following the same methods.
- generate hypotheses based upon outside sources.
- test hypotheses following the scientific method.

These skills will be especially useful when you perform and report on research in courses in the natural sciences, including biology, physics, chemistry, meteorology, and astronomy.

Sample natural sciences assignment

The following assignment was taken from a sophomore-level course in biology.

> You will be required to perform seven lab experiments during the term, each of which must be reported upon in a lab report. The purpose of a lab report is to clearly and concisely present experimental information and to carefully analyze its meaning and significance.
>
> Your report must include a title, introduction, materials and methods section, results, discussion, and summary. See your textbook for explanations of what these sections must include.

In an Introduction to Biology course, you are apt to have a workbook which includes within it a format to follow in writing a lab report. That format would include the same sections as specified in the above assignment. By the time you take a sophomore-level biology course to fulfill your general college, core, or elective requirements, however, you will be asked to write the lab report yourself. Though the above assignment is used in a sophomore-level biology course intended for prospective majors, minors, and students simply interested enough to take a second course in the Department of Biology, lab reports are routinely written in introductory courses as well.

A laboratory report is one of the major forms of writing in most laboratory science courses, including physics, earth science, chemistry, meteorology, and astronomy in addition to biology. This form of writing calls upon your ability to read carefully. In an Introduction to Biology course, you will be given fairly specific instructions about what to do in an experiment. In a sophomore-level course, by contrast, you may be given less direct advice but a specific number of research studies to read prior to engaging in your experiment. In fact, you will be required in such a writing adventure to cite sources upon which you have based your experiment. This means that you will use the following skills that are also useful in the humanities and social sciences:

- reading previous studies
- summarizing previous studies
- devising a thesis statement—in this instance, called a "hypothesis"

Since the professor wants students to follow a very tightly prescribed format, we can anticipate that students will be graded not only on the logical presentation of information but on their ability to follow that format. Even so, you can be sure that the professor expects students to perform reading tasks they should have already mastered by the time they take a sophomore-level course, skills discussed in Chapter Two.

Other skills, in addition to those you have already learned, will be stressed when you learn to perform research and research report writing in the sciences. These skills will be discussed more fully later in this chapter in preparation for extensive analysis in the later chapter "Writing in the Natural Sciences" (Chapter 7).

Exercises

1. Interview a professor at your school who teaches in the social sciences or the natural sciences. The point of your interview should be to make notes in your notebook about a research project that professor has either undertaken or studied. As far as possible, encourage the professor through your questions to indicate not only what the research entails (for example, its subject), but why (for example, its purpose) and how (for example, its methodology) it was accomplished.

2. Using the information you have gathered in exercise 1, write a short report to be shared with classmates on what you have discovered by conducting your interview, focusing on what the research entails, why it was conducted, and how it was performed.

3. Choose the assignment from this chapter (for example, humanities, social sciences, and natural sciences) that you feel best able to handle.

   If you have accesss to a computer and the World Wide Web, use a browser (for example, Netscape, Mosaic) to help you identify some of the kinds of resources currently available on the web that might help you to fulfill each of the major steps of the assignment. Browse, briefly, some of the resources that might be helpful. In your writing journal, describe these kinds of resources and indicate how you think each might support your research process.

Research in the Disciplines: Using the Library

Since each of the above assignments begins with the use of secondary sources (see page 95), you will need to familiarize yourself with your college library at some point if you hope to benefit from the various materials you might find there. Needless to say, you are wise to learn how to use your library before you actually have to do research. Still, most students learn to use the library *while* they are in the process of doing research. In a first-year composition course, for instance, one reason for assigning a research paper is to give you the opportunity to learn about the library.

No doubt technology changes so quickly that the most we can do here is provide information on general resources. We also realize that some of what follows will be fairly familiar to you. In any event, we believe that you will need some grasp of the following to function comfortably in the library:

- using the reference area
- locating books and articles using computers
- locating articles using various databases
- relying on CD-ROM and Proquest

Using the Reference Area

A reference area in a library is a place where you can get information on a topic you are required to research. As you can see, reference has is its root word "refer." The **reference area** or **reference room** is a place where materials may be found that refer in some manner to the topic you plan to explore.

When you perform library research you have to begin someplace. We recommend that you begin in the reference area. Reference librarians are perhaps your greatest resource in the library. Not only do they have the knowledge that can lead you to the material you want, but if you have a fairly good idea of what your paper will be about, reference librarians will teach you how to search through various sources.

Remember that a reference librarian can only help you if you have a fairly good idea of what you want to research. Never go to the library hoping that a forgiving librarian will provide you with a topic.

What do you need to know before seeking assistance from a reference librarian? You should have some idea about the subject—even a general idea will enable the librarian to help you, and you might decide upon a specific topic once you are under the pressure of explaining to a helpful person what you need to know. You should also have some notion about the required length of the assignment, the audience you are required to address (especially what you can assume your audience to already know about the topic), and the number of sources you will want (or be required) to use in your paper, including the kinds of sources (for example, articles, books, etc.)

The reference librarian will point you in the direction of a variety of sources, including abstracts, almanacs, atlases, bibliographies, biographies, dictionaries, encyclopedias, handbooks, indexes, reviews, and serials. Depending on the library, many of these sources will be computerized and connected to other computers, that is, on-line. In any case, some of these resources will prove more valuable to you than others in doing research in a specific discipline. Let us look at some of these general reference works that you may not use on a day-to-day basis, the way you might use dictionaries, for instance.

Abstracts and **indexes** will lead you to sources by subject and often by author. Abstracts also provide short summaries of longer works and, as a result, may save you time once you have figured out exactly what you need to know. Abstracts are also useful because they give keywords to use in database searches or in disciplinary materials (that is, they provide current "buzzwords" or jargon). Indexes point to where information might be found, including journals, magazines, newspapers, or books. Abstracts and indexes reflect specific areas of interest (for example, *Dissertation Abstracts* and *Book Review Index*).

Encyclopedias (*Encyclopaedia Britannica* and *Encyclopedia Americana,* for instance) provide another excellent place to begin research. Generally, you can count on encyclopedias to provide you with concise information on specific topics, arranged alphabetically. Encyclopedia entries not only provide general information about a subject, they also indicate other related topics which could provide you with additional sources or alternative subjects. While encyclopedias are an excellent place to begin research, they are hardly places to end your efforts.

Depending on the kind of research you are required to perform, **bibliographies** can be excellent aids. Bibliographies (for example, *Guide to Reference Books* and *A World Bibliography of Bibliographies*) will provide you with a list of books or articles on particular subjects. Most reference areas will include bibliographies for research you might choose to perform in specific subject areas in the discipline in which you are working. It is also possible that you will find bibliographical essays on particular subjects and bibliographies at the end of useful books and articles to point you to other relevant sources for your research.

Oftentimes an excellent place to begin research is by finding out something about the life of an author, a historical figure, or a scientist. **Biographies** provide you with this kind of information in both general reference (for example, *Biography* and *Genealogy Master Index*) and in more specific references (for example, *Who's Who in American Colleges and Universities*).

Once you have gathered general information on the subject, you will be ready for fuller, more in-depth treatments. If you are working on a paper that requires you to report on various views of films, novels, plays, etc., you may choose to consult **reviews** on the work. Reviews offer brief critical discussions of important works in a particular field (for example, *Book Review Digest, Book Review Index,* and *Index to Book Reviews in the Humanities*).

Still fuller critical treatments of the subject you want to research may be found in **serials**—that is, in magazines and scholarly journals that contain articles and research reports in specific disciplines. These will be discussed more fully on pages 92–93.

Locating Books and Articles Using Computers

Though it is possible that your library still uses a card catalogue, it is increasingly unlikely that they do so. In this age when information is at your fingertips, information is actually "at your fingertips."

Libraries are no longer simply places to store books. Rather, libraries are increasingly able to "access," or obtain from distant places via computer, information for you. If your library does not hold a particular book you need for your research, either you or your librarian (or, more likely, you with the help of your librarian) will be able to perform a simple computer search to find out where that book might be found. In this way, a library can bring you and a much-needed resource work together without having to use shelf space to do so.

Let us begin by considering **on-line computer catalogs** of the sort that exist increasingly in college and university libraries across the country.

More likely than not, when you walk into your college library you will see a visible sign of our times: computer catalogs. Many small libraries continue to use card catalogues, but nowadays, such card catalogues have been replaced by computerized systems.

Computer catalogs provide you with more information than students in previous generations could have ever hoped to have gotten from a card catalog. In addition to the usual information, such as the location of materials within the library, on-line catalogs enable you to find out if the book is available and, if it has been checked out, when you can expect it to be returned. If it is a book your library does not hold but that is held in a branch library elsewhere on campus or in a library with which your college has an agreement, you may be told where to find the book.

Like the old-fashioned card catalogue, on-line computer catalogs are searchable in many ways; the most popular are by author, title, and subject. Many on-line catalogues are also searchable by keywords or combinations of keywords and subjects.

Most on-line catalogues can be used by reading the menu of choices listing databases available for searching and making the appropriate selection from the main menu. Needless to say, you will need to know enough about the databases available to you to make the appropriate choice. Librarians are often willing to explain the various choices available to you in your particular library.

In addition to databases, many libraries provide access to information in other libraries through **Internet** services (see Chapter Four). The Internet is a computerized network connecting regional, national, and international sources. Once in Internet, you will be able to retrieve a far greater amount of information than is attainable using only your college's library.

You should understand immediately that different searches require different skills. Searches by subject headings, for instance, require that you familiarize yourself with headings as they will appear on the database. To do so, use *The Library of Congress Subject Headings* to identify subject areas using appropriate terminology. To search the computer database by subject heading, you need to use the subject headings actually used in the database. *The Library of Congress Subject Headings* lists these headings.

Though *The Library of Congress Subject Headings* serves as a fairly standard guide to these headings, individual databases provide indexes of keywords, called "keyword indicators" or "descriptor files," in which you may look up your subject and find out what it is called. This step greatly reduces search time and searches that yield little or no information. Also, these indexes give broader terms for topics you have chosen which are too narrow as well as related terms. Note and employ all relevant subject headings to make the maximum use of the database.

Searches by title and author are somewhat less demanding, provided you have exact information. Incorrect information, however, will be meaningless to the computer. As a result, you must make sure of the exact title if you search by title and the author's name (and the number of authors) if you search by author. You may also access materials if you have the call number or a keyword.

Remember to bring a pen or pencil with you to the computer so that you can record exact bibliographic information in the event your computer does not print out that information for you. This is especially important if there is a long list of anxious students waiting for you to get off the computer!

Since some databases permit downloading of information (see Chapter Four), you might want to bring a disk with you to the library.

Locating Articles in Serials

As we noted earlier, serials supply you with popular and professional periodicals that provide articles and research reports in specific fields. They are periodical insofar as they are printed at regular time periods or intervals, such as daily, monthly, or annually.

You may begin your attempt to locate popular articles in serials in *Readers' Guide to Periodical Literature* and *Magazine Index,* both of which will provide reference information about general-interest periodicals. For a quicker method, you can go to a computer and thereby reduce the amount of time you might spend needlessly flipping pages from each year's index.

The **Infotrack** provides two databases which use keyword/subject searches: *National Newspaper Index* and *Current Periodicals Index.* This database gives you the same information formerly found only in *Reader's Guide,* but it does so more quickly and efficiently. Often both databases give abstracts. In many cases, full citations and abstracts may be printed out to be taken to the on-line catalogue where you can find the journals themselves.

If you hope to find materials in newspapers, you might rely upon one or more of the following if your college library does not have Infotrack.

New York Times Index: lists all major articles from the *Times* dating back to 1913.

National Newspaper Index: lists articles from the *Chicago Tribune, Los Angeles Times, New Orleans Times Picayune, Washington Post,* and others.

Wall Street Journal Index: lists articles focusing on business news

Business news may also be found on a database called *A B I Inform,* a *Proquest* machine (see below) which enables you to print out entire articles.

The *Reader's Guide* and the *Magazine Index* tend to provide information of a popular sort about periodical literature. As a result, these sources may *not* be useful if your topic is technical in nature. If you are researching a technical subject, refer to articles written on the subject by experts in the field. To find those articles you will need to refer to discipline-specific materials, often found in specialized indexes and databses.

Using Other Technologies

New technologies are finding their way into libraries at a rapid rate. In fact, numerous on-line databases will be developed for use in libraries between the time we write these words and you read them. As a result, we recommend that you visit your college library and, if you are not required to tour the library as part of a course, make arrangements for a librarian to show you the facilities.

Pay particular attention to compact disk units (CD-ROMs), which are appearing with greater frequency in libraries across the country. Compact disk technology makes it possible for you to access large databases quite easily.

Finally, you might use **Proquest,** if your library has it. Proquest is a computer database which makes searching easier not only because it eliminates the physical activity of having to locate and copy source articles but also because it allows readers to access materials their libraries may not subscribe to. This computer database offers you a variety of ways to search for information stored on compact disks. Most often, you will use keyword searches, which are similar to the searches you might perform using the Infotrack machines. After you type in a keyword, the Proquest machine surveys all of the journal articles included in its database. Proquest displays the total number of "hits," or exact matches, it has found in the articles and displays citations for those articles. You may then browse through the entry titles, some of which offer abstracts, marking those essays you wish to read more closely.

After you have browsed through Proquest's preliminary findings, you may elect to read those entries you marked. If you highlight each entry with the mouse, the computer will indicate which CD you should locate from the disk tower and insert into the CD reader located next to Proquest's hard drive. After the CD is inserted and the article you want is found, Proquest displays the article on the terminal. If you decide to use the article, then you may print the entire article while you are sitting at the screen.

Another search method includes using the database to look through back issues of journals, and you may even read the table of contents for those journals if you are looking for a specific article that you cannot remember the citation for.

While Proquest provides data instantly at your fingertips, it does not survey each discipline. The machine has all but replaced the paper copies of the more general guides to periodical literature, and it also surveys several of the sciences. Business has the most advanced Proquest database, called *ABI Inform*, which surveys the largest number of discipline-specific journals. New copying agreements between the developers of Proquest and journal publishers are being reached every day, so you should check with your library to determine what its holdings include.

Exercises

1. For the purposes of learning how to use the library, research one of the following topics relying on (a) Infotrack and (b) Proquest: rap music, the failure of Baring Bank, genetic engineering. Find a minimum of four articles. Read and annotate them.
2. Write a synthesis and/or critique of the articles found in exercise 1.
3. Go to your library. With the help of a librarian or a self-guided tour, identify and try the computer-supported research tools available to you.

   Write a brief description of each resource and the help it is designed to provide. Compare your descriptions of these resources with those of other students in your writing group. Where are your lists and descriptions alike? Where do they differ?

Research in the Humanities

We begin to understand research in any field once we determine what kind of evidence is valued. Naturally, in the same way that one person's notion of what constitutes convincing evidence no doubt differs from another's, evidence that convinces a humanist differs from evidence social scientists or natural scientists find believable.

Appropriate Evidence in the Humanities

As you will learn in the courses you take across campus, a discipline's notion of evidence is directly related to that discipline's view of inquiry. In the humanities, for example, texts—rather than groups of people interacting with one another or controlled laboratory analysis—are most often studied. Needless to say, evidence in the humanities is often viewed as the least objective of the kinds of evidence discussed in this chapter since it reflects the interpreter's perspective on a work of art or literature.

No matter the discipline, we begin reading to interpret once we determine the existence of a problem, question, or controversy concerning how to read or react to a text. So we most often begin research in the humanities with some recognition in mind that an interpretation must result or that a conclusion must be reached: We employ each of the skills discussed in Chapter Two to do so.

As in the assignment from an Introduction to Philosophy course (page 84), research in the humanities is usually guided by the topic chosen for scrutiny. This topic serves to guide reading and is reflected in the kinds of annotations, notes, summaries, critiques, and syntheses a reader decides to perform.

More fundamentally, however, reading to gather information that might be used in research will involve using several related skills. For one, you must delve into other research studies in preparation for writing your own to determine and, as best as you can, to state the boundaries of a particular problem (see Chapter Five on "Critical Interpretation"). In any discipline, you must rely upon and use the language or symbols of the discipline. In the humanities, research reports will often require that you argue your position by providing examples and details as support for your thesis statement.

A study in the humanities, such as the one that will result from the philosophy assignment, will be highly subjective—that is, will evolve from individual, even personal, readings of texts. (See Chapter Five, on "Personal Reflection.") As we suggest in Chapter Two, readers quite naturally bring to any text they read prior knowledge about the subject, opinions about it, or past experiences as a reader of the kind of text being read. In the humanities, these personal experiences not only influence but, in some instances, are applied systematically and thereby constitute reading and the research study itself.

Once the topic is decided upon, the sources selected, and personal opinions and prior information understood, you will be in a good position to consider your audience and purpose.

Place yourself in the position of a student in a history course who has just been asked to write a paper on the conditions under which slaves lived. To do so, you might begin by reading a **primary source**—that is, original documents or artifacts such as poems, stories, letters, autobiographies, or newspaper articles—such as Harriet Jacobs' *Incidents in the Life of a Slave Girl*. Once you have read Jacobs' account of the times, you might deepen your understanding by reading several **secondary sources**—that is, scholarly texts that comment upon or further explain primary sources. These sources provide you with the observations of others who have not only read Jacobs' narrative, but who have read other narratives of the time, comparing them and determining which details of Jacobs' narrative support or contradict details as presented in other works written during that time period.

No doubt, in reading to gain information that later will be relayed to a reader, you will first employ the same skills you learned in Chapter Two, including annotating a text and using notecards or journals to make a range of kinds of comments about the material to be learned.

Questions Asked in the Humanities

Since research in the humanities focuses most often on texts, let us begin by briefly considering the kinds of texts you can expect to confront.

It is generally true that written texts in the humanities fall into one of three categories: creative, interpretive, theoretical.

Creative texts include primary sources such as poems, short stories, novels, non-fiction narratives, and plays. The central issue confronted by students in humanities courses is how to determine meaning in a creative text (see Chapter Five, pages 143 and 163).

As a result, humanists tend to value questions such as the following:

- What sort of creative work is it?
- How did it come into existence (for example, what cultural, historical, or sociological circumstances resulted in its production)?
- What does the work reflect about the author/artist?
- How are we to respond to it (for example, to the author's assumed intention, to the work's structure, from the reader's experiences, in terms of some theory of meaning that exists outside the text)?

Our treatments of most creative texts, then, will be efforts at **interpretation**— that is, efforts to determine the work's critical meaning and/or personal significance. Most often you can expect to be asked to support your hypothesis about a text's meaning (that is, your interpretation) by reference to the text itself.

You may also find it useful, as discussed above in reference to *Incidents in the Life of a Slave Girl,* to consult other secondary works about the meaning of a literary text. These kinds of documents, what we have above labeled interpretive texts, offer a wide range of possible interpretations of a literary text and thereby serve either as a starting place for your interpretation or as support for it. As you read these sources, consider the following questions humanists are apt to ask:

- What is this writer's interpretation?
- Does the evidence support the writer's view?
- Is the writer's view the same as mine? Are there places where our views are similar?
- Where, exactly, do our views differ? Why doesn't the writer view the text as I do?

Interpretive writing offers a critic's view of the work's meaning and significance. Your job as a researcher in the humanities is to read interpretive writing to consider the creative text from various points of view, in addition to your own.

Writers of interpretive texts must do exactly what you must do when you write a research paper in the humanities: refer convincingly to the creative text itself for support of an interpretation. As a result, interpretive texts are good models for your own interpretive writings.

The third kind of text you are apt to encounter as you conduct research and answer questions in the humanities is the **theoretical** text. Authors of these documents try to discover social and historical trends in the creative art and literature they study. Theorists ask questions such as the following:

- How does the creative text reflect the social and historical context from which it arises?
- Does the writing of the age reveal characteristics that link it to the art, music, and religious beliefs of the age?
- How is one age, as reflected through its creative texts, similar to and different from the ages that precede and follow it?

As you can see, theoretical writings attempt to take a broad look at art and literature, asking questions concerning the larger relationships you might consider as you write your research paper. In short, theoretical writing links art and literature with other subjects, such as history, sociology, or psychology.

Humanists tend to make three general kinds of inquiries: interpretations in literary and art criticism; reflections on philosophical ideas; and studies of history and culture. Your goal in doing each of these kinds of research studies is not only to deepen your understanding of creative texts, but to help others read those texts as you have learned to read them—to reflect upon the text and/or to interpret it.

Most people would agree that answers to all questions must begin with **personal interpretation.** As in reading any text, interpretations begin with understanding, and understanding arises from past experiences and prior information that influence how you might read a creative text. In short, interpretations are subjective.

Still, interpretations of art or literature are not simply a string of opinions. Rather, interpretations that convince humanists are ones that are reflected in the writing of solid arguments. While opinion leaves your writing in the realm of personal reflection where one person's reflection is as good as another's, interpretation puts your writing in the realm of criticism where critical discourse is designed to establish the superiority of one perspective over another. Such critical interpretations offer arguments then that are based on evidence your readers might be able to trace for themselves. The more completely they can trace your evidence, the more successful your critical interpretation will be.

To argue successfully to a literature teacher, you would need to offer a close reading of a text in which you follow any critical judgments about the text you are interpreting with passages from the text that will convince your audience.

The same notion of support might be adapted for interpretations of pieces of art. References you make to the painting, sculpture, or architecture must seem to your readers to truly support your interpretation.

In the following short assignment, done in a sophomore-level history class as a draft of what the student might later develop into a full research paper, the student was required to select a problem identified in Mary Wollstonecraft's *A Vindication of the Rights of Woman* and then determine if the same problem exists today, over 200 years later. Note the student's effort to argue—that is, to support her interpretation—in a manner that she believes will convince her reader.

> In *A Vindication of the Rights of Woman,* Mary Wollstonecraft writes, "It would be an endless task to trace the variety of meannesses, cares, and sorrows, into which women are plunged by the prevailing opinion, that they were created rather to feel than reason, and that all the power they obtain, must be obtained by their charms and weakness: 'Fine by defect, and amiably weak!' " The opinion that women act on the basis of emotion prevails still.
>
> Even today, women are judged to make decisions on the basis of emotion rather than logic. In a recent study, a male psychologist asked a group of girls and a group of boys to respond to the same hypothetical situation. The male researcher determined on the basis of each group's response that the boys responded to the situation in a "logical" manner while the girls answered in an emotional or "indecisive" manner.
>
> Based upon this research study, one that has been criticized for its gender bias (since whatever definition the researcher gives to the term "logical" is slanted to value the decisiveness of the boys in the study), not only did women appear to lack the ability to make logical decisions but it is assumed that logic is the best way to reach a decision. It is fair to assume that other research studies, not just in sociology or psychology, but in medicine and the sciences as well, promote this gender bias that Wollstonecraft complained about over 200 years ago.

This student completes her early draft by directly addressing the question of whether Wollstonecraft's concerns are women's concerns today. The student quotes from the essay and then shows that women are concerned that recent research suggests their inability to act decisvely (that is, logically), as that term is used generally in society. The student has rightly assessed the need to argue logically and, by referring to a recent research study by a male, appeal to the reader's sense of fair play. She has made a good start in the direction of writing an acceptable research report in the humanities.

In revision, she would need to provide a more detailed account of the research study in question, perhaps quoting directly from the report on that research, as well as further evidence that a gender bias exists in the use of the term *logic.*

As you can see by this student's response, since it is a response you might personally disagree with, no absolute proof is likely to be available in the humanities to lead a reader to an absolutely true conclusion. Instead, the student makes a claim and then offers what specific support she can to that claim. A reader agrees or disagrees primarily on the basis of whether the proof is convincing.

1. Analyze the student draft above. What is the author's chief argument? Take the opposite point of view and list points that you might use to refute her argument.
2. For practice, write a short three- to four-paragraph essay in which you refute points made in the student essay above. Rely as necessary on the list made in response to Exercise 1.
3. *If you have access to a computer and e-mail,* monitor an ongoing listserv conversation for at least three days. Save all e-mail messages posted to this discussion list. At the end of this period, write an analysis that identifies two to three of the major controversies within the discussion—issues on which people have more than one perspective. Summarize the point of each controversy and list the major arguments offered for each perspective.

Reflections on philosophical ideas

In a scene from Woody Allen's movie *Radio Days,* full-grown adults are seen arguing over which ocean is better: the Atlantic or the Pacific. In Jonathan Swift's *Gulliver's Travels,* war breaks out over which side of an egg is better to crack: the little end or the big end. Like most philosphical inquiries into ideas, absolute truth about these matters cannot be reached.

Assignments that ask students to inquire into various ideas hold more in common, generally speaking, with the Introduction to Philosophy assignment (page 84) than with the two examples above. In introductory courses, students are often asked to read statements that present various, oftentimes contradictory, views on subjects philosophers have addressed—the existence of God, proper and ethical conduct in society, matters related to what is knowable and what constitutes art—and, using these sources, argue in support of their views on the subject.

Like the two examples above, these subjects may be argued about without ever reaching absolute and incontrovertible truths. As a result, such arguments call upon the skill of the writer to employ logic in convincing the reader that proof favors one side of the issue over the other—for instance, given the intricacy of the world as we experience and know it, it must have been created and, therefore, a creator called God must exist. To argue in this manner, you must lead the reader through a series of details or examples that prove—as much as possible—a point about an issue.

A word of caution is in order, however, echoing the warnings given by the philosophy instructor in the assignment on page 84. Some topics are so overused that the details or examples that support one view of the issue over other possible views lack the convincing power of originality and, as a result, fail to demonstrate to a reader the writer's logical mind at work.

Exercises

1. All of us have engaged in arguments over ideas. Most often such arguments are unresolved. Recall one such argument you have been in or, if you cannot recall an argument, consider a topic that cannot be resolved (for instance, the existence of God). How might opposing views on this subject be argued? List arguments by drawing a vertical line down the middle of the page. Place one view on the left of the line and the other on the right.

2. Write a four- to five-paragraph essay in which you argue one side of the issue explored in exercise 1.

3. *If you have access to a computer with e-mail,* monitor an ongoing listserv conversation for at least three days. Save all e-mail messages posted to this discussion list. (If you have already done this option for the Analyzing and Writing option on page 99, exercise 3, you can use that same conversation for this exercise.)

   Isolate one important argument within this conversation, one that was not entirely resolved by the participants in the exchange and one that is represented by *at least* two sides or perspectives. In writing, identify the various perspectives on the argument and list the arguments associated with each of the perspectives. Then, identify a third or fourth perspective on this argument that manages to resolve the different perspectives offered by the participants.

Studies of history and culture

Historical and cultural research deals not only with logical arguments, but with interpretations of events as well. For instance, one assignment might require you to look into events that occurred at a particular time, such as the sequence of events leading to the release and election of Nelson Mandela in South Africa. Another might ask you to explore an individual's life, as you might the life of René Descartes in an effort to record occurrences leading to the major breakthrough in his ability to prove that he existed. Still a third might ask you to examine varying views on the causes of a historical event, such as the events leading up to and igniting World War II.

In any event, your studies of history and culture will reveal a picture of past events and ways of life that, when well done, will describe to readers and effectively recreate for them what those events and ways of living must have been like.

Some people think historians have much in common with attorneys. This comparison seems true insofar as both begin with a desire to portray a particular scenario of past events and collect data to do so. These data must be verified for accuracy: The attorney seeks witnesses; the historian reads primary and secondary accounts. Both make judgments about the information they find and offer explanations of the historical event or cultural occurrence.

Some people think historians have much in common with creative writers. Both certainly begin with verifiable fact, and both often find themselves in the position of asking, "What, given these events, must have occurred next?"—as, for instance, in reconstructing events leadng up to the start of the American Revolution. In answering these questions, both the historian and writer reconstruct a past in language that is unique to the individual.

You might begin to perform library research in the humanities by using certain specific databases. These databases include *Humanities Index, MLA International Bibliography, Art Index, New York Times Index,* and *Book Review Index,* the last of which is not on CD-ROM.

Proquest does not currently (as of this writing) have databases specific to subjects in the humanities. Its general index may provide useful sources, however. More often than not, the databases listed above will serve you well as starting places for your research in the humanities.

Exercises

1. Take any one of the three subjects identified in the first paragraph of this section (for example, Nelson Mandela, René Descartes, or the causes of World War II) and, using Infotrack and Proquest, find two interpretive and two theoretical sources you might use if you were to proceed with the writing of a research paper on the topic.
2. Write an essay in which you synthesize and/or critique the sources you have found.
3. *If you have access to the World Wide Web or Gopher Space,* use a browser (for example, Netscape, Mosaic, Lynx) to locate four historical sources and four current sources on one of the three subjects identified in the first paragraph of this section.

   Read these sources, and, using a word-processing package, write a one paragraph summary of each. Along with this summary, include a full bibliographic citation of the work. Use MLA style, and consult with your teacher if you have questions.

Research in the Social Sciences

Since research in the social sciences has as its goal the systematic study of human behavior, methods of research used to collect convincing evidence are more formal than methods used in the humanities but less formal than those used in the natural sciences. Social sciences—including psychology, political science, sociology, economics, and education—are relatively young fields which have, as a result of their newness, modeled their methods of research after the older and more established natural sciences. As a result, many social scientists study human behavior using the scientific method and conducting **quantitative research**: developing hypotheses and designing and conducting controlled experiments to test those hypotheses.

Still, because social scientists are interested in the inner workings of humans as well as outer behaviors, they have had to develop research methods natural scientists do not find relevant, **qualitative research** methods, which rely upon the researcher's ability to observe and record what is seen, either by participating in the occurrence or by interviewing or surveying those involved in it. Because natural scientists are convinced chiefly by what they can see and measure, and because they cannot see and measure the inner workings of individuals or what we describe as consciousness, many natural scientists fail to see the usefulness or reliability of qualitative research.

Most assignments in introductory courses (such as the social work assignment on page 86) are intended to get students to perform basic background work of the sort done by professionals as preparation for conducting an actual research study. They are designed, as a result, to introduce you to the three kinds of research writing you can expect to do in the social sciences: library research papers, observational (also know as qualitative or field) reports, and applications of theory reports.

In this section, we will briefly review what social scientists find to be convincing evidence for each of the kinds of research writings you might do in classes in the social sciences. We will review the methodologies that produce that evidence and consider briefly in this chapter ways of recording human behavior.

Exercises

1. Look through your local or campus newspaper and find four articles social scientists would be professionally interested in.
2. Write up a plan for investigating and observing people as they interact in the four events or occurrences listed in exercise 1.

3. Using the on-line resources at your campus library or the World Wide Web, locate and read two informational articles within the social sciences—one that focuses primarily on observable social behaviors and one that focuses primarily on nonobservable behaviors (for example, feelings, emotions, cognition). You will probably find that most articles in the social sciences are characterized by some mixture of both approaches, but choose a representative article that focuses *primarily* on each one.

   Read these two sources, and, using a word-processing package, write a one paragraph summary of each—focusing on the primary approach used to explain or interpret humans as social beings. Along with this summary, include a full bibliographic citation of the work. Use APA style, and consult with your teacher if you have questions.

Appropriate Evidence in the Social Sciences

Social scientists value evidence that leads to a better understanding of both observable "external" human behavior, often called interaction, and unobservable "internal" behavior, often referred to as human consciousness. As we briefly suggested above, social scientists and natural scientists view the issue of research into consciousness quite differently; in fact, natural scientists do not find a study of unobservable internal behaviors as the proper object of scientific inquiry. By contrast, humanists and social scientists agree that human consciousness is an important area of concern. In fact, many humanists see a work of art as an external sign of some internal behavior and, as a result, believe human consciousness is an important subject for inquiry. Social scientists conduct their research in a realm somewhere between the natural scientist and the humanist, since they are interested in understanding observable human behavior, on the one hand, and unobservable human consciousness, on the other.

From one perspective, social scientists are people-watchers. In fact, they take the observations of people interacting with each other as their special province for inquiry. Unlike the rest of us, who may also be interested in observing people interact, social scientists are not apt to be interested in random observations. Social scientists watch people in a more systematic way.

Social scientists are apt to focus their attention on human behavior in a specific **field**—that is, in a well-defined arena of human interaction—or in a **laboratory** under controlled circumstances. Under the conditions of field research, social scientists enter an environment (for example, pool hall, rural southern community, exotic Pacific island) to collect data through their observations and personal interactions but do so without predicting what they may find. In a laboratory, by contrast, social scientists perform experiments modeled after the experimentation done in the natural sciences. As a result, they begin with a prediction of the results of their experiments and then, after controlling to make certain they have eliminated any possible bias resulting from their hopes or opinions (that is, from subjectivity), perform their research.

Field research results in a kind of report simply referred to variously as a **field report,** an **observational report,** or a **case study** which reports **ethnographic** or field-based information. This kind of research is usually referred to as qualitative research since it reports not statistics or measured data but human behaviors, the quality and kinds of human interactions.

Laboratory research is reported in **lab reports** of the sort used in the natural sciences (see the biology assignment on page 87). These reports follow a very specific format (as described on pages 114–115) and are unlikely to be assigned in introductory courses in the social sciences. Instead, you can plan on being asked to write a paper in which you **apply sociological theories** read about in secondary texts or discussed in class. Each of these kinds of research studies are apt to begin with the third kind of research writing done in the social sciences, a **library research report** (see the social work assignment on page 86).

---

1. Over the next three nights, stand near an entrance to a local movie theater. Your goal will be to observe the people who enter to see different movies. In your class notebook, write down any observations you make about the kind of people who pay to see different kinds of movies.
2. Write a brief report of three or four paragraphs in which you comment on what you observed while doing exercise 1 above.

One difficulty in using observable behavior to describe patterns of human interaction is that the objective record of behavior results in an inexact picture of the way human beings function. Much of what is uniquely human occurs *inside* individuals and may be missed if only external behaviors are studied.

As a result, modern social scientists have devised methods to study consciousness, including case studies of individuals, clinical evaluation, psychoanalysis, and hypnosis. Even though these methods are highly subjective, they reveal important information about human beings nevertheless.

Besides studying individual external behavior and individual consciousness, social scientists are interested in learning as much as they can about the way people relate to one another in social situations. A large number of sociological studies have taught us about cultures familiar as well as those quite foreign to our own—everything from barber shops to sparsely inhabited islands. Wherever it is done, the study of people in groups has been intended to tell us something about the way people interact with each other.

Social scientists are interested in determining the rules and conventions that govern the way individuals in society behave in relationship to one another. For instance, one current study involves observing United States Air Force personnel isolated in Antarctica for three winter months (during which time weather prevents people from entering or exiting). The goal is to see how people in isolation interact with each other so that the social scientist involved in making the observations can use not only his observations of people in isolation, but his own experiences as one of those people, to predict how astronauts will interact with each other during extended periods in a space capsule.

With the increasing awareness that we must change the way we live on this planet or that we must leave the planet altogether, social scientists are increasingly involved in observing people in unusual circumstances in the hopes of providing insight into the way we might undergo the changes in living arrangements people will no doubt experience in the upcoming century.

1. Social scientists often enter a field to observe people interacting with each other. Go to a mall, the college cafeteria, a sporting event, or any other popular local place where people are apt to interact with each other. In your class notebook (or on anything available) make a list of the kinds of inter-actions you observe. For instance, do you notice that some people avoid making contact with others, that others try to attract attention, etc.? Once you have listed four or five different kinds of interactions, invent names for each and make notes that will remind you later of the details you have observed.

2. Write an essay of five or six paragraphs in which you report on what you observed and noted in Exercise 1.

3. *If you have access to a computer with e-mail or the Internet,* sign onto an e-mail conversation related to your career option, a MOO, a MUD, or an IRC session (see Chapter Four). If you need help accessing these kinds of exchanges, consult your campus computing center or the technical assistants in the computer-supported writing facility that you use.

   In connection with these environments, observe people interacting with others through language for two days (in the case of e-mail) or for half an hour (in the case of MOOs, MUDs, or IRCs). Make a list of the kinds of interactions that you observe, inventing labels for each kind of language behavior that you recognize (for example, asking questions, making state-ments, telling stories, complaining, referring to others, and so forth).

Questions Asked in the Social Sciences

The subtle difference between the humanities and social sciences can be seen in the questions asked in each discipline. While humanists ask about the mean-ing of human existence as reflected in creative texts, social scientists ask ques-tions that aim at explaining human behavior in a field or laboratory.

Social scientists approach an understanding of human behavior in three ways. First, social scientists believe that the behavior of individuals in society is governed by certain rules and that it conforms to specific patterns. Second, social scientists believe that when individuals interact with one another, systems evolve and likewise become rule-governed and patterned. And, third, systems change over time in response to forces that influence individuals, bringing the cycle to an end.

As a result, social scientists ask questions that fall into specific groups, such as the following.

• What characterizes the psychological behavior of individuals in isolation? Among others?

- How do groups of people formulate rules for appropriate behavior? How do individuals learn and respond to changes in these rules?
- What characterizes newly discovered or recently studied cultures? Which structures are shared by all cultures? Which structures are shared by all cultures? Which structures are unique to individual cultures? Why have they developed unique methods of relating to each other in such cultures?
- How does the commercial and economic world influence an individual's perceptions of and interactions with others?
- How do individuals behave under certain governments or in response to specific governmental restrictions or changes?

These questions might be answered in research that is done in the field or through case study of individuals or by controlled laboratory experimentation. Each of these kinds of studies begins with the reading of professional materials that might be found in the library.

Library research papers

As you can see from the assignment from a social work class (page 86), most research questions in the social sciences arise from the need to solve certain problems. A professional looking through materials in the library might discover that a certain question has not yet been answered. Such a recognition provides professionals with an opportunity to perform research that furthers our knowledge.

You might begin to perform library research in the social sciences by using certain specific databases. These databases include *Psychlit, Sociofile,* and *Public Affairs Information Service (PAIS)* on CD-ROM. Other sources not on CD-ROM at the time of this writing include *The Congressional Quarterly, West's Law Review,* and *The Supreme Court Reporter.*

In many instances, library research leads to understandings of what new and additional research needs to be done. These understandings are ordinarily expressed in the form of **research questions.** Here are two such questions.

> Two broad research questions guided the study. The first asks how men and women are portrayed in MTV commercials and hypothesizes that both men and women will be portrayed in stereotypical ways. . . .
>
> The second research question focuses on whether commercials for different types of products have a male or female gender orientation. In short, are there recognizable differences in terms of the types of products that are associated with men and women?

As you might surmise, the authors of the above two questions have used library research as a basis not only for reaching an understanding about what research remains to be done, but also as a way of establishing that the research they have performed absolutely needed to be done to answer questions other studies have left unanswered.

1. Reread the two research questions above. Go to any one of the databases identified in this section of the chapter and find four or five articles on the general subject of those questions.
2. Write a short article on the question of gender stereotypes.

Quantitative research reports

Like quantitative research conducted in the natural sciences, social scientists in conducting quantitative research predict how their research might end up. The researchers who asked the two research questions appearing on page 106 state the following five hypotheses or predictions concerning how they believe their research will turn out.

H1: Female characters will appear less frequently than male characters in MTV commercials.

H2: Female characters will be more likely than male characters to be portrayed as having very fit bodies.

H3: Female characters will be rated as more attractive than male characters.

H4: Female characters will be more likely than male characters to wear skimpy or sexy clothing.

H5: Female characters will be more likely than male characters to be the object of another's gaze.

In completing a report that answers the questions and tests the hypotheses stated above, the authors quite naturally will follow a format similar to the one required in the social work assignment (page 86).

For reports on quantitative research, the appropriate format might be described as follows:

Introduction: In this section, the authors are expected to orient their readers to the research. Why is the research needed? What research studies have been done in the area? How have they set up the research reported upon in this study? What questions will this research answer? What hypotheses seem warranted by previous studies? What hypotheses will this study test?

Methods: Simply put, in the methods section you must describe exactly how your study was conducted. Oftentimes this section is broken into subsections if needed to describe fully and accurately how the study was performed. This section, when done correctly, will permit replicability of the study.

Findings: This section presents the data produced by your study. If surveys have been used in the research, numerical results will be presented here. The goal is to provide evidence for whatever claims you might make.

Discussion: In this section, you should direct the reader's attention to significant patterns that emerge from the statistical analysis. This section will provide information that interprets results for the reader and leads to a statement of appropriate claims for your study. A statement of the research study's significance should come at the end of this section.

A generally accepted format for reporting qualitative research holds many of the above elements in common with reports on quantitative research. In both, the introduction establishes the need for the proposed study on the basis of numerous articles in appropriate journals. Since the qualitative research report highlights observations of subjects in specific environments and *does not begin with hypotheses,* you might use a subject identification section rather than a statement of hypotheses, as described below, and provide information in the methods section appropriate to the kinds of observations and interactions you as the researcher will make. In addition, rather than the traditional results section, make use of an analysis of behaviors section.

The following information should guide you in writing a research report based on qualitative research.

Introduction: This section includes a statement of the question or problem that you have studied. You should use previous research to create a foundation for this research study, suggesting that this research, as the next logical step in the ongoing search for knowledge, is both inevitable and necessary.

Subject Identification: You must provide information about the subjects studied and the environment in which they were observed.

Methods: This section must include two items: your theoretical perspective, since it is important in qualitative and ethnographic inquiry that the researcher's point of view be understood, and your method of making observations as an insider/participant to the culture or event or as an outsider/observer.

Analysis of Behaviors: You must not only report the behaviors you have observed, but analyze those behaviors as well. These analyses will provide groundwork for conclusions.

Conclusions: In this section, you must base any conclusions you reach on behaviors you analyzed and reported in the previous section.

Remember that unlike scientific research, which depends for its validity on **replicability**—that is, on another researcher's ability to repeat the study—as a basis for arguing that findings are generally applicable, qualitative research is not generalizable. Qualitative research enables researchers to reach conclusions that apply only to the specific circumstances studied.

1. Return to your list of types of interactions observed at a local gathering place. Reread your list and the report that you wrote in response to exercises 1 and 2 on page 104. If you believe it is necessary to do so, return to that place and observe the people there once more.

2. Write a qualitative report, following the format described above, in which you report on what you observed. Remember to include an introduction, subject identification, methods, analysis of behaviors, and conclusions.

3. *If you have access to the World Wide Web,* access six personal home pages that have been posted—make sure that three of the home pages are for females and three of them are for males. Look these pages over carefully, keeping in mind the following research questions: How do women and men portray themselves in the home pages they construct?

   After surveying the home pages and taking notes, write a list of at least five hypotheses associated with the research question—all of them based on your sample. Use the sample hypotheses in this section for models.

Research in the Natural Sciences

As you can tell from the biology assignment on page 87 you will be required to do a considerable amount of writing in your science courses. This writing will be the most formal writing you will do in college since so much emphasis is placed on replicability in the sciences. It will also be the most dispassionate and objective since your objectivity is required by your audience.

The natural sciences, as we discuss them here, include **life sciences,** such as biology; **physical sciences,** such as physics and chemistry; and **earth sciences,** such as geology. The insights and methods employed in these subject areas carry over as well to technological fields such as computer science and mechanical engineering.

The goal of researchers in these fields is to build upon observable and verifiable phenomena, not simply to note them. Research such as that done by natural scientists is a consequence of noting, in light of existing theories about how things operate in their field, deviations from the norm, events so incongruous that the scientist, out of simple curiosity, seeks a better understanding of what has occurred and why.

Not all research studies influence existing ideas. Rather, most studies are small steps leading to greater and deeper awarenesses of whether and how our ideas are reflected by our experiences of the world.

Your research in the natural and applied sciences may begin much as research commences in the social sciences: by an understanding, gained by extensive reading and library research, of the issues in the field. This reading will enable you to better understand the very theories your later research will either verify or call into question. Though you are unlikely to make major scientific discoveries and breakthroughs in your introductory biology course, you will build a foundation as a researcher in that course that you might use later in making an important discovery.

Once you have come to an understanding of the theories underlying your efforts at research, you will be in a position to conduct your own research. And that research will begin with a hypothesis you will test through the scientific method.

In many cases, you will be asked to keep a **laboratory notebook.** This notebook, modeled after similar scientific notebooks used by scientists who perform research in business and industry, may be used in your classes as a place where you can keep a record of your work from day to day. In business and industry, such a notebook is a legal document that might be required in proceedings concerning ownership of various trademarked materials, such as those developed by pharmaceutical manufacturers. Your use of such a notebook will be limited to keeping notes on what progress you have made in conducting an experiment, especially if that experiment cannot be completed in one session. Your notebook entries will serve both as a reminder of what you have done and as prewriting for your lab report.

As in writing done to report research in the social sciences, controlled laboratory experimentation occurs *after* the researcher has read other relevant studies. In any case, writing done in courses in the natural sciences is intended to prepare you for what you will be asked to write in upper-level courses and in technological fields as well as later on the job. As a result, you can expect to be asked to perform two kinds of writing tasks in your introductory courses in natural sciences and technology: literature review and laboratory report.

In this section of the chapter, we will explore several related issues, including what constitutes appropriate evidence in the natural sciences and technology and how to present that evidence in literature reviews and laboratory reports.

Exercises

1. Make a list of processes you know well. The list may include mechanical (for example, how to drive a car), physical (for example, how to care for a pulled muscle), or social (for example, how to train a dog) processes. Once you have made a list of five or six processes, make notes in your class notebook concerning how you would explain one of those processes to an elementary school student, ten years of age.

2. Write a letter explaining your process, addressed to a ten-year-old student in an elementary school. Make certain you begin by stating what you expect to accomplish, identifying the procedure exactly by offering a step-by-step explanation, and explaining how the process should conclude.

3. Write directions that will help a classmate learn to use one of the following applications:
   - e-mail
   - World Wide Web

- Internet Relay Chat
- news groups
- a word-processing package

When you have finished your directions, identify a classmate who does not know the application you have written about. Have this person follow your directions while you take notes on the weaknesses in your directions—the places where they cause your classmate confusion, where they lack some steps, or where they are insufficiently clear. Using these notes, revise your directions.

Appropriate Evidence in the Natural Sciences

You will be expected to conduct research in the natural sciences that conforms to certain specific expectations that, in one way or another, influence the way you will gather and present evidence.

1. You will be expected to eliminate or, at the very least, **minimize personal involvement** in your research study and present your research findings in a logical and objective manner. Unlike the social sciences, where you might need to enter the environment you intend to study and record not only what you see there but what you do, research practices in the natural sciences will require you to control all subjective factors that might influence the outcome of your experiment.

2. In qualitative research of the sort done most often in the social sciences, measurements are rarely a problem. While you must identify yourself as an influential element of the social science research environment, you do not have to make exact measurements. When you report quantitative research (as in the natural sciences and in some social scientific studies), you are required to **make precise measurements** and to do so in such a way that a member of the community for which you are writing will have little difficulty understanding how you reached the conclusions you reached. Unlike humanists or social scientists who recognize and admit to the imprecision of their senses and language, the natural scientist employs the scientific method to reduce the likelihood that language or observations might be inexact or inappropriate.

3. Research in the natural sciences is *exact*. Researchers focus on what is to be observed and then attempt to eliminate any other factors that might interfere with the results. These factors are brought under *control* by the very procedures employed by natural scientists as they conduct research.

4. Unlike humanists and social scientists, natural scientists isolate the particular variables they hope to test. As a result, rather than permitting their data to direct their hypotheses, as social scientists might, natural scientists begin with predictions or hypotheses about what they might find and then test those hypotheses. In short, while humanists and social scientists make theories from what they find in their research, natural scientists test theories they begin with.

We might add to these four features related to finding appropriate evidence in the natural sciences yet another important characteristic of research in the natural sciences: scientists strive to make their research repeatable or **replicable.** In short, if the research conducted cannot be duplicated by another scientist using exactly the same laboratory controls and research methods, your research will be called into question. Results are meaningful only if they can be obtained over and over again whenever the experiment is repeated exactly as it is described in the laboratory report.

In introductory courses, of course, you will be the one performing research that aims at replicating the studies of others. If you do not reach the expected results and conclusions, you have probably done something wrong. If, for example, after immersing an egg in water for ten minutes it is not yet hard, you probably did not actually put it in boiling water. Or, if your lab instructor asks you to find a fetal pig's stomach and you cannot, it is not likely that you have before you the only fetal pig in the room that did not have a stomach.

In any case, repeatability or replicability is an important feature of research in the natural sciences. Though we hardly expect people to make the same judgments about a poem or about their interaction with a group of individuals, we do expect them to be able to reach the same conclusions after following the same carefully controlled methods in research conducted in the natural sciences.

Exercises

1. Go with a classmate to a zoo, an aquarium, a farm, or a ranch and observe a single animal for about an hour (or just sit outside your classroom building and watch squirrels for as long as you can). In a notebook, write down detailed notes on what you and your classmate have observed.
2. Examine your notes from exercise 1 above and rearrange them if necessary to put them in order. Collaborate with your classmate in the writing of a short essay of about three or four paragraphs in which you describe exactly what you have seen. Read your essay to a group of classmates.

Questions Asked in the Natural Sciences

Questioning is essential to the sciences. In fact, professionals in the three fields of scientific inquiry identified above—life sciences, physical sciences, and earth sciences—attempt to answer questions that define the very boundaries of their fields:

- What characterizes the changes species undergo as they age?
- What forces influence the way a baseball seems to curve?
- What happens when sulfuric acid is added to sugar?
- What causes earthquakes?

Perhaps the two most important questions of all for a person who desires to conduct research in the sciences are matters of argumentation. The first involves you in noticing that something strange or out-of-the-ordinary has happened. For instance, you have poured a cup of cold coffee onto a plant in your kitchen. The next day you notice that the plant has begun to bloom. You might simply assume it was going to bloom anyway and that the fact it has bloomed the day after you have thrown coffee on it is purely coincidental. Or you might take this as an opportunity to experiment with using coffee to "water" your plants.

A second kind of question arises when you believe one thing has caused a certain kind of reaction—for instance, that something in the coffee serves to make your plant bloom. If you fail to find an explanation in horticulture books, you may then come to believe that blooming in the particular plant in your kitchen is hastened by watering the plant with coffee. A research study might arise from this hypothesis as well.

You would be wise, however, to check the available literature to determine if a research study of the sort you propose (or one similar to it) has already been done.

Exercises

1. Do you think the experiment described above is worth conducting? Why or why not? List your reasons and explanations.
2. Have you noticed strange or out-of-the-ordinary events or occurrences that, out of natural curiosity, you wanted to understand better? List them here and describe how you investigated them.
3. Using the personal home page material you wrote for the exercise on page 109, design a larger, more extensive experiment to test your hypotheses. Describe this experiment in writing. Be sure to write about why you think such research is important, how many other home pages you plan to look at, what evidence you plan to gather, and what methods you plan to use in gathering and analyzing this information.

4. Think about the experiences you have had on the Internet or the World Wide Web. Have you noticed any strange or out-of-the-ordinary events or occurrences that you would like to understand better? If so, design an experiment and write a description of it using the guidelines in the paragraph above.

The literature review

The literature review in preparation for conducting scientific research takes you to the library. Once there, you might consult databases such as *Agricola* and *Gioref* or other works designed to provide you with the specific information you need, including *Microbiological Abstracts, Chemical Abstracts, Engineering Index Annual, Physics Abstracts,* and *Science Abstracts* (see, as well, the description of library sources, pages 89–94).

Briefly put, the Literature Review brings together current knowledge on a subject. As we have already suggested in Chapter Two, you might bring sources together in one of two ways: by critiquing and classifying sources (page 71) or by synthesizing them (page 75).

Literature Reviews provide you with the experience you will need when you review relevant studies as part of your laboratory report.

Exercises

1. Go to the library to investigate literature on how plants grow and, specifically, what kinds of chemical agents stimulate growth in certain specific kinds of house plants. Find four sources that might be used in a literature review.
2. Write a literature review by synthesizing and/or critiquing the sources identified in exercise 1, above.

Laboratory reports

Lab reports in the natural sciences and technological fields are similar in format and tone to lab reports of quantitative research done for the social sciences. A laboratory report in the natural sciences is typically divided into five sections.

Introduction: In this section (as in the same section under social sciences) you should briefly state why the study was undertaken, citing relevant background facts as they lead to a statement of the specific problem you are confronting in your research.

Materials and Methods: In terms of the requirement that you make your study repeatable, this section is extremely important. Here you provide a statement of exactly what you used in your experiment and exactly what steps you took. While other portions of your report will employ argumentation as their purpose, this section will be purely informative and done in a sequence, perhaps chronological or spatial. If you record in your laboratory notebook everything you do in your experiment, you will find this section easy to write. In fact, this is where you should begin if you find it difficult to get started in writing your lab report.

Results: This is where you need to be precise. In reporting your data, you should keep in mind that you are building a case for the discussion section that will follow. As a result, you must present your data here as clearly and logically as you can. You will want to point out trends to readers and use tables and graphs to do so. Remember as well to simply *present* your data here. Interpretation will come later.

Discussion: This is where you should *interpret* your results and discuss what you believe, on the basis of data in the results section, to be their implications. You might suggest their implications by relating them to other studies done on the subject or by suggesting new hypotheses that your study make possible. This is often the longest section of your report.

Literature Cited: This section includes full citations for any works cited in your report.

You may be required by your instructor to write an **abstract** for your report, in which you summarize the problem addressed and the major findings and conclusions of your experiment.

Exercises

1. Perform the following simple experiment that you can conduct just about anyplace. Measure your pulse rate by touching the middle finger of your right hand to your left wrist. You may have to feel around a bit. Once you have found your pulse, measure it for fifteen seconds. Record in your class notebook the number of heartbeats per minute by multiplying the number you have recorded during a fifteen second interval by four. Now go for a brisk walk. Walk for about five minutes and, when you complete your walk, measure your pulse rate a second time, following the directions above. Multiply that number by four and enter the number in your class notebook.

2. Write a laboratory report on this experiment following the guidelines outlined on pages 114–115.

3. Using your campus library's on-line resources, do a totally electronic literature search on how plants grow, specifically what kinds of chemical agents stimulate growth in specific house plants. Examine the titles of the sources that you find, and identify a shorter list of the ten sources that look the most valuable to you.

4. *If you have access to a stand-alone computer,* use a word-processing package to create a questionnaire about research methods and approaches that you could use to interview a professional in the field of your choice. In this questionnaire, ask about the kinds of research questions that are standard in this field, the kinds of approaches or methods that are commonly used to answer such questions, the kinds of analyses and interpretation that are done in looking at information or evidence.

   When you have completed this questionnaire, make an appointment with a professional in the field of your choice. At the appointment, ask the person the questions you have formulated and take notes on their answers. Type these answers into the word-processing file you have created for the questions.

5. *If you have access to a computer with the Internet,* use a browser (for example, Netscape, Mosaic, Lynx) to locate information about the national professional organization representing a career in which you are interested. Find a Gopher site or a World Wide Web site that provides information about this professional organization.

Starting at this site, try to find the organization's professional style guidelines for research papers, articles, or reports. These guidelines should provide help in formatting bibliographic citations for articles or references. Using this style sheet, write up a mock bibliography (using any sources at all in the field—they need not be on any one topic) of at least twenty sources. Make sure that these citations adhere to the style sheet you have located.

6. *If you have access to a computer with the Internet,* use a browser (for example, Netscape, Mosaic, Lynx) to find out how many libraries you can access for free. Choose three of these libraries and do an on-line literature search for a research question of your choice. Make sure that the question you use is a narrowly focused one—one that yields twenty or fewer entries in the specific topic area. Otherwise, your literature search will be too extensive to manage for this assignment.

In writing, analyze and compare the list of bibliographical resources that you get from each of the three libraries you have chosen. Which library yields the most entries? Which entries seem the most useful to you? Which entries seem the most credible and why?

Finally, choose ten of the most promising resources that you have found through this exercise and create a formal bibliography for your research question, eliminating the sources that seem less than credible or that aren't focused directly on your topic. Choose a bibliographical style that has been approved by your instructor to make sure that all of your bibliographic entries are correctly and completely cited.

Universal Resource Locators (URLs)

Cautions and Reminders about Electronic Material on the World Wide Web

The specific addresses of World Wide Web (WWW) sites listed at the end of Chapters Three through Eleven are intended only as preliminary starting-point suggestions for your research. If you have access to a wide area network (WAN) and a WWW browser, such as Netscape or Lycos, you should use these addresses—also referred to as Universal Resource Locators (URLs)—to begin your exploration of the WWW. We also encourage you to identify your own favorite sites and record the URLs of these sites for future use. When attempting to access any address on the WWW, reproduce the URL exactly, with capital and lowercase letters reproduced as they have been given. Some machines are case sensitive and may not permit changes in capitalization.

However, given the dynamic nature of the WWW, the specific addresses we have provided may have changed since this book was published. The WWW represents a constantly changing collection of information, one always in the process of being composed. When consulting the site addresses we have provided, please exercise caution in evaluating the accuracy of the information found there. There is no licensing procedure for adding material to the WWW, and anybody, regardless of her or his expertise, may do so. Hence, it is important to examine and evaluate the source of the material and use it appropriately. Your instructor can help by having class discussions about ways to evaluate the appropriateness and validity of the information found in sites on the WWW. Among such strategies, we recommend cross-checking information with familiar print resources, identifying the original author(s) or sources of a text, checking copyrighted information, and considering the expertise of the site contributors.

The source of material taken from the WWW, or, indeed, from anywhere on-line, and used in print texts (or in other on-line texts) should also be cited appropriately—this includes still images and text, as well as audio and video clips. Citation provides a system for locating material efficiently, checking the accuracy and validity of information, and giving credit to authors for the original work they have done. Please refer to the electronic citation guidelines included in the appendices of this text for citing electronic materials in either MLA, APA, CBE, or Chicago formats.

URLs for Researching in the Disciplines

Library of Congress
http://lcweb.loc.gov/home page/services.html

Virtual Library
http://www.w3.org/hypertext/Datasources/bysubject/Overview/html

Research Links for Writers
http://www.siu.edu/departments/cola/english/seraph9k/research.html

WWW Research Information Locations
http://www.swin.edu.au/sgrs/research-sites.html

The HUMBUL Gateway
http://sable.ox.ac.uk/departments/humanities/international.html

Academic Libraries
http://guide-p.infoseek.com/DC/DB?C865,1584

Libraries and Reference Works
http://wws.mathematik.hu-berlin.de/~jaschke/reference.html

Libraries and References
http://www.per.dmp.csiro.au/References.html

Library and Other Research Resources
http://www.egusd.k12.ca.us/webdocs/library.html

Deja News—Usenet news archives on multiple topics
http://www.dejanews.comdndn.html

Museums
http://www.comlab.ox.ac.uk/ARCHIVE/OTHER/museums.html

Perry Casteneda Library Map Collection
http://www.lib.utexas.edu/Libs/PCL/Map_collection/map_collection.html

Lycos—Catalog of the Internet
http://www.lycos.com/

U.S. Government Information
http://techserv4.law.csuohio.edu/usgov.html

U.S. Government
http://xray1.physics.sunysb.edu/usgov.html

Written Communication and Computer Technology

Fluency, Organization, Invention, and Revision Aids

Support for Collaboration and Group Exchanges

Information and Research Aids

Problems and Challenges Associated with Computers

Some Computer-Supported Writers' Tools

Today, as the twentieth century comes to a close, it may be difficult for you to imagine writing and communicating *without* computers. And you are not alone, for professionals in almost every field take for granted an increasingly sophisticated level of electronic support. You may know friends who rely on word-processing packages to complete their writing assignments, on e-mail systems to connect them with friends and family, on Internet access to complete research projects by browsing the collections in other libraries, and on collaboration software to support their work with other writers on-line. You may also have friends who compose multimedia texts that combine graphics, still photography, sound, video, and written materials or who enjoy using listservs, news groups, and real-time conversations.

If you make only a limited use of computers to support your academic work, you should know that computer-supported writing environments can provide individual writers and writing teams a number of benefits. We cannot describe them all in detail here, but we can briefly describe a few of the reasons that writers in various fields have given for using computers in their written communications work. With this information, you might get a few ideas yourself.

One important caution should be kept in mind as you read through this chapter. A great deal of research has been conducted over the last decade to study the effects of technology on writing. However, no consistent evidence from these investigations exists to suggest that computer-supported writing— writing that generally occurs on computers with the aid of a word-processing package—improves the *quality* of written work.

There is, in other words, no reason to believe that the use of computers *alone* will help you produce more insightful or thoughtful prose, create lab reports that are more logically organized, or write papers with fewer mechanical or minor grammatical errors. We are not suggesting this caution to discourage you from using computers; they can be both useful and effective as authoring tools. We want you to know, however, that computers alone will not allow you to write documents that are of higher quality than those you created on a typewriter or by hand. As a writer, you have to depend on yourself—and a great deal of writing practice—for these results.

Exercises

1. What are the similarities and differences you have observed or experienced between writing on paper (or typing) and writing on-line?

   Using a word-processing package, make two lists, one of similarities and one of differences. Place a star next to those that seem to make an important difference in the way you think or get words down on a page.

   Get together with your writing group and, using the copy-and-paste commands in your word-processing package, create one big word-processing file into which you copy all the individual lists of differences and similarities generated by your group. Edit this file for consistency. Seek help from your teacher or a technical consultant should you encounter difficulties with this activity.

2. How much experience do you have with writing on computers? What kinds of experiences? Using a word-processing package, informally trace your own history as a writer who works on computers.

3. Have you ever had a frustrating or an exceedingly positive experience connected to writing on a computer? Using a word-processing package, write this story.

Fluency, Organization, Invention, and Revision Aids

Some of you will be happy to know that one of the most consistent effects writers have documented about using computers in a variety of disciplinary tasks is related to fluency—increased numbers of words and volume of text. This effect may be explained by the fact that many writers can produce words faster by typing than they can by writing in longhand. Computer keyboards are generally characterized by an easier action than are conventional typewriters—even the electric versions of those machines. In any case, the physical ease of text production means for many writers that they can better keep pace with the speed and complexity of thought processes, shaping ideas on a screen almost as fast as they come to mind and can be uttered in language.

For some writers, this ease of text production, or fluidity, is an aid to invention, to the creation of written text, and to an increased production of ideas. The fluidity of electronic text also encourages some writers to revise as well. In computer environments, writers often find it easier to manipulate (for example, move, reorder, juxtapose) blocks of text than they do on paper. They feel freer to try out a variety of organizational strategies to suit the information, the audience, and the purpose of the communicative situation without having to manually rewrite or retype the text blocks in question.

Finally, some writers feel that word processors that include spelling checkers and style analyzers help to increase the ease of writing and result in prose that is less error-ridden. Although these tools may appeal to some writers for their utility and convenience, again there is no consistent evidence that they necessarily result in fewer errors within written documents. Computers, indeed, have been found to generate or encourage new kinds of errors—for example, repeated words, often generated when material is cut from the middle of a paragraph or passage.

Support for Collaboration and Group Exchanges

Thus far, we have considered the benefits of computer-supported writing in fairly narrow terms—as those evident within the environment of word-processing packages. Additional benefits, however, have been attributed to other computer-based writing environments—especially to those environments that support communities of writers: environments like e-mail, listservs, bulletin boards, and on-line conferences.

Among the intriguing claims for these relatively simple uses of technology (each of which allows a writer to send messages or documents to other writers) have been the following:

- Computer-based conversations, because they support flexible connections among individuals and groups of people, may allow more people and different kinds of people to share information and form communities of writers than do face-to-face conversations.
- Computer-based conversations may help individuals and groups focus less on physical characteristics (for example, gender, race, age, disability) and more on the content of written messages.
- Computer-based exchanges transcend limitations of time and space. For some people, computer-based communication is convenient and quick.

Many communities of writers who share information on-line would not or could not have formed in traditional settings. Now, however, these writers can come together to form what are known as "virtual communities." Howard Rheingold, in a 1993 article on electronically supported groups, defined a virtual community as "a group of people who may or may not meet one another face-to-face, and who exchange words and ideas through the medium of computer bulletin boards and networks. Like any community, it is also a collection of people who adhere to a certain (loose) social contract, and who share certain (eclectic) interests."

A number of computer-based environments support such collaborative writing communities. E-mail, for example, provides a basic and relatively accessible computer environment for many collaborative writing efforts and research groups. The phenomenal growth of listservs and newsgroups, which utilize software that circulates messages from one individual to a list of subscribers interested in a topic, provides clear evidence of the usefulness of such environments. Such lists are employed by writers in every conceivable discipline. A recent publication about the Internet, Internet World's *Internet '94,* identifies more than 8,000 different groups that occupy this electronic landscape: groups formed around national allegiances (for example, Native Americans, Greeks, Algerians, Croatians, Brazilians, Cubans, Russians, Ecuadorians, Estonians, Romanians, Hungarians); literary works (for example, Chicano literature, Hebrew literature, Islamic literature, Latin American literature, Greek literature, German literature); religious topics (for example, Coptic Orthodoxy, Old Testament, New Testament, Eastern Orthodoxy, Christianity, Buddhism, Bahai, Pagan, Quakers); political interests (for example, immigration, human rights, policy making, government information, disabilities, national security, communism, feminism, family studies, gay and lesbian topics, hazardous waste management); and current events (for example, the Bosnian conflict, Somalia, Grochz Kapusta, earthquakes, cyberspace, and nuclear war).

Some businesses also provide access to more sophisticated group collaboration systems and presentation facilities. In these facilities, individual authors (often scattered across remote locations) can engage in group-based brainstorming, associational thinking, or project development planning and then project the results of this input on a large-screen presentation device that allows all group members to see the results. Such setups are now functional in a number of business and industry sites—including the Capture Lab at General Motors or the Colab at Xerox PARC—and in many educational settings.

Additional software packages and systems allow multiple authors to work simultaneously on the same material or documents. With a prototype called the Upper Atmospheric Research Colaboratory, for example, space physicists at the University of Michigan, the University of Maryland, the Lockheed Palo Alto Research Laboratory, and the Danish Meteorological Institute in Copenhagen can conduct experiments on data being gathered at the Upper Atmosphere Research Facility in Kangerlussuaq, Greenland, and exchange written information on the experiments. Another software package, Aspects, published by Group Technologies, allows multiple writers linked by computer network to write a document and comment on it simultaneously. Using a wide area network (WAN) like the Internet, collaborative writing groups can also gather to exchange information in virtual meeting spaces that allow real-time conversations.

These computer-based tools and collaboration environments have changed not only the ways in which some people write, but the relationships that bind them together within business and organizational settings, providing employees more direct access to management, encouraging collaborative team efforts across distances, and serving to flatten organizational hierarchies.

Information and Research Aids

It is clear that e-mail and other computer-based communication systems may alter the nature of the communication environment for many writers. Writers who were once limited to the data, texts, images, and information sources that they could gather in their local libraries now use computers to interview knowledgeable colleagues and experts at different sites and in various disciplines, to keep abreast of new developments via newsgroups and listservs, to access online texts and journals, and to check large infobases that contain discipline-specific information.

In addition to the general catalog systems of most modern libraries, for example, writers can now use the Internet to access the image catalogs of the Smithsonian Institute; the chromosome maps of the Salk Institute's San Diego Genome Center; the bacterial, fungi, and yeast databases of the World Data Center for Micro Organisms; all of the user manuals produced by the Space Telescope Science Institute for the Hubble Space Telescope; forecasts by the National Weather Service; the awards and requests-for-proposal announcements of the National Science Foundation; the United States Department of Agriculture's Current Research Information System; White House press briefings; and The World Factbook, produced by the Central Intelligence Agency.

Computer-based communication environments also have the advantage of supporting writers who want to take distance-learning courses from experts based in corporations or educational institutions. Many universities now offer part of their curricula within computer-supported environments; in fact, many students, especially nontraditional ones, find such classes both valuable and more accessible than conventional instruction. Some universities offer entire undergraduate and graduate degree programs in virtual environments.

Exercises

1. Individually, or in your writing group, take five minutes to draw your favorite computer-supported writing environment—the computer itself, the room in which you write, the materials you generally have at hand. Describe your drawing to your writing partner or writing group, telling why the various elements of the computer-supported writing environment are important to you as an author.
2. Using a word-processing package, work with your writing group to brainstorm a list of computer-supported writing tools that you would like to see included in standard word-processing packages during the next five years (for example, voice input, two-way video for e-mail, marginal notation, or drawing capabilities). Write a paragraph about each of these features.
3. Using a word-processing package, take a few minutes to list some of the disadvantages associated with computers as a communication tool. Choose two of these items. In a paragraph for each, tell why this particular factor is a disadvantage for your own composing processes.

Problems and Challenges Associated with Computers

The obvious potential of computer-supported writing environments—increased communication among individuals and groups on a global scale, increased productivity and access to information, sophisticated writing tools like outlining software packages and multimedia composing packages—is also balanced by obvious challenges. Although it would be impossible to list all of these challenges here, writers should become familiar with a few of the more thorny issues they may encounter when communicating in on-line environments.

Flaming

Electronic communication environments are often punctuated by flaming: the on-line use of highly emotional, often angry, insulting, and generally inappropriate language. On-line writing environments are thought to encourage flaming for a variety of reasons, one of which is the ability to use a pseudonym when sending a message.

The following quotation provides an edited excerpt from one flame that was received soon after the publication of a long profile article on Bill Gates, the Chairman of Microsoft:

> Crave THIS, asshole:
> Listen you toadying dipshit scumbag . . . look around and notice that real re-porters don't fawn over their subjects, pretend that their subjects are making some sort of special contact with them, or, worse, curry favor by TELLING their subjects how great the ass-licking profile is going to turn out. . . .

> Seabrook, J. "My First Flame." *New Yorker* 6 June 1994: 70.

Such posts, containing derogatory language and unproductive criticism, occur all too often. As Lee Sproull and Sara Kiesler, two noted experts on electronic conversations, say:

> People interacting on a computer are isolated from social cues and feel safe from surveillance and criticism. This feeling of privacy makes them feel less inhibited with others. It also makes it easy for them to disagree with, confront, or take exception to others' opinions. . . . As a consequence of the low level of social information in computer based communication and its perceived ephemerality, people lose their fear of social approbations. Moreover, they imagine they must use stronger language to get their point across. . . .

> Sproull, L. and S. Kiesler. *Connections: New Ways of Working Within the Networked Organization.* Cambridge: MIT Press, 1991, p. 49.

Flames do not go unnoticed, however, and on-line groups often chastise flame throwers or stuff their electronic mail boxes with notices to cease and desist with such behavior. In many systems, flame generators are traceable despite pseudonyms.

Surveillance

Issues of privacy and free speech also figure centrally in another problem gen-erated in computer-supported communication environments: surveillance.

As early as 1988, for example, scholars had begun to note that managers and supervisors were using computers to monitor the work of employees. The electronic surveillance of employees involved checks on productivity, speed, and accuracy in accomplishing various work-related tasks, and it took place in a range of industrial and organizational settings: banks, government offices, trucks, and supermarkets. Computers have been used to monitor the number of telephone calls that operators or reservation clerks process, the number of employee actions in assembly-line tasks, the number of keystrokes in data entry work, the caller and the recipient of telephone calls, and the punctuality of truck deliveries. Such monitoring of productivity often backfires. Workers op-erating within organizations that employ surveillance techniques often report dissatisfaction, growing out of a lack of control over their work environments.

What do such surveillance strategies have to do with writing and with writers in various disciplines? Consider these three examples: the uses of digital signature devices, message encryption devices, and time-stamping devices. Each of these devices, while providing writers with some protection against tampering with documents in electronic writing environments, also increases the possibilities for surveillance of authors and writing teams.

Digital signature devices, for example, allow authors to construct a code that will assure the recipient of the document that both the signature and the document are authentic. When important messages are sent over large, unsecured networks, such assurance is vital. Such a system, while useful to authors in electronic environments, also makes writing vulnerable to surveillance. If individuals or organizations have the ability to electronically monitor, decrypt (decode) and log (keep track of) the documents sent over a network, surveillance of writers' work becomes a reality. Within such a system, companies could record the content of documents, gauge productivity by counting documents or words within documents, identify the source and the readers of all documents to make sure that only officially sanctioned communication takes place, and search documents by keywords to locate and identify activity not authorized by a company.

Message encryption devices, such as the Clipper Chip developed by the National Security Agency (NSA), are designed to allow authors to encrypt (to code) messages, and thus make them more secure as these documents are transmitted electronically. The NSA wants not only to install a Clipper Chip in every electronic messaging device sold in the United States, but also to retain a key for these chips that law enforcement agencies could use, if necessary, to break into individuals' messages. Many writers object to such technologies because they increase the possibilities that government agencies may snoop on the writing of private citizens or organizational writers.

Time-stamping devices—which log the time a message is sent, the sender of the message, and the recipient of the message—generate similar possibilities for surveillance. Although these devices can help writers in their record-keeping, they can also help other individuals (for example, managers or even unauthorized snoopers) trace documents to authors and recipients, identify documents that are sent to personal friends rather than business contacts, and log the numbers of documents that are created and sent.

Although such capabilities may seem far-fetched to many writers, they are realities of communication in the electronic age and should not be disregarded by those who write with computers in any field.

Writing and Reading

Writing and reading on-line rather than in print create a new set of challenges for authors and audiences. These challenges, while they don't prevent people from communicating effectively on-line, do affect the complex processes associated with communication and, thus, you should be aware of them when you write in electronic environments.

Writing text on-line, for example, can lead some authors to be prematurely satisfied with a document: Justified margins, the confidence generated by spelling checkers and style checkers, and the surface-level neatness of laser-printed texts all contribute to such a phenomenon on the part of some writers. Unfortunately, as we have noted, computer-generated texts do not consistently exhibit fewer errors than do typewritten texts or handwritten texts—they just exhibit different errors! For instance, neither spelling checkers nor style checkers have the capacity to catch errors in which the author has mistakenly typed one correctly spelled word instead of another. Writing "the" for "then," for example, would not be an error that a spelling checker or a style checker would catch.

Style checkers, moreover, are problematic for additional reasons and can mislead authors who do not question their advice. In general, these software programs are not always effective because they advise without "understanding" the communicative situation within which the prose is written, the author's purpose in writing, the information to be communicated, or the intended readers' ability to understand that information. As a result of this characteristic, a style-checking program might erroneously flag the following sentences as problematic and provide this advice:

Example #1:   The **main production line set-up time** proved too long for an efficient changeover when we made a trial run on the new tire-iron product. As a result, we decided to abandon our original plans for alternating production lines on a weekly basis and reverted to a monthly changeover.

Style Checker advice: *Jargon, replace this phrase with straightforward language more appropriate to a general audience.*

Example #2:   The solution **was added** to the algae culture at six hours into the experiment.

Style Checker advice: *Passive voice. Try an active verb construction.*

Both pieces of advice are problematic. The first sentence is flagged because the program cannot take into account the communicative situation in which it was authored: The phrase was included in a memorandum written by a line supervisor to a factory floor manager. The purpose of the memo was to explain a change in production line operation. In this case, although the style checker has termed the phrase in question "jargon," both the writer and the reader of the memo know exactly what the phrase "main production line set-up time" means. These individuals, and other professionals, understand that jargon is often both a necessary and efficient shortcut that authors and readers use to establish meaning.

In the second sentence, a passive-voice verb cluster is flagged. The style-checking program tells the author to replace the cluster with an active verb because it cannot understand an accepted convention associated with writing a scientific lab report—the use of passive-voice constructions. What the program fails to take into account is that this convention, agreed on by scientists as a community of specialists, is used to encourage science writers to place the experimental processes in the foreground and keep the investigator in the background. The use of passive voice constructions is, then, an example of a style appropriate to and accepted by a specific academic culture. Chapters Five through Eleven of this book will provide further examples of how various disciplines value a variety of stylistic practices.

Reading and writing on-line may also be more difficult than doing so in print-based environments, according to some scholars. Researchers, for example, have noted that audiences may read on-line texts more slowly than print texts, may proofread less accurately, and may understand on-line texts less completely than they do printed texts. Readers may also have more difficulty getting a sense of the whole text and locating particular passages within texts when they read on-line rather than in print.

Access and Distribution

One important problem associated with the use of computer-based writing environments involves the uneven distribution of technology and access to technology in our society. Although the cost of computer equipment is dropping in some areas (for example, the cost of a personal computer or of some peripheral devices), it is rising in others (for example, the cost of access to and use of the Internet). As a result, although many educators and some political leaders see technology as having the potential to expand the democratic involvement of citizens, such an optimistic vision is not always fully warranted, according to historical or current evidence.

Numerous experts, for instance, have noted that computers are less accessible to the very populations in our country that might benefit from increased participation in a democratic society. For example, students of color, students in schools located in low socioeconomic areas, and female students often have less access to equipment, access only to older equipment, or access to less innovative uses of computers than do students in other populations.

Nor is the advent of the new Internet technologies likely to change this situation. Access to the Internet—because it is costly in terms of hardware, technical support, and infrastructure—is also expensive, and, thus, more likely to be found at large research universities and comprehensive universities than at small liberal arts institutions or historically black colleges, for example, even though the student and faculty populations at these institutions need such access and possess motivation to work in computer-supported environments.

This situation is a growing concern to a range of professionals and writers, especially as it applies in global contexts. Educators or sociologists who hope to use the Internet to correspond with colleagues or to interview experts in other countries may find that access is limited to those individuals living in developed countries or those associated with more technologically advanced university hosts. Commercial users of the Internet may find their access to individuals and divisions in certain parts of the world limited or nonexistent.

Certainly, none of the challenges that we have sketched out here indicate that on-line texts or computer-based writing environments are unworkable or that we should go back to paper and pencil or typewriters as our preferred composing medium. These challenges do suggest, however, that, as a society, we need to use, and to design, computer-based writing environments with some cautions in mind and with a productively critical understanding of both the potential and the problems associated with them.

Some Computer-Supported Writers' Tools

Within the scope of this chapter, it would be impossible to cover all of the computer-based writing tools that could support the work of writers in various disciplines. Moreover, such a task would result in a list that was quickly out of date—computer software and hardware change so fast that few of us can keep pace. It might be useful, however, for you to think of the various *kinds* of software and hardware environments offered to writers. For this purpose, we have included the following list of such generic environments and suggestions about how they may be of use to you as you write in various classes and disciplines. We also pass along a note of caution with this list: No one writer will find all of these computer-based tools to be useful. Given that writers vary so widely in the strategies they employ to compose, the information they deal with, and the situations and writing environments within which they work, each writer may indeed find different reasons to use or avoid the tools we list. Fortunately, computer-based writing environments assume almost as many forms as there are approaches to writing.

Word-Processing Packages

You probably know the most common uses of word-processing software. Some features of these packages can also be used to assist writers in many of the individual strategies they employ while composing. When writing teams want to produce a team critique or a revision plan for an in-process document, for example, they can take advantage of the chart-making feature that most full-featured word-processing packages have. Figure 4.1 provides an example.

Similarly, as teams work on documents, they may also find the annotation feature of word-processing packages to be useful. Figure 4.2 illustrates how such a feature can be employed to comment on a document draft. For those writing teams that prefer oral commentary to written commentary on in-process drafts, many full-featured word-processing packages also contain voice annotations that can be affixed to a draft document.

Another useful feature of many word-processing packages is the outliner (Figure 4.3). Outliners allow authors to show a document either in a fully fleshed-out form or in an outline form with some organizational levels hidden from view. Using these tools, writers or writing teams can take an in-process document and check its organizational framework for soundness

FIGURE 4.1

Using the "column" feature of word-processing packages to support team critiques of in-process documents

Year-End Managers' Report A. Doeth	Comments J. Tarvers	Comments J. McCune	Team Plans
Section IV.6.3 The project of cost containment in our product manufacturing efforts continues to yield positive results this year, as it did last year. By the end of fiscal year 1995, we had reduced costs in 45% of our product lines by an average of 10.3%. Next year, we have targeted five more product lines for this cost-containment effort.	Should we refer to an appendix here in which we list the product lines we targeted in 1994–95?	I agree—but the chart should also show the history of product lines targeted in 93–94 and those projected in 95–96.	Jill will mock up chart—refer to Production for exact figures in 1993–94 and 1994–95.
Individual departments also instituted cost-containment measures that were successful. In Publications, costs came down 5% in the second year of an in-house reorganization. Most of this decrease was due to the new desktop publications system that reduces the layout, mock-up, and photographic projects we have to job off-site. Quality remains a concern in these. . . .	Let's put some stats here—how many departments? Put some pressure on those who are not cooperating!	Should we give credit to Gene H. here? Might be good for his group's morale. . . .	"Five of the thirteen departments. . . ." No change.

and parallelism, reexamine the logical connections among sections of text, or rearrange elements according to their superordinate or subordinate status.

Hypertext and Hypermedia Environments for Writing and Composing

Some writers and writing groups find that nonlinear writing environments are conducive to thinking, writing, rethinking, and revising. Both hypermedia and hypertext programs (for example, Hypercard, StorySpace, Toolbook) provide environments in which authors can brainstorm ideas—as individuals or as a group—or do early drafting of sections of documents and then arrange and

FIGURE 4.2

Using the annotation feature of word-processing programs to support the team critique of documents

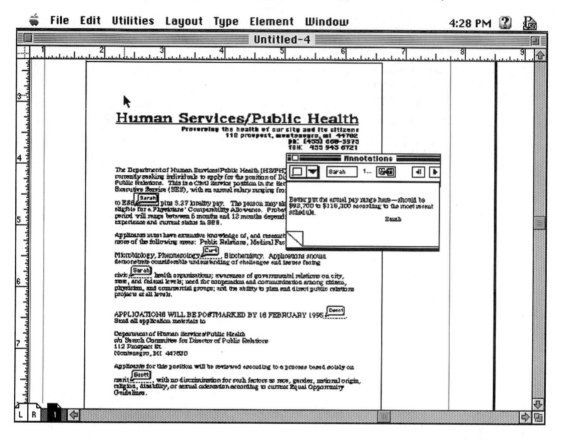

rearrange these ideas physically on a computer screen until the parts seem to form a pleasing whole. Simply put, hypertext and hypermedia documents differ from linear (page-by-page) texts in that they are composed so readers can follow their own paths through a web of information, choosing which piece of information (called a *node*) to read first and which piece of information to read next. Because individual readers' needs differ so much, no two readers will follow the same path through a hypertext.

Figure 4.4 shows a map of a hypertext document—this one in StorySpace, an Eastgate Systems package—with some of the textual elements open for reading and consideration. Electronic hypertexts, of course, can also include digitized sound, voice annotations, still images, and moving images. Writers who

FIGURE 4.3

Outliners as writing tools for checking organization, examining logical connections, and arranging superordinate and subordinate elements

Outline View: First- and Second-Level Headings Only

Introduction of Chemical Bonds

Ionic bonds
Covalent bonds
Multiple bonds

Outline View: Expansion to Third-Level Headings and Text

Introduction of Chemical Bonds (Peters, 1990, pp. 240–43)

Ionic bonds
Bonds characterized by an electronegativity difference of > 1.9 are primarily ionic.

Covalent bonds
Polar bonds
These bonds are characterized by unsymmetrical distributions of electric charges and electronegativity differences of 1.7 to 1.9.
Nonpolar bonds
These bonds, which occur between identical atoms, are characterized by symmetrical distributions of electrical charges and electronegativity differences < 0.4.

Multiple bonds
Hydrogen
Fluorine

can compose meaningful, informative, well-formed texts in multiple media will be increasingly in demand within a wide range of fields during the next decade. Organizations and companies are increasing their use of interactive, multimedia kiosks (public presentation screens) for information delivery; multimedia computer interfaces for information navigation; and multimedia manuals and expert systems for reference purposes.

E-Mail, Listservs, Bulletin Boards, and Newsgroups

E-mail, listservs (which allow one author to send a message to numerous recipients subscribed to a list), and newsgroups and bulletin boards (which both allow individual writers to access information posted about a particular subject of interest) are all tools available to writers through LANs (Local Area Networks) and WANs (Wide Area Networks). Using these tools, authors can communicate with colleagues or specialists in a particular discipline or corporation, read up on or conduct research on a topic, or post a query that results in suggestions from all over the world. Figure 4.5 represents a short excerpt from

FIGURE 4.4

Information displayed and arranged in a hypertext environment using StorySpace

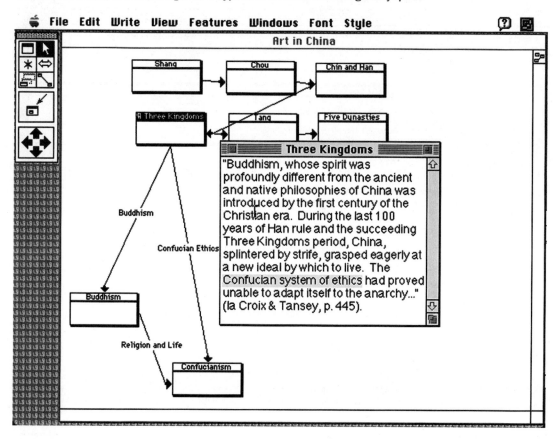

a newsgroup on alternative architecture in which one participant answers a query about the advantages of living roofs.

For information about these kinds of writers' resources, try consulting the List of Lists (listserv@bitnic.educom.edu), the List of Usenet Newsgroups (//uunet-info/newsgroups.Z from ftp.uu.net), or one of the many books about Internet resources.

Synchronous Conferencing Software

Synchronous conferencing software allows individual writers or groups of writers linked by a LAN or WAN to hold a real-time conversation (an electronic

FIGURE 4.5   Excerpt from a Newsgroup on Alternative Architecture

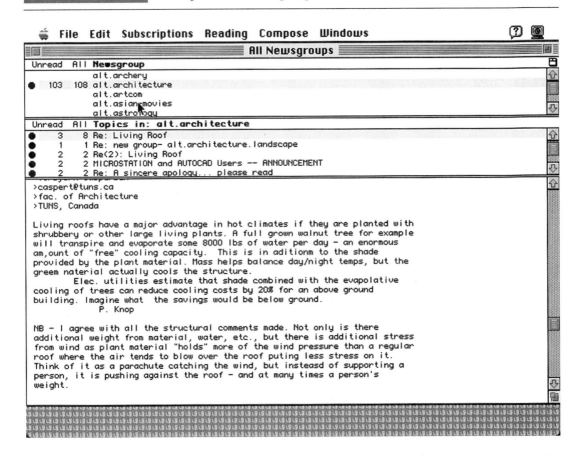

conversation that takes place with only a very short time lag, much as it would in a face-to-face situation) in writing about any topic: a writing task they are planning, a document they are revising, a research project they are undertaking. Writing teams find synchronous conferencing software to be useful for several reasons. First, such software allows writing teams in several locations to come together on-line for a conversation even if they can't meet in person. Synchronous conferencing software also allows teams to make a printed record of their conversation for later reference—a feature that helps teams track versions of a document and review decisions about revision plans. Finally, synchronous conferencing allows writing teams to consult with experts at remote locations.

Figure 4.6 represents an excerpt from a synchronous conversation involving a team of technical documentation specialists.

FIGURE 4.6 Synchronous Conferencing as a Tool for Writers' Teams

---

Drhama:

In the last version of the TextConsult software we did, there was no section on indexing, and we got plenty of customer complaints. So many people end up using this stuff for publication purposes.

Ed:

Has anyone reviewed the stuff that the design team sent us about the new version's indexing capabilities?? I'm not sure the environment is robust enough for the indexing of lengthy documents—in fact, it's pretty clumsy as I understand it.

Samantha:

Then I guess we'd better get back to Ed, Tim, and Peggi to discuss the functionality of that section?

Ed:

And I'm also not sure of the import/export compatibility for this stuff—which was another point that the user surveys have mentioned.

Drhama:

So—back to the plans for Section 3.4.2. We save some room for indexing and for indexing searches. Do we include linked TOC functionality here? Or do we save that for 3.4.3?? Sam, what's the draft outline say at this point?

Wide Area Information Service (WAIS), Gopher, and Mosaic

WAIS, developed by Thinking Machines Corporation, is a hypertext-based storage and retrieval system that allows writers to search a wide range of databases using key words. The purpose of WAIS is to make the many databases and information bases around the country accessible to users who need information for their research, projects, or reports.

For writers, the usefulness of this resource will depend on the topic under consideration. Among just a few of the databases that can be accessed through WAIS are the following: a catalogue of recent French language publications, the agricultural commodity market reports compiled by the Agricultural Market News Service of the United States Department of Agriculture, a listing of the contacts for most known organizations in the former Soviet Union having e-mail connections, a listing of compact discs, an annotated bibliographical collection of materials on cold fusion, and documents issued by the Environmental Safety and Health Information Center.

Gopher and Mosaic are tools writers can use to search the Internet for different types of information. Government documents, library catalogues, scholarly papers, maps, and the newsletters of special-interest clubs are among just a few of the many resources available through these systems.

The World Wide Web

The World Wide Web (WWW) is a vast system of computer-based documents and information that are linked electronically. The WWW is accessible through the Internet, and several programs exist to help individuals search (or browse) the WWW and navigate their way to individual documents. Among these browsing/search tools are Mosaic, Netscape, Yahoo, Lynx, and Lycos. Browsers/search tools usually operate through keyword searches of the entire WWW.

Within WWW documents, individual "hot words" (words representing electronic links to other documents) are represented in a contrasting color, often bright blue. When a reader selects a hot word in a WWW document, and thus activates a link, another document is immediately accessed. This system of webs and linkages among documents is an example of hypertext.

Documents on the WWW are often multimedia presentations that contain words, graphics, still photography, video clips, and audio clips. In this sense, WWW documents have helped to expand our definition of text to include representations through images, video, and sound, as well as through written language.

Home pages

As a method of organizing documents within the WWW, designers/authors use home pages as the starting places for related document clusters on the web. Readers often begin their use of the WWW by using a browser or search tool to locate a home page on a particular topic and then going to that home page by typing in its electronic address, also known as a Universal Resource Locator (URL). Home pages provide readers a point of access to a set of related documents through the hot-word links that authors/designers have included. Home pages can be constructed by and used by individuals, organizations, institutions, and groups of all kinds.

Suggestions on web reading strategies

There are several ways to read through a home page and the documents linked to it. One way to explore a home page, or any other web document, is to browse—clicking on the buttons that interest you, in no particular order. This is neither the most efficient way of moving through a document nor a strategy guaranteed to make sure you fully exhaust the document's possibilities. Like wandering through traditional libraries, however, it is often a strategy that can be both fun and fruitful. An alternative strategy is to click on each button on the home page in turn, following a row or a column in a systematic way. This approach, while exhaustive, may also be inefficient for your reading purposes. Most home page readers scan the available button labels quickly and then click only on those buttons that contain the information they need. This strategy is efficient, but it works only if button labels are clear and informative. In addition, to make this strategy work, readers must identify their purposes for reading. Some browsers offer a system of bookmarks that allow you to mark, and then return to, particular web pages of interest.

The home pages following page 144 will provide you a glimpse of the kinds of information that can be accessed on the WWW. We have included home pages from a variety of disciplines and interests—science, sports, a chronological period, a government organization. The possibilities for exploring and gathering information on the WWW are expanding daily. For those of you who have not experienced the WWW, we hope this section will assist you. For those who are experienced in using the WWW, we hope it adds new skills to your repertoire.

Exercises

1. Within your writing group, sit around a single computer and open a word-processing package. Have one of your group serve as a scribe. As a group, list all the ways you use computers to support your writing.

   When you are done, have each member of your group go out separately to interview someone who has considerable experience writing without the aid of computers. If both you and your interview subject have access to e-mail, conduct this interview electronically.

   When all group members have finished their interviews, make a list of all the types of writing the interview subjects remember doing.

2. As a group, write a two-page analysis that compares the two lists—the kinds of computer-supported writing you do and the kinds of noncomputer-supported writing your interview subjects did. In this analysis, try to focus on the following questions: What does this comparison tell you about writing and the ways in which writing has changed at the end of the twentieth century? What does it tell you about communicators and the ways in which their environments have changed over the last ten years? Does it reveal anything about media generations and how they might affect our success in communicating with one another?

3. Interview—by telephone, in person, by post, or via e-mail—two people in the discipline or career area you have chosen for yourself. Ask these individuals about the various uses they make of computer-supported writing environments for their own communication tasks. (If you have yet to make a choice of career paths, use this opportunity to explore some options.) Take notes on what you learn and share these with your writing group.

   Using a word-processing package, write a piece that compares and contrasts your uses of the computer to those of the people you interview. Discuss the similarities or differences with your writing group or writing class.

4. In an *on-line reading log,* identify the most important points for this chapter. Save the file each time you add material. By the time you finish this book, you should have a useful set of notes/guidelines to consult about writing.

5. *If your class has access to stand-alone computers,* create a word-processing file on a disk—one that the class can use in common to hold a group *reading-response conference.* This conference is a place for students to talk about their interpretation of the material in the chapter, a place to respond to it actively as both readers and writers. In this conference, class members can help each other understand the material in each chapter and can respond to this material by testing it against their own or others' experiences as writers. Leave this disk in some centrally accessible place—a library, a computer-supported writing facility, and so forth—and have everyone in the class put their questions, answers, and responses to the readings into the same word-processing file on that disk. By the time everyone contributes a question and some answers to this disk conference, the class will have a rich source of collective interpretive information about this book and about the human activity of writing as it is practiced by the members of your class.

   If your class has access to a computer network, create a word-processing file accessible to everyone—one that all members of the class can use to hold a *networked reading-response conference.* Use this conference for the same purpose we described above to conduct a group discussion on-line.

6. Create a *disk discussion conference* (if your class has access to stand-alone computers) or a *networked discussion conference* (if your class has access to a computer network) that starts with the following claims about computer networks:

   • Computer-based conversations, because they support flexible connections among individuals and groups of people, may allow more people and different kinds of people to share information and form communities of writers than do face-to-face conversations.

   • Computer-based conversations may help individuals and groups focus less on physical characteristics (for example, gender, race, age, disability) and more on the content of written messages.

   • Computer-based exchanges transcend limitations of time and space. They are convenient and quick.

Use these claims as springboards for a group discussion, either on disk or on-line.

   In the conference, write an entry that compares your personal experience writing on computer networks to one or more of these claims. In your experience, are these claims true, false, or both true and false? In what ways? To what extent?

   If you have not yet had the experience of writing in, or reading, an on-line conversation, you may have to do a bit of initial research in order to complete this task. To find out what writing on-line is like (for example, in an on-line discussion group or an on-line newsgroup), ask a friend or the campus computer-support people to help you get on-line and into one of these conversations. If this is impossible, go to a local computer retail store and ask the people there to show you what such a conversation looks like—they will probably have access to a commercial service such as America Online, Prodigy, or Compuserve.

If you have access to a computer network and synchronous (real-time) conferencing software—for example, access to Internet Relay Chat or to software like the Daedalus Integrated Writing environment—hold a ten-minute in-class, on-line discussion about these three claims as they connect with the personal experiences of class members. At the conclusion of the synchronous discussion, jot down what you consider to be the three most important points that were made. Use these points to continue the discussion in a traditional face-to-face format with the class.

7. Assign each person in your class one class meeting in which to act as scribe. Cover as many days as possible in your term—you may want to assign people two days of scribe duty so that all class days are covered. During each class session, the designated scribe should take notes on key ideas, controversies, assignments, and group discoveries—all in summary form.

After the class session, the scribe is responsible for transcribing his or her notes into a word-processing file and saving that file on a class disk provided by the teacher. The word-processing file for each class session should be identified by the date of the class in which the notes were taken.

At the end of the term, designate one person to copy-and-paste the materials in all of these files into a large common file. This file should provide everyone with a valuable archive of notes for the class and a record of your thinking as a class.

URLs for Written Communication and Computer Technology

Electronic Frontier Foundation (EFF)
http://www.cs.uidaho.edu/lal/cyberspace/eff/eff.html

Electronic Civil Rights
http://www.cs.vu.nl/~gerben/net-civil.html

Skim & Dive the Internet
http://www.missouri.edu/~wleric/places.html

WWW Resources for Rhetoric and Composition
http://www.ind.net/Internet/comp.html

Internet Resources for English Teachers and Students
http://www.umass.edu/english/resource.html

Writing Across the Curriculum
http://ewu66649.ewu.edu/WAC.html

Style Guide for Online Hypertext
http://www.w3.org/pub/WWW/Provider/Style

CHAPTER FIVE

Writing in the Humanities

Reflective and Interpretive Writing

Responsibilities of Humanists

Importance of Communications to the Humanist

Writing in the Undergraduate Humanities

While many of you may not decide to major in the **humanities**—that is, in English, history, communications, philosophy, music, art, dance, drama, or foreign languages and literatures—it is nearly impossible for students who plan on graduating from college to completely avoid courses in those departments. In fact, most students during their first two years of college will take one or more courses in the humanities. When they do, they will be taught to employ methods of inquiry unique to the disciplines (as we discuss them in Chapter Three) and perform the kinds of reflective and interpretive writing tasks discussed in this chapter. When you write in the humanities, you will not only be required to reflect personally on the people, institutions, occurrences, and ideas that in sum constitute culture, but to interpret them as well.

Reflective and Interpretive Writing

From one perspective, humanists attempt to **reflect on** culture, as Rick Worland promises to do in the following introductory statement from "Captain Kirk: Cold Warrier," a reflection on the way early episodes of *Star Trek* not only coincided with the "virtual declaration of Cold War in outer space," but were apparently influenced by it.

> I want to devote . . . attention to what I believe to be one of the least discussed aspects of the *Star Trek* phenomenon—the relationship of the series to the Cold War . . . especially in the context of the show's original broadcasts during the period of the greatest escalation of the Vietnam War, 1966–69.

> Worland, Rick. "Captain Kirk: Cold Warrior." *Journal of Popular Film & Television*, vol. 16, no. 3, fall 1988, pp. 109–117.

From another perspective, humanists attempt to interpret documents from the past, often using new ideas, critical tools, or recently discovered documents to do so. In "Chinese American Women Writers: The Tradition behind Maxine Hong Kingston," Amy Ling explores the relationship between Kingston and other Chinese-American women writers and their treatments of women as subservient to men. Here is Ling's view of novelist Winnifred Eaton.

> Winnifred Eaton's women are nearly always in an inferior, powerless position: social outcasts (*A Japanese Nighingale, The Wooing of Wisteria*), orphans (*Sunny-San* and *The Heart of Hyacinth*), an unwanted stepdaughter (*Love of Azalea*), a blind, homeless wood sprite (*Tama*), a geisha in bondage (*The Honorable Miss Moonlight*). Her men, in clear contrast, are invariably in positions of power and influence: princes, ministers, architects, and professors.

> Ruoff, A. LaVonne Brown and Jerry W. Ward, Jr., eds. *Redefining American Literary History*. New York: MLA, 1990, p. 223.

The goals of both of the above efforts are to clarify our recollections and to add to our knowledge about human experience and expressions of that experience.

To conduct inquiries such as the above, you must learn to think like a humanist. To understand what, exactly, that entails, consider what would happen if you were required to make a record—a kind of history—for absent class members of what transpired in a given class. Your statement of what occurred might include information such as the following, written by a student in an introductory-level art history class.

> Today we talked about John Constable. We saw slides of sketches and paintings he did of Weymouth Bay. Professor Standish made the following assignment. By next Wednesday (April 16), we must visit the Constable exhibit at the National Gallery and report on our responses to a minimum of three paintings we see there. For extra credit, we might contrast our responses to these three paintings with our responses to three paintings by Turner. Our report is limited to three to five typed pages. We cannot use secondary sources. We must rely on our own observations and information covered in today's class.

This log, or journal entry, is intended to serve as a record of what actually happened in class—as a history of a class. In it the author not only objectively describes occurrences—for instance, that Professor Standish showed slides of sketches and paintings by John Constable—but, like other historians, works subjectively in selecting which class events to include and which to exclude. As a history of a specific class meeting, this document may prove to be very important . . . or very misleading.

If two students in discussing the assignment described above disagree about some part of what they are to do—let's say, one student believes the discussion of three paintings by Turner is required and the other that it is optional, for extra credit only—they will quite naturally return to the log entry to determine who is correct. If they do not find the answer there, they might decide that the author/historian did not do a good job and undertake an investigation of their own—probably starting with interviews of people who attended that class.

The log entry above is a history, in this particular instance, that provides evidence that one student can use to support her reflection on or recollection of the assignment. Humanists similarly return to source materials for support of their observations and, when they don't find in existing sources the information they seek, undertake inquiries of their own in an effort to generate new knowledge.

As we will explain more fully below, humanists use evidence they find in past records in one of two ways: to *personally reflect on* texts, events, or occurrences and test the accuracy of their recollection, and/or to *critically interpret* texts, events, or occurrences and thereby construct new knowledge. As we point out in Chapter Three, texts used by humanists include creative texts, interpretive texts, and theoretical texts. Though three kinds of inquiries tend to take place in the humanities—interpretations in literary and art criticism, reflections on philosophical ideas, and studies of history and culture—these three kinds of inquiries are reported upon as personal reflections on texts, ideas, and occurrences and as critical interpretations of them.

Exercises

1. Read a local newspaper and make a list of news items that a historian, fifty or sixty years from now, might record.
2. Write a history of a day in your town based upon the same edition of your local newspaper as used in exercise 1.
3. Write a history of a class. Compare your history with a classmate's. What differences do you notice? Why do these differences occur?
4. *Using a word-processing package,* write a log for a class session that occurred last week. Be as complete and accurate as possible in your recollections of the important things that transpired in the class.
5. Now choose a partner from your writing group who has completed the same assignment for the same day. Use the copy-and-paste function of the word-processing package to combine the material in both files into a single file; or, *if you have access to a Windows-based system,* view the two files simultaneously on the screen. In writing, describe where you differed in your recollections, what things one of you recorded and the other did not (and why), and what areas or activities of your log might be open to more than one interpretation.

Responsibilities of Humanists

The example cited above is not really that much different from what humanists—historians, literary critics, and art critics—do professionally. Humanists often disagree, yet they do so within a shared context. To settle these disagreements, they return to evidence within that context—namely, earlier texts, ideas, or occurrences.

Let us look at the work of two professional humanists then. These views from secondary sources focus on the same primary source, the novel *Frankenstein* by Mary Shelley.

The modern consumer of film media comes to the novel *Frankenstein* conditioned to expect, first and foremost, a monster story, an entertainment. Such a tale plays on predictable human reaction to the terrifying behavior of a manlike but disproportionately powerful creature. The reader conditioned by movies mistakenly assigns the name "Frankenstein" primarily to the monster and only secondarily to the monster's creator, the mad scientist. Yet, in this contemporary perception, *Frankenstein* is not in any serious sense the monster's or the scientist's story—not an attempt, that is, to investigate the monster's feelings, challenge the philosophy of his maker, or analyze the relationship between the two.

Library of Congress Home Page
http://lcweb.loc.gov/

This home page appears exactly as it would on your screen had you searched using Netscape. We have started with this example to show some of the initial features and functions of a home page. Unless stated otherwise, "click" means clicking once on a button or area.

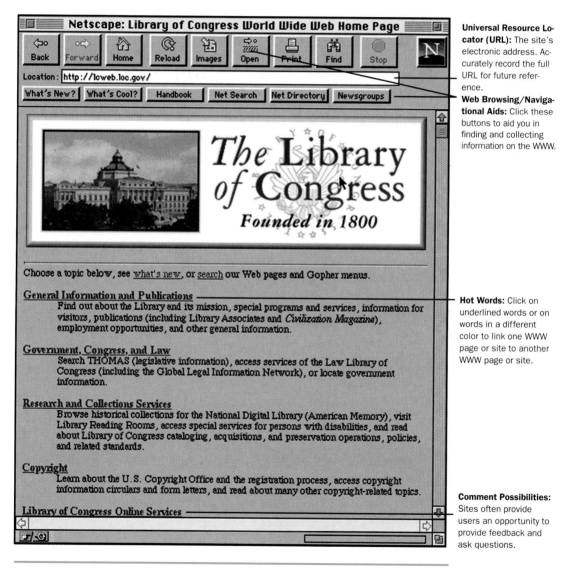

Universal Resource Locator (URL): The site's electronic address. Accurately record the full URL for future reference.

Web Browsing/Navigational Aids: Click these buttons to aid you in finding and collecting information on the WWW.

Hot Words: Click on underlined words or on words in a different color to link one WWW page or site to another WWW page or site.

Comment Possibilities: Sites often provide users an opportunity to provide feedback and ask questions.

Victorian Web Home Page
http://www.stg.brown.edu/projects/hypertext/landow/victorian/victov.html

First-level home pages provide a gateway to additional information found on
subsequent pages from the same site; a second-level page follows this example.
These first-level pages contain basic information that can be thought of as a broad
outline or structure for more specific information which follows on "deeper-level"
pages.

Buttons and Under-lined Words: Indicate a link to additional information. Note that the URL will often change from one piece of information to another.

Arrangement of Information: Whether hierarchical, linear, chronological, or one of many patterns, arrangement usually reveals the designer's approach to the subject.

Author/Designer Information: Identifies the author(s) or designer(s) of the web-page information and helps you gauge the accuracy and dependability of the information.

Additional Links: Frequently, a button at the bottom of a home page will take readers to a list of additional resources. Be sure to record immediately the URL of a new web site.

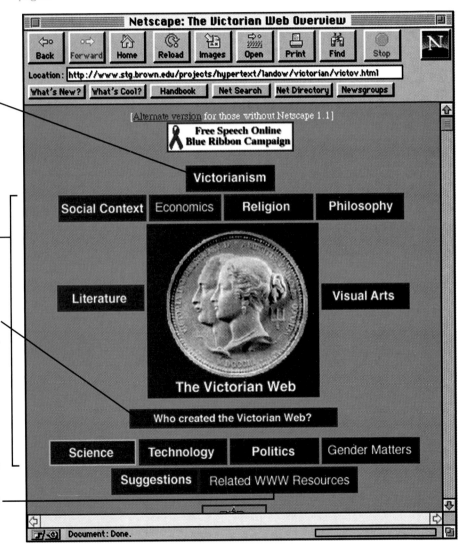

Second-Level Victorian Web Page

This annotated Victorian Web page is an example of a second-level page that provides very rich web sites which layer information in several hierarchical levels to facilitate navigation. Such sites can be described as "deep" sites because they have several levels of subordinate (secondary) and superordinate (primary) menus that readers can access. When readers first access the Victorian Web home page, they can click on the "Science and Technology" button to move to this second-level page. This second-level page provides readers with a subordinate, second-level menu of options associated specifically with science and technology topics.

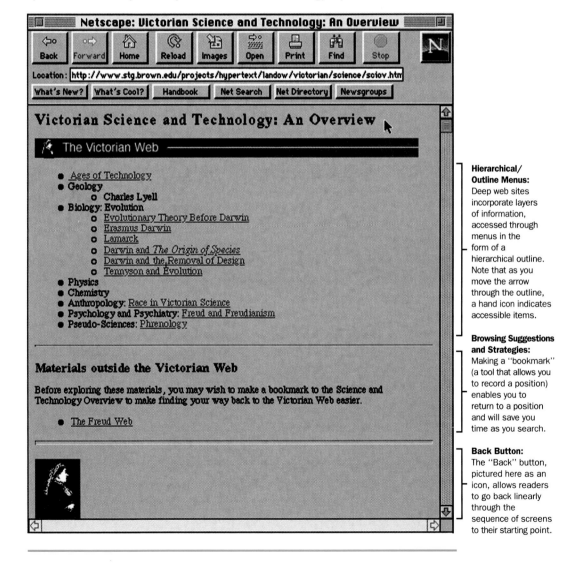

Netscape: Victorian Science and Technology: An Overview

Back | Forward | Home | Reload | Images | Open | Print | Find | Stop

Location: http://www.stg.brown.edu/projects/hypertext/landow/victorian/science/sciov.htm

What's New? | What's Cool? | Handbook | Net Search | Net Directory | Newsgroups

Victorian Science and Technology: An Overview

The Victorian Web

- Ages of Technology
- Geology
  - Charles Lyell
- Biology: Evolution
  - Evolutionary Theory Before Darwin
  - Erasmus Darwin
  - Lamarck
  - Darwin and *The Origin of Species*
  - Darwin and the Removal of Design
  - Tennyson and Evolution
- Physics
- Chemistry
- Anthropology: Race in Victorian Science
- Psychology and Psychiatry: Freud and Freudianism
- Pseudo-Sciences: Phrenology

Materials outside the Victorian Web

Before exploring these materials, you may wish to make a bookmark to the Science and Technology Overview to make finding your way back to the Victorian Web easier.

- The Freud Web

Hierarchical/ Outline Menus: Deep web sites incorporate layers of information, accessed through menus in the form of a hierarchical outline. Note that as you move the arrow through the outline, a hand icon indicates accessible items.

Browsing Suggestions and Strategies: Making a "bookmark" (a tool that allows you to record a position) enables you to return to a position and will save you time as you search.

Back Button: The "Back" button, pictured here as an icon, allows readers to go back linearly through the sequence of screens to their starting point.

The American Physical Society Home Page
http://aps.org/

"Rhetoric" is the art of effective communication. Thinking about the rhetorical context of a web page—the context for which the communication was designed—can help you read and understand a web page. Searching for rhetorical clues can help you determine the purpose of the page, its audience, the specific information it includes, and the form or style of the information.

Purpose: This section provides facts and information about the society's history, mission, members, and activities.

Audience: The 41,000 physicists who are members, or potential members, of the society. Note such topics as "Membership Information," "Meetings Information," and "Careers."

Recent Information: Information on home pages is dynamic and changes over time. Often, the first major button or link on a page will lead you to information most recently added.

Form/Style: The language, diction, font, and overall formality of this home page may reveal a good deal about the organization it represents.

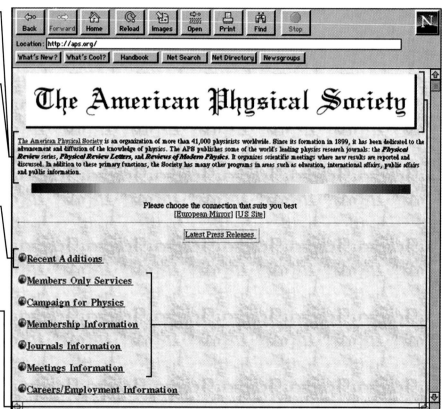

The American Physical Society is an organization of more than 41,000 physicists worldwide. Since its formation in 1899, it has been dedicated to the advancement and diffusion of the knowledge of physics. The APS publishes some of the world's leading physics research journals: the *Physical Review* series, *Physical Review Letters*, and *Reviews of Modern Physics*. It organizes scientific meetings where new results are reported and discussed. In addition to these primary functions, the Society has many other programs in areas such as education, international affairs, public affairs and public information.

Please choose the connection that suits you best
[European Mirror] [US Site]

Latest Press Releases

- Recent Additions
- Members Only Services
- Campaign for Physics
- Membership Information
- Journals Information
- Meetings Information
- Careers/Employment Information

Women's Soccer Foundation Home Page
http://www.cris.com/~jg189/wsf/

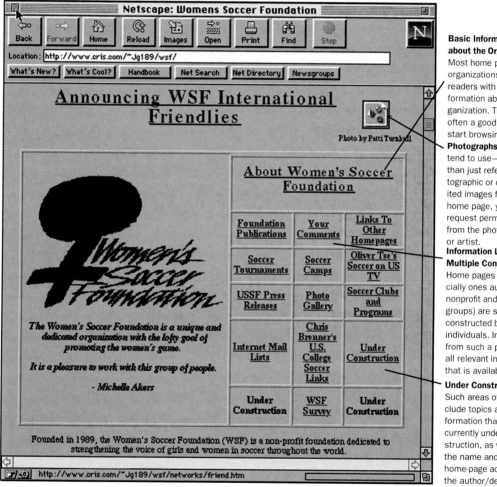

Basic Information about the Organization: Most home pages for organizations provide readers with basic information about the organization. This link is often a good place to start browsing.

Photographs: If you intend to use—rather than just refer to—photographic or other credited images from a home page, you must request permission from the photographer or artist.

Information Linked to Multiple Contributors: Home pages (especially ones authored by nonprofit and volunteer groups) are sometimes constructed by multiple individuals. In citing from such a page, cite all relevant information that is available.

Under Construction: Such areas often include topics and information that are currently under construction, as well as the name and e-mail or home-page address of the author/designer.

American Psychological Association Home Page
http://www.apa.org/

Netscape: American Psychological Association PsychNET (SM)

Back | Forward | Home | Reload | Images | Open | Print | Find | Stop

Location: http://www.APA.ORG/

What's New? | What's Cool? | Handbook | Net Search | Net Directory | Newsgroups

AMERICAN PSYCHOLOGICAL ASSOCIATION

Welcome to APA's PsychNET SM

Welcome to PsychNET SM, the Internet service of the American Psychological Association. We are continuing to regularly add a great deal of material here for the public and members. Please add us to your bookmarks and visit often.

You can also be automatically informed by email when APA's PsychNET is updated, thanks to the free URL-Minder service.

PsychNET has won a couple of awards for excellence from two independent rating organizations. For details, have a look at our "bragging page."

Our search function on the Web pages makes finding information on PsychNET easier, especially as we add material. Right now the top-level search on this page works well, as do most of the searches of subdirectory material, but there are still a few (especially the new material) where the search doesn't function yet. Please bear with us and we'll have them working soon.

readme.now

Convention
in Toronto

The APA
MONITOR

American Medical Association Home Page
http://www.ama-assn.org/

Netscape: AMA Home Page

Back Forward Home Reload Images Open Print Find Stop

Location: http://www.AMA-ASSN.ORG/

What's New? What's Cool? Handbook Net Search Net Directory Newsgroups

American Medical Association
Physicians dedicated to the health of America

What's New

Medical Science
and Education

Membership and
Constituency Groups

Advocacy and
Communications

AMA Catalogs

Links to Other
Medical Sites

JAMA   NEWS   ARCHIVES JOURNALS   JAMA HIV

Award-winning!

MAGELLAN
3-STAR SITE

About the American Medical Association
    Information about the AMA and documents of public interest
What's New
    News and notices about this site
Medical Science and Education
    Committee appointment nomination form
Membership and Constituency Groups
    Membership information and application, Federation Directory compendium of medical society information,
    Medical Student Section, Organized Medical Staff Section, Resident Physicians Section, Young Physicians
    Section

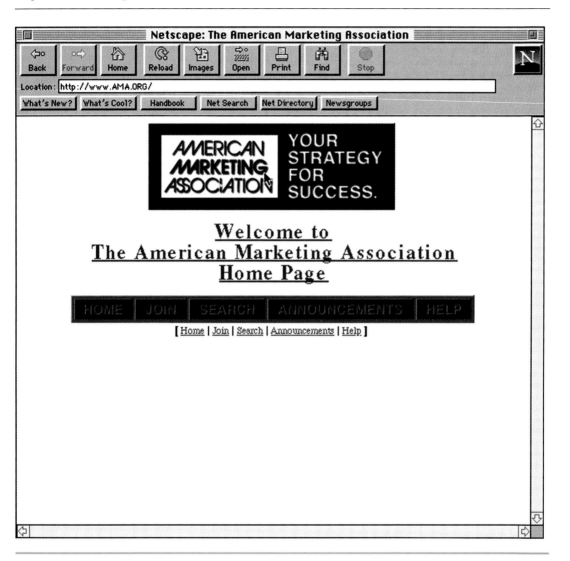

Rather, the story is "about" the fear and anguish the horrid creature elicits from his victims. Even those emotions, however, are not often closely examined and evaluated by the modern viewer.

This view of the famous story takes as its starting place a culture in which most people, even those who have never read the novel itself, have heard of the monster and, in most instances, have seen a Frankenstein movie, such as *Frankenstein, Bride of Frankenstein,* or *Young Frankenstein.* This humanist will go on to discuss how these individual experiences with the movie medium and its portrait of Shelley's novel influence the way first-time readers of the novel experience the tale.

A second analysis of the novel, however, might take an entirely different though equally valid approach, as in the following excerpt.

> It is important to note that *Frankenstein* was published anonymously, that its woman author kept her identity hidden. Similarly, no women in the novel speak directly: everything we hear from and about them is filtered through the three masculine narrators. In addition, these women seldom venture far from home, while the narrators and most of the other men engage in quests and various public occupations. These facts exemplify the nineteenth century's emerging doctrine of "separate spheres," the ideology that split off the (woman's) domestic sphere from the (man's) public world and strictly defined the "feminine" and "masculine" traits appropriate to each sphere.

As you have probably already guessed, this author will go on to discuss the novel in a manner markedly different from the way the first critic did by analyzing how the novel reflects the way the world of women was split off and forcibly separated from the world of men in nineteenth-century England.

The authors of the above two passages approach *Frankenstein* differently. In doing so, these two critics reflect the concern most often associated with humanists. They are dedicated to advancing knowledge in the humanities and to forwarding new interpretations of past events, in this instance a novel. From the perspective of many humanists, the commitment of the Modern Language Association (from the "Constitution and Bylaws of the Modern Language Association of America") may be aptly applied:

> The object . . . shall be to promote study, criticism, and research in modern languages and their literatures, and to further the common interests of teachers of these subjects.

These two approaches are more than just opinion because they go beyond simply describing the personal relevance of the novel to the critic by analyzing the patterns and themes in the work discussed. They are critical interpretations, as we discuss them below.

By contrast, the following is a statement of personal opinion insofar as it stresses the relevance of the work to an individual reader without offering textual analysis or considering the views of others who have interpreted the book.

I identified with Frankenstein's monster. The poor guy just seemed like he wanted to have friends but just didn't know how. The doctor controlled everything. He brought the monster into the world and then didn't take care of him. That's how a lot of us feel these days.

Clearly, critical interpretation is often an outgrowth of opinion. However, opinion is seldom the product of the kind of systematic inquiry and consideration of other critical views that are central to critical interpretation.

Exercises

1. Reread the three views of Mary Shelley's *Frankenstein*. Assuming that the first two views are critical interpretations and the third view a personal opinion, what do you believe to be the differences between the two kinds of inquiries conducted by humanists? In your class notebook, make a list of similarities and differences.

2. In paragraph-length responses, offer (a) an opinion about a movie you have seen recently, (b) a critical interpretation of that same movie, and (c) a comparison of these two ways of thinking—that is, of opinion and interpretation.

3. Choose a writing partner in your class who has read a novel that you have read within the last two years.

   Using a word-processing program and working separately, complete a short, one-sentence summary of the plot. When you have completed these two summaries, use the copy-and-paste function of the word-processing package to combine the material in both files into a single file; or, *if you have access to a Windows-based system,* view the two files simultaneously on the screen. In writing, describe where you differed in your summaries. Talk about what elements you included in your summary that your partner did not and vice versa. Discuss why you each included the elements that you did and why you chose to leave some elements out of your summary.

Importance of Communications to the Humanist

Humanists, including literary, art, and music critics on the one hand, and philosophers, communications experts, and historians on the other, are committed to furthering our understanding of texts, people, institutions, or occurrences so that we can think more critically and more knowledgeably not only about those matters, but about future decisions we must make. This is true even in the interpretation of events such as the history of baseball, as in the following passage, which contrasts an idealized version of why men play professional baseball with a starkly realistic view.

> The historian who studies the development of organized baseball is frequently struck by a sense of *deja-vu*. So many of the controversies of modern baseball are repetitions of earlier disputes that one wonders, finally, if baseball really has a history, or at least a history understood as change and development. "These modern ballplayers," begins a familiar lament, "care about nothing but money. They don't care about their teams, or their city, or their fans. In my day . . . they were different." But were they? This fan certainly would have no trouble finding others to agree with him. And he would feel support for his complaint if, reading the sports pages one morning, he ran across a column by a veteran player claiming that "somehow or other they don't play ball nowadays as they used to some eight or ten years ago. . . . I mean that they don't play with the same kinds of feelings or for the same objects they used to." Somewhat less encouraging to the modern fan would be the date of the veteran's letter—January 9, 1868.

Goldstein, Warren. *Playing for Keeps: A History of Early Baseball.* Ithaca: Cornell University Press, 1989, p. 1.

From this excerpt we see how humanists have not only come to understand past negotiation among baseball players and management, but recent and on-going efforts between the two groups to come to contractual agreements. In short, the research conducted by this historian reminds us that concerns we believe to be recent concerns have actually bothered people for a long time, in this case the desire to play a game for money instead of love of the game. This historian reflects upon the past, using a newspaper column published in 1868 to do so.

Humanists must also re-discover and reexamine old documents in an effort to make new knowledge. For instance, in the following excerpt, June M. Frazer and Timothy C. Frazer gain insights about "The Cosby Show" by comparing and contrasting it with "Father Knows Best," well-known situation comedies (sitcoms) from different decades in television history. The authors point out several similarities.

> The first is that we have in "Cosby," as in "FKB ["Father Knows Best"], the "normal" nuclear family, despite the fact that in the time between FKB and "Cosby" we have seen in America a tremendous increase in divorce and other social factors leading to a rise of one-parent and other forms of the non-nuclear family. Yet "Cosby" presents the mother-father-children model as the norm, just as FKB did. When so many Americans, women, men, and children, are perforce not living in the traditional nuclear family but need for the sense of belonging to feel they are part of a family, "family" for many good reasons has undergone redefinition. . . . But "Cosby" undercuts all of this.

From " 'Father Knows Best' and 'The Cosby Show': Nostalgia and the Sitcom Tradition" by June M. Frazer and Timothy C. Frazer in *Journal of Popular Culture*, vol. 27, winter 1993, no. 3, 163–72.

In brief, humanists are responsible for **reconstructing** and **interpreting**, uncovering old records and attempting to understand them, preserving what has occurred and analyzing it with current standards and tools of understanding in mind. Humanists are responsible for understanding expressions of human experience in the various forms such expressions are made.

Most writing you will do in the humanities, then, will be either a personal reflection on or a critical interpretation of texts, people, institutions, or occurrences.

To perform these writing tasks, you must possess certain reading skills, as described in Chapter Two, that might serve as starting points in reflecting or interpreting. These skills include the following.

- annotating
- note-taking
- summarizing
- paraphrasing
- synthesizing
- critiquing

In addition to these skills, most useful as you read in preparation for writing reflectively or interpretively, you will need the following writing skills discussed in Chapter One: planning through exploration, drafting, revising exploratory writing, and writing the formal paper.

More specifically, you must plan to satisfy the demands of the assignment by:

1. understanding what you are asked to do and
2. exploring the subject.

Prepare to draft the essay by:

3. devising a thesis statement and
4. supporting the thesis statement with appropriate details or examples.

Move from exploratory writing to finished drafts by:

5. writing early drafts to develop content and
6. revising appropriately to meet the needs of your audience.

Exercises

1. Reread the passage on the history of baseball (page 147). In your class notebook, answer the following questions:

   a. What does it mean to *reflect* upon a subject?
   b. How does the passage above about the history of baseball reflect on baseball?
   c. What is the author's point?
2. Reread the passage comparing "The Cosby Show" with "Father Knows Best" (page 147). In your class notebook, answer the following questions:
   a. Why do the authors contrast these sitcoms?
   b. What points do the authors make about families?
   c. Are the authors justified in making these points? If so, why?
3. *If you have access to a computer and a word-processing package,* have everyone in your writing group compose a definition of "reflect" and a definition of "interpret"—at this point, do not refer to a dictionary; we will ask you to do so later.

4. When all members of your writing group have completed exercise 3, gather around a common computer and open a new word-processing file. As a beginning for this file, look in the dictionary and record the standard defintiions of the two terms. Next, using the copy-and-paste feature of your word-processing package, add each of your individual definitions to this new file and examine the complete file.
5. Discuss how, or if, each of these definitions apply to the two previous samples in this chapter (e.g., baseball, "The Cosby Show" and "Father Knows Best"). Also discuss what features the official definition lacks that your own definitions have included.

Writing in the Undergraduate Humanities

Before examining reflective (that is, personal response) and interpretive (that is, critical analysis) writings done by professionals and students, let us briefly examine the skills necessary to write in the humanities in an effort to provide some guidance in this area.

Planning

Planning involves two tasks: (1) understanding what you are asked to do and (2) exploring the subject.

Understanding what you are asked to do is most easily managed by analyzing your assignment in terms of your purpose for writing, the audience to be addressed, and the subject you are writing about.

In Chapter One, we provide a list of words that are used most often in describing writing assignments. Familiarize yourself with those words and what, specifically, they require of you. Such descriptive words will provide you with insight into your **purpose,** or your goal, in writing for your instructor.

You might be asked to compare/contrast (see Catton pages 154–157) or discuss or interpret or examine or analyze or perform any of a number of other tasks. As you can see by reading Bruce Catton's "Grant and Lee: A Study in Contrasts," writing an essay with a specific purpose in mind usually requires that you organize your essay in a particular manner.

In addition to making an effort to understand your purpose, you should strive to understand another component of your writing assignment, **audience.** Think of audience not only as a reader, but as something a bit more complex. Think of audience as the entire set of expectations a reader has for your writing. For instance, Catton writes for a general audience familiar with Grant and Lee but not necessarily made up of experts. Carby (see pages 164–165) addresses an audience of experts in an effort to have them accept her view of slave narratives. You will no doubt write most often for your teacher, who may also grade your essay. Ordinarily in this instance, you will be told how your essay will be graded. Though their essays are not graded in the usual sense of the word, professionals who write for magazine publication spend an enormous amount of time reading the magazines they hope will publish their essays precisely to determine the editors' expectations for any essay sent to them for consideration.

When you consider audience, take the following questions into consideration:

- Does your audience know more than, less than, or the same amount as you know about the topic?
- Does your audience expect you to use the specialized language of the field or the common and day-to-day language you use when you talk to friends?
- Does your audience reward those who prepare their essays in a particular fashion better than they reward those who do not?
- Most of all, does your audience require certain expectations to be fulfilled at certain places in an essay?

This last question merits a bit more discussion here. A reader expects to be given **cues** or **signals** in the text (see the section on Skimming in Chapter Two, pages 48–49, for a systematic method for understanding cues). If you do not place cues (such as thesis statement, topic sentences, supporting details and examples, etc.) where a reader expects to see them, your reader will have difficulty reading and understanding what you have written.

Once you have decided upon a general subject for your paper, you should explore it systematically by following this sequence of tasks.

- **First,** review the primary sources involved. This task will be somewhat easier if you have already annotated the text and taken notes on it;
- **Second,** look over your notes to determine if they suggest a topic (a) that you know something about and/or (b) that interests you;
- **Third,** highlight or underline places in the primary source and your notes where you address the chosen topic;

- **Fourth,** if your assignment requires it, go to the library and read about your chosen topic (see Chapter Three). Read with an open mind, letting the secondary sources suggest to you exactly how you will focus on the material. Take notes on the information you think you might use or photocopy pertinent pages and annotate them (see Chapter Two on annotating and note-taking).

Once you have reached the point where you have decided how you will focus on your material in writing your essay, you are ready to devise a thesis statement in preparation for writing a draft of your essay.

Preparing to Draft

A thesis statement is a sentence, usually at the beginning of a paper, that declares to the reader what your essay will be about (though in lengthier essays, such as Catton's on pages 154–157, the thesis statement may appear somewhat later, though still at the beginning of the essay). Think of your first effort at writing a thesis statement as the writing of a "working" thesis statement that you may revise as you write subsequent drafts.

In some ways, however, your working thesis is more important to you than it is to your reader since a thesis statement, even a working one, is your declaration to yourself of what you are writing about. As a result, a good thesis statement at any point in your process of writing an essay indicates how you have limited the way you will treat your subject, your focus, and the purpose with which you will discuss it (for example, to compare, define, argue, persuade, and so forth). The thesis statement serves you as author by providing you with guidance as you select materials to use for support and exemplification. Still, as you draft, permit yourself to wander into new avenues of thought. If you do not find such wanderings useful, you can always delete them later. If you do find them useful, you can always revise your thesis statement to encompass an enlarged or otherwise changed subject.

In any event, one characteristic of good writers in every discipline is their ability to follow general statements, such as "Grant, the son of a tanner on the Western frontier, was everything Lee was not" (see page 155), with specific details or examples that support those general statements, such as "He was one of a body of men who owed reverence and obeisance to no one, who were self-reliant to a fault, who cared hardly anything for the past but who had a sharp eye for the future."

If you are writing chiefly from the primary source, as occurs often in introductory courses in the humanities, you should select those examples that will help you convince your audience that your thesis statement is true. Note how Pollitt has done this in Chapter Two (see pages 50–53).

Make certain to photocopy or to record on notecards, notebook paper, or on a separate sheet intended for such a purpose all of the information you will need later to document your sources.

One problem writers often must confront is how to organize supporting details and examples. An outline may help you see your material better than you can see it if you just go ahead and write, making it easier for you to arrange your support in a manner your readers will be able to follow.

An outline can be very useful provided you know when to use one. It hardly makes sense to use an outline before you have completed your research, though many writers like to use an ordered list early in the researching process to guide their research. Likewise, it doesn't make much sense to use an outline if you have a clear idea how your essay should be written, though once your first draft is written, an outline will give you a chance to double-check your organization.

An outline is most useful to writers when they have gathered materials but do not know how to present them to their readers. In this instance, we do not recommend a formal outline, which has laws to abide by that are much too complex to explain here. Rather, we recommend an informal outline that will simply enable you to look at the material you have and arrange that material in ways appropriate to the audience you are addressing.

To make the best use of your informal outline once you have written it, you must stand back and take on the role of your reader, considering from that perspective if the material is arranged in what will seem to your audience to be a logical manner.

Interestingly, this arrangement might also be suggested by your purpose. Here are some general guidelines:

- If you want to *compare* and *contrast,* you might follow a pattern similar to the one used by Catton (see pages 154–157). As you can see, Catton says something about Grant, then something about Lee, then returns to Grant, etc.
- If your purpose is to *describe* an event, you might be wise to organize in a chronological or time-based order, beginning at the beginning and ending at the end.
- If your purpose is to *inform, explain,* or *instruct,* you might work your material into patterns that move from most important to least, general to specific, or first to last.

Subject, audience, and purpose, once you know them, will help you determine the best way to organize your material.

Moving from Exploratory Writing to Finished Drafts

As in the writing that you will do in all disciplines, and as we have already suggested in Chapter One, you should begin by drafting your essay. Prior to doing so, you are apt to have already devised a thesis statement, found supporting details, and organized those details, as we have suggested. Now you must write the first draft, employing your working thesis statement, keeping in mind that you are just exploring your topic here and may write numerous drafts before you are satisfied with what you have written or before you are required to turn in a deadline draft.

Many experienced writers in all disciplines believe the adage that "writing is revising." In fact, most writers believe that revision is an absolutely critical phase in the writing process, one that often leads writers to new insights and discoveries that they can rarely reach in a one-draft piece of writing. Some of these insights and discoveries are planned results of library research. Others are products of the kind of luck that hard work during the revision process makes possible.

Sometimes writers who permit themselves to wander in their writings—a process similar to free-association thinking, but done on the page—open new possibilities that, once fully explored, provide insights into the subject that might not have occurred if they had too soon settled on a rigid organization scheme. Still, at some point, writers feel that they have satisfied the demands their subject has placed on them for developing ideas and, at that point, find an outline very useful.

When they have reached this point, writers wisely rethink their working thesis statement and revise it as necessary. Once the declaration to the reader is made, the outline can be revised so that the subject is developed in a way readers will be able to follow.

Finally, after the topic has been developed fully, most writers proofread to make certain they have met the requirements for sentence, punctuation, and spelling correctness expected by their audience.

Remember that in the humanities, you will usually be required to use Modern Language Association (MLA) style (see the Appendix). This means that you should have made certain to write down all the information you need to document your sources, both primary and secondary.

Exercises

1. Reread the section, "Writing in the Undergraduate Humanities" (pages 149–153). In your class notebook, and in your own words, summarize that section.

2. *If you have access to a computer network with e-mail or real-time conferencing software,* hold an electronic discussion with your writing group about a particular writing assignment that one of you has been given in a humanities course in the past or that your teacher has given you for this particular class. Choose a major assignment that asks writers to accomplish several kinds of activities. Before your discussion takes place, make sure to provide a hard copy or an electronic copy of this writing assignment for each member of your group.

   In your discussion, analyze what the assignment asks writers to do in terms of each of the seven guidelines identified in this section. Try to reach some agreement within your group—both about what the assignment *explicitly* asks and what the assignment *implicitly* asks—that is, what is asked for directly and what additional actions are suggested but not directly stated. For example, in order to compare the historical accuracy of the characters in two novels by the same author (a task that may be stated explicitly in an assignment) students have to be generally familiar with the historical period in question, know what people of that period were like according to other sources outside both novels, and understand what the organizational structure of comparison papers entails. These tasks are implicit in the requirements of the assignment, but not directly stated.

Make sure that someone in your group is responsible for saving or archiving your discussion.

Writing a Reflective and Reconstructive Essay

Writing from the professional's viewpoint

The following essay by historian Bruce Catton, "Grant and Lee: A Study in Contrasts," is an example of reflective writing done by a professional historian. As a writer of a reflection, Catton's goals include reconstructing the personalities of two Civil War leaders. In the process of considering evidence available to him, however, Catton had an insight important to the way historians think about these two Civil War leaders: Grant and Lee were opposite in many ways.

GRANT AND LEE: A STUDY IN CONTRASTS

Bruce Catton

When Ulysses S. Grant and Robert E. Lee met in the parlor of a modest house at Appomattox Court House, Virginia, on April 9, 1865, to work out the terms for the surrender of Lee's Army of Northern Virginia, a great chapter in American life came to a close, and a great new chapter began.

These men were bringing the Civil War to its virtual finish. To be sure, other armies had yet to surrender, and for a few days the fugitive Confederate government would struggle desperately and vainly, trying to find some way to go on living now that its chief support was gone. But in effect it was all over when Grant and Lee signed the papers. And the little room where they wrote out the terms was the scene of one of the poignant, dramatic contrasts in American history.

They were two strong men, these oddly different generals, and they represented the strengths of two conflicting currents that, through them, had come into final collision.

Back of Robert E. Lee was the notion that the old aristocratic concept might somehow survive and be dominant in American life.

Lee was tidewater Virgina, and in his background were family, culture, and tradition . . . the age of chivalry transplanted to a New World which was making its own legends and its own myths. He embodied a way of life that had come down through the age of knighthood and the English country squire. America was a land that was beginning all over again, dedicated to nothing much more complicated than the rather hazy belief that all men had equal rights and should have an equal chance in the world. In such a land Lee stood for the feeling that it was somehow of advantage to human society to have a pronounced inequality in the social structure. There should be a leisure class, backed by ownership of land; in turn, society itself should be keyed to the land as the chief source of wealth and influence. It would bring forth (according to this ideal) a class of men with a strong sense of obligation to the community; men who lived not to gain advantage for themselves, but to meet the solemn obligations which had been laid on them by the very fact that they were privileged. From them the country would get its leadership; to them it could look for the higher values—of thought, of conduct, of personal deportment—to give it strength and virtue.

Lee embodied the noblest elements of this aristocratic ideal. Through him, the landed nobility justified itself. For four years, the Southern states had fought a desperate war to uphold the ideals for which Lee stood. In the end, it almost seemed as if the Confederacy fought for Lee; as if he himself was the Confederacy . . . the best thing that the way of life for which the Confederacy stood could ever have to offer. He had passed into legend before Appomattox. Thousands of tired, underfed, poorly clothed Confederate soldiers, long since past the simple enthusiasm of the early days of the struggle, somehow considered Lee the symbol of everything for which they had been willing to die. But they could not quite put this feeling into words. If the Lost Cause, sanctified by so much heroism and so many deaths, had a living justification, its justification was General Lee.

Grant, the son of a tanner on the Western frontier, was everything Lee was not. He had come up the hard way and embodied nothing in particular except the eternal toughness and sinewy fiber of the men who grew up beyond the mountains. He was one of a body of men who owed reverence and obeisance to no one, who were self-reliant to a fault, who cared hardly anything for the past but who had a sharp eye for the future.

These frontier men were the precise opposites of the tidewater aristocrats. Back of them, in the great surge that had taken people over the Alleghenies and into the opening Western country, there was a deep, implicit dissatisfaction with a past that had settled into grooves. They stood for democracy, not from any reasoned conclusion about the proper ordering of human society, but simply because they had grown up in the middle of democracy and knew how it worked. Their society might have privileges, but they would be privileges each man had won for himself. Forms and patterns meant nothing. No man was born to anything, except perhaps to a chance to show how far he could rise. Life was competition.

Yet along with this feeling had come a deep sense of belonging to a national community. The Westerner who developed a farm, opened a shop, or set up in business as a trader, could hope to prosper only as his own community prospered—and his community ran from the Atlantic to the Pacific and from

Canada down to Mexico. If the land was settled, with towns and highways and accessible markets, he could better himself. He saw his fate in terms of the nation's own destiny. As its horizons expanded, so did his. He had, in other words, an acute dollars-and-cents stake in the continued growth and development of his country.

And that, perhaps, is where the contrast between Grant and Lee becomes most striking. The Virginia aristocrat, inevitably, saw himself in relation to his own region. He lived in a static society which could endure almost anything except change. Instinctively, his first loyalty would go to the locality in which that society existed. He would fight to the limit of endurance to defend it, because in defending it he was defending everything that gave his own life its deepest meaning.

The Westerner, on the other hand, would fight with an equal tenacity for the broader concept of society. He fought so because everything he lived by was tied to growth, expansion, and a constantly widening horizon. What he lived by would survive or fall with the nation itself. He could not possibly stand by unmoved in the face of an attempt to destroy the Union. He would combat it with everything he had, because he could only see it as an effort to cut the ground out from under his feet.

So Grant and Lee were in complete contrast, representing two diametrically opposed elements in American life. Grant was the modern man emerging; beyond him, ready to come on the stage, was the great age of steel and machinery, of crowded cities and a restless burgeoning vitality. Lee might have ridden down from the old age of chivalry, lance in hand, silken banner fluttering over his head. Each man was the perfect champion of his cause, drawing both his strengths and his weaknesses from the people he led.

Yet it was not all contrast, after all. Different as they were—in background, in personality, in underlying aspiration—these two great soldiers had much in common. Under everything else, they were marvelous fighters. Furthermore, their fighting qualities were really very much alike.

Each man had, to begin with, the great virtue of utter tenacity and fidelity. Grant fought his way down the Mississippi Valley in spite of acute personal discouragement and profound military handicaps. Lee hung on in the trenches at Petersburg after hope itself had died. In each man there was an indomitable quality . . . the born fighter's refusal to give up as long as he can still remain on his feet and lift his two fists.

Daring and resourcefulness they had, too; the ability to think faster and move faster than the enemy. These were the qualities which gave Lee the dazzling campaigns of Second Manassas and Chancellorsville and won Vicksburg for Grant.

Lastly, and perhaps greatest of all, there was the ability, at the end, to turn quickly from war to peace once the fighting was over. Out of the way these two men behaved at Appomattox came the possibility of a peace of reconciliation. It was a possibility not wholly realized, in the years to come, but which did, in the end, help the two sections to become one nation again . . . after a war whose bitterness might have seemed to make such a reunion wholly impossible. No part of either man's life became him more than the part he played in this brief meeting in the McLean house at Appomattox. Their behavior there put all succeeding generations of Americans in their debt. Two great Americans, Grant and Lee—very different, yet under everything very much alike. Their encounter at Appomattox was one of the great moments of American history.

In the same way the student who stated an opinion about *Frankenstein* offered a personal view of the novel's significance by reflecting upon and briefly reconstructing the novel, Catton reflects upon and reconstructs the encounter between Grant and Lee. Catton does not so much offer a critical interpretation of the event as rewrite and, thereby, rethink the occurrence in such a way that it allows him to show the striking contrast between these two Civil War generals. This is a highly personal record of the encounter that differs from, but does not set out to refute, other views of the Civil War commanders. Note that Catton avoids the attack that he has overgeneralized by stating in Paragraph 13 "Yet it was not all contrast, after all."

Exercises

1. Reread Catton's essay. Now, in your class notebook, answer the following questions:
   a. How does Catton's title prepare you for his essay? If you could offer a better title than the one he uses, what would it be?
   b. Find a sentence that clearly states the point of Catton's essay and either underline it or write it down.
   c. Why do you think Catton focuses in the first several paragraphs on the circumstances of the meeting between the two leaders rather than on their personal characteristics?
   d. List the points Catton uses to support the sentence you identified in response to question *b*.
   e. What justification might Catton offer for the way he has organized supporting details in his essay?
   f. Describe Catton's overall plan for developing the contrast between Grant and Lee.
2. Reflect upon two acquaintances. Write a short essay in which you compare and contrast them. Follow the process as it is described on page 148. When you draft, you might employ the same organizational strategy as Catton uses, telling a story about your friends, establishing that you will compare and/or contrast, then discussing first one and then the other. Make certain, as Catton has, to compare and contrast these people by employing comparable and contrastable details (for example, these people as athletes, students, cooks, and so forth).
3. *If you have access to the Internet,* use a network browser (for example, Netscape, Mosaic, Lynx) to explore Gopher space or the World Wide Web and find a historical piece of writing about a topic of interest to you. Make sure that the piece of writing deals with some historical event that occurred

at least ten years ago. Also choose a document that is ten pages or less. Download the document you have chosen, and print it out. If you need help with these operations, ask a knowledgeable friend, your campus computing experts, the technical consultant in the computer lab you are using, or your teacher.

After reading this piece carefully, answer the following questions in writing, using a word-processing package:

a. What does the title of the piece tell you about its contents? What does it lead you to expect?

b. Quote the one sentence in the document that clearly states the main point of the piece you have chosen.

c. List the major points that the author of the piece uses to support the thesis of the piece—to do this, quote sentences from the piece you have chosen.

d. Describe the overall organizational framework that the author uses to structure the piece. As an alternative to this task, create an outline of the piece.

e. Describe how the author uses reflection and/or interpretation in examining the subject matter in this piece.

Writing a reflective and reconstructive student essay

Now that you have examined a professional reflective writing, take a look at a reflective essay written by Lisa, a student in an Introduction to Humanities course. Let us approach Lisa's essay by examining her writing process, as the process of writing in the humanities is described above.

The assignment that produced the following draft of a short reflective essay by Lisa was given in a sophomore-level course. The assignment read:

> Write a short essay in which you compare or contrast a selection from Dorothy Wordsworth's *Alfoxden Journal* and any painting by John Constable that we have studied in class. Your goal should be to use the journal selection(s) and the poem to comment on their views of nature.
>
> In grading your essay, I will consider your understanding of the works you have selected to write about and how well you use those works to demonstrate what they reveal about Wordsworth's and Constable's views of nature. I will also take into consideration the quality of your writing.

This assignment specifies the subject—a journal entry by Dorothy Wordsworth and a painting by John Constable to be chosen from among those studied in class. The purpose is to compare or contrast the selected works so that the author can comment on each person's view of nature. The instructor is clear that he will serve as the audience.

Remember that a good way to go about understanding what you are asked to do in an essay is by determining your subject, purpose, and intended audience.

If you were asked to write this essay, you, like Lisa, would probably find it necessary to explore the subject of this assignment by studying the primary sources. As we have suggested in Chapter Two, you can save yourself considerable effort by annotating where possible and taking notes.

Lisa decided upon a pair of sources to use for purposes of contrast: Dorothy Wordsworth's *Alfoxden Journal,* February 1, 2, and 3, 1798, and John Constable's *The Hay-Wain* (see page 160).

ALFOXDEN JOURNAL

Dorothy Wordsworth

February 1st. About two hours before dinner, set forward towards Mr. Bartholemew's. The wind blew so keen in our faces that we felt ourselves inclined to seek the covert of the wood. There we had a warm shelter, gathered a burthen of large rotten boughs blown down by the wind of the preceding night. The sun shone clear, but all at once a heavy blackness hung over the sea. The trees almost *roared,* and the ground seemed in motion with the multitudes of dancing leaves, which made a rustling sound, distinct from that of the trees. Still the asses pastured in quietness under the hollies, undisturbed by those forerunners of the storm. The wind beat furiously against us as we returned. Full moon. She rose in uncommon majesty over the sea, slowly ascending through the clouds. Sat with the window open an hour in the moonlight.

February 2nd. Walked through the wood, and on to the Downs before dinner; a warm pleasant air. The sun shone, but was often obscured by straggling clouds. The redbreasts made a ceaseless song in the woods. The wind rose very high in the evening. The room smoked so that we were obliged to quit it. Young lambs in a green pasture in the Coombe, thick legs, large heads, black staring eyes.

February 3rd. A mild morning, the windows open at breakfast, the redbreasts singing in the garden. Walked with Coleridge over the hills. The sea at first obscured by vapour; that vapour afterwards slid in one mighty mass along the seashore; the islands and one point of land clear beyond it. The distant country (which was purple in the clear dull air), overhung by straggling clouds that sailed over it, appeared like the darker clouds, which are often seen at a great distance apparently motionless, while the nearer ones pass quickly over them, driven by the lower winds. I never saw such a union of earth, sky, and sea. The clouds beneath our feet spread themselves to the water, and the clouds of the sky almost joined them. Gathered sticks in the wood; a perfect stillness. The redbreasts sang upon the leafless boughs. Of a great number of sheep in the field, only one standing. Returned to dinner at five o'clock. The moonlight still and warm as a summer's night at nine o'clock.

The Hay-Wain by John Constable. National Gallery, London, Great Britain. Foto Marburg/Art Resource, NY.

THE HAY-WAIN

John Constable

Exercises

1. Study the two selections chosen by Lisa and, on the basis of your observations, devise a working thesis statement that might be used in an essay that compares or contrasts the two works. Remember, a thesis statement summarizes what the entire essay will be about and states your position or point of discussion. A working thesis statement guides you early in the writing process and may eventually be changed as your understanding of your essay changes.

2. *If you have access to the World Wide Web or Gopher space,* use a browser (e.g., Netscape, Mosaic, Lynx) to locate three historical sources that would help Lisa write this essay. In a paragraph, describe these sources, summarizing their contents and recording their locations. (To accomplish this last task, record the Gopher-site name if you are operating in Gopher space or the Universal Resource Locator (URL) if you are working on the World Wide Web.)

On the basis of her scrutiny of the two works above, Lisa has noticed that Dorothy Wordsworth and John Constable are concerned with nature and natural subjects. Lisa expresses this difference in her working thesis statement: "Nonetheless, Wordsworth and Constable share an interest in nature that is typical of early nineteenth-century art in England."

Here is a draft of Lisa's essay.

Dorothy Wordsworth's *The Alfoxden Journal* and John Constable's *The Hay-Wain,* one a journal and the other a painting, seem different in some basic ways. Nonetheless, Wordsworth and Constable share an interest in nature that is typical of early nineteenth-century art in England.

Both portray natural scenes. On February 3, 1798, Wordsworth writes about walking with her friend Coleridge. At first as they walked over the hills, their view was "obscured by vapour." But then the air cleared and she records watching the clouds sail by. Constable's painting is also of a natural scene. He too has paid attention to the clouds that dominate the right top of the canvas.

Wordsworth and Constable also stress nature's simplicity. Wordsworth records what she sees: "the sun shone clear, but all at once a heavy blackness hung over the sea" (February 1, 1798). Constable also seems focused on the horse-drawn wagon, midway across the stream, a farmer on his way home. Both portray the basic elements of the natural scene.

But both Wordsworth in her journal and Constable in his painting suggest that there is more to nature than what meets the eye. Dorothy writes, "The trees almost *roared,* and the ground seemed in motion with the multitudes of dancing leaves, which made a rustling sound, distinct from that of the trees" (February 1, 1978). By capturing the farmer half way across the stream, Constable seems to say that there's more, a moment before and a moment after, and a reason for this activity that, as we look at the painting, we are forced to determine for ourselves.

In conclusion Wordsworth and Constable are interested in nature, both as we see it and as a living thing we cannot completely understand.

Exercises

1. Reread the above draft of Lisa's essay. Annotate the essay and respond to the following.
   a. Underline the details and examples Lisa uses to support her thesis statement. If you believe she has done a good job in selecting material to support her point of view, explain why. If you believe she should revise her thesis statement, how should she revise it?
   b. Make an informal outline of Lisa's essay by placing the thesis statement at the top of a separate page and then listing beneath the thesis statement the details Lisa uses to support her thesis.

2. In a short letter to Lisa, offer advice about how this draft of her essay might be revised to meet the demands of her instructor.

3. From these two works, select details that support your thesis statement from the previous exercise. Be sure to consider your subject in terms of the features highlighted previously under "Writing in the Undergraduate Humanities."

4. Write a first draft of your essay. Have a classmate perform exercises 1 and 2 above with it, while you do the same with your classmate's draft. Be certain to give each other the best advice you can.

5. *If you have access to a computer and a word-processing package,* type Lisa's essay into a file. When you have completed this task, get your writing group to gather around a single computer with this file on the screen to conduct a draft critiquing session. As part of this session, working as a group, accomplish the following tasks:

   a. Using the font selection feature, identify the main point of this essay by changing the one sentence that represents this point into italic type.

   b. Using the font selection feature, identify the main point of each paragraph in the essay by changing it into bold type.

   c. Using the font selection feature, change all other text in this essay into six-point type.

   d. Setting the caps lock key on your computer, move to the end of the essay and write a brief comment to Lisa about how—or whether—the main points of her two paragraphs support or fail to support the broad thesis statement for her essay.

   e. With the caps lock key still active, provide Lisa with two additional details that support or illustrate the main point she makes in each of her two primary paragraphs.

   f. After each of the details that Lisa has already provided (now in six-point type), rate the effectiveness of the detail in supporting or illustrating the main point of the paragraph by putting a number from one to ten in parentheses. (One indicates poor support and ten indicates terrific support.) Arrive at this rating through discussion with your group members.

Writing a Critical Interpretation Essay

Since it is unlikely that any two readers will agree about the meaning of a literary work or a painting, humanists offer interpretations. This is not to say that one opinion is just as good as another. In fact, quite the opposite is true. As in the advice offered for writing a reflective essay, we suggest that you use supporting details and examples to prove that an interpretation is justified.

As we have already pointed out about the two interpretations of Shelley's *Frankenstein,* it is possible for two people to read the same novel and come up with completely different interpretations, both of which are valid. And, as we pointed out earlier, while personal opinions and reflections focus on the relevance of a work to a reader, they do not offer a systematic inquiry of the sort done when we write a critical interpretation.

What separates opinion from interpretation? It is the systematic use of details and examples for support of those details. Further, in writing an interpretation, authors must be aware of other critical positions taken and then place their views in relation to those positions. How do we know if an interpretation is valid? By whether we are convinced by an author's use of supporting details and examples and whether the author has responsibly attended to other known and accepted interpretations.

When you write a critical interpretation essay, think of your audience as a jury which will decide the truthfulness and honesty of your interpretation. This jury will reward careful reasoning and critical thinking as those skills lead you to judgments, especially if the judgments are supported adequately with details and examples from the text, event, or occurrence under scrutiny.

Writing from the professional's viewpoint

The writing of a critical interpretation essay is a more complex activity than the writing of personal reflections though critical interpretations often begin as personal reflections. For purposes of explanation, let us say, as the student on page 146 does, that Frankenstein's monster reminds us that we are all vulnerable and often unable to communicate to others as we would like. That observation is a personal reflection. However, if the student decides to explore that perspective on the novel further by conducting library research, finding support from other readers for that view, and then systematically supporting his thesis statement with details and examples from the novel itself, his personal reflection will become a critical interpretation. In the process of researching his personal reflection, though, the student just might decide that his view of the novel is a weak one and decide to take an altered perspective on the novel.

In short, interpretive writing requires you to approach the primary source not just to understand what it says, but to make supportable judgments about what and how it means.

What does interpretive writing hold in common with reflective writing? Both interpretive and reflective writing involve you in similar writing processes. Both require that you begin with the primary source, reading and understanding it, and then look closely for patterns of thought, theme, or technique running through it. Both kinds of writing also often require that you perform library research (see Chapter Three).

Critical interpretation, however, requires that you go a bit farther than you need to go in personal reflection. You must read and understand the words or events but attempt to find patterns or themes in them that, once discovered, will enable you to make a certain kind of sense of the work, ideas, or experiences you would not be able to make otherwise.

When you write a critical interpretation essay, you make it possible for your readers to interpret a creative text as you have and to see reasons why they should.

Sometime between reading the primary source and deciding how to interpret it, you may seek the written advice of experts in the field. If you do, you will need to go to the library with at least some general idea of what you want to find out (see Chapter Three). What you will find in the library, as the following example of interpretive writing by Hazel V. Carby indicates, is not just another opinion to lean upon as you reach some conclusions about how you will view a text. Rather, you will find in professional interpretations what you should include in your own: reasoned and well-argued beliefs, conclusions, and claims that readers will likewise see and understand.

As an example both of what you will find in the library and of a critical interpretation, read the following excerpt from an essay by Hazel V. Carby, "Ideologies of Black Folk: The Historical Novel of Slavery." Before reading it, keep in mind that in recent years slave narratives have attracted the attention of historians and literary critics alike. Because these narratives were excluded from most histories of nineteenth-century America, finding them now has (1) given historians the opportunity to study primary source materials by slaves who perceived the events of the time from a dramatically different perspective than the one offered by most historians—that is, to show that what we accept as history is not a fixed matter, but a matter of who is telling the story—and (2) given literary critics the opportunity to interpret twentieth-century writings in light of themes that can be found in slave narratives.

In the excerpt that follows, Carby nicely weaves together the concerns of the historian and the literary critic.

IDEOLOGIES OF BLACK FOLK

The Historical Novel of Slavery

Hazel V. Carby

The title "Slavery and the Literary Imagination" should generate reflection on the ways in which we, as literary critics, have constructed Afro-American literary history. Slavery appears to be central to the Afro-American literary imagination, but, as a mode of production and as a particular social order, slavery is rarely the focus of the imaginative physical and geographical terrain of Afro-American novels. The occasion for this essay is, therefore, a paradox.

One might explain this paradox in three ways. First, there is the critical influence on Afro-American literary history of the antebellum slave narrative. Henry Louis Gates, Jr., has argued in *The Slave's Narrative* that slave narratives have had a determining influence on Afro-American literature. Gates's theoretical proposition is that critical practice needs to elaborate a "black intertextual or signifying relationship" in order to produce "any meaningful formal literary history of the Afro-American tradition." Narrative strategies repeated through two centuries of black writing are seen as the link that binds the slave narrative to texts as disparate as Booker T. Washington's *Up From Slavery*, *The Autobiography of Malcolm X*, Ralph Ellison's *Invisible Man*, Richard Wright's *Black Boy*, *Their Eyes Were Watching God* by Zora Neale Hurston, and *Flight to Canada* by Ishmael Reed. As readers and as writers, then, we become receivers of a textual experience that creates the unity of an Afro-

American literary tradition, a tradition that, Gates concludes, "rests on the framework built, by fits and starts and for essentially polemical intentions, by the first-person narratives of black ex-slaves." Contemporary Afro-American literary discourse thus situates a form of cultural production that reconstructs the social conditions of slavery as the basis of the entire narrative tradition.

Second, slavery haunts the literary imagination because its material conditions and social relations are frequently reproduced in fiction as historically dynamic; they continue to influence society long after emancipation. The economic and social system of slavery is thus a prehistory (as well as a pre-text to all Afro-American texts), a past social condition that can explain contemporary phenomena. In the late nineteenth century the novels of Frances E. W. Harper, Pauline Hopkins, and Charles Chestnutt used slavery in this sense. For example, Hopkins's *Contending Forces* (1900) begins with an eighty-page slave story that acts as an overture to her tale of a black New England family at the turn of the century. Her slave prehistory provides all the necessary elements for the fictional resolutions to the novel; once Hopkins's characters *know* their history, they can control their futures. In a formal sense slavery can thus be a most powerful "absent" presence, and this device was perhaps most effectively used by W.E.B. Du Bois in *The Souls of Black Folk,* in which the slave condition, if not the slave mode of production, permeates the text.

Third, our ideas of an Afro-American literary tradition are dominated by an ideology of the "folk" from fictional representations of sharecropping. These novels, which might be called "novels of sharecropping," are those texts, central to contemporary reconstructions of an Afro-American canon, which are interpreted as representations of the Southern "folk"—a folk emerging from and still influenced by the slave condition. Indeed, I would argue that the critical project that situates the ex-slaves writing their "selfhood" or their "humanity" into being as the source of Afro-American literature also reconstructs black culture as rooted in a "folk" culture. The ex-slave consciousness becomes an original "folk" consciousness. Critics like Gates and Houston A. Baker, Jr., argue that the means of expression of this consciousness is the vernacular—for Baker it is the blues that is the "always already" of Afro-American culture—and the search for this vernacular structures and informs the intellectual projects of both critics. Intertextuality is the concept that makes the abstract theoretical proposition a material relation, which is characterized as a series of variations, or riffs, on an orginal theme to produce an Afro-American discourse, or "blues matrix."

Exercises

1. Reread the excerpt from Carby's essay. In your class notebook, answer the following:
   a. How does Carby's title prepare you for her essay? Since this is an excerpt, would a different title better prepare you for the portion of her essay you have read? If so, what title would you suggest?

b. Can you find the thesis statement? What is it?

c. List the three parts Carby uses to support the thesis you identified in question *b.*

d. How does Carby go on to defend her thesis? Why does she enumerate the parts of this excerpt?

e. Why does she support her thesis in this way? What problem in her argument is she attempting to solve?

2. *If you have access to the* World Wide Web *or* Gopher space, use a browser (for example, Netscape, Mosaic, Lynx) to locate an additional source (like Hazel Carby's essay) that would help you write an essay on female African-American writers. Print this document out.

After carefully reading the essay you have found, answer the following questions about it in writing, using a word-processing package:

a. What does the title of the piece tell you about its contents? What does it lead you to expect?

b. Quote the one sentence in the document that clearly states the main point of the piece you have chosen.

c. List the major points that the author of the piece uses to support the main point of the piece—to do this, quote sentences from the piece you have chosen.

d. Describe the overall organizational framework that the author of this piece uses to structure it. As an alternative to this task, create an outline of the essay.

e. Describe how the author uses interpretation in examining the subject matter in this essay.

Writing an interpretive essay

The student essay on pages 177–178 was written by Tim, a student in a sophomore-level Introduction to Poetry course, in an effort to interpret a collection of poems by Henry Rollins from his book, *One from None.* Since Rollins is both a rock musician and poet, Tim's task is to bring together two seemingly different worlds: music and poetry.

Before reading Tim's essay, note that there is ample precedent for the type of synthesis writing Tim performs, as the following professionally written essay by Jay R. Howard, "Contemporary Christian Music: Where Rock Meets Religion," demonstrates.

CONTEMPORARY CHRISTIAN MUSIC: WHERE ROCK MEETS RELIGION

Jay R. Howard

Religion and rock music have long had a love/hate relationship. Rock music is often charged with being a perverter of America's youth and an underminer of

Christian moral values. This fear of corruption is still evidenced today by the campaign led by Tipper Gore to put warning labels on rock recordings that contain "offensive" material. At times, Christians have cautiously accepted some rock music when artists have embraced religious themes and imagery, as in 1965, when the Byrds recorded Pete Seeger's paraphrase of Ecclesiastes 3, "Turn, Turn, Turn."

Occasionally songs with religious themes have had success on the pop charts. The Byrds' recording of "Turn, Turn, Turn" reached number one in 1965. That same year Elvis' "Crying in the Chapel" reached number three. In 1971, Ocean's "Put Your Hand in the Hand" peaked at number two. A gospel choir known as the Edwin Hawkins Singers recorded the two hundred year old hymn "O Happy Day," which peaked on the charts at number four in June of 1969. However, after the early seventies, songs mentioning Jesus or carrying religious themes made less and less frequent appearances on the pop charts (Baker).

Books on the subject of rock music have been in abundant supply on the shelves of Christian bookstores, books defending some rock music (Key and Rabey; Seay and Neely; Lawhead) and books attacking most rock music (Peters, Peters and Merrill; Larson). Television evangelists, such as Jerry Falwell and Jimmy Swaggart, have been outspoken in their denunciation of rock music.

In the midst of this controversial relationship between rock music and religious messages, and as a response to a feeling of being "locked out" of the secular music industry, there has been a burgeoning Christian recording industry using rock music, known as Contemporary Christian Music (CCM). CCM involves the pairing of a Gospel message or Christian worldview with popular forms of rock music. It is a phenomenon that first received attention during the late 1960s. In 1967, a band called People recorded an album that was to be titled, "We Need a Whole Lot More of Jesus and a Lot Less Rock and Roll." But Capitol Records, over the band's objections, changed the title to "I Love You." One of People's key singers and songwriters, Larry Norman, left the band in protest. The single "I Love You" became a top ten hit, while Norman went on to begin a solo career and a new realm of music, Christian Rock (Baker 33).

Recording artists, such as Amy Grant and the heavy metal band Stryper, have received much attention from the music industry and general public. There is also a large group of artists recording for Christian record companies (i.e., Word, Sparrow) who are being distributed to a primarily Christian audience through religious radio stations and religious bookstores. The objective of such artists is the presentation of a largely Protestant, evangelical message. Evangelization of the "lost" and the encouragement of the "saved" are the goals of the message.

CCM is representative of a large Christian subculture. The members of this subculture reject, to some degree, the values, morality and worldview of the larger society. Through the creation of their own institutions, such as a Christian music industry, members of the Christian subculture are challenging the dominant ideology of modern society. Therefore, it becomes unclear whether this is a subculture or a counterculture. For some it is a subculture sharing in the overall values of society, such as the priority of pursuing material prosperity. For others, who find their values in conflict with the larger society, it serves as a counterculture and a basis for resisting hegemonic dominance.

The CCM movement takes on added significance when one considers that social theorist Max Horkheimer felt that religion was one aspect of society that had redemptive possibilities (Horkheimer; Horkheimer and Adorno). He believed that religion might be able to challenge the closure of society via capitalist ideology. Theodor Adorno, fellow member of the Frankfurt School, also believes that the artistic realm offers the best hope of resisting the closure of society. CCM combines both of these sources of redemptive possibilities. But does CCM offer a challenge to the dominant capitalist ideology? Or does CCM merely serve, in part, to legitimate the dominant ideology, as religion and culture have been so often accused?

MUSIC AND SOCIETY

The sociology of music is more about society than about music. It is based on the assumption that social reality is embodied in an individual's activities, musical and otherwise (Dasilva, Blasi and Dees). Music is one of the ways society becomes evident to its members. Something can be understood about a society, in this case the subculture of Protestant Evangelicals, by examining their music.

In general, popular music is for entertainment purposes. But it can be, and has been, listened to and recorded for other purposes. Popular music has been used to express religious, social and political messages. Music has repeatedly been taken up by social movements to express their viewpoints as society's underdogs. Music has the potential to contribute to the "conversion" of nonmembers to the movement's position, as well as to raise the morale and express the solidarity of the movement's participants. Portia A. Maultsby has shown that "Soul Music" served these functions during the U.S. civil rights movement. Punks in England have used their music to reject the dominant values of society and to express their views (Henry). Popular music of the 1960s is another example; in this case, radical lyrics become the daily fare of the capitalist-owned media (Dasilva).

Popular music is also one way of expressing visions of a different type of society. Music has long reflected a longing for the future and lamented the fallen state of the present world. This is true of ancient hymns, of negro spirituals, of the gospel music of the late eighteenth and early nineteenth centuries and of CCM. However, there are segments of CCM that, like the "New Evangelicals" (Quebedeaux), have rediscovered a Biblical mandate for social action in addition to a concern with more traditionally viewed spiritual matters (i.e., prayer, holiness). Such artists tend to play a musical style that is closer to punk and avant garde rock than the mainstream rock of CCM. Punk and avant garde art, in general, have been argued to react against both established theories and techniques of art as well as against the larger society (Henry). CCM has expressed this rejection of society's norms in two primary ways. The first is the critique of modern society at large, pointing out the contradictions of modern society and rejecting its values and norms. The second approach is to challenge the Church itself to resist conformity to modern society and instead follow what the artists believe is a more Biblically-based role for the Church in society.

REJECTING MODERN SOCIETY

All challenges to modern capitalist society base their movements on claims of liberty, equality or fraternity and sorority (Gitlin). Capitalist society claims to offer all of these benefits, yet daily reality reveals they are lacking. Todd Gitlin has cited numerous contradictions of capitalist society. First, there is the constant urge to work hard, coupled with the proposition that true satisfaction is found in leisure. Second, there is an affirmation of authority and a contradictory affirmation of individualism and self-determination.

Among the CCM artists who have challenged the rights of hierarchical authority in their music is Steve Taylor. Taylor sarcastically mimics conservative seminar conductor Bill Gothard and Gothard's "God's chain of command" notion in his song "I Manipulate":

> 'cause a good wife learns to cower
> underneath the umbrella of power
> from the cover of heaven's gate
> I manipulate.

Rez, a heavy metal band, questions, in the song "Waitin' on Sundown," the right of the wealthy to buy up low income housing in Chicago for gentrification purposes, while making many of the inner city poor homeless:

> his wallet's a weapon
> corporation hit man
> nothin's left when he's done.

While the dominant ideology of modern capitalist society has sanctioned consumer satisfaction as the premium definition of the "good life," CCM has contradicted it (Gitlin 265). The challenge is made in both lifestyle and music. Two prominent CCM bands, Rez and Servant, have lived in intentional communities, sharing a common purse with all community members. Jesus People U.S.A., of which Rez is a ministry, choose to live in the inner city of Chicago among the city's poorest residents, thereby defying the definition of life in the suburbs as the road to happiness. Servant, until the breakup of the community several years ago, was a part of the Highway Missionary Society, an intentional community in rural Oregon. Their choice of a rural residence also rejects the definition of the wealthy suburbs as the place to fulfill the American dream of material prosperity.

Examples of the rejection of material accumulation abound in CCM:

> Mannequins on a shopping spree
> Who cares if you like it
> BUY IT! (Resurrection Band "Elevator Music")

* * *

where east meets west in a maze of pleasure
why do we feel we can live forever?
cos' they've piped in music of religious nature. (Amos)

The rejection of the drive to accumulate and the often accompanying call for
a simple lifestyle represent a partial "dropping out" of the capitalist system.
"Refuse to participate" is the message proclaimed.

Another approach to challenging society has been termed the "inversion"
of progress" theme (Bodinger-deUriarte). Several CCM artists have rejected the
hegemonic ideal of advancing technology as being in the benefit of all and
improving the general quality of life. Technology has been portrayed as a dev-
astating force that stifles humanity:

Machines remind you
that you can be replaced. (Amos)

Though progress marches on,
Our troubles still grow strong. (Amos)

In challenging these basic premises of the dominant group's hegemony, CCM
provides a space for potentially overcoming that dominance. The previously
accepted, "common sense" view of the world is open to questioning. Change
becomes a possibility.

CHALLENGING THE CHURCH AND ITS ROLE IN SOCIETY

The second approach to challenging hegemony through CCM involves the critique of the Church from the inside. This critique is offered not by groups or
individuals totally hostile to the Church, but by people who are some of the
most dedicated to the Church's mission in the world. These critiques are made
by people who want to remain a part of the Church, but refuse to let the Church
be anything less than, as it is defined in Matthew 5:13, the "Salt of the Earth."
CCM has attempted to keep the Church from ignoring issues such as Apartheid,
the arms race, the disabled, the poor and justice for the Third World.

On Apartheid:

You sow pain then pain you will receive
In the rubble of shantys in your land
Zuid Afrikan. (Rez "Zuid")

On the arms race:

When the bombs begin to fall in the middle of the night.
* * *
Put a coat over your head and paint your windows white. (Wild "Paint")

On the disabled:

Minus limbs, minus movement, minus worth
So sorry, they say but they forget me. (Resurrection Band "Chair")

On the poor:

> Little bitty beggars with the great big eyes
> I turn the channel but to my surprise
> They still press their faces to the window. (Amos)

On justice in the Third World:

> * * *
> Spoke up for the powerless for the people in need
> Oscar Romero they're coming for you (Hewitt "Oscar")

As is evident, irony and sarcasm are favorite tools for pointing out the contradictions inherent in the common sense understanding of the world. Another strategy is to place the familiar into unfamiliar contexts (Henry). For example, the punk CCM band Undercover took the over-one-hundred-year-old-hymn "Holy, Holy, Holy," a Protestant favorite, and recorded it in speed rock form. This illustrates CCM's position of being a part of the institutional church and yet radically critiquing it.

CCM has also sarcastically criticized the Church's activity, especially that of televangelists:

> Give me a bullhorn
> I'll help your kingdom come
> I get all this and heaven when I'm done. (Amos)

> It's too late for apologies
> When trust has been betrayed. (Taylor "Fritz")

In addition, CCM has critiqued the Church's failure to meet the legitimate needs of society. The Church is accused of being so preoccupied with its own agenda that it misses the opportunity and responsibility to care for those in need around them. In the song "Dancing at the Policeman's Ball," Mark Heard compared the Church's separatism with police spending all their time at the Policeman's Ball, never confronting the world, nor serving their legitimate role in society:

> Did I hear you say it is your aim
> For every night to be just the same
> * * *
> Dancing at the Policeman's Ball. (Heard "Dancing")

The aim is to get the Church to question itself, thus opening doors for radical change. By refusing to let the worldview of the Church be closed beyond questioning, avant garde CCM artists create cracks in the walls of societal hegemony. The taken-for-granted can be opened up for careful inspection.

Humility is another emphasis of CCM. Humility is needed along with a critical perspective if the Church is ever to question its own ideology or the nationalistic ideology of society.

But don't we cry alone
For the ashes and the dust
We've swept beneath the Holy throne. (Heard "We Believe")

Alongside the call for humility, there is an accompanying call for tolerance of diversity within the Church:

So now I see the whole design
My church is an assembly line (Taylor "I Want")

Draw the line and claim divine protection
Slay the one who shows the most objection. (Heard "Everybody")

Humility and tolerance must go hand in hand if the Church is ever to effectively question itself and society. The arrogance of the Church has long kept it from asking questions of itself. The lack of questioning has made the Church often irrelevant to society.

Avant garde Contemporary Christian Music offers the potential for a radical critique of the Church and society. Avant garde artists are not the dominant group in terms of record sales and religious radio airplay, but they command a significant following among Christian youth. The annual Cornerstone Festival in the Chicago area draws thousands of Christian youth to four days of nonstop rock music, camping and teaching seminars. Many of the artists referred to in this work make regular appearances in front of fanatical crowds at Cornerstone. The seeds of radical critique are being planted among the youth of the Church. Only with time will it be seen if they take root in a significant way.

WORKS CITED

Adorno, Theodor. *Aesthetic Theory*. London: Routledge and Kegan Paul, 1984.

Amos, Daniel. "Big Time/Big Deal." Newpax, 1981.
——— "Faces to the Window," Newpax, 1981.
——— "Mall All Over the World." Newpax, 1982.
——— "Incredible Shrinking Man." Twitchen Vibes Music/Snellsong, 1984.
——— "Rocket Packs." Twitchen Vibes Music/Snellsong, 1984.

Baker, Paul. "Contemporary Christian Music: Where It Came From, What It Is, Where It's Going." Westchester, IL: Crossway, 1985.

Bodinger-deUriarte, Christina. "Opposition to Hegemony in the Music of Devo: A Simple Matter of Remembering." *Journal of Popular Culture* 18 (Spring 1985): 57–71.

Exercises

Reread the essay by Howard. Then answer the following questions:

1. How does Howard's title prepare you for his essay? Would another title prepare you better? If so what title would you suggest?
2. Can you find the thesis statement in Howard's essay? If so, write it down.

3. Outline Howard's essay and write a note addressed to him discussing his organizational structure.

Now that you have read a professional essay on a topic similar to the one Tim must address, let us analyze Tim's assignment in terms of the writing process detailed earlier in this chapter. In doing so, please note that we have arranged this section so you can use it as a model in writing your own essay.

Tim's interpretive essay on Rollins' *One from None* was written in response to the following assignment.

> Write a short interpretive essay in which you analyze the thematic or technical efforts made by a poet in one of the books on the attached list. You are free to decide how to approach the book, providing you build upon methods of analysis either discussed in class or treated in the textbook.
>
> Do not just give your reader a string of unsupported opinions, however. Support your views with references to the poems themselves.

While the above assignment specifies that Tim interpret poems from a collection of poems, we can assume some liberty in the selection of a book. Tim decided on *One from None* by Henry Rollins. We have reprinted Tim's essay on pages 177–178. However, prior to reading that essay, work through the following exercises and poems. Your goal will be to devise a thesis statement based on your interpretation of the poems.

As in most writing assignments across the disciplines, the audience for Tim's essay is the instructor, whom Tim can assume knows the books on the list quite well. (Why else would an instructor limit a student to a list of books?)

The purpose—to interpret—requires that Tim work with several related purposes in mind: to analyze, to argue, and to inform.

This assignment, unlike the assignment for a reflective essay given on page 161–162, presents Tim with the responsibility for reading an entire book of poems and following the advice for reading offered in Chapter Two. Tim will read, annotate, take notes, and perhaps summarize. He will certainly need to trace from poem to poem the topics Rollins writes about and the various techniques he uses in writing about them.

Exercises

1. Read the following two poems, annotating and note-taking as necessary.
2. Devise a thesis statement that reflects the way you interpret these poems.
3. Complete this assignment with your writing group. Choose a poem that you all like and have read several times in the past. Make sure that each member of your group has a copy of this poem.

   Typing on separate computers, have each member of the group write a thesis sentence that reflects the way in which he or she interprets this poem.

Beneath this thesis sentence, have each member of the group identify at least two examples or details from the poem that support the thesis.

Now switch computers and read the thesis and the supporting details that another group member has identified. To this material, add at least two details that either support or contradict the thesis that your group member has identified.

BIRTHDAY 35: DIARY ENTRY

Fred Chappell

Multiplying my age by 2 in my head,
I'm a grandfather. Or dead.

"Midway in this life I came to a darksome wood."
But Dante, however befuddled, was Good.

And to be Good, in any visible sense,
Demands the wrought-iron primness of a Georgetown fence.

I'm still in flight, still unsteadily in pursuit,
Always becoming more sordid, pale, and acute. . . .

For all the good it does . . . I'd rather seize by the neck
Some Golden Opportunity and with a mastiff shake

Empty its pockets of change,
And let my life grow bearded and strange.

In Mexico, Hunza, or Los Angeles,
I'd smoke a ton of dope and minister my fleas.

Or retiring to Monument Valley alone
With Gauguin, I'd take up saxophone.

Or slipping outside time to a Heavenly Escurial,
I'd spend a thousand years at a Monogram serial.

For though I've come so far that nothing intriguing will happen,
Like every half-assed politico I keep my options open.

My style's to veer and slide and wobble,
Immorally eavesdropping my own Babel.

When Plato divided us into Doers and Thinkers,
He didn't mean corporate generals and autoerotic bankers;

He meant that one attunes his nerves to Mind,
Or is blind.

Will may go stupid; clumsy its dance,
Mired in marmalade of circumstance.

Abjure, therefore, no ounce of alcohol,
Keep desultory and cynical.

On paper I scribble mottoes and epigrams,
Blessings and epithets, O-Holy's and Damn's—

Not matter sufficient to guard a week by,
The wisdom I hoard you could stuff in your eye.

But *everything* means *something,* that's my faith;
Despair begins when they stop my mouth.

Drunk as St. Francis I preach to the cat.
I even talk back to the TV set.

Sometimes I even Inquisition my wife:
"Susan, *is* there a moral alternative to life?"

Partly because I want to know, partly because
I'm amused by sleazy cleverness.

I can talk till the moon dissolves, till the stars
Splash down in the filth of morning newspapers.

Talk that engenders a fearful itch
Always just barely not quite out of reach.

Talk with purposes so huge and vague,
The minor details are Om and Egg.

Surely something gets said if only in intent,
When the magnesium candle of enthusiasm is burnt.

Happy Birthday to me! At age thirty-five
I scratch to see if I'm yet alive.

Thumbing the ledger of thirty-five years,
I find unstartled I'm badly in arrears.

In fact, I'm up to my eyes in debt
Unpayable. And not done suffering yet.

But then, so what?
What you think you owe is everything you're not.

That's not true debt, but merely guilt,
Irrelevant though heartfelt;

Merely part of the noisy lovers' quarrel
We name Doctrine, Dialectic, and Moral.

I'd sleep in the eiderdown of the True Believer
And never nightmare about Either/Or

If I had a different person in my head.
But this gnawing worm shows that I'm not dead.

Therefore: either I live with doubt
Or get out. . . .

LOOKING FORWARD TO AGE

Jim Harrison

I will walk down to a marina
on a hot day and not go out to sea.

I will go to bed and get up early,
and carry too much cash in my wallet.

On Memorial Day I will visit the graves
of all those who died in my novels.

If I have become famous I'll wear a green
janitor's suit and row a wooden boat.

From a key ring on my belt will hang
thirty-three keys that open no doors.

Perhaps I'll take all of my grandchildren
to Disneyland in a camper but probably not.

One day standing in a river with my flyrod
I'll have the courage to admit my life.

In a one-room cabin at night I'll consign
photos, all tentative memories to the fire.

And you my loves, few as there have been, let's lie
and say it could never have been otherwise.

So that: we may glide off in peace, not howling
like orphans in this endless century of war.

On the basis of his reading of poems in Rollins' book, Tim has determined that one theme running through the world as Rollins' sees and writes about it is the difficulty of coping with reality. Tim expresses this theme in his working thesis statement: "The majority of his [Rollins'] poems reflect Rollins' depression and inability to cope and deal with the world around him." Here is the draft of Tim's essay.

One from None is the fourth collection of poetry from singer, writer, poet and punk icon Henry Rollins. The book, much like his others, explores the dark and brooding side of life. Rollins is not interested in painting pretty pictures. The majority of his poems reflect Rollins' depression and inability to cope and deal with the world around him.

One theme that is found throughout this book is the "Gun in mouth blues" theme. There are several poems that begin with this line. These poems show a Rollins once again pondering the possibility and ramifications of suicide. These poems oftentimes send Henry to another world. In this Universe, he is master and servant, both to himself. Distance often dominates the mood of these poems. Both physical and mental distance exist between Rollins and his evil world.

Rollins also writes a multitude of "Room" poems. It is obvious that Rollins spends lots of time in his own room, looking at the walls. He enjoys the solitude of his room. He could not live without it. In one poem, he writes, "I saw the door, . . ./I saw the world frowning at me." In another, he writes, "Mister Room, . . ./A big hollow animal, . . ./I sit in the belly and get digested." These two poems create a familiar and living creature, the room personified. It is a place where he can escape and die every day. Rollins often writes about looking out his window into the world. He talks of keeping his curtains nailed shut so the world can't get in.

Rollins also writes about his brain . . . often. He addresses his brain, wanting to change it and shape it. In one poem, he writes, "I should pull out my brain . . ./Kick it around the room to put it back in line." He often writes about his mind being a "locked room." If he could only get into this room, he could be free.

Rollins addresses women throughout his poetry. Although Rollins loves women and often lusts after them, he feels his pain and isolation preventing him from getting to know a woman truly. He often writes that he doesn't want to get to know anyone.

One from None is a book that shows and uncovers life's ugly and brutal side. Rollins' heart-felt poems are all painted black. Pain, isolation, and solitude reign supreme throughout this book. Henry Rollins does not talk about butterflies, sunshine, and happiness. He talks about rats, darkness, and depression. Rollins doesn't complain, however. He strives to fight and overcome. He draws strength and power from the darkness. *One from None* reflects the pain and torture of a powerful Henry Rollins.

Exercises

1. Reread the draft of Tim's essay. Underline the details and examples Tim uses to support his thesis statement. How well has he selected material to support his point of view?
2. Reread Lisa's essay on page 161. In what ways does Tim's essay differ from Lisa's? What do the two essays have in common?
3. Make an outline of Tim's essay. What remarks would you make to him about his organizational strategy? If he should revise, how would you advise him to go about doing so?
4. In a short letter to Tim, offer what you perceive to be the strengths and weaknesses of his essay. Recommend ways he might change his essay to improve upon this draft.
5. Return to the working thesis statement you created for the poems by Fred Chappell and Jim Harrison in the exercise on page 173. With your working thesis statement in mind, reread the poems in an effort to pick out supporting details. Be certain to consider your subject in terms of the seven elements of the writing process in the humanities.
6. Write a first draft of an interpretive essay on the poems by Chappell and Harrison. Have a classmate read your draft and answer questions 1, 3, and 4 above about what you have thus far written. You should do the same for your classmate.
7. *If you have access to a computer and a word-processing package,* choose one of the two poems we have provided in this section ("Birthday 35: Diary Entry" or "Looking Forward to Age"). Write an interpretive essay about this poem. Make sure that your essay has a thesis sentence that presents your interpretive point of view, and statements in each paragraph that present the main point of that paragraph. Make sure that you have, as well, at least two or three details in each paragraph that support the main point you make.

Exchange a disk containing your draft essay for the disk of another member of your writing group. Read the essay your partner wrote and complete the following tasks:

a. Using the font selection feature, identify the main point of the essay by changing the one sentence that represents this point into italics type.

b. Using the font selection feature, identify the main point of each paragraph in the essay by changing it into bold type.

c. Using the font selection feature, change all other text in this essay into six point type.

d. After each of the details that the author has provided (now in six-point type) rate the effectiveness of the detail in supporting or illustrating the main point of the paragraph by putting a number from one to ten in parentheses. (One indicates poor support and ten indicates terrific support.)

e. Setting the all caps key on your computer, add at least two details that support or contradict the thesis that your partner has identified. In a brief paragraph, discuss the details you chose, and tell why you feel they support or contradict the essay's main thesis.

URLs for the Humanities

The World Wide Web Virtual Library: Language and Literature
http://www.w3.org/hypertext/DataSources/bySubject/LibraryOfCongress/lali.html

Literature Directory
http://web.syr.edu/~fjzwick/sites/lit.html

European Literature—Electronic Texts
http://www.lib.virginia.edu/wess/etexts.html

English Language and Literature
http://vatech.lib.vt.edu/lib/armstrong/English_L&L.html

Humanities
http://www.einet.net/galaxy/Humanities.html

Humanities HUB Resources—Other Indices
http://www.gu.edu.au/gwis/hub/hub.other.html

Humanities, Social Sciences
http://www.lib.umich.edu/chouse/inter/408.html

Miscellaneous Humanities Sites
http://www.artsci.wustl.edu/~jntolva/misclist.html

Communication and Rhetoric Information Sources
http://www.rpi.edu/~decemj/study/cmrt/resources.html

CHAPTER SIX

Writing in the Social Sciences

Inquiring in the Social Sciences: Three Methods

Responsibilities of Social Scientiests

Importance of Communications to the Social Scientist

Writing in the Undergraduate Social Sciences

You have already learned in Chapter Three that social scientists systematically inquire into human behavior. More specifically, **psychologists** study individual personality, **sociologists** inquire into the relationships among social groups, and **political scientists** and **economists** investigate people interacting in government, labor, and trade. Please keep in mind that students who decide to major in education or criminal justice will find it necessary to employ many of the same skills useful to social science majors, as discussed in this chapter.

Inquiring in the Social Sciences: Three Methods

A convenient place to begin exploration into inquiry in the social sciences is with your day-to-day lives. No doubt many of you have learned from your day-to-day experiences the value of social scientific inquiries and, to a certain extent, you have learned how to report them. In fact, many decisions, interpretations, and judgments that you share with others result from your use of methods of inquiry that are also used by social scientists, including participant/observer, survey/interview, and statistical methods of inquiry. Writing assignments in social science, education, and criminal justice classes are designed to prepare you for reporting on your inquiries. Keep in mind, though, that you are not likely to encounter in introductory courses assignments that employ statistics. In fact, most departments will offer a statistics course to majors that prepares them for that particular kind of research.

If you are among those who believe that experience is the best teacher, you have much in common with social scientists. Many social scientists operate from a related belief: Participation in events and interaction with groups are the best methods for reaching certain kinds of understandings. This is the first kind of social scientific strategy for collecting information that most people learn and simply take for granted, the participant/observer method.

Its usefulness rests in the fact that it enables researchers to obtain first-hand experience. Using this method, you might conduct inquiries into which class or instructor to take by attending class until the last day of drop-add period and deciding then, after having participated in the class for a period of time, if it is a class you want to continue taking. Or, in deciding where to open a checking account after moving to a college town, you might use a bank for three months and then, after you have been a member of that community, decide if you want to continue or if you want to look elsewhere to satisfy your needs.

In the absence of an opportunity to participate in the group you are studying (or in an effort to find additional support for conclusions reached by personal observation), as in the two examples above, you may quite naturally employ a second method of social scientific inquiry, the survey/interview method. This method of inquiry enables you to obtain a different kind of information than you can get using the participant/observer method; because surveys and interviews enable you to ask questions of participants, these methods provide you with access to the judgments of numerous other human beings who have been in the social situation you are studying.

This approach enables you to answer questions that are not easily answered by participation alone: *Overall,* do students believe Professor X to be interesting, knowledgeable, understandable, fair? *Generally,* do students who have checking accounts at bank X believe they have been treated with respect, fairness, understanding, forgiveness?

Though surveys and interviews may be interpreted statistically, their value rests in their availability to "outsiders" as a method for accumulating judgments made by "insiders." The information obtained through surveys adds to any information obtained by means of personal observation since a researcher using surveys is able to determine from the results the views and behaviors of others. When such information reinforces what a researcher has observed as a participant, conclusions can be more forcefully argued. One line of argument in favor of using surveys is that they render greater insight into the interactions of individuals in a group than either of the other two methods.

Still, because social science is a relatively new field, modeled after natural and applied sciences, social scientists have had to fight for the legitimacy of their investigations. To do so, many rely on the third method of social scientific inquiry, a method employed in natural and applied sciences called "statistical" or "quantitative" research. In day-to-day living, you also probably have found it useful to collect and interpret numerical and statistical information for use in making judgments.

In deciding which instructor to take for a course, you might check posted grades, noting not only the percentage of A's and B's the instructor has given, but also the percentage of incompletes and withdrawals. On the basis of this information, you might decide whether to take a course from that instructor or from another whose record you have similarly studied. Or, you might decide which bank to use after moving to a new college town based upon quantifiable information available to you. Most people decide where to bank by comparing the cost of checks, the required minimum balance, and the interest that might accrue at several representative banks. They then decide to bank at a place that will assure them the least expense in obtaining the desired services.

In deciding on a range of matters, then—from instructors for a course to a place to open a checking account—you have probably relied on numerical and statistical information, what social scientists call quantitative evidence, and you have done so for good reason. Statistical information is valuable because it can be studied without too much subjectivity. Numbers seem cold, hard, and objective. A decision based upon statistical information may not only seem to you to be logical, but your process of reaching that particular decision also will be replicable by others who study the same figures.

As you probably know from your own life experiences in reaching decisions, people rely upon one or more of the above methods. Most people function as social scientists when they gather information that will help them better understand people, including themselves; or interpret behaviors, including their own; or make certain specific decisions, especially where they must reach conclusions about their interactions with others.

In short, inquiries in the social sciences, like the above life-experience inquiries, involve one or more of the following three methods.

Method 1: The Participant/Observer Method
Method 2: The Survey/Interview Method
Method 3: The Statistical Method

Furthermore, the social scientist is apt to employ these methods to solve problems that present themselves in one of two ways.

In the first, a social scientist might set out to prove something already believed to be true—for instance, it might be believed widely that if people indicate in a survey that they do not approve of a president's foreign affairs policy, that president will not be reelected come next election—and thereby test a theory.

In the second, a social scientist might work from general observations—let's say, personal interactions with individuals on certain levels of military leadership—in an effort to generate a theory about how different kinds of leadership methods result in different kinds of behaviors from subordinates.

You no doubt have worked in one of these two ways, either by testing to see if evidence you collect will prove an initial judgment correct or by making a judgment only after you have gathered adequate supporting information. In the final analysis, you probably know a great deal about inquiries in the social sciences that you can use to understand the methods of research and the value of writing in introductory courses in the social sciences, as we describe them below.

Exercises

1. Find a brochure from a local bank and analyze it to determine how and why the author(s) of the brochure used numerical information to convince you to open an account at that bank.

2. Have you ever employed any of the methods of participant/observer, survey/interview, and/or statistical inquiry in deciding on a course, an instructor, a summer job, a college, a restaurant where you might go on a date, or in making any other decision? Describe your use of the method and how things turned out. Did your methods render correct predictions? Were they unsuccessful? Read your description to a classmate, offering advice based upon your experience that will help your classmate make a decision in a similar situation.

3. *If you have access to a computer network with e-mail,* post an entry on a student-based listserv that you follow or send a message to at least ten of your friends who use e-mail. In this entry or message, ask individuals what factors they use in choosing whether to take a second course with an instructor (for example, the grade they received in the first course, the interest that the instructor fostered in the subject matter, the instructor's style) when

they have the opportunity. Ask your respondents to arrange these factors in a priority listing.

Before reading the answers that you receive, *using a word-processing package,* open a new file and write a list of predictions about the factors that respondents will provide you, and speculate about the relative priority ratings you expect to see.

Once you receive responses from at least five people, compare their answers to your predictions. In writing, discuss the ways in which they differ and the ways in which they are similar.

Responsibilities of Social Scientists

Social scientists are often interested in investigating behaviors that can be seen, reporting what they have observed. These studies are examples of **qualitative** research. Qualitative research is based upon observational techniques, such as the participant/observer method described above, and often are less structured than surveys, interviews, or laboratory experiments.

By contrast, most laboratory experiments are rigidly structured and render "hard" data characteristic of **quantitative** research. Quantitative research often requires the use of statistical manipulations of numbers that, as we have already suggested, students rarely are asked to perform in introductory courses. Rather, students majoring in the social sciences are apt to be required to take special courses in statistics as employed in their chosen field prior to taking advanced courses where quantitative research will be required of them.

Surveys, on the other hand, offer a blend of observational and statistical methods, often offering information based on the observations and experiences of those surveyed. This information is gathered in such a way that trends in the information discovered through the survey may be studied statistically for further insight into behavior.

Since you might, indeed, decide to major in the social sciences once you find out more about them, let us briefly survey types of studies reflecting each of the three above methods of inquiry.

In social scientific studies that may serve as models for what you might be asked to do in an introductory course, the social scientist leaves the laboratory environment altogether and enters a social situation or a "field" to observe behavior there. As you can imagine, this kind of research is not only a data-collecting activity, but an activity that allows the researcher to generate an explanation of why something happened (that is, a theory) as well. Rather than beginning with a hypothesis, as in the natural and applied sciences (see Chapter 7), you will more often attempt to make sense out of what you observe even as you observe it.

What kinds of phenomena have been observed in field research using the participant/observer method? In one study, Randall Alfred wanted to better understand a new social and religious consciousness. To do so, Alfred became a member of the Church of Satan in San Francisco to better understand that group. Naturally, to enter the field in an effective manner, it was important, at least initially, that members of the church not recognize Alfred as a researcher. Rather, his role was as a participant-observer.

In another study, Elliot Liebow entered the field to study childrearing practices among low-income families in Washington, D.C. Rather than entering the field as a participant as Alfred did, Liebow identified himself as a researcher and went about the task of gathering information first by winning the trust of his subjects and then by observing them in their family groups.

The survey/interview method is similarly useful in enabling researchers to explore the unspoken rules that govern behavior in society but in a less intrusive manner than the participant/observer method. Let us take an example from Criminal Justice. In one study, a criminologist surveys eyewitnesses to a crime to determine the ways responses to mug shots might be biased. Is it possible that certain behaviors by law enforcement officials bias the judgments of witnesses? Are witnesses more apt to find the correct photograph among dozens of mug shots if the photograph is viewed at the beginning, end, or someplace in the middle of a batch of photographs? Are eyewitnesses influenced by the relative clarity of the photos, the ethnicity of the people viewed, or any other factors that might be controlled in an effort to make certain the witness is making the best and most accurate judgment possible?

In a study titled "Using Mug Shots to Find Suspects," R. C. L. Lindsay et al. sought answers to the above questions by recording responses to mug shots placed before their subjects at various intervals after a staged crime was observed by the subjects. In this way, the researchers could test their hypothesis that large numbers of preceding pictures would influence their subjects' ability to identify the criminal.

Though many inquiries in the social sciences involve the use of participant/observer and/or survey/interview methods, some social scientists believe the very integrity of social scientific inquiries rests upon their use of statistical methods. In an effort to elevate their work in the eyes of natural and applied scientists, many social scientists use the methods designed for use in investigating observable behaviors.

In "Do Speed Limits Reduce Traffic Accidents?" Frank A. Haight of the Pennsylvania Transportation and Traffic Safety Center reports on his inquiry into 7,000 accidents, making before-and-after comparisons of accident rates. In his report, Haight describes experiments designed to test how specific improvements in traffic control (e.g., changed laws such as speed limit and acceptable blood-alcohol levels in drivers) affect accident fatality rates.

In another study, one that might be of interest to students who have taken the Scholastic Aptitude Test for admission to college, William H. Angoff of the Educational Testing Service shows why SAT scores are valid predictors of a student's potential performance in college. In "Calibrating College Board Scores," Angoff explains how scores by students who have taken one form of the SAT (let's say the October test) can be equated with scores by students who have taken another (say, the April test).

In discussing these studies, we should be careful not to draw too neat a distinction between research which renders quantifiable information such as statistics that may be represented in charts and graphs, and research which is solely qualitative—that is, narrative descriptions of what has been seen. In fact, some field research can be represented statistically. For instance, what percentage of Church of Satan members come from broken families? Or, what percentage of low-income families studied rely entirely on welfare for subsistence? But field researchers offer narratives that are at their best when they accurately describe the setting, characters, and occurrences as they are observed by the researcher. You are more apt to be required to record information from observations or surveys in your introductory courses in the social sciences than from statistics.

In this chapter, then, we will discuss only those kinds of writings you can expect to perform in introductory classes in the social sciences, reports that serve as preparation for more sophisticated research studies required in advanced courses. Generally speaking, you can expect to be asked to do three kinds of writing tasks in your introductory courses.

1. library research reports
2. observation reports
3. applications of theory reports

Exercises

1. Read pages 213–255 in Chapter Seven, "Writing in the Natural Sciences." What is revealed in this chapter about the way research is conducted in the natural sciences?
2. Write two paragraphs. In the first, describe the approach to research in the natural sciences and, in the second, the approaches to research in the social sciences, as described above.
3. Make a list of various groups you have entered as an outsider but have been accepted into as a trusted member. Then take any one of those groups and, using appropriate details, make one observation that you do not believe you would have been able to make if you had not been accepted as a member of that group. Consider sports teams, clubs, classes, or any other group you can recall entering. Read what you have written to a classmate, offering suggestions as to how your classmate might successfully enter that group.
4. An increasing number of social scientists use virtual (on-line) environments to study social groups. Such environments give social scientists access to many more groups than they might normally be able to study in face-to-face environments.

   If you have access to a computer network with e-mail and are a member of any on-line discussion groups or news groups, write a paragraph about an observation you can make about this group that you would not have been able to make if you had not participated in this conversation. Use appropriate details to discuss your observation.

If you do not subscribe to any on-line discussion groups or newsgroups, join one of interest to you. Monitor the conversation of this group for at least five days, and then write a paragraph about an observation you can make about this group that you would not have been able to make before you participated in this conversation. Use appropriate details to discuss your observation.

Importance of Communications to the Social Scientist

How will the ability to communicate aid you in courses and careers in the social sciences, education, and criminal justice? Aside from providing a systematic study of human behavior, these three related disciplines, when studied in the college classroom, provide you with the opportunity to learn certain specific methods of observation that, like the methods of participant/observer, survey/interview, or statistical analysis, will make it possible for you to reach decisions about and interpret the behaviors of people and events around you.

Courses in the social sciences, for instance, are uniquely valuable because they teach you strategies of observation and interpretation useful in studying human behavior. You will see that social scientists are interested in problems in society such as racism, gun control, and crime. Yet you will also see that social scientists inquire into specific behaviors, both external to individuals and internal: how societies regulate social relations, curb aggression, and maintain order.

Writing in the Undergraduate Social Sciences

In the same way that research in the humanities and the natural sciences is motivated by curiosity over something that is inadequately explained, research is conducted by social scientists when the current questions about human behavior arouse doubt and uncertainty rather than render clear and consistent answers. When they study difficult questions about human behavior, social scientists do so in laboratory environments and/or fields. In either case, social scientists begin, as do researchers in all disciplines, with an understanding of what already has been studied and researched.

Writing a Library Research Report

Since social scientists find library research valuable, you will be required in introductory classes in the social sciences to begin your investigation in the library, using the sources highlighted in Chapter Three. In fact, introductory courses in the social sciences will often begin with one of two possible assignments that require you to visit the library: (1) a summary of a specific article or (2) a synthesis and critique of several articles on the same subject.

An assignment of the first variety is almost always given in introductory courses not only in the social sciences but in education, as the following student sample shows. Such an assignment asks you to review a book, a movie, or an article, as in the following assignment from an introductory education course.

> Go to the reserve room in the library and ask the librarian for the article on reserve under my name, "Beginning Teachers and Classroom Management: Questions from Practice, Answers from Research" by Edwin G. Ralph in *Middle School Journal* (Vol. 25:1; 60–64) September 1993. Summarize the article.

Completion of this task requires that you rely upon skills (for example, the ability to summarize an article) already discussed in Chapter Three.

Here is the effort made by Gilbert, a student in an introductory education course, at completing the above assignment.

The major idea of this article by E. G. Ralph is to help beginning teachers develop an effective classroom managerial style. Mr. Ralph focuses on ways that novice teachers can identify key issues or problems that deal with obtaining and maintaining an effective classroom management style. The article explains how beginning teachers should evaluate their current style of management, identify possible alternative measures and have a way of continually monitoring both the positive and negative aspects of their program. The last point is that teachers need to be consistent in their deals with students, not to say that flexibility or modification should be thrown out. Teachers new and old alike need to reflect constantly on how they can improve their managerial style.

The author provides the reader with five of the most critical questions that beginning teachers ask when they first enter the classroom. These questions are based on his research on effective teaching and *Effective Teaching Methods* (2nd ed.) by G. D. Borich (1992). The author uses a recent survey in which 83% of the teachers polled reported having problems with student discipline. The other references the author uses offer the reader possible solutions to the questions. The author points out there are many different methods and styles that can be used to manage a classroom. The actual choice of managerial style is up to the individual teacher with the references as guides.

The author of this article, Mr. Ralph, is neither criticizing nor approving any one type of classroom managerial style. Rather, he points out five key questions that are commonly asked by beginning teachers. He offers his opinion on what constitutes effective classroom management based on years of research by experienced teachers and experts in child development. Most

of this research that Mr. Ralph offers has been conducted in the last four
years, with the older reference being that of Dr. Watson in 1968.

   The author presented the questions and problems beginning teachers face
in a well organized and factual manner. I agree that setting a positive and
stable learning environment is the best way to get results from students.
However, as the author points out, getting results is not something that just
happens in the course of a school year or term. Rather, it requires systematic
utilization of a combination of skills and techniques in order to achieve a
successful and rewarding learning environment.

Gilbert adequately meets the requirements of the first kind of assignment
you can expect in an introductory course in the social sciences. But to complete
the second kind of assignment, you must go a bit further than in the first,
beginning with summary but then moving into critique and synsthesis. Here is
an example of this second kind of library research report assignment.

Check the *Psychlit* database and find a minimum of six (6) articles on the
impact of divorce on the family. Your assignment must be completed in the
following three stages.

1. Turn in a list of articles to be used later as your Works Cited, following
   APA Style.
2. Submit summaries of each article which will be used later in your full
   library research report.
3. Devise a thesis statement that might be supported by a synthesis and/
   or critique of these articles. Make certain to have your thesis statement
   approved before writing your full report.

In the social sciences, the review of literature assignment enables you to learn
how to obtain information using pertinent sources and provides you with a
starting point in conducting research of your own.

   Read the following review of literature from Lindsay et al., "Using Mug
Shots to Find Suspects," as an example of the way library research reports are
employed in social scientific documents.

USING MUG SHOTS TO FIND SUSPECTS

Lindsay, Nosworthy, Martin, and Martynuk

Studies of eyewitness identification accuracy have generally involved the examination of lineup procedures. These studies have demonstrated that biased
lineups produce high rates of mistaken identification under a variety of con-

ditions, including when foils dissimilar to the suspect are placed in the lineup (Lindsay & Wells, 1980), when instructions are given that lead the witness to believe that the criminal is known to be in the lineup (Malpass & Devine, 1981), and when the suspect is placed in the lineup wearing clothing similar to that worn by the criminal during the crime (Lindsay, Wallbridge, & Drennan, 1987). Other studies have indicated that false identifications from lineups can be reduced if the lineup is presented sequentially. This is true whether or not other aspects of the lineup procedure are fair or biased (Cutler & Penrod, 1988; Lindsay, Lea, Nosworthy, *et al.*, 1991); Lindsay & Wells, 1985). Neither lineup biases nor sequential presentation significantly influence correct-identification rates.

Lindsay and Wells (1985) argued that the improvement in lineup performance from using sequentially presented lineups was the result of discouraging witnesses from using relative judgments. Witnesses make errors because they treat the lineup as a multiple-choice test: They select the person most similar to their memory of the criminal (relative judgment) rather than determining for each lineup member whether he or she is the criminal (absolute judgment). Biased instructions create demand characteristics that encourage the use of relative judgments, whereas poor foils and clothing bias make it easy to pick out the suspect.

Other researchers have examined the use of mug shots; however, many of them have used mug shots principally as a source of interference (e.g., Brigham & Cairns, 1988; Davies, Shepherd, & Ellis, 1979a). Subjects exposed to a target face were asked to examine pictures, not including the target, either to look for the target or for unrelated reasons, such as rating the attractiveness of the faces. In these studies, the dependent measure was accuracy of identification from a subsequent identification task, not performance on the mug-shot task. Subjects who examined photographs to seek the target were less likely to accurately identify the target later than were either subjects who had not viewed the pictures or those who had examined the pictures for a purpose other than finding the target. Brown, Deffenbacher, and Sturgill (1977) demonstrated that people were prone to selecting innocent faces from subsequent photo arrays even though they had seen the faces only during a mug-shot search. From these studies, most researchers concluded that examining mug shots is a dangerous procedure likely to result in accusations against innocent people (Wells, 1988).

Laugherty (Laugherty, Alexander, & Lane, 1971; Laugherty, Fessler, Lenorovitz, & Yoblick, 1974) explored the rate of correct identifications from mug shots. Subjects attempted to find the target face in a set of photographs, with the location of the critical picture being manipulated. As expected, the target's picture was more likely to be selected when it was presented after 50 pictures rather than 125 pictures (Laugherty *et al.*, 1971). The result prompted Wells (1988) to recommend that "no more than fifty photographs should be shown at any one time" (p. 52) in police mug-shot procedures. Similarity of the target to other faces was also examined, but the dependent measure that was used confounded confidence and selection, making it difficult to apply the results directly to forensic issues (Laugherty *et al.,* 1974).

Mug shots seem dangerous. The large size of mug-shot pools guarantees that they will contain pictures that are similar to most criminals. Despite Wells's (1988) recommendation, it would rarely be possible to limit witnesses to looking at 50 or fewer pictures. Furthermore, people who are selected from mug shots will be taken seriously as suspects unless they can demonstrate their innocence. This seems like a recipe for disaster. . . .

Lindsay et al. first present their review of pertinent literature and then state a concern they hope their research will enable them to overcome: "Mug shots seem dangerous." Since their purpose is to prepare the reader for presentation of a new piece of research, they present the current research first, establishing that because "[m]ug shots seem dangerous," this research study is necessary. Clearly, they have read relevant research studies, summarized, critiqued, and synthesized the studies, and laid the necessary groundwork for advancing work with mug shots and line-ups that has already been reported.

In introductory courses in the social sciences, you can expect to go to the library to find and report on research studies that might serve as the foundation for the kind of research study social-science majors conduct in advanced courses in their major. In introductory courses, you can expect to be asked to perform the following tasks in completion of an assignment like the one on page 194.

1. use library research tools (see Chapter Three)
2. summarize, paraphrase, critique and synthesize materials (see Chapter Two)
3. devise a thesis statement (see Chapters One and Five)
4. support a thesis statement (see Chapters One and Five)

Now read the following library research report written by Phyllis in an introductory psychology course. Keep in mind that she has already employed the process required by her instructor as mandated in the above assignment—that she compile a Works Cited list with a minimum of six works found by using the *Psychlit* database and summarize those works prior to devising an approved thesis statement.

The Broken Home

Most people assume that divorce is only a tragedy when the child is very young. Studies indicate, however, that children are affected the rest of their lives by the break up of their parents.

While very young children are not able to understand divorce, Lansky (1989) has shown that small babies can sense that something is unusual and react with bodily responses and regressive behavior in toilet training and sleep (p. 89). The babies studied by Lansky were able to "sense" almost any change in their environment.

Preschoolers often exhibit feelings of intense stress during the time of their parents' divorce. Divorce causes children to act less mature. One study of preschoolers during the time of their parents' divorce (Katz, 1984) found that the children exhibited behavior that included loss of toilet training, episodes of separation anxiety, and use of some transitional objects, such as security blankets and dolls. Some children become hostile and behave more aggressively during this time. They may hit their siblings or other children, according to Lansky (1989). Overall, preschoolers experiencing their parents' divorce also feel neglected by their parents since parents, who are often involved with their own problems, according to Segal (1989), do not pay as much attention to their children as they should (p. 22).

Children ages six to thirteen often react differently than preschoolers. They are too old to use fantasy as a means of dealing with change. They have greater difficulty denying the situation. Likewise, they are too young to remove themselves from all the implications of their parents' separation or, for that matter, to realize that they are not responsible for the rift (Lansky 1989). As Comer (1989) points out, "This is the age when significant changes in the body appear. It is a time when young people attempt to decrease their emotional dependence on parents and get more involved in relationships outside the home" (p. 93).

Children fourteen to eighteen are apt to be moralistic and judgmental about divorce. They tend to make a scapegoat of the parent they think is to blame. Lansky (1989) notes that teens will resent responsibilities dumped on them unless they are part of discussion and decision-making processes. Often young people in this age group are weakened by the demands made on them by the divorce situation. Wallerstein (1989) notes that such demands often include caring for a younger sibling or, in some instances, finding employment outside the home (p. 213).

These conditions are exacerbated for children whose parents are angry with each other. Among other problems when unresolved hostility exists among the parents, parents may tell their children bad things about each other. Johnson (1989) suggests that parents try, in this manner, to win the loyalty of their children (p. 199). Then parents may even try to "buy" their children's loyalty by taking them to special places, purchasing expensive gifts, or letting their children do whatever they want.

Divorce influences the children's behavior long after the parents have split up. In a study of more than 100 children traced after a decade (Kantrowitz,1989), almost half entered adulthood worried, underachieving, self-deprecating, and sometimes angry about relationships they have entered themselves (p. 89). Efforts to begin meaningful relationships are diminished by feelings that relationships just do not work out for some people.

Naturally, when divorce occurs, children are damaged in some way. How can the damage be diminished? Kantrowitz (1989) notes, "Caring parents make the biggest difference. There is no quick fix for the pain of divorce. But the children who feel confident of their parents' love and attention can emerge as survivors rather than victims" (p. 65).

Exercises

1. Reread Gilbert's essay and Phyllis's essay. Underline or rewrite the thesis statement of each and make an outline that reflects each author's organizational structure.

2. Make a list of similarities and differences between Gilbert's essay and Phyllis's. Compare your list with a classmate's.

3. On a separate sheet of paper, assess the effectiveness of Phyllis's library research report by analyzing her essay as follows:
   a. Select one example of a summary, and evaluate it for how effectively the author uses the summary to convey relevant information.
   b. Has she effectively employed synthesis? Where?
   c. Has she effectively employed critique? Where?
   d. What are the strengths of Phyllis's essay?
   e. What advice would you offer Phyllis as she revises this essay prior to submitting it to her teacher for a grade? Review the assignment prior to offering advice.

   Now trade your assignment with a classmate's and compare your response with that person's.

4. Do the same assignment as Phyllis has done: Check the *Psychlit* database and find a minimum of six articles on any one of the following topics: Ku Klux Klan, women's suffrage, recent trends in mortgage interest rates, lobbying, accuracy of opinion polls, effects of crime rate in countries where drugs have been legalized, reasons for raising the speed limit on interstate highways, arguments for reducing the legal drinking age, learning styles, workaholism.
   a. Turn in a list of articles to be used later as your Works Cited, following APA Style (see the Appendix).
   b. Submit summaries of each article which will be used later in your full library research report (see Chapter Two).
   c. Devise a thesis statement (see Chapter One) that might be supported by a synthesis and/or critique of these articles. Make certain to have your thesis statement approved before writing your full report.

5. Go to your library and use the electronic research tools available there to find a minimum of six social science articles on one of the following topics. Be sure to use the *Psychlit* database if it is available.
   • stalkings on the Internet
   • gender imposters on the Internet
   • pornography on the Internet
   • radical social groups inciting violence on the Internet
   • gay discussion groups on the Internet

   Print out copies of the six articles you have identified on the topic you choose. Using a computer and a word-processing package, create a file and write full bibliographic citations of each of the articles you have found. Use APA format. Also write a one-paragraph summary about each of these sources.

6. Using the same file and the same six articles, write the first draft of a library research report on the topic you chose in exercise 5. Make sure that your review contains elements of both synthesis and critique and covers all six articles that you have collected. When you have finished this draft, store it on the computer network in a place where other group members can have access to it or provide it to a specific group member on a disk.

   Take the file or the disk of a group member who has written a draft literature review. Complete the following tasks:

   a. Using the underlining feature, identify the sentence in your partner's report that seems to be the thesis sentence.

   b. In places where the author has relied primarily on synthesis, select the text and change it to italics.

   c. In places where the author has relied primarily on synthesis, select the text and change it to bold.

   d. Turning on the all caps key on your keyboard, skip to the end of the essay and write about the strengths and the weaknesses of the author's text in this current draft.

   e. Construct a sentence outline of your partner's essay at the end of his or her word-processing file. To accomplish this, select the thesis sentence of the essay and copy this text; then skip to the end of the essay and use the paste function to copy the item in the new location. Repeat these steps with the sentences that represent the main point of each paragraph.

   According to conventional outline form, indent the sentences that provide the main point of each paragraph in the appropriate way—indicating items that are subordinate by indenting them under items that are superordinate. When you are done, review this sentence outline to see if it makes sense—if the main points of each paragraph are clearly related to the thesis sentence of the essay. In places where the logic of the outline breaks down or is unclear, describe the problem to the essay's author. For this purpose, use the all caps feature and place your comments at the end of the file.

   f. Finally, at the very end of this file, provide your partner with suggestions for revising his or her essay. In providing these suggestions, refer both to the strengths of the essays and to its weaknesses. Put your suggestions in a smaller type font (use an 8 point font) to indicate that they are your text rather than the author's original words.

Writing a Personal Observation Report

Though you probably will not be asked to perform any inquiries that need statistical analysis, in some introductory social science courses you will be required to make and report on personal observations. In some instances, as in the student essay on pages 196–197 written for a psychology course, the experience will be set up for you. In other instances, you will be given only general guidelines about where to go to make your observations.

Before reading the student essay in preparation for writing an essay of your own, note how Ned Polsky describes his methods for gathering information about poolroom hustlers in his study, "The Hustler."

> My study of poolroom hustling extended over eight months. It proceeded by a combination of: (a) direct observation of hustlers as they hustled; (b) informal talks, sometimes hours long, with hustlers; (c) participant observation—as hustler's opponent, as hustler's backer, and as hustler. Since methods (b) and (c) drew heavily on my personal involvement with the poolroom world, indeed are inseparable from it, I summarize aspects of that involvement below.

Polsky, as you can see, is careful to note the combination of methods he employs in conducting his research. Now note how Vanessa responds to the following assignment, an experience set up for her and her classmates by her instructor, and the methods she uses.

> Go to the Learning Resource Center and take the Wechsler Adult Intelligence Scale–Revised. Make a personal reaction to that test, based upon the following: your test-taking experience, the application of an accepted definition of intelligence, an identification of the test's strengths, and an identification of the test's limitations.

Vanessa's instructor has specific goals in mind in making this assignment a meaningful learning experience for students. He specifies how the reaction must be made, assuring himself that his students will take into consideration pertinent information as they evaluate the Wechsler Adult Intelligence Scale–Revised. Here is Vanessa's response to the assignment.

Part I: My Test-Taking Experience

I never knew the structure of an intelligence test until given the Wechsler Adult Intelligence Scale–Revised. I went into testing not knowing what to expect and was surprised to find the WAIS–R more complex than anticipated.

I had not realized the test covered an extensive array of both verbal and performance strategies. Admittedly, the test was intellectually vigorous.

Fortunately, I had the opportunity to participate in the WAIS–R. I had never held an opinion about intelligence testing and now have strong reservations about it. From my experience with the WAIS–R, the test is an incomplete predictor of one's full intellectual capacity.

Part II: Application of a Definition of Intelligence

To gain a perspective on the criteria the WAIS–R might be testing for, I consulted Hallahan and Kauffman's working definition of the components that make up intelligence. According to Hallahan and Kauffman (1986), intellectual giftedness is defined on the basis of three principles: exceptional cognitive ability, significant creative ability, and superior task effectiveness. I concluded that perhaps the WAIS–R has structured its criteria to account for all three important factors of intelligence.

Part III: Strengths of the Test

I observed that the WAIS–R did indeed take all factors into account. The test consists of an abundance of steps testing cognitive abilities and task persistence: arithmetic, vocabulary, digit span, block design, picture arrangement, and coding. But I observed an insufficient amount testing creative and innovative aptitudes: general comprehension, similarities, and picture arrangement. In order to assess one's intellectual potential, an intelligence test should consider all three factors of intelligence. After my scores are tallied and IQ quotient revealed, I do not believe it will reflect my full intellectual capacities.

Part IV: Limitations of the Test

My full intellectual potential was not put to the test on the WAIS–R. Many steps on the test (general information, arithmetic, vocabulary, digit span, and block design) are straightforward, requiring either a right or wrong answer, leaving little room for creative and innovative thinking. I believe IQ should not be based solely on cognitive strategies and task performance.

A second problem with the WAIS–R are the questions in the general comprehension and general information sections. They are culturally and experience-biased. I did well on these portions, attributing my knowledge to a well-rounded education. The questions of literature, history, and geography were no problem. I am skeptical about people tested with the WAIS–R who have not obtained a well-rounded education. Can the WAIS–R correctly predict their IQ if they had not had the opportunity to develop it?

I did poorly on certain questions that require experience. One such question asks: ''If you are lost in the middle of the woods during the day without a compass how would you find your way out?'' Unfortunately, I never had the opportunity to acquire this knowledge; perhaps a Boy Scout could have answered correctly. Should a person be penalized due to an inadequate opportunity to acquire the necessary information?

In summary, the WAIS–R is a poor predictor of one's full intellectual capacity. I believe it does not accurately assess all the important factors of intelligence. I also believe the test to be culturally and experience-biased.

As you can see, this particular type of assignment, one performed quite often not only in introductory courses but on a grander scale by social scientists generally, requires the ability to make a certain type of interpretation of an experience, much as the humanist might interpret a literary work.

Exercises

1. Reread Vanessa's essay. Then assess the effectiveness of her essay by considering the following questions. Write your responses on a separate piece of paper.

   a. Has Vanessa followed instructions given to her in her assignment? Who has she envisioned as her audience? Has she addressed the subject as the instructions indicate she should? What seems to be her purpose in this essay? How does Vanessa portray herself through what she has written?

   b. Can you find a thesis statement in Vanessa's essay? Has she used more than one thesis statement? If so, for what purpose?

   c. Outline Vanessa's essay to see if you can figure out how her essay is organized. Are you satisfied that she has organized her thoughts appropriately? Describe her organizational strategy.

   d. What are the strengths of Vanessa's essay?

   e. What advice would you give Vanessa to help her revise this essay?

   Now compare your assessment of Vanessa's essay with a classmate's assessment.

2. Do the same assignment as Vanessa has done: Analyze any test you have taken since you have been in college (for example, a placement test, a class test, a fitness test, and so forth). Make a personal reaction to that test, based upon the following: your test-taking experience, the application of an accepted statement (for example, from a textbook) of how a test should be constructed and what a test-maker should set out to achieve, an identification of the test's strengths, and an identification of the test's limitations.

3. *If you have access to a computer and word-processing software,* open a new file and type into this file a copy of a test that you have taken sometime during the last two years in one of your high school or your college classes. Type in not only the questions that the teacher asked, but the actual answers that you gave. Use different fonts to differentiate your responses from the test questions. Don't change anything in your original responses, even if you now recognize it as erroneous. When you are done, save a copy of this file on two separate disks.

   On the first disk, review your own performance on the test. Using italics, insert annotations in specific places to indicate your first-hand observations on the test and on your responses. Make sure that these observations describe your personal reaction to the test and to its strengths and weaknesses in identifying the learning that you were supposed to have accomplished. Be sure to comment on how you think this test should be constructed to measure particular kinds of learning more effectively.

Trade the second disk with another member of your writing group— make sure that your partner has some familiarity with the subject matter of the test that you have included on your disk. On the disk from your partner, review the test that has been typed in along with the responses. On this disk, using italics, make notes in specific places to indicate your second-hand observations about the test and the answers that your partner provided. Make sure that these observations describe your reaction to the test and to its strengths and weaknesses in identifying the learning that your partner was supposed to have accomplished. Be sure to comment on how you think this test should be constructed to measure particular kinds of learning more effectively.

After completing this assignment, analyze and critique the accuracy of your own observations by speculating on the following questions, in writing: In analyzing the two tests (the one you took and the one your partner took) and the responses these tests generated, how did you differentiate between the limitations of the tests themselves and the limitations of the person taking the tests? In both tasks, what methodologies allowed you to get at these two kinds of limitations? What things prevented you from getting accurate answers to both? What problems can you see in connection with each of these two methods (that is, participant observation [looking at your own test answers] and observation and interpretation [looking at your partner's test answers])?

4. *If you have access to the Internet, use a browser* (for example, Netscape, Mosaic, Lynx) to locate five additional sources about the WAIS–R test that relate to the main points Vanessa has made in her essay. These articles should be ones that Vanessa could use in further developing the arguments she has already identified in connection with the test.

Using a word-processing package, create a new file and provide a complete citation (in APA format) for each of these articles. For each article, also provide a paragraph that summarizes the main arguments.

Writing an Application of Theory Report

In the absence of an opportunity in an introductory course to conduct statistical research of your own, you may very well be asked to write a paper that requires you to apply theories discussed in class. In some such papers, you might use personal observations, interviews, or surveys to gather information. In others, you might interpret behavior by employing a theory studied in class, in some instances, the behavior of characters in literature, as in the essay below by Tom, who has offered a psychological interpretation of Tennessee Williams' play *A Streetcar Named Desire,* "Blanche DuBois: Narcissistic Personality."

According to DSM–IV criteria, Blanche DuBois, the famous character of *A Streetcar Named Desire* clearly can be diagnosed as having a narcissistic personality disorder. In fact, she displays six of the nine DSM–IV criteria for the diagnosis of narcissistic disorder.

First, Blanche displays contemptuous and disdainful behaviors. Blanche, arriving at her sister Stella's apartment for the first time, disapproves of its lower-class condition. Blanche is shocked to find Stella inhabiting a humble dwelling, believing herself and her sister accustomed to refined accommodations.

Second, throughout her visit, Blanche displays a contemptuous attitude toward Stella's modest lifestyle and blue collar husband. Blanche lacks the kindred support that her sister needs. Her lack of understanding and unwillingness to recognize the feelings of Stella defines the second criteria necessary for the diagnosis of a narcissistic personality.

Third, Blanche believes she is unique. Her arrogant disposition causes conflict between herself and the other characters in the play. She believes herself refined and worldly, superior to the others. Blanche believes that she retains the reputation of a wealthy, high societal woman and should only associate with millionaire friend, Shep Huntleigh.

In addition, throughout the play, Blanche considers herself as possessing great beauty, magnificence, and admirers. But Blanche's youthful beauty has faded over the years and her admirers have ceased, existing in her imagination only. Blanche's fantasies of beauty and brilliance are characteristic of the fourth criteria for diagnosis.

Not only does Blanche fantasize her brilliance and charm, but she requires excess of others' esteem for her beauty. Throughout the play, Blanche expects to be complimented on her superior attractiveness. Blanche's need for extreme adoration justifies the fifth criteria for the diagnosis of a narcissistic personality. She remarks to her sister, "You haven't said a word about my appearance" (21). Seeking a compliment from Stanley, she asks, "Would you think it possible that I was once considered to be attractive?" (39). Stella constantly reminds others in the play to "be sure to say something nice" about her appearance (33).

Finally, Blanche expects others to comply with her every wish, the sixth diagnosable criteria. During Blanche's visit, she expects her sister to wait on her every need. Blanche remarks to her sister, "I have to admit I love to be waited on . . ." (79). Stella indicates that Blanche has always required favorable treatment: "I like to wait on you, Blanche. It makes it seem more like home" (79).

Blanche DuBois can be diagnosed as displaying a narcissistic personality disorder. She exhibits a prevalent display of pomposity, an excessive requirement of adoration, and a lack of understanding and support for others.

1. Answer the following questions on a separate piece of paper.
   a. What is Tom's thesis statement? Do you believe he adequately supports his observation?
   b. What theory does Tom apply to *A Streetcar Named Desire?* Is his application sensible to you?
   c. What are the six characteristics of narcisistic behavior disorder that Tom points out? List them and compare your list with a classmate's. Together with your classmate, develop a composite list.
   d. Apply four of these characteristics to any character you have read about, seen on television or in a movie, or known personally. Briefly describe how these characteristics fit the character you have in mind. In the process of applying these characteristics, you might decide that the person you have in mind is not, in fact, narcissistic.
   e. Write a short essay, about the length of Tom's, in which you apply the four characteristics of narcissism to the character identified in *d.*
2. *If you have access to the Internet,* use a browser (for example, Netscape, Mosaic, Lynx) to locate five additional sources about the play *A Streetcar Named Desire,* the character of Blanche DuBois, and narcissism that Tom could use to support the points that he makes in his essay.

   Using a word-processing package, create a new file and provide a complete citation (in APA format) for each of these articles. For each article, also provide a paragraph that tells how Tom could use this article to further develop a point that he has made.
3. *If you have access to the Internet, use a browser* (for example, Netscape, Mosaic, Lynx) to locate five additional sources about the DSMV–IV. *If you do not have access to the Internet,* go to your library and use the on-line resources to locate a similar set of sources. If your library has the *Psychlit* database, you may want to use that tool.

   Read the articles you locate, and use them to write answers to the following questions. Be sure to use the proper in-text citation format to document the sources for the information you paraphrase, quote, or summarize. Consult your grammar book or your teacher for help in this matter.
   • What is the DSMV–IV and what is it used for? By whom?
   • What have critics identified as the strengths and the weaknesses of the DSMV–IV?
   • Why was the DSMV recently revised? What are the important issues associated with its revision?

Now read Ned Polsky's study of poolroom hustlers on the following pages. Note how Polsky adapts theories of occupational sociology to approach hustling as an occupation.

THE HUSTLER*

Ned Polsky

Such a man spends all his life playing every day for small stakes. Give him every morning the money that he may gain during the day, on condition that he does not play—you will make him unhappy. It will perhaps be said that what he seeks is the amusement of play, not gain. Let him play then for nothing; he will lose interest and be wearied.

—Blaise Pascal

They talk about me not being on the legitimate. Why, lady, nobody's on the legit when it comes down to cases; you know that.

—Al Capone[1]

The poolroom hustler makes his living by betting against his opponents in different types of pool or billiard games, and as part of the playing and betting process he engages in various deceitful practices. The terms "hustler" for such a person and "hustling" for his occupation have been in poolroom argot for decades, antedating their application to prostitutes. Usually the hustler plays with his own money, but often he makes use of a "backer." In the latter event the standard arrangement is that the backer, in return for assuming all risk of loss, receives half of the hustler's winnings.

The hustler's offense in the eyes of many is not that he breaks misdemeanor laws against gambling (perhaps most Americans have done so at one time or another), but that he does so daily. Also—and again as a necessary and regular part of his daily work—he violates American norms concerning (a) what is morally correct behavior toward one's fellow man and (b) what is a proper and fitting occupation. For one or another of these related reasons the hustler is stigmatized by respectable outsiders. The most knowledgeable of such outsiders see the hustler not merely as a gambler but as one who violates an ethic of fair dealing, they regard him as a criminal or quasi-criminal not because he gambles but because he systematically "victimizes" people. Somewhat less knowledgeable outsiders put down the hustler simply because gambling is his trade. Still less knowledgeable outsiders (perhaps the majority) regard hustlers as persons who, whatever they may actually do, certainly do not hold down visibly respectable jobs; therefore this group also stigmatizes hustlers—"poolroom bums" is the classic phrase—and believes that society would be better off without them. Hustling, to the degree that it is known to the larger society at all, is classed with that large group of social problems composed of morally deviant occupations.

---

[1]The Pascal quotation is from Pensées, V. Al Capone's remark is quoted in Paul Sann, *The Lawless Decade* (New York: Crown Publishers, 1957), p. 214.

However, in what follows, I try to present hustlers and hustling on their own terms. The material below avoids a "social problems" focus; to some extent, I deliberately reverse that focus. Insofar as I treat social problems, they are not the problems posed by the hustler but for him, not the difficulties he creates for others, but the difficulties that others create for him as he pursues his career.

This approach "from within" has partly dictated the organization of my materials. Some sections below are built around conceptual categories derived less from sociologists than from hustlers, in the hope that this may help the reader to see hustling more nearly as hustlers see it. The disadvantage for the scientifically minded reader is that the underlying sociological framework may be obscured. Therefore I wish to point out that this framework is basically that of Everett Hughes's approach to occupational sociology.

I try mainly to answer three types of questions: *(a) The work situation.* How is the hustler's work structured? What skills are required of him? With whom does he interact on the job? What does he want from them, and how does he try to get it? How do they make it easy or hard for him? *(b) Careers.* Who becomes a hustler? How? What job risks or contingencies does the hustler face? When and how? What is the nature of colleagueship in hustling? What are the measures of success and failure in the career? In what ways does aging affect the hustler's job skills or ability to handle other career problems? What leads to retirement? *(c) The external world.* What is the place of the hustler's work situation and career in the large society? What changes in the structure of that society affect his work situation or career?

PREVIOUS RESEARCH

A bibliographic check reveals no decent research on poolroom hustling, sociological or otherwise. Apart from an occasional work of fiction in which hustling figures, there are merely a few impressionistic accounts in newspapers and popular magazines. With a couple of exceptions, each article is based on interviews with only one or two hustlers. No article analyzes hustling on any but the most superficial level or provides a well-rounded description. The fullest survey of the subject not only omits much that is vital, but contains numerous errors of fact and interpretation.[2]

The desirability of a study of hustling first struck me upon hearing comments by people who saw the movie *The Hustler* (late 1961, rereleased spring 1964).

---

[2]Jack Olsen, "The Pool Hustlers," *Sport Illustrated,* Vol. 14 (March 20, 1961), pp. 71–77. Jack Richardson's "The Noblest Hustlers," (*Esquire,* Vol IX (September, 1963), pp. 94, 96, 98) contains a few worthwhile observations, but it is sketchy, ill-balanced, and suffers much from editorial garbling, all of which makes it both confusing and misleading for the uninitiated. One article conveys quite well the lifestyle of a particular hustler: Dale Shaw, "Anatomy of a Pool Hustler," *Saga: The Magazine for Men,* Vol. 23 (November, 1961), pp. 52–55, 91–93. Useful historical data are in Edward John Vogeler's "The Passing of the Pool Shark," *American Mercury,* Vol. 8 (November, 1939), pp. 346–51. For hustling as viewed within the context of the history of pool in America, see Robert Coughlan's "Pool: Its Players and Its Sharks," *Life,* Vol. 31 (October 8, 1951), pp. 159 ff.; although Coughlan's account of the game's history contains errors and his specific consideration of hustling is brief (p. 166) the latter is accurate.

Audience members who are not poolroom habitués regard the movie as an accurate portrait of the comtemporary hustling "scene." The movie does indeed truly depict some social characteristics of pool and billiard hustlers and some basic techniques of hustling. But it neglects others of crucial importance. Moreover, the movie scarcely begins to take proper account of the social structure within which hustling techniques are used and which strongly affects their use. *The Hustler* is a reasonably good but highly selective reflection of the poolroom hustling scene as it existed not later than the mid-1930s. And as a guide in today's hustling scene—the terms on which it presents itself and on which the audience takes it—the movie is quite misleading.

METHOD AND SAMPLE

My study of poolroom hustling extended over eight months. It proceeded by a combination of: (a) direct observation of hustlers as they hustled; (b) informal talks, sometimes hours long, with hustlers; (c) participant observation—as hustler's opponent, as hustler's backer, and as hustler. Since methods (b) and (c) drew heavily on my personal involvement with the poolroom world, indeed are inseparable from it, I summarize aspects of that involvement below.

Billiard playing is my chief recreation. I have frequented poolrooms for over 20 years, and at one poolroom game, three-cushion billiards, am considered a far better than average player. In recent years I have played an average of more than six hours per week in various New York poolrooms, and played as much in the poolrooms of Chicago for most of the eight years I lived there. In the course of traveling I have played occasionally in the major rooms of other cities, such as the poolrooms on Market Street in San Francisco, West 25th Street in Cleveland, West Lexington in Baltimore, and the room on 4th and Main in Los Angeles.

My social background is different from that of the overwhelming majority of adult poolroom players. The latter are of lower-class origin. As with many American sports (e.g., baseball), pool and billiards are played by teenagers from all classes but only the players of lower-class background tend to continue far into adulthood. (And as far as poolroom games are concerned, even at the teenage level the lower class contributes a disproportionately large share of players.) But such differences—the fact that I went to college, do highbrow work, etc.—create no problems of acceptance. In most good-sized poolrooms the adult regulars usually include a few people like myself who are in the poolroom world but not of it. They are there because they like to play, and are readily accepted because they like to play.

The poolroom I play in most regularly is the principal "action room" in New York and perhaps in the country, the room in which heavy betting on games occurs most often, sometimes, particularly after 1:00 A.M. the hustlers in the room well outnumber the non-hustlers. Frequently I play hustlers for money (nearly always on a handicap basis) and occasionally I hustle some non-hustlers, undertaking the latter activity primarily to recoup losses on the former. I have been a backer for two hustlers.

I know six hustlers well, and during the eight months of the study I talked or played with over 50 more. . . . It seems safe to assume that the sample is at least representative of big-city hustlers. Also, it is probable that it includes the majority of part-time hustlers in New York, and certain that it includes a good majority of the full-time hustlers in New York.

THE HUSTLER'S METHODS OF DECEPTION

The structure of a gambling game determines what methods of deception, if any, may be used in it. In many games (dice, cards, etc.) one can deceive one's opponent by various techniques of cheating. Pool and billiard games are so structured that this method is virtually impossible. (Once in a great while, against a particularly unalert opponent, one can surreptitiously add a point or two to one's score—but such opportunity is rare, usually involves risk of discovery that is judged to be too great, and seldom means the difference between winning and losing anyway, so no player counts on it.) One's every move and play is completely visible, easily watched by one's opponent and by spectators; nor is it possible to achieve anything via previous tampering with the equipment.

However, one structural feature of pool or billiards readily lends itself to deceit: on each shot, the difference between success and failure is a matter of a small fraction of an inch. In pool or billiards it is peculiarly easy, even for the average player, to miss one's shot deliberately and still look good (unlike, say, nearly all card games, where if one does not play one's cards correctly this is soon apparent). On all shots except the easiest ones, it is impossible to tell if a player is deliberately not trying his best.

The hustler exploits this fact so as to deceive his opponent as to his (the hustler's) true level of skill (true "speed"). It is so easily exploited that, when playing good opponents, usually the better hustlers even disdain it, pocket nearly every shot they have (intentionally miss only some very difficult shots), and rely chiefly on related but subtler techniques of failure beyond the remotest suspicion of most players. For example, such a hustler may strike his cue ball hard and with too much spin ("english"), so that the spin is transferred to the object ball and the object ball goes into the pocket but jumps out again, or he may scratch (losing a point and his turn), either by "accidentally" caroming his cue ball into a pocket or by hitting his cue ball hard and with too much top-spin so that it jumps off the table, or, most commonly, he pockets his shot but, by striking his cue ball just a wee bit too hard or too softly or with too much or too little english, he leaves himself "safe" (ends up with his cue ball out of position, so that he hasn't another shot). In such ways the hustler feigns less competence than he has.

Hustling, then, involves not merely the ability to play well, but the use of a kind of "short con." Sometimes the hustler doesn't need to employ any con to get his opponent to the table, sometimes he does; but he always employs it in attempting to keep his opponent there.

The best hustler is not necessarily the best player among the hustlers. He has to be a very good player, true, but beyond a certain point his playing ability is not nearly so important as his skill at various kinds of conning. Also, he has to possess personality traits that make him "rocklike," able to exploit fully his various skills—playing, conning, others—in the face of assorted pressures and temptations not to exploit them fully.

JOB-RELATED SKILLS AND TRAITS

Although the hallmarks of the good hustler are playing skill and the temperamental ability to consistently look poorer than he is, there are other skills and traits that aid him in hustling. Some are related to deceiving his opponent, some not.

Chief of these is argumentative skill in arranging the terms of the match, the ability to "make a game." The prospective opponent, if he has seen the hustler play, may when approached claim that the hustler is too good for him or ask for too high a spot (i.e., one that is fair or even better). The hustler, like the salesman, is supposed to be familiar with standard objections and "propositions" for overcoming them.

Another side of the ability to make a game reveals itself when the prospective opponent simply can't be argued out of demanding a spot that is unfair to the hustler, or can be convinced to play only if the hustler offers such a spot. At that point the hustler should of course refuse to play. There is often a temptation to do otherwise, not only because the hustler is proud of his skill but because action is his lifeblood (which is why he plays other hustlers when he can't find a hustle), and there may be no other action around. He must resist the temptation. In the good hustler's view, no matter how badly you want action, it is better not to play at all than to play when you are disadvantaged; otherwise you are just hustling yourself. (But the hustler often will, albeit with much argument and the greatest reluctance, agree to give a fair spot if that's the only way he can get action.)

The hustler, when faced, as he very often is, with an opponent who knows him as such, of course finds that his ability to make a game assumes greater importance than his ability to feign lack of skill. In such situations, indeed, his gamemaking ability is just as important as his actual playing ability.

On the other hand, the hustler must have "heart" (courage). The *sine qua non* is that he is a good "money player," can play his best when heavy action is riding on the game (as many non-hustlers can't). Also, he is not supposed to let a bad break or distractions in the audience upset him. (He may pretend to get rattled on such occasions, but that's just part of his con.) Nor should the quality of his game deteriorate when, whether by miscalculation on his part or otherwise, he finds himself much further behind than he would like to be. Finally, if it is necessary to get action, he should not be afraid to tackle an opponent whom he knows to be just about as good as he is.

A trait often working for the hustler is stamina. As a result of thousands of hours of play, all the right muscles are toughened up. He is used to playing many hours at a time, certainly much more used to it than the non-hustler is. This is valuable because sometimes, if the hustler works it right, he can make his opponent forget about quitting for such a "silly" reason as being tired, can extend their session through the night and into the next day. In such sessions it is most often in the last couple of hours, when the betting per game is usually highest, that the hustler makes his biggest killing.

Additional short-con techniques are sometimes used. One hustler, for example, entices opponents by the ancient device of pretending to be sloppy-drunk. Other techniques show more imagination. For example, a hustler preparing for a road trip mentioned to me that before leaving town he was going to buy a soldier's uniform. "I walk into a strange room in uniform and I've got it made. Everybody likes to grab a soldier."

Finally, the hustler—the superior hustler at any rate—has enough flexibility and good sense to break the "rules" when the occasion demands it, will modify standard techniques when he encounters nonstandard situations. An example: Once I entered a poolroom just as a hustler I know, X, was finishing a game with non-hustler Y. X beat Y soundly, by a higher margin than a hustler should beat anyone, and at that for only $3. Y went to the bathroom, whereupon I admonished X, "What's the matter with you? You know you're not allowed to win that big." X replied:

> Yeah, sure, but you see that mother-fucking S over there? (nodding discreetly in the direction of one of the spectators). Well, about an hour ago when I came in he and Y were talking, and when S saw me he whispered something to Y. So I had a hunch he was giving him the wire (tipping him off) that I was pretty good. And then in his middle game it looked like Y was stalling a little (missing deliberately) to see what I would do, so then I was sure he got the wire on me. I had to beat him big so he'll think he knows my top speed. But naturally I didn't beat him as big as I could beat him. Now he'll come back cryin' for a spot and bigger action, and I'll nail him.

And he did nail him.

THE HUSTLER AS CON MAN

As several parts of this study illustrate in detail, hustling demands a continuous and complicated concern with how one is seen by others. Attention to this matter is an ineluctably pervasive requirement of the hustler's trade, and is beset with risks and contradictions. The hustler has not only the concerns that one ordinarily has about being esteemed for one's skills, but develops, in addition to and partly in conflict with such concerns, a complex set of special needs or desires about how others should evaluate him, reactions to their evaluations, and behaviors designed to manipulate such evaluating.

The hustler is a certain kind of con man. And conning, by definition, involves extraordinary manipulation of other people's impressions of reality and especially of one's self, creating "false impressions."[3] If one compares the hustler with the more usual sorts of con men described by David Maurer in *The Big Con*, part of the hustler's specialness is seen to lie in this: The structural contexts within which he operates—the game, the setting of the game within the poolroom, the setting of the poolroom within the larger social structure— are not only more predetermined but more constraining. Structures do not "work for" the poolroom hustler to anywhere near the extent that they often do for other con men, and hence he must involve himself in more personal ways with active, continuous conning.

The point is not simply that the hustler can't find an ideal structural context, but that much less than the ordinary con man is he able to bend a structure toward the ideal or create one *ab ovo* (come up with an analogue of the con man's "store"). That is, the hustler is far less able to be a "producer" or "director" of ideal social "scenes." To a much greater extent he must work in poor settings, and to a correspondingly greater extent he must depend on being a continuously self-aware "actor."[4]

The hustler needs to be continually concerned about evaluation of him by other persons. But the nature and degree of his concern vary with the particular kind of "others" that these persons represent. The victim or prospective victim, the hustler's orientation toward whom we have discussed at several points, is only one kind of other. Obviously the hustler must take cognizance of at least two additional types of significant others: outsiders and colleagues. . . .

CONCLUSIONS

. . . Here I would like to point out certain other findings that seem to have no analogue in the literature of occupational sociology.

(1) The work situation. We saw that the hustler must be not only a skilled player, but that he must be skilled at pretending *not* to have great playing skill. . . . As far as I know, this hustling reliance on competence at feigning incompetence is unique, and nowhere treated in the occupational literature.

(2) Careers. Certain occupational roles require youthfulness by definition (e.g., acting juvenile parts), and thus enforce unusually early retirement. In

---

[3]Of course, conning is only a matter of degree, in that all of us are concerned in many ways to manipulate others' impressions of us, and so one can, if one wishes, take the view that every man is at bottom a con man. This form of "disenchantment of the world" is essential to Herman Melville's *The Confidence Man* (one of the bitterest novels in all of American literature) and to the sociological writings of Ervin Goffman. It's principal corollary is the view expressed by hustlers, by other career criminals, and by Thorstein Veblen, that all businessmen are thieves.

[4]The kinds of structural problems faced today by the pool or billiard hustler are by no means all endemic. Some are the result of recent social change. On the other hand, such change does not create structural problems for all types of hustling. Today the golf hustler, for example, finds that with precious little "acting" he can (a) get heavy action from non-hustlers, (b) lose the good majority of the 18 holes and still clean up, and at the same time (c) not be suspected as a hustler. The structure of the game of golf itself, the peculiar structurally predetermined variations in the betting relationship as one makes the round of the course ("presses," etc.), and the present setting of the game within the larger society—all these combine to create a situation that is tailor-made for hustling. But that is another story.

certain other occupations (airline pilots, for example) age-related career contingencies also force early retirement. It is common to cite competitive sports or games requiring high physical skills as examples of this type—but pool or billiard playing doesn't fit the pattern.

(3) The external world. We saw that changes in American sporting life over the past three decades have severely damaged the hustler's work situation and career. These changes have reduced the number of places he can hustle in, the time-span in which he can stay unknown, the number of people he can hustle, and the average amount of money he can get from someone he hustles. Hustling is a dying trade.

Whenever an occupational group faces a disappearance or major decline of the market for its skills and a consequent inability to make ends meet, we conceptualize this situation as "technological unemployment." But this concept doesn't fit the situation of hustlers at all well. They suffer not from a shift in technology but from a shift in America's demographic structure, i.e., the decline of the bachelor subculture that populated poolrooms so heavily, and secondarily from a shift in fashion, i.e., the decline in the average amount of money bet on poolroom games. . . .

A more general lesson of this essay is that sociology has unduly neglected the study of people who engage in sports or games for their livelihood. The sociological reason for this neglect is that sociology is compartmentalized into "fields" that tend to make such people, for all their visibility to the sociologist as citizen, invisible to him in his role as sociologist. Such people are neglected by students of leisure because the latter are by definition concerned with sports involvement only in its impact on avocational life, and because sports involvement is for the very great majority of people strictly avocational, and those who earn a living at it constitute a minuscule fragment of the labor force, the study of the latter is neglected by occupational sociologists. Thus a largely unexplored area of social research consists of the people who work at what most of us play at.

Exercises

1. Reread Polsky's study and then answer these questions on a separate sheet of paper.
   a. What is Polsky's thesis in his study of poolroom hustlers?
   b. How does he support his thesis? Describe by outlining what organizational strategy he follows.
   c. Make a list of similar "occupations" you know about.
   d. Make a list of occupations that interest you.
2. Using Polsky's study as a model, write an analysis of any one occupation listed in *c* or *d* above. You should gather information first in the following sequence.
   a. Use the library to discover what has already been written about the occupation you have chosen to study.

    b. Contact a person employed in the occupation you intend to study and interview that person. Be sure to make a list of questions that will satisfy your need for specific information.

    c. Organize your paper as Polsky has organized his and as discussed below: introduction, previous research, method and sample, special occupational information (for example, "the hustler's methods of deception"), job-related skills and traits, and conclusions.

Introductory Material: Note that in Polsky's introduction he makes certain specific points about pool hustling as an occupation: how the hustler makes a living, how the professional pool hustler is viewed by others (that is, the pool hustler's status in American society), how he intends to study pool hustlers, what his approach will entail, and what kinds of questions he plans on answering. Your introduction should attempt to include these general categories of information as well.

Previous Research: This section has many characteristics in common with what we have described in this chapter as the library research study (see pages 188–190). This section gives the writer an opportunity to cite relevant research studies and, in so doing, make the point that the research to be reported is the next logical step in ongoing inquiries into the subject. Unlike the library research report, which begins with a thesis statement and then uses research studies for support, this section of Polsky's report uses research studies to lead up to a thesis or, in the social sciences, a hypothesis.

Method and Sample: In this section, Polsky simply identifies how he has gathered information. In his case, Polsky has used direct observations, informal talks, and participation to better understand pool hustlers as professionals.

Special Occupational Information: Some occupations require certain behaviors that might be reported upon in this section. The poolroom hustler uses deception as a part of his occupation. Polsky, as a result, discusses in depth this particular essential component of the poolroom hustler's skills.

Job-Related Skills and Traits: Polsky describes certain skills poolroom hustlers possess, in addition to "playing skill and the temperamental ability to consistently look poorer than he is. . . ." These skills include argumentative skill in arranging the terms of the match and an ability to adjust the argument to meet specific demands of the hustler as Polsky describes them.

Conclusions: Polsky enumerates his conclusions, reflecting the three questions highlighted in the introduction. He reaches conclusions about the work situation, careers in poolroom hustling, and the way poolroom hustlers are viewed in the external world. For Polsky, however, a more general service has been performed: He has demonstrated that "sociology has unduly neglected the study of people who engage in sports or games for their livelihood."

3. *If you have access to the World Wide Web or Gopher space,* complete an electronic version of exercise 1*d*—that is, use *only* electronic sources to complete your study of an occupation that interests you. You can gather information from your library using on-line resources such as the *Psychlit* database, use a browser on the Internet to gather information about the profession you have chosen, use e-mail to contact and correspond with people in that profession, use a word-processing package to write an anlaysis of the profession. Make sure that you identify and use no fewer than eight substantial on-line sources to write the draft of your essay. Also be sure to include complete bibliographic citations on these sources.

Organize your paper as Polsky organized his, using the following sections: introduction, previous research, method and sample, occupational information, job-related skills and traits, conclusions.

When you have completed your essay, compare the results you have gotten to those that Polsky reports by using nonelectronic sources. In writing, discuss any differences and similarities that you can identify.

4. *If you have access to the World Wide Web or Gopher space,* use a browser (for example, Netscape, Mosaic, Lynx) to locate five additional sources that you can use to further develop Polsky's essay. *If you do not have access to the Internet,* go to your library and use the on-line resources to locate a similar set of sources. If your library has the *Psychlit* database, you may want to use that tool.

As an exercise in imitating a professional social scientist and his style, use the information in these sources to write five paragraphs that could be inserted into Polsky's essay at various points—use a word-processing package. Make sure that the style of these paragraphs—as well as their organization, tone, use of detail, voice, and perspective—matches that of Polsky's writing as closely as possible. Your purpose is to write five new paragraphs based on the additional sources you find that a casual reader would think that Polsky himself wrote. You will also want to indicate exactly where you would insert these paragraphs in Polsky's essay.

Remember that this is just an exercise in imitation to sharpen your skill in writing like professional social scientists, and you will not want to use a similar approach when asked to undertake your own original work. Under these circumstances, merely imitating other professionals—adhering slavishly to others' perspectives, style, or insights without contributing original thinking and observations of your own—is considered unacceptable and wrong. When you are just beginning to learn how to write like a social scientist, however, such an exercise can be useful, especially if you take care to recognize both the benefits and the limitations of imitation, and to identify your own work as yours and others' work as theirs.

URLs for the Social Sciences

Social Sciences—General Resources
http://bib10.sub.su.se/sam/ssdata.html

Social Sciences—Anthropology
http://www.einet.net/galaxy/Social-Sciences.html

WorldWide Guide to Social Science
http://www.theworld.com/HUMANITI/SOCIALSC/SUBJECT.HTML

Humanities, Social Sciences
http://www.lib.umich.edu/chouse/inter/408.html

Di's Online Cafe—Social Science
http://www.dibbs.net/socsci.html

More Social Science Links
http://sun.soci.niu.edu/other/socilinks.html

Social Sciences—General Resources
http://bib10.sub.su.se/sam/ssdata.html

Other Social Science Mosaic Sites
http://augustus.csscr.washington.edu/personal/fred-mosaic/other_ss.html

Sociology
http://hakatai.mcli.dist.maricopa.edu/smc/ml/sociology.html

Cool Social Science Links
http://bowler.dacc.wisc.edu/coollinks.html

Sociology/Social Work
http://www.lib.lsu.edu/soc/sociology.html

CHAPTER SEVEN

Writing in the Natural Sciences

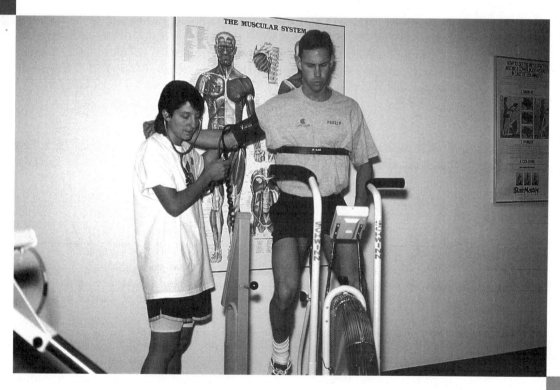

Divisions between the Humanities and the Sciences

Responsibilities of Natural Scientists

Importance of Communications to the Natural Scientist

Connecting Writing in Liberal Arts and Social Sciences
to Writing in the Natural Sciences

The Writing of a Professional Scientist

Writing in the Undergraduate Natural Sciences

Many of you have chosen or are considering choosing a major in a scientific field that will require you to take advanced courses in that area. After graduation you may choose to enter a career related to those majors. These choices may lead you to very important positions, for advanced societies place great value on the knowledge represented in these scientific disciplines. In order to understand the work done by scientists, their relationship to other professions, and the place of scientists in our society, let us begin with the following quotation. Almost forty years ago, the eminent British scientist and writer C. P. Snow identified a problem in *The Two Cultures* which still concerns us today.

Literary intellectuals at one pole—at the other scientists, and as the most representative, the physical scientists. Between the two a gulf of mutual incomprehension—sometimes (particularly among the young) hostility and dislike, but most of all lack of understanding. They have a curiously distorted image of each other. Their attitudes are so different that, even on the level of emotion, they can't find much common ground.

Divisions between the Humanities and the Sciences

In his remarks, Snow addresses an issue which still divides much of the academic and professional communities of many countries: Those who are trained in the liberal arts (for example, literature, art, music) and those trained as scientists (for example, chemists, geologists, biologists, and physicists) are often at odds concerning the exploration of ideas, the value of specific kinds of knowledge, and the roles of scientists and humanists in society. In truth, the rapid growth of technology over the past forty years and the increased emphasis on math and science education have created even deeper rifts in some communities. Importantly, however, some organizations are beginning to bridge these splits to find common ground for exploring ideas.

As the world is made increasingly smaller through telecommunication and global competition, many scientists and humanists are recognizing their shared interests and the necessity to promote those interests to achieve both individual and organizational success. Further, as research in the sciences reveals such far-reaching knowledge as the biochemical and neurological structure of human beings and the molecular structure of agricultural food stuffs, discussions focusing on the ethical issues related to scientific work and the application of the work in society have assumed an important place in academic institutions, in many corporate and business organizations, and in society as a whole. In other words, various cultures are debating these critically important questions, the answers to which will dramatically affect our future and the future of the planet.

College students have not been immune from the effects of the decades-old division. Often, students in the sciences view those in the humanities as taking "soft" courses which rely on "natural" talents, related to speaking and writing, while many humanities students think of science majors as weird people who spend all their time in laboratories, separated from the joys of youth. And, often, both groups of students are resistant to courses which they view as foreign to their interests. For students in the sciences, such courses as sociology, literature, and, yes, writing are frequently included in that group.

Regardless of their attitude toward writing, most college science students know that they will be required to write laboratory reports; more and more, however, science faculty require their students to write not only laboratory reports, but also term papers, critical reviews of journal articles, essay answers on examinations, and an increasingly popular form in science classes, the "micro theme." Like engineers, professional scientists must maintain a record of their work which can be legally certified. Thus, partly as a means of preparing them for their work as professional scientists, many professors require their students to keep a journal in which they record observations on experiments and fieldwork. Over the past ten years, college science faculty have turned increasingly to writing assignments for the following two major reasons:

1. to determine whether their students understand and can apply the course material, as opposed to simply memorizing a set of facts; and
2. to prepare their students for the tasks they will assume in graduate and professional schools, as well as their work as college-educated professionals schooled in the sciences.

In this chapter we shall cover examples from both points. Before doing so, we ask that you consider the following list of occupations entered by persons who obtain majors in science. It should provide a clear indication of not only the job possibilities for science majors, but also the potential tasks fulfilled by such persons.

Health Fields
medicine, dentistry, chiropractic, nursing, physical and occupational therapy

Business and Industry
agri-chemical, household and personal products, food production, manufacturing

Education and Government
K–12 teaching, post-secondary education
Departments of Agriculture, Wildlife, Natural Resources

Sales
pharmaceuticals, agri-chemicals, military products, food products

Responsibilities of Natural Scientists

While the previous list doesn't cover all the careers entered by science graduates, it does provide a glance into the diversity of positions held by such graduates.

The range of work and work environments for scientific professions is, indeed, broad. Some work directly with engineers, such as those in food industry positions, where a chemist might serve on a product-development task force with manufacturing engineers who design the machines that produce the food products. Other scientific professionals enter medical fields and become dentists, surgeons, optometrists, or podiatrists. Some become wildlife biologists and work either very close to urban areas or in wildlife areas deep into back-country sanctuaries, while still others become salespersons for pharmaceutical or agri-chemical companies and interact with a myriad of other professionals.

As you can probably tell from the list of potential careers, all of them bear directly on the quality of our everyday and future lives. Whether these graduates go into sales, become educators, or test products critical to our personal health, all bear substantial positions of responsibility. Since very few of us produce our own food; construct our vehicles; or grow, harvest, and refine our medicines, we depend directly on these professionals for our well-being. Thus, we expect them—and, of course, many of you will become "them"—to be knowledgeable in the subject matter of their fields, as well as ethical in their concern for the general society.

Moreover, like almost all occupations today and in the foreseeable future, graduates of scientific disciplines will find themselves working daily with persons from a variety of specialities; all of this work will be communicated either verbally or in writing, or both. Additionally, many scientific professionals communicate regularly with a wide range of other people—for example, customers, government and media representatives, and employees of other companies.

Exercises

1. Discuss the following questions with a partner or group: Do you know a college graduate who majored in a scientific field? If so, what kind of work does that person do? With whom does the person work? Have you ever seen any writing that the person has done? Based on your answers to these questions, together with your partner (or group members) write a description of the person's work.

2. Discuss the following questions with a partner or group, and write down your answers to them. Have you done any science writing, either in school or for a job? If so, what characterized that writing? Who were the audiences? How did that writing differ from writing you have done for another academic discipline? If you have written for science classes, what criteria were used to evaluate the writing? Make a list of these specifics by question and share them with the other groups in the class.

3. Quite often the popular media will carry a story on a person who has discovered a problem related to developing a product for their company. Oftentimes, this person is a scientist or a person who is trained as a scientist and who has determined that the product as developed may pose a threat to the proposed market for the product or for another group in the general

population. Using your college library or other search sources (for example, an on-line search service), find an example of such a case and write a one-paragraph summary of the case and how the person communicated this problem to the media.

4. *If you have access to a computer network with e-mail,* locate and subscribe to an on-line discussion or newsgroup that involves individuals working in a field of the natural sciences in which you are interested. Use the list on page 215 for help in thinking of such fields. For help in locating an appropriate on-line discussion, go to the library or a local bookstore and find a book on the Internet that provides a subject-focused index of on-line discussions and newsgroups. Seek help from your campus computing experts, knowledgeable friends, the technology consultant in the lab you use, or your teacher in subscribing to the list.

   Closely observe the conversation on this list for four days. Then, using your observations, write a summary about the kinds of work the scientists on this discussion list do, the kinds of questions and problems they pursue, and the kinds of people with whom they work.

5. *If you have access to a computer network and access to the Internet,* use a browser (for example, Netscape, Mosaic, Lynx) to search Gopher space or the World Wide Web and locate five sources on professions (or a profession) in the natural sciences, sources that would let other students know what scientists do, where they work, what professional options they can choose from, what problems they are currently attacking.

   Explore each of these five sites, and, using a word-processing package, write a summary paragraph describing what you found there. Be sure to record the Gopher-site address or the Universal Resource Locator (URL) address on the Web.

Importance of Communications to the Natural Scientist

While there are numerous differences among the scientific disciplines, there are two common points shared by all the sciences:

1. Scientific knowledge is based on observation and experimentation.
2. Scientific knowledge must be communicated to take its place in the field of knowledge.

Consider for a moment the massive amount of information necessary to communicate one scientific principle or law.

If you wanted to communicate to someone the law of gravity, how would you do that? Would you simply point to the sky and say that anything that's in the sky will fall? How fast would the object fall? Would factors affect the speed of the falling object? Of course, we know the answers to most of these questions because we have taken physics or physical science courses in school.

Also, we know the answers to these questions because scientists grappled with them for centuries until Isaac Newton conducted the appropriate experiments, observed the phenomena, recorded the results, retested what he believed were the results, recorded those results, then postulated the theory we now regard as a law of physics. Had Newton not recorded any of his observations, how would he have known exactly what happened from one experiment to the next? In short, science as we know it could not exist without recording information and then shaping that information into clear explanations and persuasively structured arguments. Thus, scientific writing involves much more than just reporting what has happened. It is the *careful presentation of observations, tests, hypotheses, theories, and laws.* As we proceed in this chapter, keep in mind the following personal definition of science offered by chemistry professor Roald Hoffmann from Cornell University, for we shall touch upon all of the points of his definition. In part, he says:

1. Science is the acquisition of knowledge about the world.
2. Science is part discovery, part creation.
3. Science is done by human beings and their tools.
4. Science proceeds in part by rules.
5. Science depends on argument.
6. As a system, science works.

Exercises

1. Have each member of the group choose one of the tenets in the above definition of science and write a brief statement explaining how the tenet might help them to understand the work of scientists.

2. *If you have access to the Internet,* use a browser (for example, Netscape, Mosaic, Lynx) to locate an example of writing in the natural sciences—a document, a report, a letter, an e-mail discussion list, or a committee paper. Make sure the document is no longer than ten pages. Print this document out and read it carefully.

   In writing, analyze the language features of the document you have found. Try to describe the following items:
   - sentence length
   - use of professional vocabulary
   - sentence structure (for example, Does the subject come first in most sentences? Are the sentences simple or complex?)
   - organization (for example, use of thesis sentences, transitional devices, sections, headings, and so on)
   - paragraphing (for example, long or short, construction, focus)

3. *If you have access to the Internet,* use a browser (for example, Netscape, Mosaic, Lynx) to locate a copy of an experimental report in a field of the natural sciences that you find interesting. Print this document out and read it carefully. *If you do not have access to the Internet,* find such a document

in your library, using on-line sources only, if possible. Make a copy of the document you find and read it carefully.

Using a computer and word-processing package, make an outline of the major sections of the experimental report. Do not outline every detail of the report; note only the major sections with headings. Under each outline item, include one sentence summarizing, in your own words, the contents of that section.

Connecting Writing in Liberal Arts and Social Sciences to Writing in the Natural Sciences

A final note as we move toward a presentation of examples from writing in the sciences. The first two discipline-specific chapters in this book explored writing in the humanities and the social sciences, two disciplines which are very different in many respects from the sciences. However, when we look at what constitutes sound writing in the three areas, we find substantial similarities among them. You will find that most science faculty and scientists outside the university value many of the same traits in finished pieces of writing as does your composition teacher: clarity, focus, organization, appropriate detail, sound reasoning, attention to audience, and grammatical correctness. Note that in the personal definition of science on page 218, valued characteristics of science include discovery, the acquisition of knowledge, and a reliance on argument. We believe that these same characteristics are valued in your writing course. What we attempt to do in this chapter, as well as in all the other discipline-specific chapters, is to provide you with specific examples of writing from a variety of courses and disciplines that students often enter. In short, we hope to help you prepare both generally and specifically to think critically and write skillfully no matter what major you choose.

As a means of preparing for our exploration of writing from science classes, let us now turn to examples of writing done by a graduate of a zoology program who now works for a state game and fisheries department. In order to demonstrate the application of general principals we have introduced in the text, we shall consider several written documents authored by this scientist.

The Writing of a Professional Scientist

We present the writing of one professional in order to portray in a unified manner the kinds of writing tasks often fulfilled by graduates of science programs. As we said earlier, most science majors are aware that they will have to write laboratory reports, but they may not be aware of the variety of writing tasks for which they will be responsible, both as undergraduates and later as professionals. The following documents should show very clearly the benefits of preparing to write in a variety of formats, through a range of complexity, and to a diversity of audiences.

Writing in the Community

Let us begin this section with a piece of writing which you might not guess a professional scientist would write:

Mrs. Singh's Class
January 12, 1993

I had a marvelous time talking to your class. Your students are so well-behaved and inquisitive; you must be proud of them! This letter responds to follow-up questions contained in their letters, and I wondered if you would mind reading it to them.

Mrs. Singh's Class: I hope you had wonderful holidays—I'm sure your holidays were good because you were all so well-behaved when Tony-the-snake and I were there (which made our job fun and easy). A couple of you had follow-up questions in the letters you wrote to me, and I have answered them below.

Emily B. asked: How do the suction cups (on the tree frog) work, and how can they walk up glass? Are the suction cups small?

The tree frog's toes have a natural glue which helps it stick to smooth surfaces like glass, but in addition to this "glue" the toe tips are large and have very small bumps on the skin that act like thousands of tiny suction cups which help hold the frog to the glass.

Emily B. also asked are there lots of frogs in Tucson?

Since there is not a lot of water in Tucson, you wouldn't think that there would be many frogs. While there are not a lot of frogs in southeast Arizona compared to the rain forest, you would be surprised at the large numbers of frogs and toads that can be found around temporary ponds. The best time to see frogs in Tucson is during the summer rains.

Drew H. asked: Are all of those frogs (and Tony) mine? Where could I get a frog of my own?

I keep them because I enjoy watching them and they help teach classes like yours important ideas about animals and the planet they (and we) live on. Having a frog of your own is a BIG responsibility! If you would like to have a frog, you should read a book that explains basic care of frogs. If your mom and dad see how much you know about frogs, they might let you buy one! When you think you are ready for a real frog, look in a local pet shop for one.

Thanks again for having me up to talk to all of you. Oh—by the way, Tony says HI.

Sincerely,

Amphibians and Reptiles Field Projects Coordinator
RMR:ms

As we said, you might not have guessed that a graduate of a zoology program would have an occasion to write to an elementary-school class. While, admittedly, the level to which this letter is written is considerably below the level of education attained by the wildlife specialist, it does emphasize a particular fact about the writing done by professionals. We have said elsewhere that most college graduates write for a variety of audiences who have varying degrees of knowledge about the subject specialty of the writer (see Chapter One for an early discussion of the importance of audience). This letter provides a vivid demonstration of that fact. The biologist was asked by the teacher to give a presentation on frogs and snakes—something that is sure to provoke interesting reactions from children!

Let's look quickly at some of the features of this letter by responding to the following exercises.

Exercises

1. In a small group discuss the language features of the letter. Comment on the word choice and sentence structure. Which words seem very much addressed to this particular audience? What other stylistic features of the letter seem directed specifically to this audience?
2. Write in a journal or class notebook: Can you recall any demonstration in one of your grade-school classes which was similar to this one, one which involved animals? How did you and your classmates react to it? Did you do any writing related to the experience?
3. Choose a scientific topic about which you know a good deal or select a topic from a college science textbook, scientific journal, or popular market scientific magazine and write the following letter: a letter to a sixth-grade class explaining the scientific principle involved in your topic. Make sure you indicate to the class why knowing about this principle is important to them.

Writing to Expert Audiences

While some professionals write for audiences who know less than the writer, many professionals write for expert audiences. The following section from an article written by biologists exemplifies their most formal writing. We have included enough of the article to familiarize you with the general layout, specific sections, and level of writing in a journal article, and we would like you to turn to that section now and scan the selection. Keep in mind that the authors wrote this article for an audience with advanced knowledge of the subject area, in this case, herpetologists.

THE INTERACTION OF PREDATION, COMPETITION, AND HABITAT COMPLEXITY IN STRUCTURING AN AMPHIBIAN COMMUNITY

Michael J. Sredl and James P. Collins

We examined effects of predation and competition on population dynamics and community structure in an aquatic system in central Arizona by measuring how refugia for tadpoles (Hyla eximia) *influence predation by larval salamanders* (Ambystoma tigrinum). *Using field enclosure with three densities of A. tigrinum and two of H. eximia and two degrees of habitat complexity, we measured the effects of predation, competition, and habitat complexity on four components of fitness in larval amphibians: mass at metamorphosis, growth rate, length of larvel period, and survival.*

Hyla eximia had low survival where salamanders were present. Tadpoles in treatments with two or four salamanders had one-fifth the survival of tadpoles in treatments with no salamanders. We found some evidence of density-dependent effects in Ambystoma. *Mean salamander mass was negatively affected by salamander density. Density-dependent effects in* H. eximia *were weak. Habitat complexity alone did not affect any response variable but interacted with salamander density and tadpole density in a complex, nonadditive fashion.*

Many studies that have examined the relative importance of predation and competition in structuring amphibian communities have ignored habitat complexity. Our experiment, which examined different degrees of habitat complexity, suggests that the relationship between predation and competition may be nonadditive depending on the degree of habitat complexity.

Factors that contribute to the stability of predator-prey relationships could alter the importance of predation in shaping population or community structure. In simple laboratory environments, elimination of the prey species and extinction of the predator is the usual outcome (Gause, 1934; Huffaker, 1958). Coexistence of laboratory predator-prey systems has been prolonged by addition of physical refuges sheltering part of the prey population from the predator (Gause et al., 1936), reduction of the frequency of contact between predator and prey (Luckinbill, 1973), or addition of structural complexity to the experimental design (Huffaker, 1958). Refugia and habitat complexity are also important in stabilizing predator-prey populations under natural conditions (Connell, 1970; Murdoch and Oaten, 1975).

Amphibian larvae have been used as model systems to assess the relative importance of predation and competition in structuring populations and communities (e.g., Wilbur, 1972, 1984; Morin, 1983). Predation and competition often interact in a complex manner. Without predators, larval densities may be so high that competition slows growth, resulting in low survival and small mass at metamorphosis (Brockelman, 1969; Wilbur and Collins, 1973; DeBenedictis, 1974). With predators, larval densities may be reduced such that competition is unimportant (Wilbur, 1972; Calef, 1973). Predation may even reverse the outcome of competition, allowing a competitively inferior species to dominate (Morin, 1981).

In amphibian communities, relative importance of predation or competition may depend on pond duration. In ponds of long duration where predators can become established, predation may be more important, whereas in ephemeral ponds competition may be more important (Heyer et al., 1975; Wilbur, 1980; Smith, 1983). This generalization overlooks the importance of refugia in stabilizing predator-prey interactions. In complex environments, predators may restrict prey to less productive microhabitats. Mittelbach (1981) estimated that juvenile bluegills could increase their net energy gain up to 50% by feeding in open water on zooplankton instead of feeding in vegetation but did not do so because of higher predation rates in open water. *Ambystoma tigrinum* alters its diel foraging pattern in the presence of a predaceous diving bettle (Holomuzki, 1986; Holomuzki and Collins, 1987). Tadpoles of *Hyla crucifer* alter their microhabitat use when exposed to predatory *Notophthalmus viridencens* by spending greater amounts of time in leaf litter (Morin, 1986). Stenhouse (1985) found that refuges improved survival of *A. maculatum* in the presence of a predator. Studies examining factors structuring amphibian communities have focused on predation and competition; few have considered the role of habitat complexity in altering the interaction of predation and competition (but see Heyer et al., 1975; Stenhouse, 1985).

We used *A. t. nebulosum* Hallowell (Arizona tiger salamander) and *H. eximia* Baird (=*H. wrighotorum* Taylor, mountain treefrog) to examine how habitat complexity shapes predator-prey interactions. *Hyla eximia* occurs in the mountains of central Arizona and western New Mexico, and south in the Sierra Madre Occidental to Guerrero, Mexico (Duellman, 1970; Stebbins, 1985). In central Arizona, breeding occurs sporadically over a few weeks in temporary and permanent ponds where the degree of habitat complexity varies. Breeding commences with the summer rains in early July, and larvae metamorphose in late Aug. *Ambystoma tigrinum,* an early spring breeding species, is found in many of the same habitats (Collins, 1981). Larval *Ambystoma* are characteristically the top predators in fishless aquatic habitats of Arizona, undergoing substantial ontogenetic change in size and diet (Collins and Holomuzki, 1984; Holomuzki and Collins, 1987).

We studied the relative roles of competition and predation in structuring this amphibian community and how the interactions of these factors affect larval fitness components. We examined the effect of habitat complexity in predator-prey interactions by manipulating habitat complexity in field enclosures. We tested for the presence of competition between tadpoles and then determined whether the strength of the predatory interaction between larval frogs and salamanders was related to the degree of habitat complexity. Finally, we show how different densities of predators and prey, coupled with different degrees of habitat complexity, increase the complexity of predator-prey interactions.

MATERIALS AND METHODS

Site description.—We conducted enclosure experiments in Lake 1 (Coconino County, Arizona, 30.5 km SW of Heber, 34°18′02″N, 110°53′00″W, elev. 2304 m) on the Mogollon Rim in central Arizona. This area is the southern edge of the Colorado Plateau and supports Rocky Mountain (Petran) Coniferous Forest dominated by ponderosa pine *(Pinus ponderosa)* (Pase and Brown, 1982). Lake 1 is a natural sinkhole formed by piping in Coconino Sandstone (Cole, 1983) with a maximum depth in early spring of 1.2 m and a maximum area of 4.0 ha. Its initial water level is determined primarily by winter snowfall (Whiteside, 1965), and its duration can depend on summer rains. Lake 1 fills with aquatic macrophytes (*Utricularia vulgaris, Potomogeton natalis, Sparganium androcladum, Eleocharis* spp. *Carex* spp., *Scirpus pallidus*) by late June.

Experimental design.—The experiment was a 3 × 2 × 2 factorial design replicated three times. In each enclosure, density of salamander larvae (0, 2, 4) was crossed with density of tadpoles (20, 40) and habitat complexity (low, high). Salamander and tadpole densities were within limits found in the field (Gehlbach, 1969; Whitaker, 1971; Smith, 1983). Treatments were randomly assigned to one of three spatial blocks.

We collected salamanders as larvae from Lake 1 on 30 July and Lonesome Lake (Coconino County, Arizona, 34°17′02″N, 110°51′05″W) on 5 Aug., and kept them in enclosures in Lake 1 until the experiment began. Snout-vent length varied from 25–35 mm at time of collection. We randomly assigned salamanders to enclosures on 11 Aug.

We collected frogs as eggs from nearby Grasshopper Lake (Coconino County, Arizona, 34°17′29″N, 110°52′53″W) on 23 July, brought them to Lake 1, and allowed them to hatch in a small enclosure. We also collected tadpoles from a nearby meadow, Hole-in-Ground (Coconino County, Arizona, 34°20′39″N, 110°58′29″W), on 11 Aug. Tadpoles used were about 4 mm total length and prestage 25 (Gosner, 1960). These groups were mixed and randomly assigned to enclosures on 11 Aug.

Habitat complexity of an enclosure was low or high. Habitat complexity was increased by adding 18.9 liters of loosely packed wheat straw on 10 Aug. Wheat straw was chosen to increase habitat complexity because it is a natural material that created a habitat similar to that of natural ponds without appreciably increasing nutrients compared to other natural materials. The straw was spread on the water surface; some stems became waterlogged and settled within

24 h, whereas others remained partially buoyant, creating a complex three-dimensional habitat for most of the experiment.

We constructed enclosures (1 m × 2 m × 0.6 m) with nylon window screen (7 strands/cm) attached to the top, bottom, and sides of wood frames (see Sredl and Collins, 1991). A layer of 0.1 mm clear polyethylene plastic prevented aquatic macrophytes from growing through the bottom screen. Three rows of four slits, 5–8 cm long, in each piece of plastic allowed gas and water exchange with the bottom of the lake.

We placed enclosures in the littoral zone on 7 Aug. Depth and distance from shore were nearly equal for all enclosures. The bottom screen was weighted to ensure contact with the substrate. Enclosures had 200–400 liters of water depending on depth of the lake during the experiment. We checked enclosures between 0800–1000 h three times weekly beginning 7 Aug., then six times weekly beginning 16 Aug. We considered frogs metamorphosed when their tailbud was ≤5 mm (≥Gosner stage 44, Gosner, 1960). All animals were collected and preserved in the field, measured in the laboratory, and stored in the Lower Vertebrate Collection at Arizona State University (ASU Catalog nos. 25913, 25823). The experiment began on 11 Aug. Metamorphosed frogs were collected from 16 Sept. to 9 Oct., and metamorphosed salamanders on 30 Sept., 3 Oct., and 8 Oct. On 15 and 16 Oct., all remaining salamander larvae were collected and preserved. We terminated the experiment on 16 Oct. after all frogs had metamorphosed.

Response variables.—We assessed experimental effects on *H. eximia* by mean length of larval period, mass at metamorphosis, growth rate, and by proportion survival to metamorphosis. These variables have important fitness consequences for amphibians (Wilbur and Collins, 1973; Smith-Gill and Gill, 1978; Collins, 1979). Frogs were preserved in 10% formalin, then transferred to 65% ethanol. We determined preserved mass (=0.1 mg) of animals stored in alcohol after blotting each dry with a paper towel. The date we collected a tadpole minus date we placed it in an enclosure (11 Aug.) equaled length of larval period. Growth rate equaled mean mass at metamorphosis within an enclosure divided by mean length of larval period for that enclosure.

Because mass, length of larval period, and growth rate for *H. eximia* are highly correlated, and probability of a type I errors increases with multiple univariate tests, we analyzed the overall response of these variables as a MANOVA. Means of mass, length of larval period, and growth rate were approximately normally distributed and were not transformed (Sokal and Rohlf, 1981). We used the mean of individual responses for each enclosure as a measure of the response for that experimental unit to avoid a pseudoreplicated design (Hurlbert, 1984). We examined survival for *H. eximia* by an ANOVA on the transformed survival (2 × arc sine square root transformation) of each enclosure (Neter et al., 1985).

Response variables measured for *A. tigrinum* were similar to those for *H. eximia,* but because the experiment was terminated before many *A. tigrinum* metamorphosed, primarily larvae were measured. We measured mass of

animals collected and preserved in 10% formalin using the procedure as for
Hyla. Mass and survival were analyzed as separate univariate ANOVAs. Mass
was approximately normally distributed, but we 2 × arc sine square root transformed survival of *A. tigrinum* in each enclosure (Neter et al., 1985). All statistical procedures used Statistical Analysis System (SAS Institute, Inc., 1985).
Type III sums of squares were used for all hypothesis tests (Freund et al., 1986).
Any multiple comparisons used Ryan's Q test (Einot and Gabriel, 1975; Day
and Quinn, 1989).

RESULTS

Hyla eximia responses.—Initial tadpole density, salamander density, and habitat complexity had no significant effect on mass at metamorphosis, length of
larval period, and mean growth rate of *H. eximia* (Table 1, MANOVA). There
were no significant block effects or interactions when mass, larval period, and
growth rate were analyzed simultaneously as a MANOVA.

Results from the univariate ANOVA support the multivariate results. No
factors, or interactions of factors, significantly affected length of larval period
of *H. eximia* (ANOVA, $P > 0.05$). ANOVA suggested that salamander density
influenced length of larval period (ANOVA, $F_{2,15} = 2.86$, $P = 0.093$), but the
3.2 d difference between the means of the highest and lowest larval period
suggests salamander density could be important when both salamander density
and tadpole density are high. No factor or interactions of factors affected mass
at metamorphosis or growth rate of *H. eximia* (ANOVA, $P > 0.05$).

Survival to metamorphosis for *H. eximia* was strongly influenced by predation (Table 2; ANOVA, $F_{2,22} = 8.65$, $P = 0.002$). Survival in enclosures with
no salamanders was 21.8%, in contrast to survival in enclosures with two
(4.1%) or four (4.5%) salamanders. Survival of *H. eximia* in blocks 1, 2, and
3 was 4.1%, 8.8%, and 14.9%, respectively. These differences were suggestive
but not significant (ANOVA, $F_{2,22} = 3.13$, $P = 0.063$). The source of these
minor differences is unclear.

Ambystoma tigrinum responses.—Mean mass was significantly affected by
salamander density (Table 3). Mean mass of salamanders in enclosures with
two salamanders ($\bar{x} = 3.7$ g) was signficantly greater than that with four salamanders ($\bar{x} = 2.9$ g). This relationship, however, was not linear because of
the significant S*F*H interaction (ANOVA, $F_{1,14} = 5.50$, $P = 0.034$, Fig. 1).
This interaction was primarily caused by differences in the way habitat complexity affected mass in the treatment with two salamanders. In simple habitats,
increasing tadpole density had a positive effect on salamander mass. In complex
habitats, an increase in tadpole density had the opposite effect. Where there
were four salamanders, habitat complexity and density of tadpoles had little
effect on salamander mass.

Salamander survival in all treatments averaged 93.8%. Although no factor
significantly affected salamander survival, density explained the greatest
amount of variation in survival (34%, ANOVA, $F_{1,14} = 3.15$, $P = 0.098$),
suggesting increased densities of salamanders could reduce their survival.

Table 1. RESPONSES OF *Hyla eximia* TO SALAMANDER DENSITY (S), TADPOLE DENSITY (F), AND HABITAT COMPLEXITY (H). When H = l habitat complexity is low; when H = h habitat complexity is high; n = number of enclosures. Treatment mean ± one standard error of the mean, SEM.

S	F	H	Mean larval period (d)	Mean mass (mg)	Mean growth rate (mg/d)	n
0	20	l	41.8 ± 1.2	416.8 ± 34.7	10.02 ± 1.08	3
0	20	h	40.6 ± 2.4	396.2 ± 18.8	9.77 ± 0.12	2
0	40	l	45.8 ± 1.0	337.0 ± 37.4	7.35 ± 0.74	3
0	40	h	42.4 ± 1.2	372.0 ± 28.3	8.79 ± 0.77	3
2	20	l	41.9 ± 0.9	390.4 ± 62.1	9.36 ± 1.68	2
2	20	h	37.8 ± 0.0	411.9 ± 0.0	10.90 ± 0.0	1
2	40	l	37.8 ± 0.2	391.4 ± 6.2	10.37 ± 0.23	2
2	40	h	40.1 ± 2.6	382.9 ± 33.1	9.53 ± 0.29	3
4	20	l	41.9 ± 1.6	399.9 ± 13.4	9.54 ± 0.04	2
4	20	h	37.7 ± 0.7	344.9 ± 42.9	9.14 ± 0.98	2
4	40	l	42.0 ± 0.6	448.9 ± 3.1	10.68 ± 0.07	2
4	40	h	43.1 ± 2.4	371.6 ± 35.7	8.69 ± 1.31	2

MANOVA: length of larval period, mean mass, and mean growth rate

Source	Wilks' λ	F	df	P
Block	0.5915	1.10	6.22	0.3931
Salamander (S)	0.5510	1.27	6.22	0.3098
Frog (F)	0.7460	1.25	3.11	0.3393
S·F	0.6054	1.05	6.22	0.4235
Habitat (H)	0.8389	0.70	3.11	0.5691
S·F	0.6095	1.03	6.22	0.4325
F·H	0.8108	0.86	3.11	0.4926
S·F·H	0.5143	1.45	6.22	0.2424

Table 2. SUMMARY OF TREATMENT MEANS OF SURVIVAL FOR *Hyla eximia*. Treatment mean ± SEM, symbols same as Table 1.

S	F	H	Survival	n
0	20	l	0.30 ± 0.05	3
0	20	h	0.18 ± 0.09	3
0	40	l	0.30 ± 0.07	3
0	40	h	0.19 ± 0.11	3
2	20	l	0.08 ± 0.06	3
2	20	h	0.08 ± 0.08	3
2	40	l	0.03 ± 0.02	3
2	40	h	0.07 ± 0.02	3
4	20	l	0.08 ± 0.04	3
4	20	h	0.07 ± 0.04	3
4	40	l	0.08 ± 0.04	3
4	40	h	0.05 ± 0.03	3

Table 3. SUMMARY OF TREATMENT MEANS OF MEAN MASS
FOR *Ambystoma tigrinum.* Treatment mean ± SEM,
symbols same as Table 1.

S	F	H	Mass (g)	n
2	20	l	3.37 ± 0.10	3
2	20	h	3.99 ± 0.29	3
2	40	l	4.50 ± 0.40	3
2	40	h	3.07 ± 0.42	3
4	20	l	3.08 ± 0.14	3
4	20	h	2.87 ± 0.50	3
4	40	l	2.84 ± 0.39	3
4	40	h	2.88 ± 0.09	3

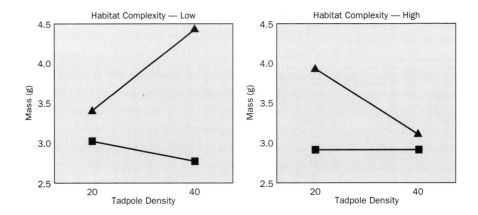

FIGURE 1 Salamander mass (g) plotted against tadpole density (tadpoles/enclosure) for each habitat Symbols are salamander density: triangle is treatment mean of enclosures with two salamanders, square four salamanders. Left graph: habitat complexity is low; right graph: habitat complexity is high.

DISCUSSION

Salamanders strongly affected survival of *H. eximia.* When salamanders were absent, survival was nearly five times greater than when two or four salamanders were in an enclosure. The fact that *H. eximia* is so strongly affected by salamander predation is interesting considering that *H. eximia* breeds in two distinct aquatic habitats. The first type, of which Lake 1 is an example, is a long duration site with a complex fauna. Many animals in these lakes in addition to salamander larvae prey on tadpoles, including odonate nymphs, notonectids, dytiscid beetles, and leeches. The probability these lakes will dry in any year is low. The second type of breeding habitat is ephemeral: rainpools, natural depressions in meadows, or drainage ditches. Short duration sites do not develop a density of predators as high a predator density as the more permanent breeding sites (M. J. Sredl, pers. obs.; Sih, 1987; Wilbur, 1987).

Two apparent differences between these habitats are duration of aquatic habitat and level of predation. In any one year, breeding success of *H. eximia* depends, in part, on the relative risks of predation and desiccation in these two habitats. In years of abundant rainfall, survival of *H. eximia* tadpoles at permanent habitats is probably low compared to temporary habitats because of high densities of predators. . . .

Now, let's review several sections of the article to determine the distinguishing features of this type of writing and to learn more about how such writing reflects the discipline and culture of science.

After you scan the title and authors' names, look at the **abstract** from the article, that portion of the article that summarizes in broad detail the task undertaken, the scope, findings, and potential importance of the task. The abstract is particularly important for scientists—and for all advanced scholars, for that matter—because it allows them to read quickly the most fundamental level of the work done. They can then decide whether they should study the article in depth. You will find, in fact, that, as you begin to do research on various subjects, abstracts will be very valuable aids in operating efficiently.

Exercises

1. With a partner, look at paragraph three of the abstract. Do you see a particular word which connotes caution about the study done by these two scientists? What is the effect of this word? Why would these researchers use this cautious term, as opposed to another, more emphatic term?
2. *If you have access to the Internet,* use a browser (for example, Netscape, Mosaic, Lynx) to locate a copy of the abstract of an experimental report in a field of the natural sciences. Print this abstract out and read it carefully. *If you do not have access to the Internet,* find such a document in your library, using on-line sources only, if possible. Make a copy of the abstract from the document you find and read it carefully.

    Using a computer and word-processing package, make a detailed outline of the abstract, using the following items for major headings and filling in short quotes from the abstract underneath each:
    - Introduction (problem statement, focus of experiment)
    - Experimental Materials and Methods (what was done, what was measured, how the experimental methods were conducted)
    - Results (findings)
    - Discussion (conclusions, importance of findings)

Formatting Scientific Writing

Another important feature of scientific writing is the arrangement of elements on the page. Unlike writing in the humanities, for example, which is almost always structured around paragraph format, scientific writing must include several mediums of expression and communication in the presentation of scientific ideas and information. The pages from the article on pages 226–227 of this chapter reveal this important feature of scientific writing, whether that writing is done for your college science courses or as a job responsibility. Study the **format**—the arrangement of text, graphs, and figures on these pages.

Now think of how that format might compare to a page of an article from another discipline. You have probably noted that the pages from this article emphasize **visuals** as well as writing. The use of such visuals—tables, charts, graphs, photographs, and so on—is crucial to successfully communicating information and developing knowledge in the sciences. In fact, one could argue that to some extent, many disciplines rely heavily on different types of "languages" to convey messages and meaning. In this case, writing and visual language have been used together to convey very complex scientific information about the interaction of two groups of animals within two habitats. The importance of using visual language is demonstrated clearly in the example. Try this exercise as a means of determining whether the information in the chart should have been presented differently.

Exercises

1. If you were given the task of conveying the information in Table 3 (page 228) in a standard paragraph format, how would you structure that paragraph? Try writing a prose version of Table 3. What difficulties did you have to overcome to convey this information in prose? How would the changes you made affect a reader?

2. Make some observations about your own pulse rate, collecting data every half hour, as long as you are awake, for two days. This should be the first thing you do when you wake up in the morning (even before you get out of bed or move) and the last thing you do at night (just before you drop off to sleep). Record these data in writing and provide them to the members of your writing group.

   Using the table-making function in your word-processing program, have each member of your group—working independently—design a chart that represents the data from all members of the writing group in a clear and understandable manner. Make sure that you include the following items in your chart:
   • a title or caption that explains the subject of the chart
   • two axes, labeled carefully
   • all the data that you collected
   Working with the other members of your writing groups, compare the charts that individuals made. In writing, analyze the ways in which they are alike and different.

You have probably determined from exercise 1 above that changing to a paragraph format is inadvisable. While it is possible to convey information in several different forms, it is also true that sometimes certain types of information and messages are more suitably conveyed in either written, visual, or mathematical language. Appropriate charts, tables, graphs, and photographs convey at a glance what would take considerably more time and space to convey in writing. Additionally, as we shall see a bit later in this chapter, mathematical language is often integrated into scientific text.

Before we leave this example, we should point out the basic divisions within the article, for they represent the traditional format of the scientific report, one that you will encounter in either full-form in upper division science courses or in abbreviated form in your lower division courses.

Typically, the traditional science report is divided in the following way:

Introduction: a basic description of what has been measured or evaluated

Experimental Materials and Methods: a summary of what was used and the manner in which the experiment was conducted

Results: a simple statement of what the research found—often expressed in numerical or factual narrative

Discussions: the most complex part of the report—considers the goals of the experiment, often presents comparisons and considers uncertainties

Understanding these divisions is critically important, for without an understanding of the function of each part, one cannot understand the way scientists structure the knowledge which comprises their discipline. In Chapter One, "Writing in the Disciplines," we proposed that understanding the cultural values of a discipline enabled one to better understand the way disciplines explored and communicated knowledge. The sections of this professional article provide a map to the way professional scientists perform experiments and the manner in which they arrive at decisions about their research. No scientist could imagine, for example, conducting an experiment without recording in precise fashion the methods used to collect data. Without this exact information, other scientists would be unable to evaluate the research or attempt to replicate—to reproduce—the results in their own experiments. If you think of the vast potential for error in conducting experiments, you can probably understand why scientists are so adamant concerning procedures and formats.

One last point before we move to the next example of writing from this scientist. Most professional articles include an **acknowledgments** section which thanks those people who have advised and assisted the researchers as they went through the experiment. Additionally, these acknowledgments can lend a voice of authority to the article. As in all disciplines, there are important figures in the specialties in science. If one or more of those figures has played some role in your work, you might gain a more attentive audience by acknowledging their contribution. Thus, we see that there is a human element in all endeavors. That you understand this about science is particularly important, for some mistakenly believe that science is a completely objective field, governed by absolute procedures, as well as laws that govern the physical world. Perhaps those of you who major in one of the sciences or those who take such courses as the History of Science will have the opportunity to explore in detail this misconception. The last example from our scientist may shed some light on this issue.

Writing in the Workplace

Exercise

So that you may study this document without any more prompting from us, we would like you to read the following letter before we comment further. Take your time as you go over the letter and think about the issues covered in this text concerning such topics as subject, audience, purpose, format, and so on. Your class may decide to form into groups to discuss the letter, but we would suggest that you first study the letter individually. As you think about the letter, jot down some notes to share with your classmates.

A Game and Fish Department inter-office memo

To: Non-game Branch Chief
From: Amphibians and Reptiles Program Manager
      Amphibians and Reptiles Field Projects Coordinator
Subject: Use of formalin
Date: June 15, 1995

Proper use of voucher specimens is essential to the success and validity of inventory projects, and the projects within the Amphibians and Reptiles Program have collected specimens when necessary. Removing and killing animals from wild populations is not something our program takes lightly, and, once removed, the value of that animal is only as high as the quality of its preparation as a biological specimen. Through various experiences in museums and graduate school, preparation of herpetological specimens is a topic with which we have had considerable experience. While alcohols, including isopropyl, are frequently used as long-term storage fluids, we know of no reference which recommends using isopropyl as a fixative (see attachments).

There is a great deal of confusion regarding the appropriate use of fluids in wet specimen preparation. Much of this confusion has been caused by imprecise terminology. The first and most important step in specimen preparation is fixing the soft tissues. This is most effectively done by cross-linking adjacent protein chains, something formalin is very good at doing. The next step is placing the specimen in an appropriate long-term storage fluid. Here is where confusion sets in. Some call this long-term storage fluid a preservative, while this word conjures up fixing in the mind of others (even amongst curators of major museums). While it is true that alcohol is an appropriate preservative (=storage fluid) for some specimens, it is a poor fixative.

Our program purchases full strength formalin (=37% formaldehyde) and prepares a 10% buffered solution for FIXING all reptile and amphibian specimens. As a long-term storage fluid, we use 65% ethanol—that's pure, not denatured. The only specimens we store in formalin for the long-term are amphibian eggs and larvae. We seldom have more than 5 gallons of full strength formalin on hand and periodically generate "waste" 10% formalin.

Current inventory:

    5 gallons full strength formalin (=37% formaldehyde)
    6 gallons used 10% buffered formalin
    ½ gallon 10% unused buffered formalin

In addition to being knowledgeable about specimen preparation, Sara Fentress has taken considerable time to investigate the safe use of the chemicals used in this activity, and has developed guidelines for their safe use in the West Road wet lab (see attached guidelines). She has coordinated carefully with Dave Tapani and even had the lab inspected for worker safety.

RMR:rr
cc
attachment

Frequently within organizations, difficulties will arise which must be responded to in official ways. Because all organizations are composed of individuals, departments, divisions, and so on, it is a mistake to think of any organization as always behaving as a unit. Frequently, individuals within organizations, no matter what the size, hold radically differing points of view on the same issue. Thus, official communications which travel from one division to another or which move up or down in the structure of an organization must be very carefully considered and executed. If not thoughtfully handled, such occasions can lead to extremely volatile situations.

So, given your reading and thoughts on the letter and the points made in the discussion, what have you decided about the letter? Did you consider and discuss any of the following: What was its purpose? Was it informational? Argumentative? Descriptive? The heading reveals that it was written to a branch chief by a manager and a coordinator. Of what importance is that flow of authority or power? What do you suppose happened to require that such a letter be written?

We suspect that you've already surmised a good deal about this document. Here are a few particulars about it:

1. Someone within the organization questioned the use of what they considered a potentially toxic fluid. Particularly disturbing to the person was the danger posed by storing large quantities of the fluid.
2. Since the organization is an entity of a state government some individuals were concerned that any use of a potentially controversial fluid was unwise.
3. The chief to whom the complaint was directed thought that the situation was best handled by employees who were directly involved with the collection, handling and preservation of specimens.

While there is much more we could say about this letter, we believe by now you have seen the types of issues and the related writing tasks which scientists must sometimes address. If you major in science and become a scientific professional, you are very likely to encounter such communication tasks as the ones presented in this section.

Exercises

1. Review the section on the writing of professional scientists (pages 219–234) and respond to the following questions in writing:
   a. What is your reaction to the claims we have made about the importance of writing to scientists?
   b. Does the material presented provide you with enough information and examples for you to decide whether that material accurately represents the tasks of scientists?
   c. Does the material correspond with what you know about the work of scientists?
   d. What have you learned about the work of scientists?

2. This exercise will be an extension and a variation of exercise 4, page 217. In that exercise, we asked that you locate an online discussion group of scientists, monitor that list for several days, then summarize your observations of the work the scientists do, the questions and problems they pursue, and the kinds of people with whom they work. Refer to that exercise if you need a detailed reminder of the exercise's content.

   After observing the list for four days, post a query which asks the individuals on the list to comment on the range of writing tasks that they do as scientists. Save all those responses.

   Using a word-processing package, list all of the kinds of writing that have been mentioned in the responses; be as complete and specific as possible. Surveying the list when it is done, note the natural groupings of these writing tasks, and at the end of the file, create a shorter list of headings under which several of the various writing tasks can go. Then, using the cut-and-paste function, place each of the kinds of writing in your original long list under the appropriate heading in the shorter list. Compare your new list—organized into natural groupings of writing tasks with headings—with the lists of other members in your writing group.

3. *If you have access to e-mail or real-time conferencing software,* hold a discussion among the members of your writing group about the kinds and the amount of writing that scientists do. In this discussion, make sure to include what you have learned about the writing demands that scientists face by looking at the documents in this chapter, by searching the Internet for documents that scientists have written, and by following the discussion lists that involve scientists. Tell what surprised you, what seemed strange, what you have learned about the work of scientists, what appeared most difficult to you, what challenges you noted as interesting. Save this discussion.

Individually, *using a word-processing program,* analyze this discussion. Note especially what most group members found surprising about the writing and the work of scientists, what they did not know before they started their reading and observations in this chapter.

Writing in the Undergraduate Natural Sciences

Like all college-educated people, graduates of science programs are responsible for a wide range of intellectually demanding tasks. And like all other professionals, scientists are best prepared to fulfill their role as skillful communicators if they have prepared for those tasks prior to accepting positions after graduation from college. Having taken that position, let's turn now to some typical writing assignments and examples of student writing from undergraduate science programs. Although these examples come from across the country and from a range of academic institutions, they do not exhaust the possibilities you may encounter in your classes. We do believe, however, that they are representative of the writing you will be assigned.

If you intend to major in a science curriculum, you will probably take thirteen to twenty science courses. Those who do not major in a science will probably take at least two courses, perhaps as many as four, just to fulfill the college's general requirements. Regardless of which group you fall into, you will write in many of the courses you take. Over the past decade large numbers of science educators have called for increased emphasis on critical thinking and thoughtful writing in science curricula. The assignments in this section represent many of those voices. These scientists know that having their students write in a variety of forms, in addition to the traditional lab report, intellectually engages students in ways which multiple choice and one-phrase-answer testing cannot. The remainder of this chapter will consider some of these assignments.

Many of you are taking or have taken first-year science classes. Typically, students take either biology, chemistry, earth science, or physical science. Less frequently, such courses as astronomy, physics, and geology are offered. Depending on your college, you may be in a large-size lecture session, with up to 400 students enrolled, and then attend a laboratory section which enrolls from twenty-five to forty students. Most of these classes will require short "write-ups" of the laboratory experiments, and often these assignments are limited to one to two pages. Thus, a premium is placed on brief, clear, well-organized writing which responds directly to the questions posed by the lab instructor. In this section we shall review two assignments related to lab sections and one which is used throughout science curricula.

Laboratory Summary Assignment

In addition to requiring a laboratory notebook in which students record such specific information as measurements and values, lab instructors frequently require that students turn in a written summary of the work performed, at least in some of the lab sessions.

Exercises

1. Take a few minutes individually to study the example on page 237, jotting down your impressions of it, then, as a class respond to the following:
   a. What are the strengths of this summary?
   b. What is your evaluation of the formatting of the information?
   c. What suggestions for improvement would you make?
   d. If the maximum points possible were 10, what grade would you assign this summary? Why?
   e. After the class has discussed the summary, begin a class discussion during which the following activity is planned: Divide the class into groups of four to five people who are all currently taking the same science course or who have taken a similar course, so that each person will understand material from that discipline. The group's task is this: Select a concept, process, or experiment and write a document which contains both summary and comment sections. Write your document to provide information which is both substantive and readable.

2. In your writing group, make appointments to visit and interview several of the natural science professors on your campus or individuals who work as natural scientists in the community where you live. Make sure that every group member visits one individual. Make sure that you mention the purpose of your visit and interview. Coordinate your visits with your teacher so that no one individual is visited by more than one student—these are busy people who need to do their own work as well.

   In the interview meeting, ask the professor or the scientist for a copy of one of two things: 1) a format sheet that details the organizational structure for a lab report or 2) a copy of a lab report that the individual has written.

CH100 Sec. 01
Experiment #1

Summary

The objective of this experiment was to learn how to properly assemble a boiling point apparatus, to practice calculating densities and determining solubility, and to use these physical properties to identify an unknown chemical substance.

The unknown was determined to have an average density of .74 glmL and an average boiling point of 80.0°C. These were determined over two trials. The unknown was found to be soluble in cyclohexane, slightly soluble in ethanol, and insoluble in water. Through these physical properties, the unknown was identified as being cyclohexane.

Although cyclohexane's (C_6H_{12}) physical properties were the closest to the experimentally calculated ones, there were some deviations in them. For example, the true density of C_6H_{12} is .779 glmL, which is .039 glmL higher than the experimentally calculated one. This is due to the fact that a graduated cylinder, which is less accurate, was used in place of a 10.00 mL pipet because the student had trouble using the pipet and in the process spilled some of the solution leaving less than 10mL left. The boiling point was only .74°C off and could have resulted from not recording it at the exact moment the bubbles ceased to escape and before the liquid entered the capillary tubes. Also, it was determined that the unknown was slightly soluble in ethanol, but in actuality C_6H_{12} is soluble in ethanol. This could possibly be from adding too much solute causing oversaturation.

Ask the individual to explain the document that she or he provides, talking you through the various parts of it. Take notes.

Share the document you get with the other members of your group. Together, sitting around a common computer and using a word-processing package, write a document for students in the natural sciences that accomplishes the following tasks:
• describes the purpose of laboratory summaries or reports
• provides an outline of the typical sections in such a report
• explains what kind of information goes into each section and how it should be presented
• provides hints about the characteristics that make up a successful lab summary—including the style, the tone, the vocabulary, the organizational structure, etc.

Your class discussion has probably yielded a fruitful critique of the above summary, so let's focus on a point which someone may have already raised. In the third paragraph this writer does something more than summarize or report what was done or what happened. Notice that the student spends some time discussing probable reasons for some of the "problems" raised by the experiment. The student deals with the variance in boiling point, which seemed to have been off only slightly, addresses the deviation of measured density to true density, and then takes up the solubility of ethanol. In all these problems, the student is offering possible answers to the questions raised by differences between ideal and experimental results. This is a very simple example of a very profound principle of science: Science is part discovery, and discovery must at some stage undergo questioning and speculation based on sound observation and reasoning. This first-year student is engaging in a valuable exploration, one which in more advanced courses builds in complexity but which still follows the same scientific methodology.

Laboratory Notebooks

The **laboratory notebook,** another popular source of writing and learning in the sciences, serves as both a place to record observations and a source for information which may later be integrated into a formal lab report. One of the characteristics of this writing is that it often incorporates a kind of "shorthand" which the student can ultimately shape into formal prose in the Methods and Materials section of a report. In this practice, the style of the notebook is similar to that used in lecture or reading notes, the kind of style which allows writers to record information in a rapid manner so that later they can return to the notebook and translate the information into more formal prose. While the style of the laboratory notebook is informal, it is not as informal as it would be if the writer were the only person to see or use the notes. Remember that most often the laboratory notebook is turned in to the professor.

Exercises

1. Study the example on page 239 and list the characteristics of the laboratory-notebook style. If you have ever recorded observations in a notebook, what connections do you see between notebook style and learning in the sciences? What benefits did you derive from the activity? If you were to revise notebook writing into formal scientific writing, what strategies would you employ?
2. Go back to the summary in the previous exercise and revise a section into a laboratory-notebook entry, then compare the two documents. What would you say are the chief advantages of one form compared to the other?

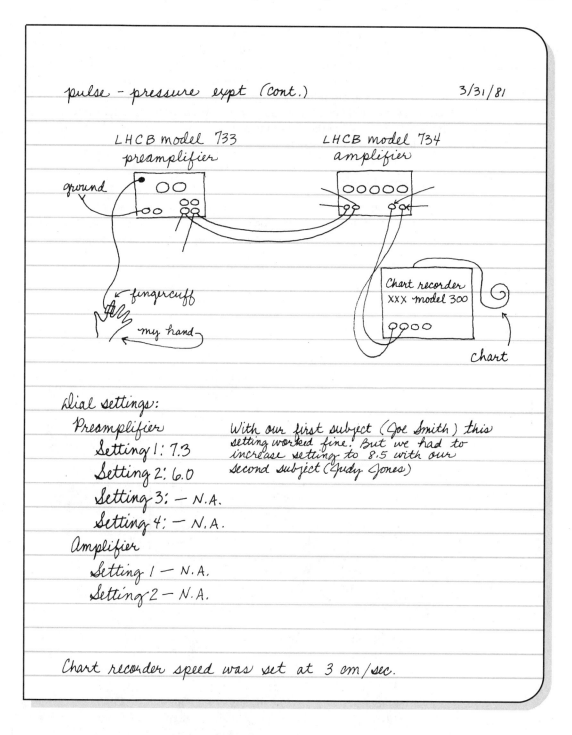

pulse – pressure expt (cont.)   3/31/81

LHCB model 733
preamplifier

LHCB model 734
amplifier

ground

fingercuff

my hand

Chart recorder
XXX model 300

chart

Dial settings:

Preamplifier

Setting 1: 7.3
Setting 2: 6.0
Setting 3: — N.A.
Setting 4: — N.A.

With our first subject (Joe Smith) this setting worked fine. But we had to increase setting to 8.5 with our second subject (Judy Jones)

Amplifier

Setting 1 — N.A.
Setting 2 — N.A.

Chart recorder speed was set at 3 cm/sec.

The laboratory notebook is an extremely important tool for science students. Primarily, it provides practice in one of the mainstays for all scientists: recording scientific observation and work. Without this repository of information, scientists simply would not be able to carry on the highly detailed work which characterizes their discipline. Thus, students who record observations of their laboratory or fieldwork experiences are participating in a scientific culture. They are learning what the discipline values and understanding the role of those values in forming a scientist.

The Microtheme

The **microtheme** is a very popular assignment among those professors who value student creativity and who believe that students need to articulate their knowledge of science in some form other than a test. These assignments are limited to a paragraph or two responding to a specific question which has no right or wrong answer. Instead, the answer reveals the student's imaginative thinking about a real science problem or principle. One assignment of a microtheme follows.

Quandary-Posing Microtheme for Introductory Physics

Suppose you put a big block of ice in a bucket and then fill the bucket with water until the water level is exactly even with the edge of the bucket. (The ice, of course, is now floating in the water.)

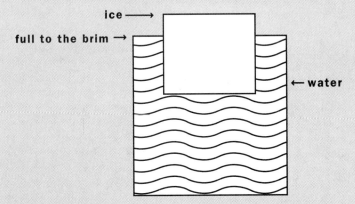

Now we will wait for several hours for the ice to melt. Which of the following will happen? (Neglect evaporation.)
1. The water level in the bucket will remain exactly the same.
2. The water level in the bucket will drop.
3. Some water will overflow the sides of the bucket.

Your Task: After deciding upon your answer, explain it in writing. Imagine that you are writing to a classmate who doesn't yet understand flotation and who is arguing for what you consider the wrong answer. Your task is to explain your reasoning so clearly that your microtheme serves as a little text-book, *teaching* your classmate the physics principles involved. Thus, your microtheme will be judged *not simply* on whether or not you figure out the correct answer, but also on whether or not you can write clearly enough to *teach* a fellow classmate.

1. Try the Quandary Microtheme assignment (many of you have had a high school or even a college physics course). After you write a consensus group answer, have each group appoint a spokesperson to read your imaginative responses.

2. This activity requires that each person in class have a partner; at least one of the partners should currently be taking a science course. Select a topic from your science course and review your course notebooks for notes on that subject. Working with your partner, compose a three-part document containing the following:
   - informal notes which cover the fundamentals of the subject and record any individual thoughts you and your partner may have on it
   - a summary of the material contained in the informal notes, including vi-sual and mathematical language where appropriate
   - a microtheme on an interesting and challenging aspect of the subject (we suggest that the first two parts be team-written but that each person write his or her own microtheme)

3. *Using a computer and a word-processing package,* and working individ-ually, write an assignment for a microtheme that is suitable for a com-munity-based science class in a local science museum, a nature center, a community education course, a planetarium, a hospital, an arboretum, or a garden club. Make sure that the assignment is appropriate for an audience (and experimenter) who has no formal training in the natural sciences field. Make sure that the microtheme assignment has the following characteristics:
   - deals with a specific question about a natural phenomenon that has no right or wrong answer
   - requires no complicated scientific apparatus to complete
   - identifies an audience other than a teacher or a student in the same class (for example, someone's mother, a younger brother, a class of elementary school students, a group of senior citizens)
   - can be completed in two or three paragraphs
   - identifies a question and offers methods that investigators can use to an-swer the question

   To get some ideas about an assignment, go to the library and look at some natural sciences textbooks written for children or nonscientsts or con-sult a science textbook that you used in secondary or elementary school. *If you have access to the Internet,* use a browser to locate a Web site that presents science projects to children or nonscientists.

In your writing groups, exchange these assignments with another individual. Using a word-processing package, complete the assignment of your partner by writing the two or three paragraphs it requires. When you are done writing your microtheme, meet with your partner to discuss any rough spots you found in the assignment—things that are unclear, elements that are difficult to accomplish, important instructions or materials that are left out.

Using the feedback you receive from your partner on the rough spots within your assignment, revise your own original assignment to improve it.

Two final assignments will be covered in this chapter: a critique of a journal article and a formal laboratory report. While both are assigned less frequently in lower division than in upper division classes, the principles involved in each are often integrated into lower division course assignments. Moreover, since both assignments focus on the formal-report format and address the sections of a formal report, they both prepare students for writing professional journal articles and reports required in both private- and public-sector laboratories. Let's start by spending a bit of time reviewing some of the benefits of the critique.

The Journal Critique Paper

On the following pages we have included both a journal critique assignment and a student's response to it. Begin by reading the professor's introduction to the assignment, then respond to the questions in the Exercises.

Critique Paper

Vertebrate Zoology 370

I. INTRODUCTION TO THE ASSIGNMENT

For class you will be expected to critique two (2) scientific papers on almost any aspect of vertebrate biology you desire. Specifically, the papers you will critique MUST (a) be published in a peer-reviewed journal, (b) contain the sections Introduction, Material & Methods (=Methods), Results, Discussion, and Literature Cited (References), and (c) be published recently (1990–1995). This exercise is valuable because it requires that you use critical thinking (e.g., accepting or refuting claims) and, therefore, differs from the typical term papers that you have done since grade school (uncritical thinking?). A common claim in scientific papers, for example, is the hypothesis, but other types of claims can be presented. An important part of this exercise is that you must judge or determine whether or not claims presented by the author(s) are supported by evidence. In other words, are the claims presented reasonable? To a large extent, this is nearly identical to the process done when a manuscript's worth is refereed by two to three experts for possible publication in a journal; hence, the name peer-reviewed journal. This type of exercise is applicable to many other areas outside the realm of biology, and for this reason alone its importance and utility is increased. To help you begin this assignment, I have placed on reserve at the main library an example of critiques done by former students. Also, I have provided an extensive list of peer-reviewed journals available on all campuses that often contain papers on vertebrates.

To begin this assignment, I expect you to bring to me several photocopies of papers that you would WANT to critique. I will then determine their suitability. A decent-sized paper is ten to fifteen pages in total length. I recommend that you choose a subject you feel comfortable with—but do not hesitate to explore something new. I will not place a grade on the first draft; instead, I usually comment extensively and discuss with you face-to-face the merits/weaknesses of your critique. The second draft will be returned for a grade (25 possible points). The second critique will not require a draft, but I will inspect it prior to submission.

The approach I recommend is to read first the photocopied sample of the paper you have chosen. Do this several times in a quiet and familiar setting, with some coffee or a soda. Put it away for one to two days, let it incubate in your mind, then read it again. Next, prepare notes on the paper itself. These notes should be placed along the margins of the paper and will concern the information presented by the author(s)—I recommend this be done on a paragraph-by-paragraph basis. It is important to do this to (a) record your thoughts, and (b) maintain some type of order. From these notes, you might consider writing them again onto a new sheet of paper so you can see/read them together. I find this procedure to be extremely helpful when I review large manuscripts that are data rich. From these notes you will be developing your critique.

II. FORMAT OF THE EXERCISE
You will be expected to submit to me a typed (ten to twelve point), double-spaced, 1 inch margins, critique paper. It must have the following sections.

1. COVER PAGE (Separate Typed Page—Page 1)
   The cover page must have the following elements:

   TITLE of paper you critiqued
   AUTHOR(s) of paper
   JOURNAL that published the paper (Name, Volume, Number, Pages)
   YOUR FULL NAME
   SUBMITTED TO: Dr.   Spring 1995
   CRITIQUE NUMBER 1 or 2

continued

2. INTRODUCTION (Pages 2–3)

The introduction must introduce the subject and research of the author(s). Most good introductions (a) state and review the problem/issue, (b) discuss the specific reasons for conducting the present research, and (c) present a formal hypothesis or goal. This is an important section in that the remaining paper is developed from the introduction. In your critique, discuss whether the author(s) thoroughly and effectively present areas a–c above. If so, explain how this was accomplished. If not, also explain. Your explanations are not to be simple regurgitation of the work, but your judgments. Further, I expect you to challenge information and ideas that you suspect are either wrong or placed out of context. Importantly, do not be inhibited regarding your comments—you will not be penalized for trying!

3. MATERIALS AND METHODS (Page 4)

The M&M section should reflect information presented in the introduction. Do the methods make sense to you? Are they presented fully? In some ways, it will be hard to make these and other conclusions, but try. Once the Results section has been read and analyzed (in part), reread the M&Ms section to see if anything is missing or incorrect.

4. RESULTS (Pages 5–6)

The results should only present the information and should not contain discussion of those data. Results are generally presented in two formats: tables and figures. Figures can be either line-drawings or photos (halftones). Ask yourself, do these data make sense in the way that they are presented? Could they be presented more clearly? How would you do this? In the latter case, show me your suggestions. Clearly, there are many more questions that could be asked. One good method is to spell them out on paper prior to writing the critique.

5. DISCUSSION (Pages 7–8)

In this section the results are discussed with respect to hypotheses/goals presented in the introduction and, perhaps, in other papers. You are to determine whether or not the data are discussed adequately. Do the data the authors provide support their hypotheses/goals? How? If not, explain. Do they discuss all possible interpretations or scenarios? If not, what other interpretations can you suggest? List them and explain why they are important.

III. PHOTOCOPY OF CRITIQUED ARTICLE

Staple the article you examined to your critique. This will allow me to judge better the work you have done. Critique papers without the photocopy of the article will not be accepted. If you have any questions regarding this assignment, do not hesitate to ask me.

What do you think are the professor's major goals for this assignment? What kind of tone is the professor trying to set for this assignment? What do you think the students will gain the most from this assignment? After you have finished discussing the points, write a synthesis answer from your group.

Here are the professor's major goals for this assignment:

1. Familiarize students with the form and function of the experimental journal article.
2. Allow students to practice reading for both detail and summary skills.
3. Provide students with practice in critical appraisal, as opposed to accumulation of data.
4. Promote the notion of science as a process.

Did your lists of goals resemble the professor's? As you read the Introduction section, could you tell that the professor seeks something other than having students repeat back what they have heard in class lectures? In paragraph two of the instructions, for example, the professor indicates emphatically that the articles should be ones the students *"want to critique."* Thus, it seems clear that the professor is seeking involvement from the students; moreover, it seems clear that students are required to think critically about the assignment. Can you determine what kinds of thinking are being required?

Now read the student's response to the assignment on the following pages.

Critique:
Causes of divorce in the monogamous willow tit, *Parus montanus,*
and consequences for reproductive success
Markku Orell, Seppo Rytkonen & Kari Koivula
Animal Behavior, 48:1143–1154 (1994)

INTRODUCTION

Causes of divorce, or previous-year mate rejection, in the willow tit, *Parus montanus,* were examined by Orell, Rytkonen and Koivula. The low divorce rate of this species (12%) makes divorce the exception rather than the rule. In this paper, the authors seek to find the behavioral conditions under which that rule is broken.

Relevant background information included studies that showed willow tits to be highly site-tenacious. This information was important in

---

continued

determining the status of a mate as dead as opposed to divorced. Other studies provided criteria and interpretation of social dominance within this species of tit. Further studies reveal flocking patterns throughout the year, which were helpful in understanding timing of territorial establishment.

Several hypotheses have been proposed to explain why divorce would occur in a pair of birds. The 'incompatibility hypothesis' suggests that a pair that does not breed successfully together initiate both birds to choose another mate to improve success. According to the 'better opinion' hypothesis, only one member of the pair would improve its reproductive success by deserting its mate. The authors of this paper seek to understand the adaptive forces behind the exceptional action of divorce, with consideration given to breeding success, cost vs. benefit of new pairing, territory enhancement, and rank improvement.

Within this study the authors altered the breeding success of divorced and monogamous groups by manipulating brood sizes. From their data, they concluded that there was no correlation between divorce and previous breeding success. This left improved breeding success in the future to be considered. It was assumed that the factors involved in future breeding output, either directly or indirectly, were the only considerations the willow tit had for choosing mates. It was these factors that the authors studied as divorce-initiating in this research.

The authors do not directly state a hypothesis; they investigate certain factors, with a leaning towards the 'better option' hypothesis as a starting point to begin testing by manipulation and observation. If this hypothesis is valid, they expect to find victims, usually the male, who do not benefit by the divorce. But this is not all they did in this paper. They looked for the initiating factor that promotes the time and energy-consuming decision to divorce. They assume, as such, it is adaptive and, therefore, ultimately will lead to increased future reproductive success.

METHODS

This research was conducted on a willow tit population in the conifer forests of northern Finland (65°N, 25°30′E) during 1986–1992. For further information about the habitats, this paper refers the reader to another paper. It may have been redundant to repeat the habitat description here, but might have given insight to territory differences and possible preferences leading to social-order questions.

Observational data were used to determine breeding status and success. The parameters of breeding success were: data of laying, clutch size, number of hatched and fledged young. Experimental data on 45% of the broods were manipulated by randomly transferring two 1–3 day old chicks between two nests. This percentage seems an adequate amount to ascertain the effect of a decrease in number of hatched on the breeding pair.

The continuous monitoring of the birds over a six-year period gives the reader confidence that the interpreted social ranking and data concerning divorce times for the pairs were well determined, though the average lifespan of a willow tit was never mentioned.

Also, the determination of mate-change costs was fairly justified. Change in nesting success was investigated from the following angles: between the first year of a new mate to that of the last year of an old mate and those who had stayed together for two successive seasons.

It is within the paper's Materials and Methods section that I first came across the first definition of "divorce." I understand it being covered here because of its connection to the counting procedures, but it left me well into the paper imagining little bird attorneys squabbling over chick support. The authors assumed the reader knew what divorce means in the willow tit world.

Because of the manipulation of breeding success by the moving of chicks, adjustments were made when analyzing variance in the numbers of fledged young. The authors chose to use least square means to simulate no removal of chicks from some broods and correct differences between manipulated and control broods. I had a general idea of this procedure after reading it over several times, but a sample calculation or graphic might have helped here.

RESULTS

There were a total of 28 pairs of breeding birds that divorced between 1986–1992. This was the population that is represented in Table I. This table does not account for all the divorced pairs, so I was left to wonder what happened to 13 pairs, assuming the whole time that the paragraphs covering the topic were clear and I cannot count when it entails word problems. This whole section concerning breeding seasons and timing of divorces could have been presented more clearly.

From the above population, more data were collected. Age relevance to divorce rate was analyzed by log-linear models and presented in an easy-to-read histogram on page 1146. The relationship between male and female age combinations relating to marital status is quickly recognizable from this graph. It is apparent that old age is correlated to staying together, whereas juvenile mates strongly tended towards divorce.

From Table III relating frequencies of different-aged new mates to that of the previous, the authors suggest a role of social hierarchy in divorce

continued

initiation to explain a choice of a younger mate. They cite one documented case when an old female chose a younger but high-ranking male as a mate. This case hardly seems significant enough to support the suggestion. What is significant is the great preference of divorced male birds for younger mates. Though ranking criteria are not detailed in the paper, one might suspect that most of the old male to young female matings were not due to attempts at enhancement of rank.

The results of survival rates per year were interestingly displayed in Figure 2, and were significant in that there were no great sex-ratio differences possibly leading to correlation with divorce rates.

Divorce as related to breeding success is illustrated in Table IV and discussed in the Discussion section. All I can say is that I will just have to take their word for what is significant and what is not. To me, unless otherwise told, negative numbers are significant, no matter what the P value says. The authors maintain that there was no correlation between divorce and breeding success using the standardized breeding parameters listed previously.

My confusion was furthered by the next section describing pair type (+/−Juv, and +/−Exp) as strongly influencing breeding success. I concluded from Figure 1 that juvenile/juvenile pairs were the most unstable. From Figure 3, I conclude that juvenile/juvenile pairings have the lowest breeding success. Though the authors attribute this to "the significant female effect," to me it seems to be a way of not saying breeding success is related to divorce. Similarly, old/old pairings breed successfully and have the highest stay-together rate.

DISCUSSION

From the title of this paper onward, confusion reigns due to the usage of nonscientific words to describe animal behavior. According to Funk and Wagnalls' standard dictionary, divorce is the dissolution of a marriage bond by legal process or accepted custom. This process is obviously necessary to keep the willow tit monogamous, or of the condition of having only one wife or husband at a time. Oh boy!

Past the terminology problem, I had a conceptual block. Though the connection between breeding success rate and divorce rate in juvenile/juvenile parings did not explain divorce in older bird pairs, that divorce rate may be due to a related reason. The authors claim that their data showing females increasing their breeding success after divorce may be ambiguous. If shown to be true, it would also point to enhanced breeding as an initiator for divorce.

I truly got lost in the jargon of this paper. I cannot see how one minute a scientist can say breeding success does not affect divorce rates, but pairs divorce to increased reproductive output. And since all roads are hypothesized to lead to breeding success, how can one support a hypothesis that states divorce is an action to gain a higher-ranking mate, not improve breeding success? Why is a higher-ranking mate important anyway? The author concedes it is to insure protection from aggression from other flock members and to attain better nutrition. What do secure, well-fed female willow tits do . . . plan corporate careers? It seems we're still on the Road to Rome.

As you read this student's critique, you probably saw that there is no lack of involvement on her part. She writes on page 247 that by waiting until the reader of the article is "well into the paper," the authors "assumed the reader knew what divorce means in the willow tit [*Parus montanus*] world" She also takes the authors to task for not providing a "sample calculation or graphic [which] might have helped. . . ." One might argue that the student's comment ignores the primary audience, scientists who might know more than she does about *Parus montanus* for the article, but one cannot argue that she is not involved in her work. In her Discussion section, she goes on to criticize the authors for developing a confusing argument and trying to establish a faulty hypothesis.

This paper was written by a third-year student who had taken the introductory biology courses. We would assume, then, that she had some familiarity with this type of journal article, as had most of her classmates. However, the professor says that very few students at this level ever critique the ideas and data they find in such articles. Rather, they simply accept the substance of such work as being factual and valid. The professor sought, then, to make critics rather than recorders or repeaters, of his students.

Learning to critically research and question is one of the most valuable abilities you can develop during your college years. Such skills are central to posing questions, gathering and evaluating information, and making judgments. This professor is not alone in providing opportunities for students to think critically, to question the merit of ideas and positions, and to examine the basis upon which those ideas and positions are founded. This professor, as well as many others in the sciences, is turning increasingly to writing as a medium for establishing those skills within the specific context of science.

The Laboratory Report

The final assignment we will consider in this chapter will be the formal laboratory report. Most colleges require students to take at least one year of a laboratory science course, and most students fulfill this requirement by taking biology, physical science, or chemistry. Although many science faculty no longer require formal laboratory reports in their first-year courses, some still believe that the report provides an important way to determine whether the student has understood the laboratory experiment and has gained facility with scientific process.

Earlier in this chapter we used a professional journal article written by two practicing scientists to present the basic format of the scientific report. As you move through this section, refer to that earlier section to compare the two reports. Since we established the principles involved in a scientific report in that earlier section, we ask that you refer to pages 229–236. We ask, also, that you treat that division as preparation for the activities in this section, for we shall use this student report as a basis for the final writing assignment in this chapter.

Finally, read the report in its entirety, for the final writing exercise in this chapter will involve writing a similar report. Also, we suggested in Chapter Two, "Reading in the Disciplines," that skimming can be an excellent preparation for more detailed reading, so you might skim the entire report before you read it carefully. As you read, answer the following questions in a notebook and use the answers to the questions as guides to analyzing and understanding the report and to preparing for the final writing assignment.

Guide to analyzing and understanding a laboratory report

1. In Chapter Three, "Researching in the Disciplines," we offered the following definition of the purpose of a laboratory report: The purpose of a lab report is to *clearly and concisely present experimental information and to carefully analyze its meaning and significance.* How well does this report fulfill this purpose? Can you cite specific areas of the report which aid in fulfilling this purpose? Are there areas which do not fulfill this requirement?

2. As well, in Chapter Three, we specified the following as sections of a laboratory report: *title, introduction, materials and methods, results, discussion,* and *summary.* Does this report meet these requirements? If not, why do you think the writer changes the established format?

3. Scientists value clear, concise, well-organized writing. Critique the writing in this report. Consider such features as *word choice* appropriate to the discipline, clear *sentence structure, organization* of sections (paragraphs, lists, and so forth), *format* (arrangement of elements, spacing, use of bullets and other markers).

4. Earlier in this chapter we said that the discussion section was perhaps the most important section in the scientific report. This student discusses a number of issues in his "Discussions" section, as well as raising several alternative hypotheses. How successful is this major section? Does the student present sound evidence and reasoning? Are his hypotheses presented logically?

First-year Biology Laboratory Report

John Meyers
B10 100 LAB
Dr. Bishop
Final Lab Investigation
April 5, 1995

What Variables Affect the Rate of Photosynthesis?

Casual Questions/Introduction

Plants are the only known species on planet Earth which are capable of producing their own food. These green plants contain tiny chloroplasts which are contained in the cell membrane of the plant. They use these chloroplasts to produce their food. Plants are able to do this because of a process called photosynthesis. This process gives off oxygen and appears to only be carried out when light is present. The chloroplasts use the photons which are presumed to come from within the light itself. The energy source for photosynthesis appears to be the light. However, do all the colors in the spectrum of light contribute to photosynthesis? Does each color get used up equally? Are there certain colors which assist photosynthesis more than others? Does the intensity of the light play a factor in the process of photosynthesis? *What Variables Affect the Rate of Photosynthesis?*

Alternative Hypothesis

I. Red light is known to have more energy than any of the other colors in the light spectrum. Therefore, photosynthesis is carried out best under red light.

II. Light is not the only factor aiding in photosynthesis. The heat given off by the lamp also affects the process of photosynthesis. As the heat is increased, photosynthesis is increased.

III. Green light is reflected by the plant. Therefore, the process of photosynthesis is not capable under green light.

IV. The intensity of the light affects photosynthesis. Therefore, the greater the intensity of light (the closer the lamp is to the plant), the more photosynthesis gets carried out. The less intense the light (the farther the lamp is from the plant), then the lower photosynthesis gets carried out.

continued

Experimental Procedure

I. I tested hypothesis IV. I collected all of the materials I needed to carry out the experiment. Below is a list of materials I used.

    100ml glass jar (approximately)
    200ml glass jar (approximately)
    special carbonated water solution (provided)
    an aquarium plant
    a ruler
    a tiny glass beaker (to fit at end of funnel)
    glass funnel (provided)
    white light source (provided)
    light stand (provided)
    timing device (stop watch)

II. Next I took my 200ml jar and filled it with regular water about 1.5″ full. I then placed my aquarium plant in my 100ml jar and covered it with the funnel, placing the wide end at the base of the jar. Next I filled the 100ml jar with the special water solution and filled it up to about 2.5″ deep. Then I filled up the glass beaker with the same special water solution and used it to cap off the thin end of the inverted funnel. Do this in such a manner that the water in the beaker remains in it as it is inverted too. There should only be about .5″ of air at the top of the inverted beaker. I then placed the 100ml jar into the 200ml jar, creating a water bath for the 100ml jar. This bath will prevent the element of heat from being a factor in the results of the lab.

III. I began my experiment by placing my light directly over my jars. I immediately began timing how long I was shining this white light on the plant. As I timed it, I counted the number of bubbles I saw rise from the plant. When photosynthesis is being carried out, oxygen is released from the plant. I recorded the number of bubbles (oxygen) that I saw in one minute and recorded the distance from the light to the jar. This distance is the intensity of the light. I repeated this last step of timing and counting the bubbles for five more intensities (heights) and recorded the data respectively.

IV. My independent variable for this lab was the intensity for my light. I changed my intensities of light. The dependent variable for this experiment was the amount of oxygen bubbles given off for each different light intensity. I had no control over how many oxygen bubbles were given off. I wrapped aluminum foil around the big glass jar to keep the outside light from reaching the plant and affecting its photosynthesis. The plant is still in the small glass jar, inside the big glass jar. With the use of the aluminum foil wrapped around the big jar, the only light that reaches the plant is that which comes from the lamp I used. It comes from directly above the plant and is the only light present in the experiment.

Expected Results

I. IF red light is known to have more energy (the greater the energy, the greater the results of photosynthesis) than any of the other colors in the light spectrum, AND I plant two plants, shining one with only red light, and the other with any other color from the spectrum of light, THEN the plant provided with only red light should photosynthesize better than the other plant.

II. IF the amount of heat given off by a light source affects the process of photosynthesis (the greater the heat, the greater the results of photosynthesis), AND I plant two plants supplying one with plenty of heat and the other with no heat at all, THEN the plant I supplied with the heat should photosynthesize better.

III. IF light intensity affects photosynthesis in plants, AND I expose my plant to different light intensities, THEN there should be more photosynthesis taking place in the plant during its exposure to the greater light intensity compared to its exposure of low light intensity.

Actual Results

My actual results were similar to my predicted results, which were: that there would be more oxygen bubbles, resulting from photosynthesis, with more intense light than with lesser intense light. The differences between intensities are illustrated in Graph 1.1. Table 1.1 breaks this data into numerical values.

Discussion and Conclusion

My actual results are the same as my expected results. There was more photosynthesis being carried out in the plant while it was exposed to strong light intensity and less photosynthesis while it was exposed to low light intensity. I conclude that light intensity does affect the rate of photosynthesis. My actual results are consistent with my hypothesis and, therefore, they support my hypothesis.

My actual results are what I expected to find. I saw more oxygen bubbles given off by the plant when it was exposed to strong light intensity than when it was exposed to low light intensity. These bubbles indicated that photosynthesis was taking place. None of my above alternative hypotheses could be supported by my collected data and therefore should not be tested in the future; however, there is another hypothesis which could be tested with these results: that as the light gets intense, so does the heat, and therefore the greater the heat, the more photosynthesis is taking place, and vice versa with less intense light causing less heat, causing less bubbles. These two hypotheses can be tested and compared and therefore should be enough for the data to support them. They can both be tested using the experimental procedures as listed above.

continued

Why does greater intense light cause more photosynthesis to take place in plants than lesser intense light? This cannot be explained with my data and should be tested with another experiment. One hypothesis for this question might be that there is stronger radiation from the light the closer and more intense it is than the further and less intense it is, resulting in weaker radiation. Some other hypotheses might be: 1) Why does the variance in heat from the light source cause photosynthesis to fluctuate depending on the temperature? 2) Why does a plant use light to carry out photosynthesis? Why doesn't it use water?

The above information can be helpful for anyone trying to construct and operate an artificial greenhouse for plants, or for the average houseplant which needs light to survive. My casual question is intriguing and simple to test if you take every precaution and every detail of the experiment into account.

Exercises

This last activity will ask that you bring together all the information and knowledge you have gained about the writing, reading, and researching process and *apply* that process to writing a scientific report. The activity is best carried out if you work in groups of three students who will share research and reading tasks and who will serve as critics for the paper each of you will write individually.

Each group should select a topic which interests them and which can be researched by using sources within the college community or the immediate geographical area. We suggest two groupings of students:

- If three students are taking the same laboratory science course, have taken the course recently, or are familiar with the course material and procedures, they may use any of the topics of their laboratory or class work as the foundation for the report.
- Those who are not currently enrolled in a science course could select a topic which can be carried out through both field research and such other sources as library resources; interviews; local, county, and state offices (agriculture, natural resources, etc.); college departments and institutes; and electronic media resources.

Selecting a topic: Groups should be free to select a topic which focuses on one discipline or one which spans disciplines but which uses one particular science as a base for certain knowledge. For example, for those not currently taking a science course, animal-language research is based both on biology and linguistics and could be researched through both scholarly and popular sources. Try to select a topic which involves laboratory or fieldwork—or both—or research which involved such work.

Basic Guidelines

a. Set up a format for the report which follows or adapts the basic scientific report format provided in the Guide section above.

b. Write the report for an audience of your peers, preferably for classmates in this course.

c. Write the report to emphasize both clear expression and sound organization, but also pay attention to formatting that will appeal to the readers.

d. Establish as a class the schedule for completing the stages of the writing process and grading criteria for the entire project.

e. Specify the responsibilities of each group member.

f. Try to use as many of the writing and learning elements and techniques as you can: notebooks, journals, note cards, discussions, interviews, varied media, drafts, varied means of presenting material (prose, visuals, audio and video tapes, CD-ROM and other computer tools).

g. Finally, understand that you are not expected to be expert scientists at this point; your main goal should be to explore an interesting topic and communicate your findings in a scientific format.

URLs for the Naturual Sciences

The Academy of Natural Sciences Related Links
http://www.acnatsci.org/links.html

The World(TM) Guide to Natural Science
http://www.theworld.com/SCIENCE/NATURALS/SUBJECT.HTML

Natural History Resources
http://ucmpl.berkeley.edu/subway/nathist.html

National Academy of Sciences
http://www.nas.aas.org/

Science and Technology
http://www.voicenet.com/tech/

NASA Kennedy Space Center Library
http://www-lib.ksc.nasa.gov/lib/science.html

The USDA Research Database
http://cos.gdb.org/best/fedfund/usda/usda-intro.html

CHAPTER EIGHT

Writing in Mathematics and Information Technology

t_1

ω_2

An accelerating bicycle wheel rotates with angular speed ω_2 at time t_2.

Responsibilities of Mathematicians and Information Technologists

Importance of Communications to the Mathematician and Information Technology Professional

Writing in Undergraduate Mathematics and Information Technology Programs

Writing in Computer Science and the Decision Sciences

In this chapter we will consider writing in two related areas: mathematics and information technology. You are, no doubt, familiar with the first of these from such previous courses as basic mathematics, algebra, geometry, and calculus. You are probably less familiar with the second area, which includes computer science, management information systems, decision sciences, and industrial technology—all of which apply computer technology to solve problems in a specific field or discipline. We have put them together in this chapter because they either focus exclusively on mathematics or use mathematics and computing as a foundation.

Throughout this book, we try to show that writing is useful to both students and graduates in such diverse fields as social sciences, humanities, engineering, health sciences, business, and natural sciences. Most of you might even have realized before the semester started that writing plays a central role in learning, expressing knowledge, and communicating in most of these disciplines. However, if we had provided a list of all the disciplines covered in this book and then asked students to indicate which ones were least likely to involve writing, mathematics and information technology would probably have been selected unanimously. Many students might argue that mathematics and information technology areas depend completely on numbers, symbols, equations, and mathematical models to solve problems, express mathematical functions, and write coded programming. Thus, those students might argue that writing plays no role in such areas. As we have done in previous chapters, let's look to the actual professional responsibilities of graduates in these programs as a means of considering these assumptions.

Responsibilities of Mathematicians and Information Technologists

One way to understand the occupational, professional, and ethical responsibilities assumed by people in their chosen careers is to consider how specialists define their disciplines. In turn, knowing these definitions enables us to understand the uses of writing and other forms of communication in those careers. Study the following definitions and then complete the exercise.

Mathematics: The science of numbers and their operations, interrelations, combinations, generalizations, and abstractions and of the space configurations and their structure, measurement, transformations, and generalizations.

Computer Science: The discipline of computing is the systematic study of algorithmic processes that describe and transform information: their theory, analysis, design, efficiency, implementation and application. The fundamental question underlying all of computing is, "What can be automated?"

From "Computing as a Discipline," A Report of the ACM Task Force on the Core of Computer Science.

Industrial Technology: The application of computing theory, processes, and practice to design, implement, and develop technological solutions to industrial problems.

1. After carefully studying the definitions, list what you think might be the responsibilities of people who work in these areas. If you know people who work in occupations related to these areas, think of what their jobs entail. Have you read about any of the responsibilities associated with careers in these areas? How might the responsibilities of these people determine the writing they do? What types of writing do you suppose they do?

2. Does your list reveal connections among any of the three disciplines above and disciplines covered in previous chapters? If so, compare one of the above disciplines to one of the disciplines from Chapters Five through Seven.

3. *If you have access to the Internet,* use a browser (Netscape, Mosaic, Lynx) to locate five Gopher sites or World Wide Web sites of interest to students pursuing one of the following careers:
   • computer science
   • mathematics
   • information technology
   Explore each of the five sites you locate, making sure to record their Gopher site address or their Universal Resource Locator (URL).
   Using a word-processing package, write a paragraph that summarizes the contents of each of the sites you have found and describes the materials that are contained within them. Make sure to include the address of the site.

4. *If you have access to a computer network and e-mail,* locate and subscribe to an on-line discussion or newsgroup that involves individuals working in one of the fields listed above. For help in locating an appropriate on-line discussion, go to the library or a local bookstore and find a book on the Internet that provides a subject-focused index of on-line discussions and newsgroups. Seek help from your campus computing experts, knowledgeable friends, the technology consultant in the lab you use, or your teacher in subscribing to the list.
   Monitor the conversation within this discussion or newsgroup for at least three days. At the end of this period, *using a computer and word-processing package,* identify the issues that have been covered in this conversation, providing a one- or two-paragraph summary description of each.

The responsibilities of those who get degrees in mathematics are related directly to the jobs they hold. We all know that many who major in mathematics go on to teach, either grades 1 through 12 or in college. The responsibilities of these graduates are the same as those of other teachers and professors in that they must meet the same ethical and professional standards required of any educator. That mathematics is the second most commonly taught subject in college, as well as in grades 1 through 12, should tell you the importance that not only educators but the public, as well, place on learning mathematics. Aside from those who become educators, many other mathematicians go on to work in business, health sciences, industry, or government. While the careers of people with mathematics degrees are probably as diverse as those of any major, a large percentage of mathematicians work directly with scientists, health professionals, and engineers. Thus, they fulfill responsibilities similar to those groups. Significantly, virtually none of those careers operates solely in a purely numerical or mathematically symbolic environment.

Whether the graduate becomes a statistician in an insurance company, is a member of a project team along with engineers and physicists in an automobile company, or works with health scientists developing prediction models for disease control, mathematicians spend major amounts of their time *communicating,* both in speaking and writing, with coworkers from many fields, and are frequently called upon to explain and clarify important issues to the general public.

What is true for business, social sciences, engineering, and all other majors covered in this book is true for mathematics majors: Almost all college-educated people work closely with a wide range of other professionals and play important roles accomplishing the goals of their organization. Like all other professionals, mathematicians depend heavily on sound communciations skills to succeed. This is also the case with those who major in the growing field of information technology.

Comprised of such areas as computer science, manufacturing and industrial technology, decision sciences, and management information systems, this growing academic field emerged from the rapid development of computers in the past twenty years. As both the capacity and capability for computers to process and store information, compute vast amounts of data, and model potential solutions to problems has grown, education, business, industry, and government have created enormous demands for computer technology and software. Chapter Four of this book offers a brief glimpse into the significant impact of computers on writing. The effect of computers on industry and business has, if anything, been even more dramatic. Over the past decade, Computer-Aided Design (CAD) and Computer-Aided Manufacturing (CAM) have revolutionized industrial processes, while companies have integrated computer-related procedures into virtually every aspect of their businesses.

Like any other revolutionary development in our society, such changes carry with them enormous responsibility for those who create and control the instruments of change. As this change relates to writing and communication in general, those who work in these new fields are challenged with communicating very complex knowledge to a variety of audiences, both within their own organizations and to customers, public officials, and the general public. In the case of those in decision sciences, for example, clear communication of the benefits of their product determines whether their customers can understand and use the product or whether they will be baffled by the language intended to explain the product's use. In other words, if a company does not clearly communicate and support its products, they will not stay in business.

Lastly, these graduates hold key positions in science, business, health care, industry and education—all critically important areas to citizens. Therefore, they have an important responsibility to use and communicate their knowledge to the benefit of society, as well as to the benefit of themselves and their employers.

1. Many of us have experienced the frustration of grappling with instructions or directions intended to guide us through the use of a computer or a computer software package. Find an example of both a successful and an unsuccessful computer-related document that seeks to explain, describe, or guide users. Working with a partner, analyze the two examples to determine why one is successful while the other is not. What characterizes the differences between the two examples? What specific features make the reading and understanding of the unsuccessful example difficult? Rewrite the unsuccessful example so that it possesses the positive attributes of the successful document.

2. *If you have access to a word-processing package,* work with a writing partner to compose a short tutorial that would take first-time users of this package through the process of loading up the package, creating a file, writing a sample paragraph in the file, printing a file, and saving a file.

   When you have a draft of this tutorial, test it on a user. Identify a friend, classmate, high-school student, or acquaintance who does not know how to use the word-processing package. Make an appointment with this individual for a user-testing session. Have one of your team sit next to the user and take notes about where the instructions are incomplete, inadequate, or confusing. Hold an interview with your subject after the task is done to get additional feedback.

   Using the feedback from this session, revise your tutorial.

3. *If you have access to a computer network and the World Wide Web,* work with a writing partner to create a short beginner's tutorial for using a browser (for example, Netscape, Mosaic, Lynx). In this tutorial, provide directions about how to search the net by topic and how to locate a specific site by using its Universal Resource Locator (URL).

   Complete the rest of the assignment as described in the second and third steps of exercise 2.

Importance of Communications to the Mathematician and Information Technology Professional

Interestingly, mathematics is regarded by all mathematicians as a "language" in its own right. Whether it is algebra, geometry, calculus, differential equations or combinatorial mathematics, all involve specialized languages to express solutions to problems. Certain mathematics courses focus on such languages. Note the following course description:

> A theory of grammars: methods of syntactic analysis and specification, types of artificial languages, relationship between formal languages and automata of computer science.

The course described above is not from an English department, rather it is from a university mathematics department and describes a senior-level course entitled Theory of Formal Languages. Notice, however, that the description includes terms similar to those used to describe courses we usually think of as grammar courses, "syntactic analysis," for example.

Like the above course, information technology courses are intricately involved with languages. Whether the language is one of the numerous mainstream programming languages (for example, COBOL, FORTRAN, SNOBALL, BASIC, and C which are used to develop applications that then run on their own) or one such as an EXCEL or LOTUS macro language that may only be used with a specific application, languages form the crux of all disciplines and occupations. Remember, as we saw in Chapter Seven, highly scientific and technical fields rely extensively on visual, graphic, and mathematical languages.

Those of you who do not major in mathematics or in one of the information technology areas may never take a course which employs such high-level mathematical languages or advanced programming languages. Most often, these languages are used to collect data, form hypotheses, build data structures, and test models. However, the results of all this "language" manipulation are found in thousands of common devices–from watches and microwave ovens to the most complex space vehicles. All electronic mechanisms are, in fact, controlled by languages because the computers themselves are controlled by programming languages. Therefore, the specialists who create and use these languages are experts in this particular type of language use.

Despite the complexity and mathematical orientation of these disciplines, not all the ideas communicated among these specialists depend solely on mathematical language for their success. Mathematicians and information technologists accomplish much of their work through clear, concise documents which employ both mathematical languages and their country's written language. Additionally, in both informal workplace conversation and in formal meetings, they exchange ideas through verbal language. In short, mathematicians and information technologists move back and forth between languages, integrating the languages in order to successfully communicate.

Exercises

1. Solving a mathematical problem depends greatly on being able to read the problem and integrate both the mathematical and verbal languages used to

pose the problem. In other words, the interaction of both languages contributes to your understanding or, at times, your lack of the same. Locate a mathematics textbook and select a problem which uses both verbal and mathematical languages. After carefully studying the problem, describe the ways in which the two languages contribute to your understanding of the problem and to any difficulties you may have with the problem.

2. If you have taken a mathematics course in which the teacher included writing of any kind, summarize your response to that part of the course. Do you think writing helped you in the course? Did writing about the problems and solutions provide you with a different view of them? How did other students respond to the assignments?

3. *If you have access to a word-processing package,* browse through your current mathematics textbook and find an equation for a type of problem that you already know how to solve. Create a file, and write this equation at the top of that file. Shutting your math book, type below this equation a description of how to solve it—using words only. Imagine the audience for your writing to be a student who has not yet completed the mathematics unit that deals with the equation in question—one who may know some mathematics, but is not familiar with the particular kind of equation on which you are focusing. In your description, try, as well, to provide your audience with a real-life example of a situation in which they could use the equation.

When you are done with your description, compare the two kinds of expressions you have in front of you—the equation, consisting of one kind of symbolic representation in the language of mathematics, and the description, consisting of another kind of symbolic representation in words. Write a paragraph that reflects on two things: first, the differences between these two modes of representation, and, second, the usefulness that each manner of representation may have in different situations.

Writing in Undergraduate Mathematics and Information Technology Programs

In the remainder of the chapter we will explore writing assignments from three academic areas, presenting examples from mathematics, computer science, and decision sciences. While mathematics professors do frequently assign writing in such courses as History of Mathematics and sometimes require students to write reviews of scholarly articles, most of the writing assigned in undergraduate mathematics courses may be classified as "writing to learn" activities, including journal entries and annotations of problems; therefore, we shall emphasize those types of assignments. The examples from computer science and decision sciences have been chosen not only because they represent assignments from undergraduate courses but also because they often demonstrate the kind of writing required of graduates from these programs. Writing in such courses is very much directed at the professional responsibilities of the program's graduates, so the examples used will mirror the writing required of professionals in these fields. Thus, in this chapter, we have chosen to integrate the presentation of professional and academic writing.

Writing in Mathematics Courses

Short written responses

Some of the most frequently used writing assignments in mathematics classes involve very short written responses. Figure 8.1 shows an example of a chart used in an intermediate algebra class:

FIGURE 8.1   Algebraic Expressions Exercise

#	EXPRESSION IN WORDS	EXPRESSION IN ALGEBRA
1.	half of a number	$n/2$
2.	six more than half of a number	$n/2 + 6$
3.	half again as much as a number	$1.5\,(n) = 1.5n$
4.	three less than one-third of a number	$n/3 - 3$
5.	a number squared	n^2
6.	twice as much as the square of a number	$2(n^2) = 2n^2$
7.	the square of twice a number	$(2n)^2$

Exercises

1. What are the benefits of first showing the expression in words and then asking students to write the expression algebraically? Are there, in fact, additional ways which would express in words those algebraic expressions? After each student writes answers to these questions, compile a list of all the possible benefits of expressing algebraic equations in both writing and algebraic notation. What does the list reveal about the relationship between mathematical problem solving and the use of written expressions?
2. *If you have access to a word-processing package,* browse around in your mathematics textbook and find an equation for a particular kind of problem that you already know how to solve. Create a file, and author two word problems that require the use of the equation you have chosen. Make sure that the word problems you create are real-world problems—ones that students you know might encounter in their daily lives. Imagine the audience for these problems to be advanced high-school mathematics students.

While Figure 8.1 appears to show very simple examples of writing to express algebraic expressions, the examples exemplify two of the major attributes of skillful writing about mathematics: clarity and brevity. For example, is there another way to write the example given in number 7? If so, is that way as concise and clear as "the square of twice a number"? Does the expression "two times a number squared" convey the same meaning as the previous phrase? Or in number 1, does the expression "a number divided by two" possess the same meaning as "half of a number"? As you study the column "Expressions in Words," do you see any patterns in word choice (diction) or the arrangement of words and grammatical parts (syntax) that would explain the choices? Is there any significance to the absence of such mathematical terms as "times" and "divided by"? Your answers to these questions should help reveal the value of precision in expressing mathematical expressions verbally and in writing.

Exercises

1. Here are some of the remaining items from the intermediate algebra "expressions" exercise (Figure 8.2.) Try them on your own, then compare your answers with a partner's.

FIGURE 8.2   Algebraic Expressions Exercise

#	EXPRESSION IN WORDS	EXPRESSION IN ALGEBRA
8.	fifteen less than half of the square of a number	
9.	fifteen miles per hour	
10.	nine miles per hour for 6 hours	
11.	twice as many dimes as nickels	
12.	half as much as three years ago	
13.	more than 6 times as much as it was five years ago	
14.	doubles every year	

2. *If you have access to a word-processing package,* work with your writing group to create a file that contains twenty algebraic expressions of the kind represented in this section. Represent ten of these expressions in words only and ten of them in algebraic symbols. In the prose descriptions, try to come up with expressions that will challenge the algebraic knowledge of a first-term college student.

Exchange this file, on disk or via a network, with another writing group. Each group should translate the expressions provided to them—changing the ten algebraic expressions into linguistic representations and the ten language expressions into algebraic expressions.

Another way to briefly respond to mathematical problems is to provide short explanations, or what mathematicians sometimes call justifications, for mathematical calculations. The next example (Figure 8.3) is taken from the same algebra class as Figures 8.1 and 8.2. Note that the arrows leading from the left to the right column indicate steps in the mathematical solution and the corresponding reason for the calculation.

FIGURE 8.3   Work/Justification Exercise

work/calculations	reason/explanation/justification
p. 300/#5 $\quad\quad\quad 0 = 5y^2 - 20$	
$0 = 5y^2 - 5.4$	→ re-write w/coefficients factored
$0 = 5(y^2 - 4)$	→ remove common factor using distrib. property
$0 = 5(y + 2)(y - 2)$	→ factor binomial as difference of 2 squares
$5 = 0, y + 2 = 0, y - 2 = 0$	→ zero-product rule
$\downarrow \quad y + 2 - 2 = 0 - 2, y - 2 + 2 = 0 + 2$	→ move constants using addition prop. of equations
no sol'n., $y = -2, y = +2$	→ write in solution form
p. 303/#11	
$(x - 6)(x + 1) = x(x - 8) + 5$	
$x^2 - 6x + x - 6 = x^2 - 8x + 5$	→ expand in order to group terms
$x^2 - 5x - 6 = x^2 - 8x + 5$	→ combine like terms on ea. side
$-x^2 \quad\quad\quad\quad -x^2$	
$-5x - 6 = -8x + 5$	→ subtraction property of equ'n.
$+ 8x \quad\quad\quad\quad + 8x$	
$3x - 6 = + 5$	→ addition property of equ'n.
$+ 6 \quad\quad\quad\quad + 6$	
$3x/3 = 11/3$	→ addition property of equ'n.
$x = 11/3$	→ division property of equ'n

This exercise requires that the student specify (or rewrite) each step of the algebraic solution. Sometimes called annotating (see Chapter Two for our first discussion of annotating), this procedure provides the student with another means of understanding the steps involved in solving the problem. The mathematics teacher who assigns this exercise believes that requiring students to translate the algebraic operations into written language allows them to think more carefully about the steps and to connect the steps of the solution more logically.

Exercises

1. Study the annotations for each of the two problems. In Chapter Two, Reading in the Disciplines, you learned that successful reading and understanding depend on observing cues in the reading that alert you to important features of the material and that can enable you to predict what will come next. Are there such cues in the annotations to these problems? Has the writer constructed thoughts which allow a logical progression through the steps?

2. We might think of annotating as a means of commenting on—or, as we shall see in the computer-science section of this chapter, of documenting steps in—a process. Our understanding of process is almost always increased if we see clearly the coherent relationship among the parts. Can you think of a process for which commenting or documenting would provide insights and help establish relationships among the parts? Working with a partner, select a process or a step-by-step problem-solution and write and annotate it. Remember: Clarity and brevity are prized in this type of writing.

3. *If you have access to a word-processing package,* look through the homework you completed for your most recent mathematics class. Find a problem that was complex and that took numerous steps to complete. Using the word-processing package, create a file and, in it, show the steps you took in solving this problem. Use mathematical notation as you would on a quiz to get partial credit for the processes involved in solving a problem. When you are done, recheck the problem to make sure that you recorded each step of the problem's calculations as you solved them.

   Next, if your word-processing package has an annotation feature, identify in words the specific justification for each step in the problem-solving process. See our example on page 266 for an illustration of this process.

4. *If you have access to a word-processing package,* create a file, and, using only words (and nonmathematical picture elements, if you choose), author a paragraph or two that describe to a second-grade student the easiest way of estimating the answer of multiplication problems involving the number nine and a double-digit number (for example, 9×27, 33×9). Explain not only how to estimate the answer, but what an estimation is. In addition, tell your audience why this process of estimation works and why it is important that they learn this process.

   When you are done with this explanation, try to find a second-grade student who can read and learn from your explanation. Have this student read your writing out loud and try the technique that you have identified. If you cannot find a second-grade student locally, try this exercise out with a younger member of your family, the children of friends, or your own children. As you watch the student read your explanation, identify the areas in which it is unclear, incomplete, or confusing for your audience. Revise your explanation after this user-testing experience.

Journals and guided inquiry writing

In Chapter One, Writing in the Disciplines, we noted that the Mathematical Association of America believes so strongly that writing is important in learning mathematics that they published a book entitled *Using Writing to Teach Mathematics*. This book, a direct result of presentations at the Association's 1989 conference where about forty mathematicians described how they used writing to teach mathematics, includes examples of writing in mathematics courses from all four years of the undergraduate curriculum. Let's look at an example from the book which demonstrates how writing promotes the learning of mathematics.

One of the most popular methods used by mathematics professors to integrate writing into their courses is the use of journals, which many professors view as a means of getting students to *think* about problems and solutions rather than searching randomly for an answer. Most students who take math courses are probably familiar with the statement, "You must show your work in order to get full credit for your answer to this problem." The two earlier exercises from the intermediate algebra class are examples of such practices. Most of the teachers who require this do so not because they want to make sure you have done the work yourself, but because they want to make sure you truly have understood the solution to the problem. Without seeing the steps you have gone through, teachers cannot tell how your thinking has developed. Journals can accomplish a similar goal.

In the following example from a calculus class, students were asked to solve a problem about the speed of an airplane with respect to the ground and to write about their solving process in a journal. One student's journal entry revealed that she first attempted to solve the problem by drawing a picture: "So that's the picture I come up with." However, even the drawing didn't initially help, for she subsequently wrote, "Now I want to find the speed of the plane with respect to the ground. . . . I'm not really sure about this problem. I don't know what the 'respect to's' mean." After more thought, the student wrote, "What I should have done to make things more clear to myself is I should have labeled things like letting V_{pa} be the velocity of the plane with respect to the air and let V_{ag} be the velocity of the plane with respect to the ground." Once the student began to realize that labeling parts of the problem and following the hints provided in the problem statement provided a path to solving the problem, she quickly did so by combining her new insights and previous knowledge.

This student's experience in using her own writing as a learning tool is not unusual. As is the case in other disciplines, writing in academic journals often assists students in discovering what they do and do not understand about a subject or, in this case, a problem. Many mathematics teachers regularly ask their students to write about solving problems—what strategies they use, what is working, and what's not. The following problem and a student's response to it show yet another benefit of writing about problem solving:

Problem: The perimeter of a combined figure formed by a rectangle and a square is 34; the two figures share one common side. The perimeter of the rectangle is 26. Find the sides of the square and the rectangle.

Guided Inquiry Writing: How would you solve the problem? Can you think of more than one way to solve it? Write out your solution(s) to the problem.

Now look at this math student's response to the same problem (Figure 8.4):

FIGURE 8.4   Student's Written Response to a Math Problem

Visualizing this type of problem can be an effective way to solve it. First, draw a picture of the combined figures and label the sides with two variables. Here is what such a picture would look like:

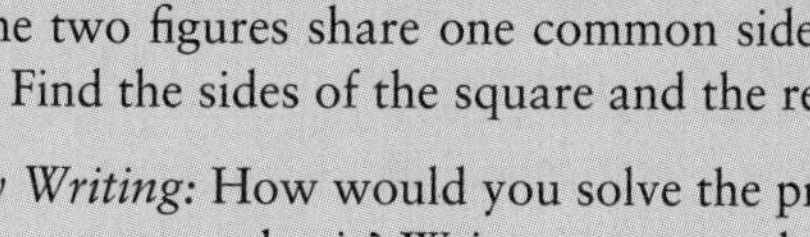

Then, use the perimeter formula for rectangles to subtract the rectangle from the combined perimeter:

$$P = 2L + 2W$$
$$(L + L + W + W)$$

$$\begin{array}{r} 4a + 2b = 34 \text{ combined perimeter} \\ -(2a + 2b = 26) \text{ perimeter of rectangle} \\ \hline 2a \qquad = 8 \end{array}$$

Now, just solve for your variable ($a = 4$) and substitute that answer back into both equations to find the length of the sides of the square and rectangle. Of course, you can also use the formula without the drawing to create your equations directly, but drawing the figures can sometimes help you see the problem more clearly.

This student's response powerfully demonstrates the integration of the several languages employed by scientists, technologists, and mathematicians: visual, mathematical, and written. Note how she moves from stage to stage, through the presentation of first the visual (the drawing), then the mathematical (the formula), and finally the written (the words themselves). Note also that as she moves from one stage to the next in her explanation, she links the three language presentations together by markers or cues: "First," "Then," and "Now." Such markers usually indicate that the writer has fashioned a well-organized plan and clearly understands the purpose of each section of the document. Even in this informal piece of writing, the writer demonstrates a strong sense of how each of the three languages she uses contributes to her explanation.

Final comments on writing in mathematics courses

Although writing throughout the mathematics curriculum is far more varied than we have presented here, the content of most of that writing was far too advanced for our purposes in this textbook. Nevertheless, we should mention some of those assignments. Most mathematics majors take courses in the history of mathematics and in the theory of formal languages which require writing essays, reports, and, perhaps, an argumentative paper. Occasionally, senior-level mathematics students are required to write papers which follow the format of a professional journal article. Since we have covered all these types of writing in other chapters and since the mathematics required to construct such papers is so advanced, we have chosen not to cover them as they would occur in mathematics courses. Remember, as well, that mathematicians work closely with a wide range of other professionals, so the writing done by mathematics graduates often results from collaborative writing tasks with scientists, engineers, medical researchers, and businesspersons. Mathematics graduates, must, therefore, be prepared to write to other mathematicians, coworkers from many disciplines, and occasionally to those who know far less mathematics than they do. Their writing tasks are, then, very much like those of almost all other college graduates: varied, frequent, and often collaborative.

Writing in Information Technology Programs

It is difficult to imagine any course of study more language-intensive and more dependent on sound written and verbal communication than those programs which focus on information technology. Starting with the field of computer science and extending to such applied fields as management information systems, decision sciences, and computer information systems, these technology- and language-based programs have grown dramatically over the past decade. Responding to demands from both the public and private sectors for computer-based data and information systems specialists, college programs preparing students for work in these areas have been hard-pressed to meet the demand for their graduates. Students in and graduates of these programs spend almost all their study and work time learning, creating, applying, or communicating in a growing array of languages, and also in learning and creating structures for those languages.

In previous chapters we touched on the importance of computers and information systems, both to you as a student and to the society as a whole. From supermarket check-out procedures to deep-space satellites, computers and the languages used to operate them significantly affect our daily lives and possess the potential to do so for the world community. While this may sound like an overly dramatic portrayal of the importance of computers and computer systems in our lives, a look at our daily lives may prove the validity of the statement. The following exercises should help you begin to think about writing related to information technology.

1. Divide into groups of four or five and make a list of everyday devices and situations that depend on computers.

    After the list has been constructed, have each person choose a device that requires you to read instructions in order to operate it. Write a paragraph addressing the following questions: How would you describe the writing in the manual or guide? Is it easy to read? Does it provide clear and complete directions? Is the writing aimed at a general level of understanding? Did the instructions assist you to your satisfaction?

2. Science fiction books and films regularly portray civilizations brought to ruin by computer technology. Can you think of actual world events which have been affected by computers or computerized systems? Are there direct correspondences between the creative versions of computers' capabilities and the actual capabilities? As a group, make a comparison and contrast list which you could use as the basis for an essay.

3. Find a set of directions or a user's manual for a commercial product you have recently purchased—a wristwatch, a VCR, an alarm clock, a calculator, a CD player. Choose a short section of these directions that you feel is particularly misleading, incomplete, or vague—for this activity, you will be revising this section of the directions. Using the word-processing package, type in the section of the original directions that you are going to revise. If your word processor has an annotation feature, use it to identify the specific points at which the directions are incomplete, vague, unclear, or misleading; describe the particular problems in evidence at each point of the original directions. In these annotations, consider the directions from the point of view of a consumer who must be able to understand the directions in order to use the product effectively and safely.

    Next, below the original section and your annotations, rewrite the directions to address the specific problems you have identified.

    When you have completed your revision, exchange your work with a writing partner. Using the annotation feature of the word-processing program, comment on the effectiveness of the revision, indicating the specific points at which the revised directions remain problematic in some way. In your annotations, consider the revised directions from the point of view of a consumer.

Writing in Computer Science and the Decision Sciences

Looking at the courses a computer science or decision sciences major takes in the first two years of college provides a clue to the emphasis on language in computer science and information technology programs. For example, in courses numbered 100 or 200 in Arizona State University's Computer Science and Engineering curriculum, no fewer than nine computer programming languages are taught. Therefore, many of the assignments in these courses focus on introducing students to such specialized languages as COBOL, BASIC, FORTRAN, LISP, PROLOG, and APL and on testing their understanding of these languages. Additionally, the introductory courses focus on problem solving, design, mathematical systems, and data structures. As we have seen, these are concerns in other disciplines. Thus, the study of computer science and information technology combines approaches and strategies used in science, mathematics, engineering, business, and communications studies. The successful computer-science student, then, must possess a range of knowledge and must develop a range of learning and communication skills. Let's look at a few representative examples of assignments that demonstrate some common practices in computer science and information technology courses.

The writing of those who work in the computer field is similar to scientific and technical professionals from other fields in that it spans a variety of audiences and encompasses a variety of formats. In fact, many faculty try to simulate these features in their assignments. Here is a list of writing formats from computer science and decision sciences courses, first-year through senior level:

essay exams	article reviews
memos	proposals
programming	case studies
documenting programming	test reports
recommendation reports	procedures manuals

You will note that many of these formats are covered in chapters on writing in natural sciences, business, health sciences, and engineering. Therefore, much of what applies to writing memos in business and management and engineering, for example, can be transferred to writing memos in the information sciences. Thus, knowledge you have gained about these formats from these other disciplines is especially applicable for this reason: As we have pointed out, computer science and information technology draw on several disciplines to establish their means of acquiring and communicating knowledge; therefore, they will share certain strategies, structures, and formats with these related disciplines.

While the final section of this chapter will present writing assignments from both computer science and decision sciences courses, we will concentrate primarily on examples from decision sciences for several reasons. First, the subject matter is more accessible to most first-year students than is computer science, which concerns itself with application, functional, or assembly languages. Second, over the past decade, programs which prepare people to work as informational specialists in specific environments—business and industry, in particular—have assumed more and more prominence. This area is, therefore, very representative of a major swing in information technology programs. Adding to this popularity is the shift from highly coded, machine-readable languages to ones increasingly similar to commonly spoken and written languages. Third, to an extent, your work in this chapter will prepare for assignments in Chapter Nine, Writing in Business and Management, for, as we have noted, decision sciences and business programs are closely connected.

However, to begin, let's look at a few assignments and sample writings from computer science which will provide a sense of how writing is used in the discipline.

Writing in Computer Science

Informal learning logs

Students in introductory computer science classes are often asked to summarize lectures, concepts, or readings in what humanities faculty might call a *journal,* whereas faculty in the sciences would probably prefer the term *learning log.* Regardless of the term used to designate the source, the general purpose remains the same: writing in a journal or log provides an opportunity to test understanding. The following entry is representative of one from a first-year student's learning log.

"Let's see, the diff bet'n digital and analog computers. Well we learned in class that a digital computer works with symbols such as #s or letters that are used to translate data into a form that the computer can read. It then takes the translated data and manipulates it in the desired fashion. An analog comp. works with quantities such as lengths and current to solve a certain problem, like an engineering design problem. The signals from an analog comp. don't jump around like the ones in a digital comp. I guess that's because they change more smoothly. I guess. The part I don't quite understand is why the signals on a digital comp jump around more than the ones in an analog comp. Karen, my friend, who's a EE [electrical engineering major] says it's because the quality of the signal in an analog is a continuous signal but the digital signal is interrupted. Come to think of it, if the analog signal is smoother and better then why wouldn't they make all computers that way?

This brief statement of the difference between digital and analog computers suggests several possibilities.

1. Working with a partner, list answers to the following questions:
   a. Which parts of the statement seem to be in a student's own words and which parts might be a teacher's words?
   b. Are there signs that the writer doesn't really understand the difference between the two types of computers?
   c. Does this writer seem interested in understanding the difference between the two types of computers?
2. If either you or your partner knows the difference between digital and analog computers, write a paragraph explaining the differences.

3. *If you have access to a computer network and to the World Wide Web,* use a browser (for example, Netscape, Mosaic, etc.) to explore at least ten Web sites that might be of interest to students seeking a career in information technologies. After you have made a preliminary exploration of these sites, choose five of the most interesting ones to annotate for other members of your class. Explore each of these sites more fully, taking notes as you go. Write a paragraph that summarizes the materials found in each of the sites, the issues covered there, the benefits that the site has for students, the interesting features of the site. Don't forget to identify the Universal Resource Locator (URL) for each site.

   In your writing group, add your list of annotated sites to those of the other members of the writing group. As a group, visit each of the sites and create a new list of the top three sites that the members of your group agree on as being most interesting for students. Add these top three picks to those produced by the other writing groups in your class to create a combined list of WWW sites that students interested in information technologies might want to visit.

Your answers to the exercise questions may have cited some of the major benefits of this type of assignment, one of which is that it allows the writer to bring up important issues not directly raised by the question. For example, had the student been asked to merely list the characteristics of the two types of computers, he would probably not have explored what he didn't know. Listing is, of course, a frequently used testing technique and a useful way of determining whether students have read the material or listened to the lecture and taken accurate notes. However, listing is not generally regarded as an effective means of determining to what extent someone actually understands the material and its application.

This example shows only a small portion of the benefits of this type of assignment in technical areas. Learning logs are valuable in information technology courses precisely because they allow students to put into their own words what they do and do not understand, what confuses them and what has been clarified. These are critically important issues in highly technical courses, for too often students believe that memorizing lists of traits and procedures constitutes learning in technical disciplines. Whether the field is engineering, science, or information technologies, the important issues are how well information and knowledge are understood, applied and communicated. Learning to accomplish those goals through writing is important to the success of any scientist or technologist.

Programming and documenting

No presentation of writing in computer science would be complete without at least mentioning programming. One of the main tasks learned by computer-science students and certainly one of the most important duties of a large number of computer-science graduates, programming may be defined as *creating a series of coded steps to predetermine the operations of a computer*. Programming is accomplished by writing instructions to direct the computer's functions or operations. Those of you who have done any programming know that in order for the program to run correctly, the programming must be absolutely correct. The instructions must be precise and error-free. In fact, you may have heard a computer programmer say that computers are only "dumb machines" since they only do what they are told to do. In other words, if you try to program a computer to execute a task it cannot do, very frustrating or bad situations can result! Here's a section of programming from a simple language called C (see Figure 8.5, page 276). This section is written to perform one simple operation: It is intended to supply an English-formatted "string" (a series of alpha-numeric characters comprising a unit—in this case the unit specifies complete date and time) generated from the operating system's date and time. We have annotated a few of the features of this bit of programming to provide some idea of the requirements placed on programmers, and to indicate some of the very basic features of the programming.

Programmers must be absolutely precise when they write programming code: Marks of punctuation and other markers are used with absolute consistency. For example, brackets are always used to designate a particular element in a series. If a programmer were to substitute a semicolon for brackets, misplace a comma, a period, or a bracket, the program would contain a "bug" and the program must be "debugged"—corrected—to run properly.

Different marks indicate different operations within the program code. The lines beginning with a "//" indicate lines of documentation, comments written by the programmer to assist the operator in carrying out the task. Notice the left brace ({) at the beginning of the eighth line of the programming section, just below the line that reads, "void main(void)." That brace marks the beginning of the programming; any line previous to that line is not a command, but rather a line of documentation or the title for that particular programming task. In this case, the title is "main," and the two terms before and after "main" tell what information, or types of information, will be exchanged with the

FIGURE 8.5   Annotated "C" Programming

Identifies language used, "C"

```
// ASCTIME (C*/)
// uses asctime() to get system time; the re-formats it into
//desired format
#include "stdio.h"
#include "time.h"
#include "conio.h"
void main(void)
{// ——————— needed by asctime()
    time_t lt;
    struct tm *ptr;
// ——————— needed for re-formatting of date
    static char time_string[30];
    static char date_string[32]
    static char asc_dayname[10];
    static char asc_month[10];
    static char asc_day[3];
    static char asc_year[4];
    char *weekday[] = {"Sun","day","Mon","day",
            "Tue","sday","Wed","nesday",
            "Thu","rsday","Fri","day",
            "Sat","urday"};
    char *month[] = {"Jan","uary","Feb","ruary",  ← note comma punc
            "Mar","ch","Apr","il",
            "May","","Jun","e",
            "Jul","y","Aug","ust",
            "Sep","tember","Oct","ober",
            "Nov","ember","Dec","ember"}; ← note ";" punctuation
int i, j;
(//)——————— get and save system time in ASCII format
    lt = time(NULL);
    ptr = localtime(&lt);
    strcpy(time_string, asctime(ptr));
/*  puts(time_string); */
// ——————— day of week
    for (i=0; i<3; i++) // collect the abbreviation supplied by
        asc_dayname[i] = time_string[i]; // asctime()
    i=0;
    while(strcmp(asc_dayname, *(weekday+i))!=0)
        i+=2; // look for a match in the weekday array
    strcat(asc_dayname, *(weekday+i+1); //add it to my_string
// ——————— month
    for (i=4; i<7; i++) // collect the abbreviation supplied by
        asc_month[i-4] = time_string[i]; // asctime()
    i=0;
    while(strcmp(asc_month, *(month+i))!=0)
        i += 2; // look for a match in the month array
    strcat(asc_month, *(month+i+1)); //add it to my_string
// ——————— day
```

Bracket marks → *(brace enclosing lines from* `// ASCTIME` *to* `void main(void)`*)*
beginning of
programming task

Slashes denote → *(pointing to the* `(//)` *line)*
documentation

Programming → *(brace enclosing the "day of week" section)*
codes note
consecutive
"string" of text

computer. Had we continued this example until the end of the programming direction, a right brace would have indicated the end of this programming task.

All this is, of course, very detailed work, the kind you might think leads to nothing but dreary hours spent behind a keyboard, churning out thousands of lines of programming and documentation. Well, not always. The following "apology" was written anonymously by a programmer after the release of a software program which was designed to execute engineering problems. The program was, shall we say, less than successful.

SORRY FOLKS !!!

AHPLSIM, contrary to the supplied documentation, does not support the following features:
1. FUNCTREG's are not in any way supported—either through library or user-defined routines.
2. CLUNITS may not be nested. (I.e., INC(DCD(A[5:2])) will not work, even though this physically implies that the outputs of the decoder are the inputs to the incrementor, which is clearly ok.) (Note: This is not in the documentation, but is so useful that it should be supported.)
3. The NODELAY statement doesn't work.
4. The SUPPRESS command doesn't work.
5. LABELS don't work.
6. (I'm on a roll!)
   Transfers with a vector length of more than 32 bits are parsed correctly, but execute improperly. (Extra bits get zeroed.)

Your frustrated AHPL buddy,

P.S. #1 Other than this it's a great simulator, and that's why I'm rewriting it!!

P.S. #2 Hex constants are illegal in-line. (Just thought I'd throw that in!)

This apology is not as atypical as you might think. Many computer science graduates write directly to their company's clients or to general audiences who are learning how to use software packages. Often, the writers try to make the instructions—or in this case, the follow-up apology for incomplete instructions—humorous.

We can see, then, from just these three examples that writing in computer science can be diverse and challenging, with many of the assignments being similar to ones you will write in other disciplines. Because computer science shares characteristics with mathematics, sciences, and engineering, computer science faculty often value formats, style, and conciseness as do those other disciplines. Yet because computer science also depends so much on careful, persuasive writing, it shares certain preferences with disciplines that value the clear presentation of argument. In light of this, consider the following question and then turn to the next set of exercises: Given the seeming difference between writing programs and documenting code on the one hand and writing well-crafted essays as they are traditionally conceived on the other, what might possibly connect these two tasks?

1. Make a list of the possible connections between writing in programming languages and in written English. Compare your list to two other classmates' and discuss how you would develop a short essay from them.
2. One of the most common assignments in upper-division computer science courses is the review article. (See Chapter 7, page 245, for a similar assignment, the "Critique of an Article.") When students write their reviews, they often spend all their time presenting the specifics of the article and then neglect the careful organization and coherence of their review. The following paragraph is the first of such a review. Even though it would have been written for a 300-level class, you should be able to comment on weaknesses in the paragraph's organization and coherence. Read the paragraph carefully, then suggest changes that would improve it.

Review—Peter J. Denning: Third Generation Computer Systems

In this paper, Peter Denning examines the features of third generation operating systems, that is, systems that were designed later than 1964. He first takes a broad look at different types of systems and the properties that they all have in common. The first of these properties is concurrency, the ability of a system to support several simultaneously operating activities or processes, which may or may not be progressing simultaneously. In the second common property, automatic resource allocation, the operating system controls the allocation of resources, thus freeing programmers from making such (possibly inefficient) decisions. This can be very helpful, especially when we view many different areas of system operation as resource allocation problems. Sharing, the simultaneous use of resources by more than one process, is the third common characteristic. The advantages of sharing include the ability to use subroutines written by someone else, the sharing of a central data base, and the removal of redundancy. According to Denning, the techniques for implementing sharable subroutines are similar to those for recursive subroutines, which can be called many times before even a single return is executed. The fourth common property, multiplexing, takes on many different forms. Basically, it involves the division of time into many disjoint intervals. A resource can be assigned to at most one process during each time interval. There are several techniques used for sharing and multiplexing. Under multiprogramming, many different programs may reside simultaneously in main memory. This implies the necessity for location independent programming and special switching mechanisms. With multiaccessing, many users are allowed simultaneous access to the system. Multitasking involves the support of more than one active process by a system. Multiprocessing is the process by which several processes are supported by the system. The next common property of third generation systems allows many users interaction with their processes. This interactive computing is known as remote conversational access. Nondeterminacy is another common characteristic. Simply stated, it is the unpredictable order in which resources may be assigned, shared, accessed, and released. The final common property is long term storage, which gives users the ability to store programs and data for long periods of time.

3. Choose any computer software package you are familiar with—perhaps a word processing program, a spreadsheet program, or a home management program—and select a task you have had some difficulty performing in it. Write a brief, step-by-step program for executing the task and include short documentation for several of the steps. Try to specify and maintain rules that remain consistent throughout the process. Remember: As a programmer and documentation specialist, your job is to simplify the life of the user, but you should also feel free to "liven up" the task for the user.

4. If you are taking, or have recently taken, a programming class, find an example of a program that you have written and had graded. If your word-processing package has an annotation feature, write documentation for each of the major sections or parts of this program that would be apppropriate for explaining to a nonprogrammer what is being accomplished and why each major element is important to the overall function of the program. At the beginning of the program, include a short descriptive statement, again for a nonprogrammer, about the program as a whole and its purpose. Your annotations should focus on the function of the program in a real-life situation and should not contain jargon unfamiliar to nonprogrammers.

5. If you are taking a computer science course, identify a writing partner with whom you can do this exercise. Each day after class, for a week, identify two to three questions that you have about the day's lecture or instruction— focus on concepts you did not understand, relationships between ideas that seem unclear to you, sections of the book that did not make sense. *Using a*

word-processing program, write out these questions and exchange them, on disk, with your partner.

Using a word-processing program, answer the questions your partner has given you on his or her disk. If you need help with these answers, consider the following possibilities: Ask the computer science instructor; a friend who has already taken and passed this course with a B or better; your study group; or, if this option is available to you, a tutor at the learning center that provides additional help with the assignments for this class. When you have answered your partner's questions clearly and completely, pass the disk back to your partner. Your partner will, in the meanwhile, answer the questions you have written and return the answers to you.

Writing in Decision Sciences

It is, perhaps, fitting that the final section of this chapter presents assignments from a discipline which we might say represents a growing trend in interdisciplinary approaches to educating people for the twenty-first century. Growing out of computer science and aligning itself with business and management departments, decision sciences is built both on theory and practice. The student who majors in decision sciences must be well-versed in the conceptual foundations of computer science, while also preparing to address both the immediate and future needs of business organizations. Here is the way one university describes its decision sciences major:

> The major prepares students for professional careers involving the analysis, configuration, programming, and database aspects of the design and implementation of computerized business information systems. The course work prepares students for a career in business computer information systems and for admission to graduate programs in computer information systems or management information systems.

This description points out two connections between the careers of decision sciences graduates and writing. First, the emphasis on information systems indicates clearly that students who major in decision sciences will assume major responsibilities in shaping and delivering usable information to clients—a job that demands specific writing skills. Second, graduates of this program may be involved in all aspects of such systems, so they will work with employees from many areas of their organization—a task for which sound communication skills in all areas are critical.

Writing from an introductory decision sciences course

Having established a context for the writing of decision science students, let's look at some representative assignments from an introductory decision sciences class. To begin, let's review the syllabus from this course to get an idea of how writing fits into such a course.

School of Business
Department of Decision Sciences
DSCI 3063 (MIS I)
Fall, 1995

I. Instructor:

Office: GCB 3104
Phone: 757-6410
Office Hours: MWF 8–9, M 2–3, W 5:30–6:30 (and by appointment)

II. *Course Objectives:* To gain knowledge of fundamental concepts and issues in information systems development. Students will gain hands-on experience using 4th generation development tools.

III. *Required Course Textbooks:*
1. Laudon and Laudon, *Essentials of Management Information Systems,* Prentice Hall, Inc., 1995.
2. (2) 3.5" DS/HD (1:44MB) disks.

Recommended—Birmele, *QuickStart, Access 2 for Windows,* Que Press, 1994, or any other Access 2 manual.

IV. Requirements and Evaluation: This evaluation of work in the course is based on performance in three major areas over the semester.
First, three examinations will be given: 2 exams during the semester and a final exam. Exams will deal with concepts discussed in class. The final exam will be comprehensive. Students should bring a blue book, blue bubble sheet, and a No. 2 pencil to each exam. There are NO makeups! If you are going to miss an exam, you must contact me prior to the exam time for any special consideration.
Second, five computer assignments will be assigned. The computer assignments will provide the student with an opportunity to learn basic features of Microsoft Access. The computer lab is located in GCB 3001. Each team member will present at least one assignment. Most of the assignments will be graded as you present them, thus assignments will not be accepted late.
Third, participation in class discussions is expected. Attendance will be required. There will be several opportunities for in-class discussion on current computer-related issues. Repetitive absence will result in a reduction in your grade.

continued

Grading		Grade Scale	
2 exams @ 20% each	40%	A	90–100
Final Exam	10%	B	80–89
Group Evaluation	5%	C	70–79
5 Assignments @ 3% each	15%	D	60–69
Final Project	30%	F	below 60
TOTAL	100%		

V. *Assignment/Study Recommendations*
1. Do not wait until the last minute to do your work. Lines for the computers can get long when assignments are due, so start early.
2. For a class of this type, it is expected that the average student will need to spend 2 to 3 hours outside for each class hour, in order to receive an average grade (C). For this course, that translates to about 6 to 9 hours a week of outside work.
3. This syllabus is tentative and subject to change, if necessary. Changes will be announced in class. If you miss class you are still responsible for any changes.

VI. *Class Schedule*

VII. Your final project will be a complete system that will be turned in on a disk along with a documentation notebook containing the following:
1. An overview that describes the original problem and the business and system objectives of the new system.
2. A system diagram with a description of the problem in systemic terms.
3. Data Flow Diagrams, Data Structures, Data Model, and Structure Chart of the proposed system.
4. A user section providing printouts of each screen with explanations and instructions

I will provide you with forms with which you will rate your team members based on their contribution to the project. Each team member will receive the final project grade unless the contribution of one or more team members is significantly different (higher/lower) than those of the others. In that case the grade will be adjusted to reflect the situation.

If you refer to the "Grading" section on the syllabus, you will notice that at least 80% of the credit in the course is earned through writing, 50% for essay exams and 30% for the final project. While some teachers might not weigh writing quite so heavily, the prominence given writing in this course is not at all unusual. Most professors assume that students will acquire the facts and general information of the subject. What faculty will really want to know is whether students can turn those facts and information into knowledge through such acts as expressing, applying, analyzing, and evaluating.

In this class, the essay tests and the final project are the means through which students demonstrate these skills. The essay examinations are composed of both short-answer and longer, essay-answer questions and place strong emphasis on clarity and brevity. The final project contains a range of elements, each designed to highlight a particular aspect of knowledge or information expression. We will first look at some questions from the exams to understand the types of writing and thinking this professor values, then briefly look at a document used with the class presentation. Finally, we will review some specific features of the final project that will provide a look at an important writing assignment in decision sciences.

The essay examination

Read through the following essay exam from a decision science course.

DSCI 4133—Exam 2

Short Answer

1) Briefly (describe) what is meant by "data definition inconsistency." What major problem does it cause?

2) Briefly (compare and contrast) the three DBMS models.

3) (List) the four types of information. Give a one sentence definition of each type.

4) We use internal and external measures to evaluate the operational performance of a system. (Define) what internal and external measures are and give one example of each.

5) What four factors have been identified as contributing to the efficiency of IS operations?

6) (List) the three characteristics that all prototyped systems share.

7) (Compare and contrast) the evolutionary and revolutionary viewpoints on system development.

8) (What) are the guidelines you should follow in planning for multimedia systems?

9) (Why) do structured development techniques emphasize early error detection?

10) (How) does object oriented programming emphasize reusability?

Essay. Choose 3 of the 5.

1) Data is a valuable corporate resource that requires protection. (Describe) the internal and external options available for disaster recovery planning. What criteria would you use to select an option for your firm?

continued

2) Describe function point analysis. Include in your discussion an explanation of the five types of function points, as well as how they can be used to compare programmer productivity on simple and complex programming jobs.

3) CASE tools have received a lot of press in recent years. How do CASE tools improve programmer efficiency? List and describe the four major parts of a CASE tool. Why has CASE not been widely accepted?

4) In most organizations, system maintenance is viewed as a necessary evil. Describe how this traditional approach to maintenance can lead to inflexible systems and discuss the 5 tactics that IS managers can use to develop higher quality and more adaptable systems.

5) It is difficult to run an unattended distributed system. Briefly describe what an unattended distributed system is and discuss the unique technical problems one faces in such a setting.

We have circled some of the words which specify the types of responses the professor expects. A number of the questions ask students to "describe" functions or approaches. While we would have to know exactly how the teacher defines this term in order to understand fully what is required, "describe" often indicates providing characteristics or recounting the features of something. Notice, however, that the students are asked also to "define," "compare and contrast," and "discuss," as well as to "answer" the questions what, why, and how. In short, the professor requires written responses that demonstrate an ability to write clear, concise, but substantive answers. Below is a sample essay question from a similar class taught by the same professor and an answer which represents the type of response the professor expects:

Question: Describe the process by which an organizational strategy set is transformed through the MIS strategic planning process into a MIS strategy set. Include in your discussion how the stakeholder analysis is an integral part of this process. At what point would one use CSF's?

Answer: The heart of the MIS strategic set is changing the organizational strategy set into systems objectives, systems constructs and systems strategies. The organizational set is comprised of the missions, objectives, strategies and other organizational strategic attributes.

A MI designer must devise a process to make sure the plan to change the organizational set isn't deficient. The stakeholders are an integral part of this process. First, you must delineate the claimant structure. This means you must identify the stakeholders of the organization. Secondly the stakeholders' mission, goals, and objectives must be identified. Thirdly, the organization's mission must support the stakeholders' goals, missions, and objectives. You would use CSF to identify key areas and help with the planning process. The process of transferring the organizational strategic set into the MIS strategic set is illustrated below. Below is a flow chart which represents the transforming process.

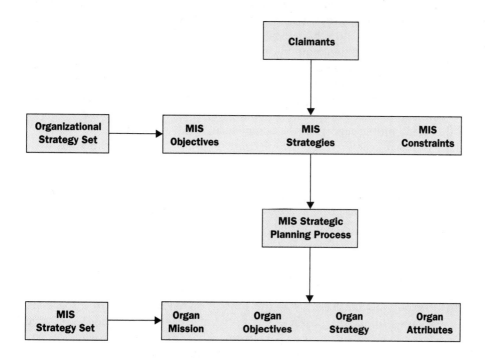

You have seen throughout this book (particularly in Chapter Two) that learning to read assignments and questions skillfully enhances your ability to write successful papers and answers. This essay question contains cues which should alert the student to issues and ideas the professor expects the writer to explore.

Exercises

1. Carefully read the essay question to determine which cues would aid the student in understanding the professor's expectations. After determining them, critique the essay answer. Does the answer address the issues the professor cued for the student? Do you have enough knowledge of the subject to tell whether the student has succeeded in this answer?

2. In previous chapters (see Chapter Two, for example), we covered issues concerning jargon. Some beginning students will simply acquire terms and

then use them without any real sense of their meaning. Critique the diction of this answer. Can you tell whether this student clearly understands the term used in the answer?

3. Did you notice that the term "process" is used several times in the question? If you were writing an answer to the question, you would, no doubt, want to focus on the processes involved in the different strategies and plans. How successfully did the student incorporate a discussion of process in the answer? What strategies and means did the student use to show how process works? Was the flowchart the student positioned at the conclusion of the answer successful in communicating anything more about the process than does the written answer?

4. Read the essay answer carefully, then prepare an outline of the written answer. How does your outline compare to the flowchart? Is there a direct correspondence? A slight correspondence? If there is a difference, what is its effect on the success of the complete answer?

5. *If you have access to a word-processing program,* complete this activity with the other members of your writing group. In a word-processing file, using the circled words on pages 283–284, create a glossary of essay-writing terms that would be useful for students taking this particular class. For each of the circled terms, provide a definition and an extended example that will help students understand what is required in an essay answer that asks for discussion, comparison and contrast, or an explanation of how something happens. In each definition, discuss the attributes of an excellent answer, an acceptable answer, and an unacceptable answer.

Exchange your writing group's glossary for the glossary of another writing group in your class. Using the annotation feature of a word-processing package, critique the glossary. In your critique, be sure to provide productive revision suggestions that will help the other group revise their glossary. When you are done, exchange your work once again. Revise your glossary using the suggestions provided by the other group.

Like all professors who assign essay tests, this professor wants students to demonstrate their understanding of the course material through written expression. However, essay tests are only one means of evaluating the work of students. Many faculty in decision sciences know very well that most of their students will move directly from the undergraduate degree to a job in business or industry. Therefore, many of the assignments in their classes provide direct preparation for the writing tasks faced by employees in information technology areas. The writing we will consider in the rest of this chapter fits that definition.

The end-of-term project

Before we begin our discussion of the final project in this course, refer again to the syllabus on pages 281–282 for the description of the final project.

Many courses in information technology programs will require term-end projects that integrate visuals, written language, computer languages, and technology-based operations and techniques. This project involved all of those areas. The report is divided into four parts:

- Part 1 (Overview): requires students to provide a prose description of the problem and the objectives of the proposed system.
- Part 2 (System Diagram): asks students to integrate written discourse and visual display (the system diagram).
- Part 3 (Data Flow Diagrams): requires students to represent visually the flow of information and processes, as well as representing models and structures.
- Part 4 (User Section): calls for a combination of visual representation (screen printouts) and written explanations and instructions.

The material from the report should provide a sense of what is expected from students involved in such a project and also allow you to critique features of this report.

Assignments of this type are often written for and submitted to actual clients or to mock clients. Whenever possible, third-year and fourth-year classes in decision sciences, as well as the other information technology areas, solicit projects from agencies, offices, and companies. Students meet with representatives from the organization to determine the client's needs, gather information for the report, and establish a constructive relationship with the client. When an actual client is not available, the professor will have the students construct a fictitious client. In either case, students put together documents that would appeal to a real audience.

In addition to writing clearly and presenting information accurately, writers often try to liven up their reports with humor. While such attempts give the documents something of a nonacademic flavor, they may provide some audience appeal. The cover of one report from this class is shown in Figure 8.6. As you can see, sometimes a little humor goes a long way! Whether or not you found the attempt humorous, it illustrates the different ways in which the writing task is regarded by various disciplines.

Exercises

1. The audience for any document is critically important. In the case of this final project, there are two audiences, the professor in the course and the mock clients who work in the placement office at Big State University. The group's task was to produce a manual that would provide clear information and instructions for employees operating the database. Study Figure 8.7, and, working with a partner, answer the following questions.

   a. Are the information and instructions presented in clearly organized ways? Does each paragraph focus on one subject? Should they in this type of document?

FIGURE 8.6   Report Cover

USER'S MANUAL

Big State University's
Career Placement Database

T A R G E T
P L A C E M E N T
Version 1.0

The Career Placement Database System
for Microsoft Access

    b. What general suggestions would you offer to improve the material on page 1?

    c. In several of the chapters in this book, formatting has been presented as a key to successfully designing reports. What comments and suggestions would you make concerning the arrangement of material on this page?

2. *If you have access to a word-processing package,* identify what you consider to be the most problematic paragraph on the first page of this manual. Create a file, and type this original paragraph into that file. Using the

FIGURE 8.7 Final Project, page 1

Getting Started

System Overview

The Target Placement system is a Microsoft Access relational database application designed for Big State University's Career Placement Office. The purpose of the database is to improve the efficiency and effectiveness of entering, manipulating, and storing information for use in the matching of registered applicants with prospective employers. The database is designed for adding and modifying information, tracking current employment information, and printing reports concerning the following information:

1. Applicants
2. Employers
3. Positions
4. Interviews
5. Work Experiences
6. Education Experience

The program is a menu-driven system that allows the user to easily navigate throughout the different modules of the application. Command buttons are used to accomplish this task. Each command button has a specific navigation function. The button is activated by clicking on its icon. Please refer to the next section for specific information on the function of each button. Help buttons are located throughout the application to provide general explanations for a variety of common tasks.

When adding information, forms are used to easily identify the required fields for each new entrant. The fields on each form can be accessed by clicking on the field box with the mouse. Also, the fields on each form are assigned a vertical tab order, allowing the user to navigate within the form by pressing ENTER when data entry is complete. This task can also be accomplished by depressing the tab key.

When modifying information, drop-down lists allow the user to select existing records. This eliminates the risk of miskeying information. In cases where a yes/no response is required, check boxes are provided. Check boxes are activated by clicking on the box to the right of the descriptive field. An 'x' in the box indicates 'yes.' An empty box signifies 'no.'

Application Layout

By double-clicking on the database icon, the system is automatically activated. At this point, the user is introduced to the title page, where he/she can move to the Main Menu by pressing the Main Menu button. Here, the navigational layout of the database is shown and can be accessed.

As follows, the Main Menu contains seven selection areas: applicant information, interview, employer information, position information, create reports, help, and exit. By double-clicking on each respective area of interest, the user can enter that module of the database.

1

continued

FIGURE 8.8 Final Project, page 2

Applicant Module
This module allows the user to add, modify, or delete applicant demographics, educational experience and work experience.

Employer Module
This module allows the user to add, modify, or delete employer information.

Position Module
This module allows the user to enter, modify, or delete positions posted by active employers.

Interview Module
This module allows the user to enter, modify, or delete interview information based on currently posted positions.

Print Reports Module
This module allows the user to print various reports based on the four modules above.

Report Descriptions
Nine automated reports can be printed using the Print Reports Module. These reports satisfy specific objectives of the placement center. Please refer to Appendix A for a sample of each of the following reports.

Applicant Reports

Active mailing labels — This allows the placement office to send current position information to the applicants.

Inactive mailing labels — This allows the placement office to send letters to inactive applicants in order to determine if they were satisfied with the services they received, or if they need to be reactivated.

Education report — This allows the placement office to send information about current applicant's educational information to prospective employers.

Employer Reports

Active mailing labels — This allows the placement office to send the education report to active employers (those who have hired someone from Big State University from the date specified by the user).

Inactive mailing labels — This allows the placement office to send letters to employers who have not hired an employee from Big State University since the date specified by the user.

Position Reports

Current listing — This prints a listing of all open positions, with the educational requirements, as of the date specified by the user.

Old listing — This prints a listing of all positions with a closing date earlier than the date specified from the user. . . .

2

annotation feature of the word-processing package, identify the specific parts of this paragraph that are problematic. When possible, use the criteria identified in the questions following this exercise to discuss these problems in the annotations you provide.

Next, below the original paragraph and your annotations, write your own revision of this paragraph. Make sure your revision addresses the problem areas you identified and annotated in the original version.

What decisions did you reach about the format of the text? When you revised a section, for example, did you place parts of the section in lists? Did you use bullets or numerals to set off items from one another? Paragraph two contains several sentences conveying information on the function of "command buttons." These writers have chosen to place that information in a paragraph form. If you were to revise the paragraph (or section) to include bullets and offset the points, would the information be more clearly presented? One of the main uses for this document would be as a reference source; that is, users would reach for it when they have forgotten a procedure or were unclear about a function. Are the details in these sections presented as clearly as possible for quick reference? Remember: (1) such documents seek to communicate as clearly as possible; (2) users want help and they want it quickly; and (3) they do not want to have to search for the information they need.

Focus on the above user needs as you study page 2 of the document, Figure 8.8.

Exercises

1. Both the module descriptions (which begin on page 1) and the report descriptions, contain phrases that are repeated numerous times. What is the effect of these repetitions? Write a critique of these sections that would help the writer to revise for clarity, brevity, and emphasis.
2. *If you have access to a word-processing package,* create a new file and revise page 2 to eliminate the unnecessary repetition and redundancy.
3. If you have access to a desktop-publishing, page-layout, or page-design program, create a file in which you use graphic elements (for example, boxes, bullets, icons or symbols, lines, and so forth) to make this revised page 2 clearer, more understandable, more graphically appealing for a reader.

Finally, since instructional documents use visuals to convey much of their information, the writing that accompanies these visuals must complement the images by adhering to the same demands for clarity and brevity required in all technical documents. The "Applicant Selection Form," Figure 8.9, and "Main Menu Screen," Figure 8.10, provide examples of such complementary text.

FIGURE 8.9   Applicant Selection Form

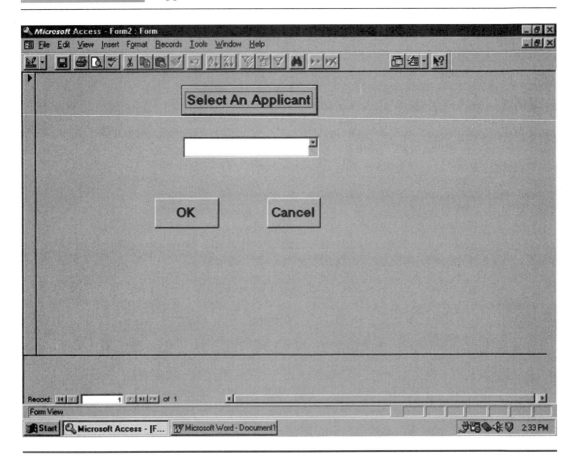

Applicant Selection Form
This form has a drop-down box, which allows the user to choose which active applicant to modify.

Select An Applicant Button:
The select an applicant button is activated by simply clicking on the down arrow and then clicking on a specific name. To actually choose this applicant to modify; the OK Button must be activated after choosing the applicant.

OK Button:
Once the correct, complete information is entered, click "OK". The OK button, when activated, will save the current information and turn to the next form (Educational Experience Modify Form).

Cancel Button:
If at any point the information entered is found to be inaccurate, click the cancel button. The cancel button, when activated, eliminates the information entered, and the program returns to the previous form (Applicant Information Form Link).

Help Button:
Help buttons exist throughout the program. They open new screens with information to assist the user on specific forms.

FIGURE 8.10   Main Menu Screen

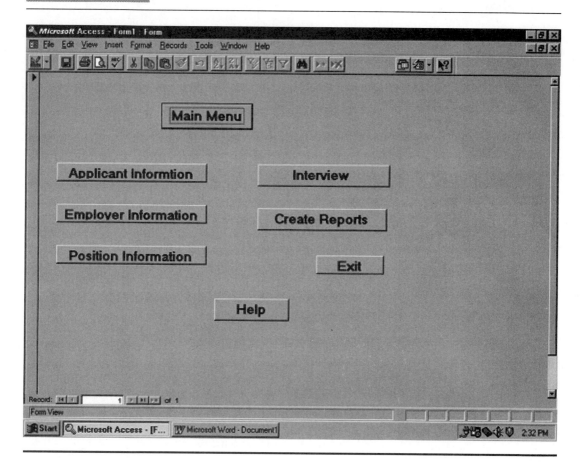

Main Menu Screen
This screen allows the user to choose the type of information to be added or modified.

Applicant Information Button:
The applicant information button, when activated, opens the Applicant Information Link Form.

Interview Information Button:
The interview information button, when activated, opens the Interview Information Link Form.

Employer Information Button:
The employer information button, when activated, opens the Employer Information Link Form.

Position Information Button:
The position information button, when activated, opens the Position Information Link Form.

Create Reports Button:
The create reports button, when activated, opens the Create Reports Link Form.

Exit Button:
The exit button, when activated, closes the Main Menu Form and the database application.

Help Button:
Help buttons exist throughout the program. They open new screens with information to assist the user on specific forms.

Group Exercise: Figures 8.9 and 8.10 present information both visually and in writing. Are they equally successful? What are the strengths of each screen? What are the weaknesses?

Much of the writing required of majors in information technology programs requires the skills to produce concise, clear and visually attractive writing. While you have worked a good deal on the first two requirements, you have probably not spent a lot of time gaining skills in the latter. With the advent of sophisticated word-processing programs, however, more and more opportunity develops to produce eye-catching documents. Such programs present us with the possibility to position lists, highlight words and sections, change font style and size—all of which allow us not only to write substantively but to present our essays, proposals, letters, and reports in ways that attract readers and make our writing more pleasing. While almost all writing in technical areas establishes clear communication as its highest priority, remember that it is people who read writing, and people respond positively when they are pleased.

Exercises

1. Group Assignment: One of the most interesting and representative writing assignments for decision sciences majors is the recommendation report. Written to respond to a request for proposal or a call for action, this project requires a comprehensive approach to solving a client's problem. Although the structure of the report will vary somewhat from project to project, there are usually the following parts:
   - **Problem statement**   A precise statement of the problem the organization wishes to solve or the change it wishes to effect
   - **Background**   A summary of the organization's goals, mission, history, and current condition
   - **Analysis**   A description of the problem or desired change and its relation to the organization's current state
   - **Recommendations**   A series of steps or actions suggested to solve the problem or reach the desired change

   While recommendation reports are almost always linked to computer automation in the real world, yours does not have to be so directed, though computer solutions are certainly welcome for this assignment. Here is a list of suggestions for the assignment:
   a. Structure the report around the traditional format of such a report or an adaptation of one.
   b. This assignment would work well for a group of 3–5, depending on the scope of the task. Like many other actual researching, solving, and writ-

ing tasks faced by decision scientists, this one requires teamwork and planning.

  c. The written document should be accompanied by an oral presentation in which all team members participate.

  d. Grading criteria and individual responsibilities should be determined before beginning the project.

Here are two basic topic areas we suggest:

Computer systems topics   Almost all colleges are struggling to keep pace with the rapid changes brought on by the need and demand for computer facilities and services. Research this situation at your college to determine current demands and needs, as well as projections of the same. Select a topic which can be explored both through local sources and through library resources.

Topics not necessarily related to computers   Use the basic structure of the recommendation report to propose a solution to a local or college problem. Essentially, this approach would follow a Problem-Solution or a Needs Assessment-Recommendation model, both of which can be structured similarly to the structural outline we propose. Suggested possibilities: problems faced by campus student organizations, local volunteer organizations, local school districts. Your topic should involve a business practice or procedure or a communication situation or strategy; you may, of course, include both of these.

2. *If you have access to the Internet,* select a campus problem for this activity that is a common problem at other schools as well (for example, the availability of student parking, high tuition costs, the reselling of textbooks, problems with the quality or the variety of food in the dorms). Once you have chosen a problem on which to focus, e-mail three to five individuals (for example, friends, high school acquaintances, friends of a friend, relatives) from other colleges or universities to discuss this problem. Make sure you contact individuals at schools generally comparable to your own in size, focus, and composition. Ask these individuals how their school handles this problem. Ask whether attempts at solving the problem have been successful or unsuccessful and why. Include the information you get from these contacts in your group's recommendation report.

URLs for Mathematics and Information Technology

A Catalog of Mathematics Resources on WWW and the Internet
http://mthwww.uwc.edu/wwwmahes/files/math01.html

Mathematics Resources
http://www.cs.dal.ca/math.html

Mathematics Resources
http://www.lib.lsu.edu/sci/math.html

Mathematics Resources
http://macs01.mathcs.citadel.edu/math.html

Mathematics Resources
http://doppler.thp.univie.ac.at/math.html

Other Mathematics Resources
http://www.cs.gsu.edu/math/othermath.html

History of Mathematics: NonWeb Resources
http://aleph0.clarku.edu/~djoyce/mathhist/nonwebresources.html

Welcome to ERIC National Clearinghouse—Mathematics Education
http://www.ericse.ohio-state.edu/

Mathematics Resources
http://math.liu.se/math.html

Science and Mathematics Resources—K-16 Science Resources
http://www-sci.lib.uci.edu/

Education Library & Information Technology
http://teach.virginia.edu/curry/resources/

Instructional Technology Resources
http://interact.uoregon.edu/MediaLit/ITF/ITResource

Instructional Tools on the Web
http://www.utirc.utoronto.ca/InsT/web_resources.html

Information Technology—Related Sites
http://www.envision.net/osites/infotech/inforela.html

CHAPTER NINE

Writing in Business and Management

Responsibilities of Business and Management Professionals

Individual and Collaborative Writing

Importance of Communications to the Business and Management Professional

Miscommunication is among the most costly problems in business and management, not only damaging the efficiency of a company's internal operations, but hurting its reputation with its clients as well. So well-known and widespread are difficulties associated with reading and writing that most business majors nowadays are required to take courses specifically designed to teach them how to perform these tasks on the job.

These courses are taught in the belief that employees who work in business and management will be required to write once employed. Such writers tend to fall into one of two categories. One is made up of specialists in writing for business and industry who are experts at performing the kinds of writing tasks expected of them on the job. Most of these people are trained in technical writing programs. In the other category are the large majority of employees who write in business and industry, those for whom writing is an inevitable requirement of their jobs. Until recently, most employees in business and management were not trained as writers beyond freshman composition or on-the-job training. More recent generations of business majors, however, have been required to take at least one writing course, usually called Writing for Business and Industry or simply Business Writing, after taking freshman composition.

The skills discussed in this chapter are important for another reason, however, besides their usefulness on the job; these skills are universally applicable. Most of you—whether you decide ultimately to enter business or teaching or health sciences or engineering—will be called on to perform the kinds of writing tasks discussed in this chapter: the writing of memorandums, letters, and reports. What's more, because these writing tasks require certain thought processes valued in making day-to-day decisions about how you might present yourself to others or how you might decide on an item to purchase, time invested in mastering the skills treated in this chapter is time well spent.

Responsibilities of Business and Management Professionals

The increased number of writing specialists employed in business over the past twenty years reflects an effort by businesses and industries to make certain they are represented as a group of literate professionals. You may decide during college to specialize in technical writing and take courses that will prepare you to oversee a company's communications. Though the notion of specializing suggests that such writers spend much time alone, **technical writers**—often employed as corporate trainers, public information officers, or public relations specialists—rarely work in isolation, except in the writing of short documents such as memos and letters. In fact, their jobs may entail a wide range of responsibilities, from coaching others who must write on the job, to collaborating with support personnel and department heads, to devising formal reports in conjunction with specialists in preparing visual and graphic aids. Writing is one of the most difficult jobs in business and management, and such specialists must be able to work closely with others to accomplish it.

Most students who major in business and management are in a slightly different situation than the corporate trainer, public information officer, or public relations specialist. Nowadays in business and industry, most employees are required to be (or become through on-the-job training) skilled writers, capable of performing writing tasks required on the job. In fact, in many businesses, writing performance is one area of annual evaluation. Though you will on occasion work independently, you more often will be required to serve as a team or group member, contributing to that group's writing requirements.

Writers under either set of the above circumstances—that is, writing specialists or employees who must write on the job—must meet the most fundamental challenge for writers in business and management in the twenty-first century: communicating with various audiences while, at the same time, adjusting to shifting organizational structures. Rarely will the image of the lone businessman working late at night in the solitude of his office be used in the twenty-first century to communicate what goes on in business and management.

Rather, by choosing to enter business and management in the twenty-first century, you have chosen to learn how to work on teams and in groups. The ability to collaborate, then, is a critical skill for you to possess.

Exercises

1. Interview someone you know who works in a local business or industry. Consult with that person to answer the following questions.
   a. Where does that person work? What kind of job does that person perform at work?
   b. What kinds of writing does that person do on the job? What kinds of reading?
   c. How did that person learn to perform the required reading and writing? (for example, did the person learn in college, during on-the-job-training, from a supervisor, by reading numerous other documents written by others on the job, or in some other way?)
   d. What is that person's writing process, starting with the moment she or he knows a writing task must be performed and ending with the task's completion? How does reading enter into his/her writing process?

2. Interview someone you know who is employed by a business or in an industry. Ask that person the following questions in preparation for writing a paragraph-length report: Is a company better off hiring a small number of trained writing specialists or making certain that those employees they hire are able to perform the writing tasks required of them on the job? Why?

3. *If you have access to the World Wide Web,* use a browser to locate home pages for five corporations and/or commercial businesses. Explore these home pages. Pick two of these businesses or corporations (perhaps ones in your chosen career field), and e-mail the contact person listed on the home page. Ask who wrote the information on the home page and who designed

it. E-mail these people to ask what additional kinds of writing are required by various members of their firms.

Next, e-mail your findings to the other members of your class. In your e-mail message, describe the sites you chose, give their Universal Resource Locators (URLs), describe the contact you had with the companies, and describe what you found out about the kinds of writing that are commonly done by people within these companies.

Individual and Collaborative Writing

In the writing classes you will take as a business major, you may be asked to work in one or both of the situations described previously—**independently,** where you will be required to do all of the drafting, or **collaboratively,** where you will have to work closely with others. In most instances, teachers strive to create both kinds of situations: You may be required to work independently in the writing of short documents such as memos and letters, but to work collaboratively in the writing of longer documents such as reports or proposals that must be completed in multiple stages over an extended period. In any case, you can expect to perform the following kinds of writing tasks in your business writing courses, each of which we will discuss at length.

1. memorandums
2. letters
3. formal and informal reports

Memos and letters are usually short communications written by a single author. On some occasions, they must be approved by a supervisor prior to being distributed or mailed. **Memos** are written to meet specific organizational goals. They are characterized by being *internal* to the company, *brief, focused on a single topic,* and highly *predictable.* Memos are most often used in informational or instructional communications. For instance, an informative memo might be written to tell employees that the business will close on Christmas Day. Or you might use an instructional memo to teach employees proper emergency procedures. But memos also can be used with a range of other purposes in mind, sometimes even to persuade a supervisor to change her view on a given issue.

If it is true, as we suggest in Chapter Two, that reading occurs when readers respond to certain specific cues in a document, then one of the first cues readers are apt to notice is what kind of document they are receiving. The decision to write a memo signals to the reader that the document will be different in certain fundamental ways from letters or reports or proposals.

A reader receiving a memo will automatically make several predictions. First, the reader will know immediately by the form of the communication that it is from inside his or her business. Second, the subject is probably a matter that requires some sort of formal documentation, enabling the reader to predict that the memo will deal with a limited number of topics. And, third, the matter discussed is simply too complex to be conveyed through electronic mail (e-mail).

Like the memo assignment, you are more apt to be asked to write a letter by yourself than with a team or group. A letter is used to convey information to people outside the company, to formally document a transaction, and to deal with a matter too complex for phone conversation.

While it is possible, if somewhat unlikely, that on-the-job memos and letters will be written by committees, a professor will want at least some of the business writing in your course to be done by you alone. Documents you write independently will enable your teacher to provide you with more focused attention, making better instruction possible.

Still, many instructors want to provide business and management students with an opportunity to experience the dynamics of group communication. You are apt, then, also to be asked to work either as a primary author working with experts or specialists on the report topic and/or the report design, or as a partner with a team of others who perform an equal amount of research and writing.

When working as a primary author in a collaborative writing effort, you will be responsible for drafting the document. When this is done in business or industry, the author often consults with specialists at various stages in the writing process. Those with particular expertise concerning the subject of a document are usually the first whom a writer consults. Later, artists and printers may be contacted for assistance with polishing and finishing the piece of writing. And certainly a writer drafting a document will feel free to consult others whenever necessary to make certain the information conveyed is correct.

When this method of collaboration is employed in a business writing course, it is usually discussed in class, and students often decide which role they want to play in the writing process. Each individual might be given a specific task. Perhaps two or three people will survey different sources in the process of gathering information, giving that information to the writer who drafts, revises, edits, and prepares the final copy.

A second kind of collaboration in business writing courses occurs when you are asked to work jointly with one or more coauthors who undertake the writing of a document as equals. Instead of breaking the writing process itself into its components, the coauthors divide the *parts* of the document so that each person will be responsible for one or more parts, or they work through drafts of the entire document together.

In either case, collaboration is not an easy undertaking. People seldom agree about anything, especially what to emphasize about a topic and how to say something. Less obviously, people seldom relate as equals in groups. Someone quite naturally leads, and often the politics of collaborative writing assignments—not the document that is supposed to be written—become the central focus.

Regardless of which collaborative method you are involved in, such efforts can be accomplished with less stress if team members follow mutually agreed-upon rules or guidelines such as the ones that follow.

1. Remember that collaboration is a strategy that is employed on a project to solve certain problems. On the one hand, the project may be too large, or the time constraints too severe, for one person to handle. On the other, the project may require that various skilled personnel be involved or that different views be incorporated into a single statement.
2. Team members, unless instructed otherwise, should operate from the perspective that all members are equal.
3. One member should be designated by the group or by a supervisor (see the project that follows) as a team leader or team coordinator. The leader does not have more authority than the others in making decisions. Rather, the leader is responsible for performing simple administrative tasks (for example, calling meetings, coordinating team responsibilities, and so forth).
4. Early in the project, team members should decide on their goals by broadly outlining the task and identifying the project's duration, audience, purpose, and scope.
5. Early in the project, assignments should be given to team members. The team leader should record these assignments, making certain that no task is duplicated or left unassigned. A written statement of these assignments should be made available to team members to avoid misunderstanding later.
6. Once assignments are made, the team should draft a schedule explicitly stating deadlines for drafts, reviews of drafts, and revisions. The team leader should make certain that each team member has a copy of dates for deadlines.
7. In reviewing drafts, team members should be open-minded in accepting recommendations of peers for revision.
8. Team members should strive to limit conflict.

As you read the memos provided in the following exercises, please note Memo Three in particular and the way in which it solves the problem of who is in charge. In this modification of the first method of collaboration described above, collaborators consult and work closely with the company's writing specialist. The writing specialist's level of involvement will depend on the group's needs, just as a business writing teacher's might be.

Exercises

1. Read the three memos that follow. What is the purpose of each? What elements do they have in common? What differences do you note between them?

Memo One

FROM: Theresa Walters
TO: Department Heads
DATE: February 15, 1992
SUBJECT: Work Permits

It has been brought to my attention that the mechanics are having difficulty in contacting the shift supervisors when they have mechanical work to do in the area and need permits signed. I would like all supervisors to employ the following guidelines in the future.

Before coming to the main building, the mechanics will contact the shift supervisor on the radio and arrange to meet him/her in his/her office or in the work area. If the supervisor has to leave the area for meetings, classes, etc., for more than a one-hour period, he/she should leave his/her radio with the assistant, who will assume the shift supervisor's duties until his/her return.

Let's try to assist the mechancs in completing their jobs with the least amount of lost time—this will benefit all of us.

Memo Two

FROM: Frank Hawkins
TO: All Building #3 Personnel
DATE: July 25, 1993
SUBJECT: Traffic Behind Building #3

During recent years, the area behind Building #3 has changed from a roadway and storage area to a chemical recovery, waste disposal, and staging area. This change makes it necessary to apply restricted access controls and safety requirements similar to those used in other chemical processing areas.

We recommend that additional gates and signs be installed to restrict access to the area behind Building #3. Enforcement of restricted access and safety equipment (hard hats and safety glasses) requirements should be implemented immediately.

Memo Three

TO: Don Green
FROM: Susan Boyd
DATE: April 19, 1990
SUBJECT: Advertisements for WWTP Program

I read your memo and charts. The information certainly indicates impressive increases in efficiency and decreases in Biochemical Oxygen Demand and Total Suspended Solids. However, conveying this message to certain audiences could be a problem.

My first question to you is who is your intended audience?

The charts you have would be appropriate for Commissioners, students studying wastewater treatment, environmentalists, and reporters doing a story on discharges. In other words, this audience would have to have a certain reservoir of interest and knowledge before the charts would make sense. The people in this audience would have to know what BOD means. (Most people probably think a BOD is something that looks good in a bikini.) And they'd have to understand that low BOD is good. The same with TSS. Will the audience you hope to reach know what these mean?

The charts as they are right now (maybe with BOD and TSS written out at the bottom) would be fine for the audience mentioned above. If you're aiming for a more general audience, the charts would need some modification. You'd have to assume that the general public doesn't know the first thing about wastewater treatment, and that they all slept through chemistry. You can't underestimate their intelligence. It's just a matter of what he or she has been exposed to and is interested in. You have to assume that the general public doesn't know anything about your subject and start from there.

If I can help in any way as you adapt your materials to a more general population, please let me know.

---

2. *If you have access to a computer and a word-processing package,* choose one of the three memos provided in this section, and type it into the computer. Next, using the annotation feature of a word-processing package, annotate the memo as if you were using it to teach a high-school business writing class how to write an effective memo. In your annotations, you will want to identify the important parts of the memo and describe the salient characteristics of each part. You will also want to annotate any unusual features, talk about the importance of purpose and audience, and provide

the high-school students with hints about how to make sure their memorandums work well.

When you are done with annotating your memo, share your comments with your writing group members, and get their comments for revision. Revise your annotations according to this input, and provide your teacher a copy.

3. *If you have access to a word-processing package and e-mail,* print out an e-mail message you have recently received (avoiding messages that are highly personal), and either cut-and-paste it into a word-processing file or—if this is impossible—retype it into a word-processing file. Next, using the annotation feature of the word-processing package, annotate the e-mail message as if you were using it to teach a high school business writing class how to write an effective e-mail message. In your annotations, you will want to identify the important parts of the message and describe the salient characteristics of each part. You will also want to annotate any unusual features, talk about the importance of purpose and audience, and provide the high school students with hints about how to make sure their e-mail messages work well.

When you are done annotating your annotations, share your comments with your writing group members, and get their comments for revision. Revise your annotations according to this input, and provide your teacher a copy.

Importance of Communications to the Business and Management Professional

It is common in business and management to create a paper trail of documents that, when pieced together, form a history of a particular event or transaction. In business and management, such a paper trail may include some or all of the following: e-mail, memos, letters, proposals, and reports.

Let us trace such a history by looking at documents written by team members in the process of hiring a firm to conduct a survey of customer satisfaction. To do so, and to begin the entire process, much internal correspondence took place, as the heavy reliance on e-mail and memos highlighted below indicates.

Writing Memorandums and E-Mail

Once Broadway Wholesale Warehouse decided to survey customers and a RFP (Request for Proposals) was drafted, the general manager sent the following pieces of electronic mail that, in form anyway, look like memos. Let us begin with e-mail and then distinguish the uses of e-mail from the uses of memorandums.

TO: Julie Brown, Public Information Officer
FROM: Tom Feeney, General Manager
cc: Bill Tyson
DATE: November 2, 1994
SUBJECT: Customer Survey

The draft Request for Proposals you sent to me appears to be very satisfactory to send to interested firms (this includes the sample questions). The next step is to identify qualified firms to which we can send the Request. It was my understanding that you have already had discussions with Gerace and Associates to get the name of firms that might be interested in doing what we need done. There may be other firms as well, but I don't know how to identify them. I also heard that Dr. Mike Myrick, professor of marketing at Tristates, might have some interest in this type of survey. May be worth investigation. At the very least, he may be able to identify some firms which might be interested.

Note that the above piece of e-mail is intended as an informal method of communication. As a result, adherence to rigorous standards of correctness is not necessary. Additionally, the author may feel that he is permitted to discuss several different topics, rather than one, suggesting that e-mail is not confined to a single topic and that the author is free to roam randomly through the elements of those topics. Abbreviations often are used in e-mail and grammatical correctness, proper spelling, and other qualities usually valued in writing are of less importance than simply making contact with someone and conveying bits and pieces of information.

But there is even more to discover by reading the above e-mail. We also find out a great deal about the hierarchy of Broadway Wholesale Warehouse, especially the role of the people involved in this communication. For instance, the general manager is responsible for delegating authority, approving various documents before they are sent out, and providing guidance to subordinates. Though Julie Brown is the public information officer who has written the RFP, she is simply the liaison between the company and the marketing research firms contacted. As a result, she must receive her supervisor's approval prior to mailing any official documents.

TO: Brenda Tyson, Public Relations and Sales Supervisor
FROM: Tom Feeney, General Manager
cc: Julie Brown
DATE: November 2, 1994
SUBJECT: Customer Survey

I would like for you to head up the consultant selection process. I will serve on the committee and suggest you, Julie Brown, Jim Kirkland, John Grillo, and I. You need to develop a selection schedule which should either be attached to the Request for Proposals or included in the cover letter to interested firms, which should go out under my signature. Because of the estimated dollar amount of this work, I don't think we have to be "real" formal in the selection process. Rather, we should simply select the firm which we think will give us the best job. (About the schedule . . . you need to give them a "gross" estimate of the contract period . . . e.g. we estimate the entire project from date of notice to proceed should be completed within a three-month period.)

The general manager's e-mail to Brenda Tyson, above, similarly delegates authority, establishing that she will head up a management team to select an outside consultant to conduct the survey.

A memo on the same subject would differ in some basic ways. First, a memo would be more formal than e-mail. Second, a memo would demonstrate greater concern with correct form than the above e-mail correspondences. And, third, in a memo the author would be more apt to take a tone appropriate to his place in the company's hierarchy of authority.

Not surprisingly, in addition to corresponding through e-mail, the general manager found it necessary to communicate directly with management team members, instructing them as to their responsibilities. Since the information is internal, brief, and focused in its scope, the general manager wrote a memo—which in most businesses is slightly more formal than e-mail—carrying the tone of authority befitting a general manager and employing the usual standards of correctness.

A memo has certain other benefits. By sending the same memo to all team members, the general manager can be certain they all receive the same information. Pay particular attention to the tone of authority of the following memo and the increased sense of the author's concern for formal correctness.

> TO: Department Heads
> FROM: Tom Feeney, General Manager
> DATE: October 5, 1994
> SUBJECT: Customer Survey
>
> Broadway Wholesale Warehouse seeks continually to be responsive to the needs of its customers. A customer opinion survey provides us the opportunity to identify those needs and to monitor customer trends, issues, and concerns.
>
> As you know, we conducted our first customer opinion survey in 1990 as a pilot project. It was a learning experience. Soon we will be able to apply what we learned about the process when we conduct our second survey in December 1994.
>
> We are in the process of focusing on topic areas for the new survey. Your suggestions for topics and issues that we might address are needed. Cost and space limitations will prohibit us from addressing every topic of concern, but we would like to get a representative sampling.
>
> On the attached form, please indicate items that you feel should be addressed in our survey, and return the form to Julie Brown by October 19. Your cooperation is appreciated.

In writing a memo for your business writing course, you should keep in mind, as Tom Feeney has in the above document, that readers will expect that certain information will be given at specific, predictable places in the text of what you write. To demonstrate this point, take a minute and read the following memo, which has been segmented for you, one line at a time. For purposes of seeing exactly how reading is a kind of prediction based on certain cues placed in the text (see Chapter Two), you might take a sheet of paper and cover the entire memo, moving down the page only far enough to predict what will follow, as you answer the questions following each segment.

> TO: Donald Palumbo, Assistant Director of Training

Based on the author line, what do you think this document will be about? What do you predict to be the purpose?

> FROM: Al Muller, Head of Personnel

Based on the recipient line, what do you think this document will be about? What do you predict to be the purpose?

> SUBJECT: New Position, Quality Products and Service Program

On the basis of this subject line, what do you predict this document will be about?

> The attached requisition for Help and Position Description identifies the requirement for a new position at the Greensboro site. This position is necessary

What do you think will follow?

> to ensure that a Total Quality of Products and Services program is implemented at the Greensboro site.

On the basis of paragraph one, what do you think paragraph two will be about?

> A total Quality of Products and Services program will allow Carolina Textiles to gain a competitive edge on the textile industry through

What do you think will follow?

> cost reductions, quality improvements, and productivity increases. It will also ensure complete adherence to regulatory compliance.

What do you predict paragraph three will be about?

> The program, once designed and implemented, will address and improve productivity, quality, team building, employee development, and communication issues. It will also identify real needs and budget requirements and will reduce waste and redundancy.

What do you predict will come next?

> We at Carolina Textiles have to direct our efforts to produce and deliver to our customers a top-quality product in a cost-effective and timely manner. In order to accomplish this, we have to involve employees at all levels. This program allows that involvement, and this position will ensure it.

As you can no doubt see for yourself when you read this memo, reading *is* a process of predicting what will come next in a document based on the cues a writer inserts at particular places. Among those cues is the form of the document itself. Just by acknowledging that the document received is a memo indicates to readers that the document is internal to the company, focuses on one subject, and will unfold in a predictable manner.

An experienced reader of memos knows that the author line and the subject line are important indicators of the document's contents. If the author of the memo is the general manager, a reader will expect one range of possible topics. If the memo comes from the head of security, the reader will expect another range of topics. And still another range of topics might be predicted if the memo comes from the head of personnel, as the last memo did. When the subject line is read, the range of possible topics is narrowed even further. The subject line should, in a maximum of seven to eight well-chosen words, indicate to the reader what to expect in a document.

Further, the first paragraph should have one sentence that repeats the subject of the memo so that the reader whose eyes jumped over the subject line will be properly oriented. In addition, the opening paragraph should also indicate to the reader why the document has been written.

A reader familiar with memos will expect the body of the document to be an analysis of the stated problem and the conclusion to describe follow-up actions.

Consider the wisdom, then, of making certain that specific cues are in a memo by further analyzing the memo Tom Feeney, General Manager of Broadway Wholesale Warehouse, sent to department heads soliciting questions for the survey. A reader receiving this memo will know immediately that it is an important document dealing with problems company-wide since it is from the company's general manager. Further, the subject line makes it possible for the reader to further limit the possible range of matters addressed to the customer survey. And for those who missed the subject line, the first paragraph of the memo provides a reminder of the memo's subject. Needless to say, a reader will anticipate being asked to do something to help the survey procedure along.

Guidelines for Writing Memos

1. Use memos for in-house correspondence.
2. Route memos through the accepted chain of command.
3. Remember that your memo is apt to become part of a file. Be careful not to say anything you do not intend to have recalled months or even years later.
4. A memo is less formal than a letter and does *not* include a return address, inside address, or salutation.
5. The format for a memo includes heading material as follows:

   TO:
   FROM:
   DATE:
   SUBJECT:

6. Memos follow a block format—that is, all information is placed flush against the left margin.
7. Whenever necessary, the document may be subdivided by use of headings for ease of reading and to help readers anticipate the topic of each section and how many sections there will be.
8. Remember your readers. Make certain you have included proper signals so they can predict what will come next in your memo. These signals include, in addition to the author's name, the subject line, an introductory statement of purpose, a body which elaborates on the one subject introduced, a description of follow-up actions to be taken, and a summary.

Exercises

1. Read the following memo and write a brief analysis of its effectiveness. Focus on the author's success at including cues and on your ability as a

reader to predict the direction of the memo based upon those cues: author line, subject line, statement of intent in paragraph one, focus on a single topic for the duration of the memo, suggestion of a course of action. Then, after analyzing the document, write a memo back to the author suggesting ways the memo might be improved.

TO: Richard Hauser, Shift Supervisor
FROM: Dan Schisler, Quality Assurance Department
DATE: November 14, 1993
SUBJECT: Summer Work Schedule

The summer work schedule, now firmly established at Lawless Container, consists of four consecutive ten-hour days. At the discretion of the department head each department follows this schedule. Many employees are able to choose between the four-day summer schedule and the regular five-day work week. However, in critical areas—such as production—there has been no freedom of choice.

All production personnel must adhere to the four-day work week. Employees without young children simply adjust their personal schedule for the summer to accommodate their work. On the other hand, this schedule poses a serious problem for parents of small children. Production personnel are hindered by the summer work schedule since day care centers do not offer flexible hours of operation.

A solution to the summer work schedule is an in-house day care center for children of working parents which will operate on a temporary basis during the summer months. In order to be of maximum cost efficiency the day care center should support only those employees who have no freedom of choice over their working hours. The location of this center will be the present Quality Assurance building, and the center will open once the move to the new Quality Assurance building is complete. Additionally, this new day care center will improve Lawless's community relationship as it will be staffed by college and high-school students at the time of year during which the most students are searching for temporary employment.

---

2. Draft a memo to your teacher in which you identify a subject you would like to investigate and write a formal report on (see pages 321–339). This subject must be a problem in need of a solution. The problem might involve anything, from which camera to purchase to where to shop for vegetables to why a stoplight should be installed somewhere on campus to anything you would want to see changed or improved on your college's campus. Remember in writing your memo to include all the cues your reader will need to be able to read your document.

3. *If you have access to a work-processing package,* type the memo in exercise 1 above into a word-processing file. Then, use the annotation feature of a word-processing package to complete the analysis of the various parts of that memo and their relative effectiveness.

When you have completed this exercise, exchange your annotated memo with other members of your writing group, and examine their annotations. Discuss those annotations that are common in the group, and those on which members of the group seem to disagree.

4. *If you have access to a word-processing package,* write a memo to the president or the governing board of an organization to which you currently belong. In this memo, identify a problem that the organization faces and suggest some solutions to address this problem.

Writing Letters

While memos are the basic means of communicating within organizations, letters are the basic means of communicating between organizations. In fact, most of the work of transferring information from one place to another among organizations is done through letters.

Letters, then, can serve any number of purposes. Generally, though, most people agree that letters can be classified into three general types: those that attempt to *persuade* a reader to act in some way (for example, collection, complaint, application, solicitation, credit, and inquiry letters), those that *convey good or neutral news* (for example, acceptance or transmittal letters), and those that *convey bad news* (for example, refusal or rejection letters). Each kind of letter, as you might imagine, is structured in some slightly different way.

Let us understand the usefulness of these three types of letters as means for communicating between organizations by continuing to follow the management team as it attempts to get firms to bid on the job of surveying their customers.

The management team met their charge as it was given by their general manager by drafting a formal RFP and sending it to several marketing research companies. Though the RFP was a collaborative effort of the sort described on page 301—where each team member contributed information, suggested revisions, and assisted with editing—the public information officer, as the company's writing specialist, performed the actual writing. Additionally, she drafted a cover letter for the General Manager, which he read, made suggestions about, and ultimately approved and sent out under his name.

A letter serves the following purposes and makes it preferable to memos or reports for some kinds of communication—including transmittal, rejection, and acceptance, for the following reasons.

1. Letters constitute a permanent, written record of a business transaction. Though persons involved in the transaction may discuss matters over the

phone or in person during interviews, the transaction is not official in most instances until one party sends the other a written notice of the transaction, usually in a letter.

2. The cliché "put it in writing" has a special significance in business since letters reflect the commitment on the writer's part to follow through with some part of an agreement.

3. Letter writing is convenient, especially as a follow-up for salespeople who travel three or four days a week. One day can be set aside to catch up on paperwork, usually including correspondence through mail.

4. Letters can create and continue goodwill even where bad news has been communicated, as we will illustrate later.

5. Letters provide authors with an opportunity to say exactly what they mean. Unlike spoken words, a letter can be revised until it says exactly what is intended.

Like memos, letters have the benefit of being predictable in some ways. A letter has specific parts a reader looks for and responds to.

Letters begin with a **heading,** which includes the writer's full address (for example, street, city and state, zip code). Obviously, if you are using company letterhead, you will not need to employ an additional heading. Include the **date,** though, directly under the heading, whether you type the heading or it is a part of the letterhead.

You will, under any circumstances, need to include an **inside address.** The inside address includes the recipient's full name and address. This should be two lines below the date.

Two lines below the inside address, you should include a **salutation,** or greeting. The salutation usually uses the recipient's title and last name, followed by a colon. If you do not know the person, use a title appropriate to the context of the letter (for example, "Dear Client," "Dear Customer," "Dear Manager," etc.).

The **body** of the letter is what the letter is about. The body should begin two lines below the salutation. Use single lines within paragraphs and double lines between them.

Two spaces below the body of your letter, you should employ the **complimentary close.** This portion of the letter format is simply the "good-bye." Most businesses employ standard expressions such as "Yours truly," "Sincerely yours," or "Respectfully yours."

If a letter requires a second page, carry at least two lines of the body to the second page. You should have a heading on the second page that states the recipient's name on one line, followed by a line identifying the page number and a line with the date. The heading should go in the upper left-hand corner or across the page on a single line. Never use letterhead for a second page.

In the correspondence below, note that a letter was used instead of a memo because the correspondence was with someone *outside* the company. As an example of a letter designed to persuade people to act on the RFP, the letter is arranged in a particular fashion. Some call this method of organization **AIDA,** since it attempts to get a reader's **Attention**, arouse **Interest**, create in them a **Desire** to comply, and convince them to take **Action**. Here is the general manager's letter.

Broadway Wholesale Warehouse
3232 Independence Avenue
Charlotte, NC 28223

August 20, 1994

To Whom It May Concern:

In March and April of 1990, Broadway Wholesale Warehouse conducted its first-ever customer survey. The original purpose was to determine public attitudes toward Broadway Wholesale. The information would allow us to identify the effectiveness of our public information efforts. The first survey was also to be used as a base of information against which future surveys could be compared.

We now wish to conduct a second survey of our customers and have identified your firm as a prospective consultant to prepare, conduct, and analyze such a survey. We have provided you with a general statement of the purpose of this project, our most recent annual report, and proposal requirements.

Julie Brown, BWW's public information officer, will oversee the project and serve as the primary contact for the consultant selected. If you have any questions, you may contact her at 555-7453.

We certainly hope that you will submit a proposal for consideration of award of this project.

Sincerely,

Tom Feeney
General Manager

attachments

As you can see, a cover letter was sent with the Request for Proposals. This was done for three reasons. First, the general manager is the only person in the company who can authorize such a request. Second, because he knows the history of customer surveys at his company and the purpose of this survey, the general manager is in a position to provide background information. And, third, the seriousness of this effort is underscored by the fact that a person of such high standing in the company has initiated contact with these firms.

The team decided to attach to the letter information concerning the purpose of the survey and how a firm might submit a bid, including what specific format to follow in offering a proposal.

By the December 10 deadline, five firms had submitted proposals which, over a three-week period, the management team reviewed. The team decided to award the contract to O'Day and Associates. Though phone conversations,

Broadway Wholesale Warehouse
3232 Independence Avenue
Charlotte, NC 28223

December 28, 1994

Dr. Collett Dilworth
Dilworth Marketing Consultants, Inc.
111 Martha Drive
Manassas, VA 22110

Dear Dr. Dilworth:

Your proposal to conduct a survey of customers for Broadway Wholesale Warehouse has been rejected. A proposal from another firm was better than yours.

Sincerely,

Julie Brown
Public Information Officer

visits, and interviews took place, vital official business—that is, awarding the job—was accomplished through a letter.

A business is always interested in establishing goodwill with the outside community. This desire is more complex than it might at first seem: If one firm is awarded the contract, four must be told that they were not selected to conduct the customer survey. As a result, the public information officer had not one, but two types of letters to write: a good news letter and a bad news letter.

In composing the bad news letter, as you might in your business writing course and again later on the job, the public information officer wanted to make certain she could keep a working relationship with the firms that would not be offered this contract. For one thing, other Requests for Proposals would be written in the future for other jobs; a wise business will want to assure itself that future bids will be competitive so that the best proposal can be rewarded. For another, the business community is surprisingly small. Thoughtlessness and mean-heartedness are often responded to in kind, that is, by other thoughtless and spiteful behaviors.

The letter on page 316 is an example of a thoughtless rejection letter that is not apt to engender goodwill. Perhaps the best that can be said about the letter is that it is short. Brevity enables the author to get to the point without mincing words. But the writer has failed to establish goodwill. The letter lacks an expression of regret, appreciation for the effort put into the proposal and, most basic of all, concern with how Dr. Dilworth will feel about being thus rejected.

Worse yet, the author writes as though there may never again be a reason to solicit a proposal from Dilworth Marketing. The news is all bad in the above letter, employing a bad news/explanation/close pattern.

We recommend that bad news be given more carefully than in the above letter. Begin with a paragraph-length **buffer,** that delays bad news and offers a positive tone. Then give an **explanation** that develops the facts logically enough to make the **bad news** that inevitably must follow understandable; **reestablish goodwill** in the conclusion.

A better bad news letter, the one actually written by Julie Brown, is shown on page 318. Note that in this letter, the first paragraph serves as a buffer for the bad news. Paragraph two offers an explanation of why the contract was not awarded to Dawson Marketing Research. And the conclusion reestablishes goodwill with the company.

Good news letters are not only more fun to write, but are easier to send and receive. Good news hardly ever needs a buffer. In fact, we recommend that you give the good news immediately so readers will pay closer attention to the details or terms of the agreement that usually follow. An appropriate pattern for good news letters begins with the **news,** offers an **explanation of pertinent facts,** and ends in **goodwill,** as in the following award letter (page 319) sent to O'Day and Associates.

All letters you write must be accurate since they constitute a written record and, in many instances, make up some portion of a paper trail. Remember that

Broadway Wholesale Warehouse
3232 Independence Avenue
Charlotte, NC 28223

January 10, 1995

Mr. Douglas Handy
Dawson Market Research Inc.
1 Magnolia Circle, Suite 239
Orlando, FL 32803

Dear Mr. Handy:

Thank you for submitting a proposal to conduct our survey of customer attitudes. We received numerous proposals, all of them offering excellent services.

After careful consideration of these fine proposals, our selection committee has chosen O'Day and Associates of Raleigh, North Carolina, as the firm that best suits our needs.

Again, thank you for your interest in the survey, and perhaps a future project will give us the opportunity to work together.

Sincerely,

Julie Brown,
Public Information Officer

the person whose name is signed to the bottom of the letter is the one responsible for what the letter says. That person must be certain the letter reflects the kind of thinking it should.

But there's another kind of accuracy to check for, mechanical accuracy. Unlike a phone call or conversation, business letters must be checked for correct punctuation, sentence construction, and spelling. A messy letter suggests careless thinking and general unreliability.

Broadway Wholesale Warehouse
3232 Independence Avenue
Charlotte, NC 28223

January 11, 1995

Dr. Felix O'Day, President
O'Day and Associates
2110 Edenton Street
Raleigh, NC 27695

Dear Dr. O'Day:

After careful review, our selection committee has chosen O'Day and Associates to conduct our customer survey, and our Board of Directors has approved that choice. Based on your excellent proposal, the favorable impression from my visit to Raleigh, and the positive comments from several references, I have every confidence that our project will be in good hands.

Enclosed is a copy of the contract signed by Tom Feeney, General Manager. I look forward to working with you and, if you have any questions, please contact me at 555-7453.

Sincerely,

Julie Brown
Public Information Officer

Guidelines for writing letters
1. Follow the proper format for letters (see page 314).
2. Determine your purpose (to persuade, to convey bad news, or to convey good news) and arrange your information appropriately.
3. Properly assess your audience's level of knowledge about the subject, role in the transaction, and position in the company hierarchy.
4. Check for accuracy of content and mechanics.

Exercises

1. Read through all of the documents related to Broadway Warehouse's efforts to hire a marketing research firm to conduct a customer survey. Then read the following e-mail and determine where in the developing history of this search for a marketing firm the e-mail should be placed. Write a memo to your instructor explaining why you have decided to place the correspondence where you have in the evolving history of this search.

FROM: Julie
TO: Tom Feeney
SUBJECT: Survey

I'm planning to go to Raleigh, NC, on January 3 and meet with the people at O'Day and Associates on the following day. Please review the O'Day proposal and let me know any questions you'd like me to ask or anything that needs to be clarified. I'll be on vacation from Dec. 24—Jan. 2, so please just send me your questions in an e-mail message or by mail before Jan. 2. Thanks.

---

2. Compare the memos pertaining to Broadway Wholesale by answering the following questions:
   a. What are their purposes?
   b. How do they differ from e-mail? from letters? from Requests for Proposals?
   c. Briefly characterize each memo's author in terms of level of authority, kind of task undertaken in writing the memo, writing skill, tone, and understanding of audience
   d. Which is the best written memo? Which is the worst?
3. Rewrite the memo you believe to be the weakest of those related to hiring the marketing research firm.
4. *If you have access to a word-processing program,* write one of the following letters:

   • a letter to the president of your university describing some problematic policy you know of that adversely affects the quality of student life on your campus and suggesting some changes you think might help
   • a letter to your campus newspaper describing a problem you perceive on campus and suggesting some changes you think might help
   • a letter to the local newspaper describing a problem you see in the local community and suggesting some changes you think might help
   When you have written your letter, exchange it with a member of your writing group. Using the annotation feature of a word-processing program, critique your partner's letter focusing on the Guidelines for Writing Letters

we provide on page 319 of this section. In these annotations, discuss with your partner whether or not the letter's various parts seem to accomplish the purposes for which they are intended, and provide some specific suggestions for revising the less effective parts.

Writing Informal and Formal Reports

Reports, ranging from informal to formal, are used to document some of a company's most important information. The writing of such reports is, therefore, a critical activity for anyone hoping to work in business and management.

In a report that must be written over an extended period of time or that involves multiple steps, team members need to be informed as to the status at regular intervals, perhaps at time periods the team designated early in the process of completing the project. The team leader usually takes responsibility for updating the team on the status of a project by writing a status or progress report.

Team members will want to know the project's current status, if it is within the budget, and if it is on schedule. If a series of progress reports must be written, each report must have the same format.

The standard format for a progress report includes an **introduction** that identifies the subject, the methods employed to complete the project, and the projected date by which the project should be finished. The **body** of the progress report should describe the project's current status, including any difficulties with scheduling or funding. And the **conclusion** should suggest any recommendations for changing the methods employed in completing the project, the schedule, or any other adjustment that needs to be made or reminders that must be given. Of course, you may in the best of circumstances use a progress report to reassure team members and supervisors that everything is progressing at the anticipated rate.

Here is an example of a progress report written by Julie Brown of Broadway Wholesale Warehouse.

December 11, 1994

TO: Customer Survey Selection Team
FROM: Julie Brown
SUBJECT: Project Status Report

Our deadline for receiving proposals from firms interested in conducting our customer survey was December 10. We sent RFPs to twelve firms.
We have currently received proposals from five firms. Two firms responded that they do not do surveys. State law prohibits the Regional Development Institute from submitting a proposal. Four other firms have not responded at all.

continued

> The survey selection committee is scheduled to meet on Friday, December 14, at 10 a.m. to discuss the proposals. To make that meeting more efficient, I am providing you with summaries as well as copies of the complete proposals ahead of time.
>
> We budgeted $12,000 for a customer survey, so bear that in mind when you review the summaries and proposals. If you have any questions, please call me.

You can expect to be asked to write some kind of report for your business writing class. The report you write may be assigned to you for independent research, or you may be asked to collaborate with others in your class. In any case, your assignment will be something along the lines of the one below, given in a course called Writing for Business and Industry.

> Your technical report is a recommendation report that is eight to twelve pages long. It should solve a problem by comparing two or more products or systems which are similar, but—perhaps—not the same. For instance, you would want to compare two nineteen-inch color TV's rather than one thirteen-inch and one projection-screen TV. The criteria and their development should be obvious to readers in the findings section of the report.
>
> Within the findings, writers should explain terms that their target audience would not understand. Their audience should be described (usually in one sentence) in the purpose section of the Introduction.
>
> The report itself must follow the format I will give you. Besides the text, you must include graphics, Table of Graphics, and Table of Contents.
>
> The report must be documented—failure to use internal documentation is grounds for failure—and it should follow MLA style. The writing should adhere to the basic conventions of standard written English, avoiding errors in punctuation, grammar, spelling, usage, etc.

The format given to students who must complete the above assignment is fairly typical of formats used in business writing courses. You should note, however, that many companies have their own formats for reports that should take precedence over any format offered in any book.

The standard format for a formal recommendation report includes the following:

1. **Table of Contents:** In some instances, it is wise to write the table of contents last, after you have decided on a clear system of headings within the report. The headings you have created should be indicated in the table of contents along with the page on which that section begins. Use exactly the same

format in the table of contents as on the page where that section can be found.

2. **Introduction:** As with all section headings, "Introduction" must be indicated at the top of the page, centered, and must begin on a page of its own. The introduction should include the following: a statement of the problem, a statement of the project's purpose, identification of methods employed in gathering information for the report, a statement of its scope and its limitations, and an explanation of how the report is organized.

3. **Findings:** By findings, we mean the data observed, discovered, or created. In the report on the customer survey, the data is simply what O'Day & Associates found out. For instance, O'Day & Associates may have accumulated data such as the following: Only 12.5% of those surveyed believe Broadway Wholesale Warehouse is concerned about their customers' satisfaction. (Interpretations of the results *do not* belong here. Interpretations belong in the conclusion.)

4. **Conclusion:** This section interprets the data reported in the Findings. Conclusions are the meanings you assign to what you have found out. The conclusions must be stated clearly so the reader can see how and why you interpreted your findings as you have. For instance, O'Day & Associates might conclude from their findings that Broadway Wholesale Warehouse needs to do something to make customers feel that their satisfaction is important.

5. **Recommendations:** A recommendation is simply a suggestion about how things should be done in the future. O'Day & Associates might have suggested that Broadway Wholesale Warehouse attempt to improve its image by undertaking a serious public relations effort, for instance.

In some reports, such as the one that follows, you might be asked to write an **abstract,** which serves as a brief technical summary of the report. In an abstract, you should describe the problem, important results, conclusions, and recommendations. Additionally, some instructors will expect you to include tables and charts and a table of graphics, as in the following report, written in response to the assignment on page 322.

Guidelines for writing a recommendation report

1. Find a problem in need of remedy. This problem may be a personal matter (for example, Which camera should I purchase from among two or three similar ones?) or school-related (for example, Should condoms be made available in dormitories?) or job-related (for example, Which computer system is best for my place of business? Which system will best prevent theft at the place where I work?) or community-related (for example, Why should a stoplight be put up at a particular intersection? Why should a community-based teen center be established?).

2. The problem should have several alternative solutions you can study by observing, interviewing, surveying, or reading.

3. Follow the format described on pages 322–323.
4. Remember that findings are raw, uninterpreted data.
5. Remember that conclusions are efforts to interpret or to find meaning in collected data.
6. Remember that recommendations are courses of action that seem a logical consequence of conclusions you have reached.
7. Revise, proofread, and edit.

Pages 325–338 show an example of a recommendation report written by a student in a business writing course.

Technical Report

Inventories Are Falling
and
Shoplifting Rising

April 21, 1996

Submitted to:

Dr. R. Chappelle

1.0   Abstract

This technical report compares four possible methods of security for Sports Unlimited. Closed circuit televisions, android surveillance, plainclothed officers, and uniformed security officers were compared to find the most effective method of security. Costs, installation, benefits, and drawbacks were all taken into consideration before making a recommendation. Through my research I discovered that CCTV systems were most expensive yet most effective in preventing shoplifting.

2.0   Table of Contents

1.0   Abstract 1
2.0   Table of Contents 2
3.0   Table of Graphics 3
4.0   Introduction 4
    4.1   Problem 4
    4.2   Purpose 4
    4.3   Plan and Organization 4
    4.4   Method 4
5.0   Findings of Investigation 5
    5.1   Closed Circuit Television (CCTV) 5
        5.1.1   Costs 5
        5.1.2   Installation 5
        5.1.3   Benefits 5
        5.1.4   Drawbacks 5
    5.2   Uniformed Security Officer 5
        5.2.1   Costs 5
        5.2.2   Benefits 6
        5.2.3   Drawbacks 6
    5.3   Plainclothed Officer 6
        5.3.1   Costs 6
        5.3.2   Benefits 6
        5.3.3   Drawbacks 6
    5.4   Android Surveillance 7
        5.4.1   Costs 7
        5.4.2   Installation 7
        5.4.4   Benefits 7
        5.4.4   Drawbacks 7
        5.4.5   Construction 7
6.0   Conclusion 8
    Graphic 9
    Graphic 10
7.0   Recommendation 11
8.0   Works Cited 12
    Graphic 13

3.0   Table of Graphics

Figure 1   Money lost on a national level due to shoplifting   9
Figure 2   Percentage of effectiveness   10
Figure 3   Price for Possible Security Method   13

4.0   Introduction

4.1   Problem

As Sports Unlimited begins to expand and the size of stores increases, employees themselves are no longer enough to stop the ongoing dilemma of shoplifting. The focus of this report is on finding the most efficient and reliable method of security possible.

4.2   Purpose

Security for Sports Unlimited has become a primary topic of discussion. The report discusses four major areas of security in hopes of finding the most reliable and efficient source for preventing shoplifting. The four security methods are as follows: closed circuit televison (CCTV) units, plainclothed officers, uniformed security officers, and android surveillance.

4.3   Plan and Organization

The material is divided into four major headings; each possible security method follows the heading individually. Subdivisions of the four major topics include the cost, installation, benefits, and drawbacks. The security android includes subdivisions concerning its means of installation and construction. Following the findings, a conclusion and a recommendation are presented. After the recommendation is the works cited page.

4.4   Method

The following sources I used to gather information were obtained by a series of telephone interviews, personal knowledge of security devices, and the television show *I-Witness Video.*

5.0 Findings of investigation

5.1 Closed Circuit Television (CCTV)

5.1.1 Costs

When covering a store of 30,000 square feet, numerous monitors and cameras are essential. Listed below is the average cost for one CCTV system:

Camera	$600.00–$1000.00
Switcher	$200.00– $500.00
Monitor	$300.00– $500.00
Recorder	$1000.00–$3000.00

5.1.2 Installation

For a store the size of Sports Unlimited, one day is needed just to run the necessary cable. An average of $45 per hour is the basic rate. One hour is required per camera and monitors; recorders and switchers average twenty to thirty minutes per unit.

5.1.3 Benefits

Using the CCTV unit gives you a clear, overall view of the entire store. Recorders provide the store manager with solid evidence that will stand in the courtroom for prosecution. With shoppers able to see the cameras, a visual deterrent is present as well. Other benefits follow: simple operation, easy installation, and great dependability.

5.1.4 Drawbacks

With certain benefits, drawbacks as well are usually evident. Persons are required to watch the monitor, and with the activity in a store of this size it would seem impossible for someone to maintain constant watch. A job of this type can become very boring and someone who is monitoring the CCTV tends to become easily distracted and often uncaring.

5.2 Uniformed Security Officer

5.2.1 Costs

The cost for a uniformed security officer varies greatly. If hired by a private security firm, hourly wages can range from $10 to $15 an hour. A police officer who does this type of work in his or her spare time can range in salary from $4.50 to $5.50 an hour (MacKenzie).

5

5.2.2 Benefits
The primary benefit of a uniformed security officer is the visual deterrent that is present. Security cars, and on occasion police vehicles, are parked immediately in front of Sports Unlimited; this in turn lets the shopper know that authority is present. Another major benefit is public humiliation. When an arrest occurs, shoppers who witness the act begin to think twice about shoplifting. Public humiliation is another form of visual deterrent.

5.2.3 Drawbacks
The major problem I found with uniformed security officers is that one person cannot cover 30,000 square feet thoroughly. An experienced shoplifter knows where the security guard is at all times. The security guard needs breaks and a lunch hour, and an experienced shoplifter will wait and then make his or her move. A less critical problem I found was that security officers tend to mingle with store employees rather than patrol the store looking for shoplifters.

5.3 Plainclothed Officer

5.3.1 Costs
After conducting an interview with a personal friend, I found that a large majority of stores, including Sports Unlimited, are beginning to use plainclothed security officers. The cost, based on an hourly wage, is in the neighborhood of $6.50 to $13.00 an hour (Garrison).

5.3.2 Benefits
Obviously the most relevant benefit is the unknown and secret security officer. Posing as an ordinary shopper, the plainclothed officer is able to wander about the store undetected. If the shoplifter is unaware that someone is watching, he or she is more likely to steal or make an attempt. You may never know that someone is watching your every move. Although the hourly wage tends to be high, the rate of success tends to be high as well.

5.3.3 Drawbacks
With plainclothed officers the immediate visual deterrent is not present. No one suspects any authority to be within the store. Once again the plainclothed officer needs to take breaks, including a lunch break; this becomes a vulnerable spot in security. Constantly walking and being on one's feet all day, one tends to get very tired and then one's attention begins to wander as well.

6

5.4 Android Surveillance

5.4.1 Costs
To acquire the android surveillance unit will cost you somewhere between $2,000.00 to $5,000.00 per system (*I-Witness Video*). Sports Unlimited, consisting of 30,000 square feet, would take ten androids to cover the entire store. The cost for ten android units can run as high as $50,000.

5.4.2 Installation
After the construction of the android is complete, the installation is the easiest step. All that is required is to dress each android and then place it in the appropriate position. Monitors, cameras, and recorders are placed in the head and controlled from a single unit.

5.4.3 Benefits
What normal shopper would ever guess that the mannequin is actually a surveillance unit? Simple installation and low cost become very appealing to the store manager. The android requires no vacation, will not call in sick, and needs no lunch break. With recorders that videotape the action, these tapes are submissible in court as evidence.

5.4.4 Drawbacks
Only being able to monitor through their eyes, the androids become vulnerable to blind spots. The android needs to be placed in a prime position to achieve maximum efficiency. There is no visual deterrent that is noticeable to the shoppers. One way to eliminate this problem would be to advertise the security android. It would be wise as well to use the surveillance unit with a CCTV system.

5.4.5 Construction
As simple as it may seem, a lot of tedious hours go into the completion of the security android. The actual bodies are assembled at the mannequin factory and then shipped to the security store for completion. Cameras are placed in the eyes of the android, with a microphone in the nose of the android. A monitor is then linked to the android so that activity can be monitored. Transmitters and switchers are assembled in the head of the android for convenience purposes.

7

6.0   Conclusion

While collecting the information necessary, I found none of the four methods of security to be 100% effective.

The CCTV unit is the highest priced but also the most effective. The cost of each security system varies greatly; the uniformed officer and the plainclothed officer were the cheapest of the four methods. They were also the least effective of the four compared. The android surveillance unit is much cheaper than the CCTV unit by several thousand dollars. All units have their benefits, but the CCTV and android surveillance were more effective considering the benefits. Coverage of the entire store was the largest benefit both could offer. With benefits come drawbacks. The CCTV unit and the android surveillance had too many blind spots to be 100% efficient. Uniformed and plainclothed officers could not cover the entire store as well as the CCTV and the android units. Both required various breaks and a lunch hour as well; . . . therefore, the store would lack security at these times. Installation of the android unit compared to the CCTV was much easier and less time consuming.

The following recommendation is presented to maximize the efficiency of the CCTV unit. Protection of inventory is essential to all stores, large and small.

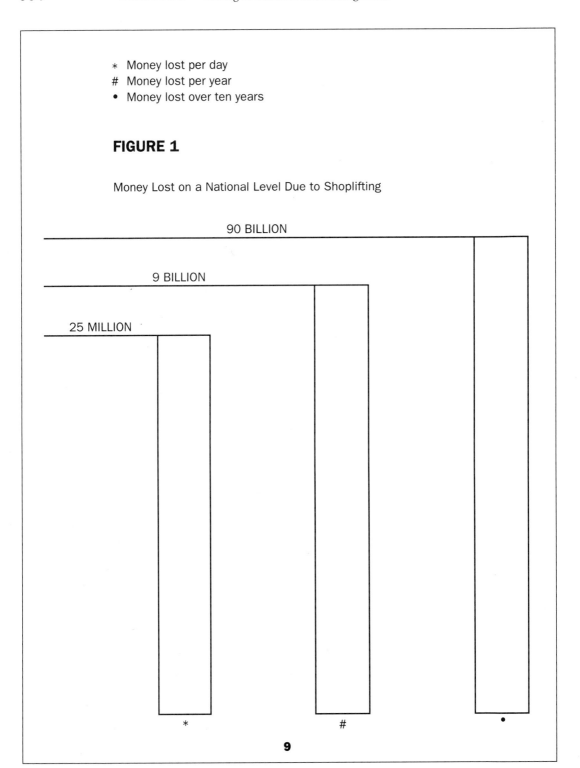

∗ Money lost per day
\# Money lost per year
• Money lost over ten years

FIGURE 1

Money Lost on a National Level Due to Shoplifting

90 BILLION

9 BILLION

25 MILLION

∗

\#

•

9

FIGURE 2

Percent of Effectiveness

CCTV—Closed circuit television
USO—Uniformed security officer
PCSO—Plain-clothed security officer
AS—Android surveillance

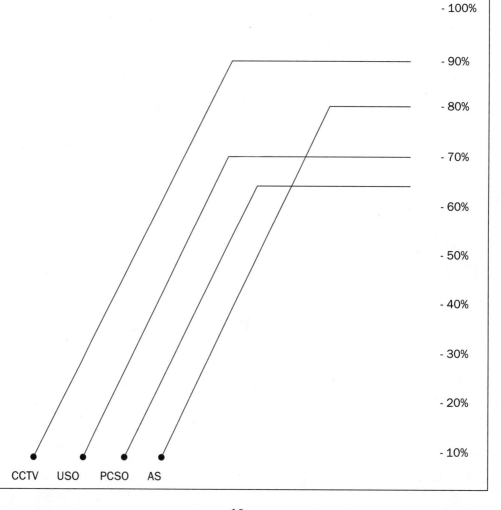

7.0   Recommendation

Results of my findings have suggested that the CCTV system would be most effective in the security of Sports Unlimited Sporting Goods Co. Though the CCTV unit is the most expensive, it can cover the entire store, a quality the other three lacked. True, it is the most expensive and the installation takes longer, but in the long run the store manager can rest easier knowing that his or her inventory is being monitored at all times.

11

8.0   Works Cited

Campbell, Melinda. Personal Interview. Sports Unlimited Store Manager. 16 June 1989.

Garrison, Harry. Personal Interview. Mecklenburg Co. Police Dept. 20 December 1990.

I-Witness Video. Television show. 5 April 1992.

MacKenzie Security. Telephone Interview. 18 March 1992.

Security Alert. Telephone Interview. 18 March 1992.

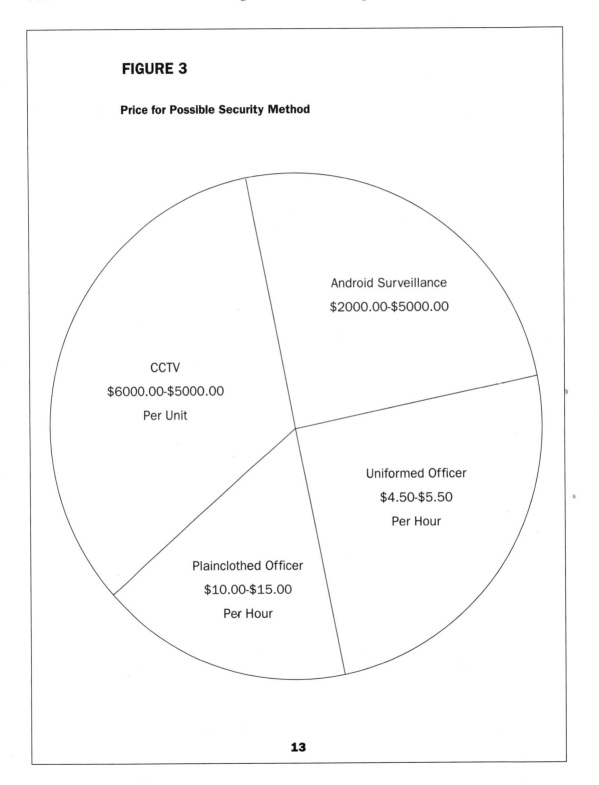

FIGURE 3

Price for Possible Security Method

Android Surveillance
$2000.00-$5000.00

CCTV
$6000.00-$5000.00
Per Unit

Uniformed Officer
$4.50-$5.50
Per Hour

Plainclothed Officer
$10.00-$15.00
Per Hour

13

This draft of the student report satisfies many of the requirements of the stated assignment. The student has succeeded in finding a problem in need of a solution. What's more, he offers several alternative solutions and investigates them without judgment or preconception. He follows the format as it is described by his teacher.

More specifically, the components of the report are structured with the reader in mind. A reader can turn to the abstract to determine the report's merits and relevance. The table of contents follows the same format as on individual pages, reflecting the report's organizational structure. The table of graphics likewise refers to specific graphic aids used to demonstrate visually what the report states in narrative fashion.

A good introduction to the report identifies the problem, states the purpose of the investigation, identifies the plan and organization of the report, and states the specific methods the investigator employs in gathering information.

The body of the report, the findings, adheres to the requirement that raw, uninterpreted information be presented to the reader without any intrusion of judgment or preconception by the author. The conclusion, then, serves as a place where the investigator interprets the data found in the findings and offers certain meanings and interpretations of what has been found. The recommendation section that follows is a place where, on the basis of conclusions made by analysis of data, a solution is offered to the problem identified in the introduction. As you can see, all parts of a good technical report are interrelated.

Note also that since the teacher has identified MLA documentation style as the format to be used in this report for citing references, the final section is entitled Works Cited.

Exercises

1. Reread the student recommendation report. Write a memo to the student offering two kinds of observations: a statement of what has been done well in the report and a statement of how the author might improve her report.
2. Write a recommendation report. Be certain to follow the seven guidelines for writing a recommendation report.
3. *If your writing group has access to a word-processing package,* identify some of the major challenges that student writers have in adapting to the kinds of writing required of them in their first year of college on your campus. In a word-processing file, take notes that define these problems, provide evidence of these problems, identify some solutions for addressing these problems in first-year writing classes and in other classes, and offer some recommendations about the first-year writing curriculum that students need. Provide a copy of these notes to each student in the writing group.

   Over the course of several days, working individually, have each member of the writing group draft their own recommendation report using these notes.

Exchange your recommendation report draft with another member of the writing group. Using the annotation feature of a word-processing package, critique your partner's report draft. For this purpose, use the guidelines on pages 322–323 for writing a recommendation report. In your annotations, provide commentary on each section of the report that tells what parts are most effective and why, and what parts are least effective and why. Also be sure to include specific suggestions for revision.

Revise your draft report using the recommendations your writing partner provided.

4. *If you have access to a computer network and real-time conferencing software,* hold a 20-minute, full class, on-line discussion about the writing problems first-year students experience when they come to your campus. Focus on identifying these problems and identifying some instructional approaches that might help students address these problems in productive ways. When this discussion is complete, archive it so that all class members have access to the transcript.

Over the course of several days, working individually, have each member of the class draft their own recommendation report using the transcripts and the ideas from the discussion.

Exchange your recommendation report draft with another member of the class. Using the annotation feature of a word-processing package, critique your partner's report draft. For this purpose, use the guidelines on pages 322–323 for writing a recommendation report. In your annotations, provide commentary on each section of the report that tells what parts are most and least effective and why. Also be sure to include specific suggestions for revision.

Revise your draft report using the recommendations your writing partner provided.

URLs for Business and Management

Finance: The World Wide Web Virtual Library
http://www.cob.ohio-state.edu/dept/fin/overview.html

Business Administration (Business and Commerce)
http://andromeda.einet.net/galaxy/Business-and-Commerce/Business-Administration.html

Council of Better Business Bureaus Publications
http://www.bbb.org/bbb/pubs.html

Business and Finance
http://128.172.69.103/cworld/Business.html

WorldWide Guide to Business
http://www.theworld.com/BUSINESS/SUBJECT.HTML

The Business Page—Worldwide
http://www.sgn.com/4reps.html

Business General Resources (Business and Commerce)
http://www.einet.net/galaxy/Business-and-Commerce/
Business-General-Resources.html

Business Resources
http://www.rutgers.edu/newark/DANA/njone.html

Business and Economics—Special Fields
http://bib10.sub.su.se/sam/sbspec.htm

Business Resources
http://darkwing.uoregon.edu/~kbrink/

CHAPTER TEN

Writing in the Health Sciences

Responsibilities of Health Sciences Professionals

Importance of Communications to the Health Sciences Professional

Writing in the Undergraduate Health Sciences

Newspaper headlines on just about any day are apt to focus on issues of importance to health science professionals. Consider debates over the past decade concerning AIDS and the cost of AZT, a national health care system, life-prolonging techniques and organ transplants, life-ending techniques and euthanasia, the sale and consumption of tobacco and alcohol, and the effects of ultraviolet rays on your skin. Health scientists are interested in these issues and often enter public dialogue concerning them.

If you enter a field in the health sciences, communication skills will be very important to you. As a health sciences major, you not only will be required to perform the writing tasks most often required in the natural sciences (see Chapter Seven), but you must also learn how to complete certain specific writing tasks in introductory courses in your major field, whether it be nursing, occupational therapy, physical therapy, sports medicine, exercise physiology, health education, or recreational therapy.

Writing skills that you will gain in health science courses are designed to prepare you for your chosen profession. If you hope to become a nurse, therapist, or trainer, you can expect to write assessments, health plans, and other documents that will become part of a patient's records.

On the other hand, you may plan to use your undergraduate training in these health-related fields as background for entry into advanced study programs. You may study health sciences as an undergraduate in preparation for becoming a doctor, dentist, or other trained medical specialist. You will need to know how to perform the writing tasks described in Chapter Seven, including laboratory notebooks, laboratory reports, microthemes, and critical reviews. In addition to the kinds of writings required of scientists, you will be expected to know how to observe a patient, diagnose an illness, and design a health care plan for that patient as well.

If you take courses in the health sciences under either of these plans of study, you can expect to perform some writing tasks similar to those required in other disciplines. For instance, the library research paper, assigned in introductory courses in most disciplines, will also be assigned in health science courses. Such an assignment is designed to provide you with skills that will enable you to stay current with information that might one day influence decisions you make as a professional, not only about how to treat a particular illness or injury, but also about how to treat a particular patient.

Some assignments will only *seem* to you to be similar to assignments in other disciplines. For instance, observation is required in most disciplines. But in the health sciences, you will be asked to observe individuals in need of health care as well as groups of employees at businesses or in industries that desire wellness programs. As a student, you will need to observe health educators and report on what you have observed (see pages 368–369). Your observations will be reported systematically, in any case, as a basis for deeper understanding of the situation, leading to diagnosis and treatment, both on the level of the individual patient and on the level of the large organization.

Still other writing tasks, such as certain discipline-specific health care plans, are clearly unique to individual areas of concentration in the health sciences, such as nursing and recreational therapy. These will not be discussed at any length in this chapter, since they are not apt to be required of you in your introductory courses in the health sciences. Preparation for the writing of recreational therapies assessments, new patient evaluations, and nursing care plans (see pages 346–352) is the goal of writing instruction in introductory courses. These more sophisticated documents require exact description of what has been observed and explanation of how certain decisions were reached, including the various steps you as the health professional have taken in treating a patient. As preparation for writing these documents, you will be asked to observe closely and make judgments that reflect what you have learned about wellness.

Responsibilities of Health Sciences Professionals

Writing tasks in the health sciences are apt to begin with library research, then proceed to observation and judgment, and finally conclude in plans or treatments. Often these phases of documentation begin when a nurse, doctor, or therapist dictates what needs to be written, proceed to a secretary who transcribes that dictation, and finishes with the doctor who reviews the document.

Some of the documents a health professional might write, then, will serve as a record of a patient's history. These records will be stored in a file and used at some later date by colleagues in determining, on the basis of the patient's history, what steps to take in treating an illness. While doctors can expect to compose such documents, they are often assisted in their writing by other health personnel, as in the new patient evaluation form on page 348, which is typical of what might be spoken by a doctor into a dictaphone, transcribed by a secretary/transcriptionist, and finally proofread by the doctor.

If you choose to become a doctor, you may find the ability to compose aloud to be invaluable. On the other hand, you still may find yourself working partially or even exclusively in research, perhaps at a university or at a pharmaceutical company. Such scientists should plan on writing research reports to share innovations and discoveries with others in the field. Increasingly, even in industry, publication of research is required for pay increases and promotions.

All in all, if you major in the health professions you can expect to perform a considerable amount of writing. Not all of it, however, adheres to the rigid requirements of most composition courses taught in English departments. In fact, many of the specific departments in the health sciences employ a kind of shorthand understood by others in the discipline.

To better understand the specific writing skills health science majors must obtain, we will examine three samples—a therapeutic recreation assessment written by a certified recreational therapist, a new patient evaluation dictated by a doctor to a secretary, and an excerpt from a health care plan written by a student in a nursing program. These examples (Figures 10.1, 10.2, and 10.3) reflect in content, style, format, and tone the range of writing tasks done in most professions in the health sciences.

FIGURE 10.1   Sample Therapeutic Recreation Assessment Form

DATE REQUESTED: _____5/2/91_____ REFERRED BY: _____N/A_____ CASE MANAGER: __N/A__

REFERRED FOR ASSESSMENT IN: _____ OCCUPATIONAL THERAPY
　　　　　　　　　　　　　　 _____ MUSIC THERAPY
　　　　　　　　　　　　　　 __✓__ THERAPEUTIC THERAPY
　　　　　　　　　　　　　　 _____ HORTICULTURE THERAPY
　　　　　　　　　　　　　　 _____ OTHER _____

COMMENTS: _____

_____

_____

ACTIVITY THERAPIES DISCIPLINE ASSESSMENT:

Mr. Worth received Therapeutic Recreation yearly update on December 2, 1991. Evaluation was completed by J. Phifer, CTRS. The evaluation techniques included TR Assessment Guide, Patient Interview, Observation of Participation in TR Group sessions, review of medical chart.

Mr. Worth . . . has been hospitalized most of his adult life (since age 17). He has a history of inappropriate sexual behavior such as grabbing and pinching females and inappropriate sexual comments. Current diagnosis: Schizophrenia, Disorganized Type.

THERAPIST OBSERVATION/PATIENT INTERVIEW:

During interview, Mr. Worth was oriented X3 (person, place, time). Attention span—fair. He was cooperative but appeared nervous as evidenced by wringing of hands. During interview and overall assessment of Mr. Worth his communication skills are poor. He has a low monotonous voice and often speaks in a rapid manner. Therapist has noted patient mumbling to himself at times. He will follow directions but repeats a question or instructions several times. He can usually be seen with a grinning and peculiar facial expression. Mr. Worth appears to lack appropriate socialization skills as evidenced by his being more isolated and withdrawn and his episodes of bizarre behavior, particularly inappropriate sexual behavior (history of grabbing and pinching females). Upon observing Mr. Worth in TR sessions, he is very regimented in his way of doing the assigned tasks, and does not like to veer from his particular pattern. When questioned about work experiences he stated he . . . has never been publicly employed.

STRENGTHS
1. oriented X3 (PPT)
2. cooperative
3. ambulatory

NEEDS
1. To increase appropriate socialization skills
2. To channel nervousness into appropriate outlets
3. To decrease bizarre and inappropriate actions

continued

FIGURE 10.1

PLAN

Mr. Worth will attend TR Exercises and Movement I on Tuesday, Thursday, and Friday from 2–3 p.m. with therapist J. Phifer. This involvement is designed to meet the following goals:

Long-Term Goals: In 6 months, Mr. Worth will increase appropriate social interaction by becoming more verbal and by decreasing bizarre and inappropriate actions.

Short-Term Goals: (in 3 months)
   Mr. Worth will increase appropriate social interactions by initiating 1–2 conversations per session.

   Mr. Worth will channel nervousness into appropriate outlets as evidenced by successful completion of his exercise and movement tasks 100% of the sessions.

   Mr. Worth will decrease bizarre and inappropriate actions to no more than 1 to 2 episodes during a 3-month period.

Strategies: Therapist will encourage patient involvement in Therapeutic Recreation and will give positive enforcements for appropriate attendance, participation, and behavior. He will also be reminded when behavior is inappropriate and intolerable.

_____

Certified Recreational Therapist

Keep in mind, however, that you are unlikely to be required to write these kinds of documents in introductory courses. The writing you are most apt to do in introductory courses is designed as preparation for writing these more sophisticated documents later in your program of study.

These documents are similar in tone, style, and form to texts written by therapists, doctors, nurses, and other health professionals who offer various other kinds of therapies (for example, occupational, physical, and so forth). In fact, once on the job in the health professions, you can expect to spend considerable time diagnosing illnesses (as in the new patient evaluation), assessing patients' conditions (as in the therapeutic recreation assessment), devising health care plans (as in the nursing care plan), and, generally, recording your observations and your insights to be read sometime in the future by your colleagues in helping that same patient. As a result, your training as a writer in the health sciences is designed to prepare you for the writing of such texts once you have graduated and taken a job.

As you can see, both the therapeutic recreation assessment form and the new patient evaluation combine narrative and fill-in-the-blanks. The goal, of course,

FIGURE 10.2 New Patient Evaluation Form

ALLERGY, ASTHMA and IMMUNOLOGY CLINIC
NEW PATIENT EVALUATION

Patient Name:
Date of Visit: 05/23/95
MPI#:
DOB: 07/11/54

HISTORY OF PRESENT ILLNESS

The patient is a 40-year-old white male with an 8-year-history of rhinitis symptoms. He reports rhinorrhea, sneezing, itchy eyes, nasal congestion, and postnasal drip with year-round symptoms that exacerbate in the spring and in the fall. There is a history of wheezing and chest tightness ×3; one time requiring oral prednisone and a nebulization treatment. His symptoms are worse outside the home and worse in the early morning. He has recently noted an increase in nocturnal wheezing symptoms. Beconase has been very effective in the past as have bronchodilators by metered dose inhaler. There is no history of frequent colds, no recent sinus x-ray, and no recent antibiotic use. Nonsteroidal antiinflammatory drugs do not exacerbate symptoms. There are no associated symptoms with food and there is no history of urticaria. Currently he has a cough productive of yellowish sputum but no frequent headaches. The cough has improved with Beconase use. There is a history of some reflux symptoms associated with spicy foods.

PAST MEDICAL HISTORY

Medical—As noted in HPI.
Hospitalizations—None.
Emergency Room visits—None.
Pneumonias—None.

REVIEW OF SYSTEMS

Noncontributory.

SURGICAL HISTORY

Status post surgery on the hand and chin.

IMMUNIZATIONS

PPD negative, date unknown; tetanus toxoid up to date; influenza—yearly; reactions to these injections—none.

FUNCTIONAL

Loss from daily routine—None.

IMMUNOTHERAPY

He was on immunotherapy for two years as prescribed by an allergist in Temple, TX. He stopped two years ago. He felt that it was very effective and had grasses, cedar, and dust.

CURRENT MEDICATIONS

Beconase AQ 2 sprays to each nostril p.r.n.; Tylenol ES 1 p.o. p.r.n.; Multivitamin 1 p.o. q/day.

ALLERGIES TO MEDICATIONS None.

FAMILY HISTORY

Paternal grandmother with asthma and a child with allergies.

SUPPLEMENTAL HISTORY

Occupation—Sales manager for two years in Hilton.
Home Environment—He lives in a vinyl-sided home with new carpet, central heat and air; mattress with foam and feather pillow. The patient was advised to discard the feather pillow.
Smoking—He is exposed to smoke at work. He was advised to avoid smokers as much as possible.
Alcohol—Rarely.
Pets—Outside dog which does not exacerbate symptoms.
Hobbies—Gardening and woodworking.

PHYSICAL EXAMINATION

VITAL SIGNS: BP 120/80; TPR 98.3-80-20; peak flow 550, predicted 610; Hgt. 71″; Wgt. 255.5 lbs.

FIGURE 10.3   Health Care Plan

EAST CAROLINA UNIVERSITY
SCHOOL OF NURSING
CLIENT/FAMILY NURSING CARE PLAN

NURSING DIAGNOSIS/PC# _Ineffective airway clearance R/T excessive and tenacious exercises_

FUNCTIONAL HEALTH PATTERN _Activity-Exercise_

DEFINING CHARACTERISTICS: MAJOR _Ineffective Cough and Inability to remove airway secretions_ **MINOR** _Abnormal breath sounds_

CLIENT GOAL AND/OR DISCHARGE GOAL _The client will demonstrate effective measures to cope c̄ ineffective airway clearance due to secretions._

OUTCOME CRITERIA	INTERVENTIONS	RATIONALE WITH DOCUMENTATION	IMPLEMENTATION	EVALUATION
1. The client will demonstrate effective coughing and increased air exchange in the lungs, within one week.	1. Instruct the client on proper method of controlled coughing. a. Breathe deeply and slowly while sitting up as high as she can. b. Teach to use diaphragmatic breathing.	1. Uncontrolled coughing is tiring and ineffective, leading to frustration (Carpenito, p. 108, 1995). a. Sitting up high shifts the abdominal organs away from the lungs, enabling greater expansion (Carpenito, p. 108, 1995). b. Diaphragmatic breathing reduces the respiratory rate and increases alveolar ventilation.	1. Nurse told client that an effective cough would be less tiring than an unproductive cough, and nurse demonstrated cough for client. a. Nurse showed client how to breathe deeply and slowly and instructed client to sit up high while doing so, in order to promote expansion. b. Nurse showed client how to properly breathe diaphragmatically and instructed the client verbally also.	1. Client could explain why an effective cough would be useful. a. Deep breathing in an upright position was accomplished and client told nurse that greater expansion was provided in 2 weeks. b. Diaphragmatic breathing was accomplished by client within 2 weeks.

continued

FIGURE 10.3

EAST CAROLINA UNIVERSITY
SCHOOL OF NURSING
CLIENT/FAMILY NURSING CARE PLAN

NURSING DIAGNOSIS/PC# _____

FUNCTIONAL HEALTH PATTERN _____

DEFINING CHARACTERISTICS: MAJOR _____ MINOR _____

CLIENT GOAL AND/OR DISCHARGE GOAL _____

OUTCOME CRITERIA	INTERVENTIONS	RATIONALE WITH DOCUMENTATION	IMPLEMENTATION	EVALUATION
2. The client will be able to relate the proper strategies to help decrease tenacious secretions; hydration and humidity of air; within 2 weeks.	2. Teach client the measures that should be taken to reduce the viscosity of secretions. a. Maintain adequate hydration by increasing the fluid intake to 2–3 qts. per day. b. Teach to maintain the proper humidity of inspired air.	2. Thick secretions are difficult to expectorate and can cause mucous plugs, which can lead to atelectasis (Carpenito p. 108, 1995). a. Thick secretions are difficult to expectorate and can cause mucous plugs, which can lead to atelectasis (Carpenito p, 108, 1995). b. Thick secretions are difficult to expectorate and can cause mucous plugs, which can lead to atelectasis (Carpenito, p. 108, 1995).	2. Client and nurse discussed effective strategy in order to help decrease thick secretions. Nurse told client that thick secretions can be problematic, causing mucous plugs and atelectasis. a. Nurse instructed client to drink at least 2–3 qts. a day in order to decrease secretions. Nurse often offers client H_2O. b. Nurse and client discussed the importance of the humidity factor in the inspired air. Nurse	2. Explanation was clear on how to try and ↓ secretion consistency the idea of hydration and proper air humidity in 2 weeks. a. 2–3 qts. a day of fluid was consumed by client at the end of 2 weeks. b. Importance of humidity of inspired air was recognized by client. Client ran warm H_2O in sink and breathed deep while holding face over H_2O. (Take place of shower at this pt.)

continued

FIGURE 10.3

EAST CAROLINA UNIVERSITY
SCHOOL OF NURSING
CLIENT/FAMILY NURSING CARE PLAN

NURSING DIAGNOSIS/PC# _____

FUNCTIONAL HEALTH PATTERN _____

DEFINING CHARACTERISTICS: MAJOR _____   MINOR _____

CLIENT GOAL AND/OR DISCHARGE GOAL _____

OUTCOME CRITERIA	INTERVENTIONS	RATIONALE WITH DOCUMENTATION	IMPLEMENTATION	EVALUATION
3. Client will verbally explain to the nurse the importance of each medication that she is currently on within 2 weeks.	3. Explain to client the importance of the meds. she is on and have her recall this info. and explain it to the nurse.	3. Clients need to understand the importance of taking the prescribed regimen of drugs to obtain maximum effectiveness (Lewis and Collier, p. 520, 1992).	recommended a steamy shower when possible. 3. Nurse explained to client the need and importance of each medication she was on at the time. Nurse wrote brief summary of side effects to look for in order to warn the client.	3. An explanation of the reasons why she is on the meds. she is on was provided to the nurse by the client at the end of 2 weeks. Understanding of the importance of each of them is present by the end of 2 weeks. The client has reached her goal of demonstration of effective measures to cope c̄ ineffective airway clearance. We will continue to progress in order to expectorate secretions.

continued

FIGURE 10.3

EAST CAROLINA UNIVERSITY
SCHOOL OF NURSING
CLIENT/FAMILY NURSING CARE PLAN

NURSING DIAGNOSIS/PC# _____

FUNCTIONAL HEALTH PATTERN _____

DEFINING CHARACTERISTICS: MAJOR _____ MINOR _____

CLIENT GOAL AND/OR DISCHARGE GOAL _____

OUTCOME CRITERIA	INTERVENTIONS	RATIONALE WITH DOCUMENTATION	IMPLEMENTATION	EVALUATION
	c. Instruct client to hold her breath for 3–5 sec. and slowly exhale as much as she can through the mouth, so that lower abdomen and rib cage sink down. d. Instruct client to take a second breath, hold it, and then cough from the chest; not the mouth or throat; c̄ 2 short, forceful coughs.	c. Increasing the volume of air in the lungs promotes the expulsion of secretions (Carpenito, p. 108, 1995). d. Increasing the volume of air in the lungs promotes the expulsion of secretions (Carpenito, p. 108, 1995).	c. Nurse instructed client to take slow deep breaths and hold for 3–5 sec. c̄ an exhale that's slow, through the mouth in order to ↑ air in lungs to ↑ expulsion of secretions. d. Nurse instructed client verbally and visually on the process of taking a second breath, holding it, and coughing 2× forcefully from the chest.	c. Slow, deep breaths were accomplished holding for 3–5 sec. and client exhaled slowly through her mouth in 2 weeks. Accomplished deep breath and cough from the chest in an effort to cough up secretions.

is to offer an accurate, accessible, and understandable picture of the client based not only on what the therapist or doctor has observed, but on what others have observed previously about the patient. In fact, both documents require the author to construct a brief history of the patient: The therapeutic recreation assessment has space for "activity therapies discipline assessment," which summarizes the patient's history, while the new patient evaluation has two relevant sections, "history of present illness" and "past medical history," intended for the same purpose. This combination is fairly standard in assessment forms employed widely in health science professions.

The nursing care plan, written by a senior nursing major, more clearly than the other documents demonstrates the need to observe and then accurately describe those observations. In a nursing care plan, a nurse must determine what kinds of changes need to take place in the patient, what activities will result in the desired changes, and why she believes the actions she intends to take are warranted. Since she is a student, the rationale for her suggested actions or interventions must be documented—that is, she must cite a source that proves she has suggested the correct interventions. Her teacher will then review the health plan and make recommendations as to how the student's observations and goals can be improved.

No matter the specific field, there is little doubt that the authors of the previous documents followed a process in addition to the writing of drafts that occurs in most disciplines. On the basis of the information provided, we can assume that these three authors have reviewed past texts concerning their patients, gathered new information through observation and interview, thoughtfully considered past texts and new information in light of up-to-date procedures for dealing with patients such as these, written out the document, and then rewritten it or revised it where necessary. Likewise, the doctor who composed the new patient evaluation may have halted while speaking into the dictaphone and edited (revised) anything from a word to the entire idea she was trying to communicate.

To perform this kind of writing on the job, a therapist must have access to the patient's history, as often recorded on other assessment forms filed under the patient's name. In the absence of such prior observations, or in addition to them, the therapist must interview the patient. Additionally, the therapist must have access to an environment where new observations might be made, and must stay abreast of the most current thinking done on the problem of how to remedy that patient's malady.

To better understand the writing demands made on health professionals, consider the following activities.

Exercises

1. Reread any one of the documents in Figures 10.1–10.3. On a separate sheet of paper, analyze exactly what has been accomplished in the document. Consider the following questions in writing your analysis:

a. Who does the therapist address? How does she envision her audience in terms of their prior knowledge of the patient and his illness and in terms of their level of education?

b. Look at each individual section of the report you have selected. What is the author's purpose in each section? Do you believe the author succeeds at what she sets out to accomplish?

c. Note how the information is presented. Identify the formal elements of each section.

d. Make a separate list of words you believe to be part of a system of shorthand used by the therapist/author. Which words give you the most difficulty in figuring out what the author means?

e. What is the general subject of each section? Do you get a clear picture of the patient's condition? Can you pick out several details used by the author that show, rather than tell, something about the patient or the proposed treatment? List two or three such details.

f. Describe the author of this document as you perceive her, based on the words she uses. Is she widely experienced with problems of the sort she notes in this patient? Is she observant? What has she observed?

g. If asked, what specific advice would you offer this therapist about how to make her writing more understandable to you?

2. *If you have access to the Internet,* use a browser (Netscape, Mosaic, Lynx) to locate five Gopher sites or World Wide Web sites of general career interest to students pursuing one of the following careers:

• recreational therapist
• physical therapist
• nurse
• physician's assistant
• emergency medical technician
• medical technologist or technician
• physician

Explore each of the five sites you locate, making sure to record their Gopher site address or their Universal Resource Locator (URL).

Using a word-processing package, write a paragraph that summarizes the contents of each of the sites you have found and the materials that are contained within them. Make sure to include the address of the site.

3. *If you have access to the World Wide Web,* use a browser (e.g., Netscape, Mosaic, Lynx) to locate a World Wide Web site for one of national or international professional societies that serves a career listed in the last activity. Make a careful survey of this particular site, taking notes as you go.

Using a word-processing package or a drawing package, create either (1) an outline or (2) a representational diagram of the site. The home page will serve as the starting point for your outline or diagram. From this point, outline or diagram all the major links that extend to other places, documents, or organizations in the site. As a part of this outline or diagram, write a one-paragraph description for each of the major links contained within it.

Finally, be sure to record the Gopher site address or the Universal Resource Locator (URL) address on the web.

Importance of Communications to the Health Sciences Professional

Health science professionals advise and foster well-being among individuals, not only those who require special assistance as they attempt to overcome various illnesses, but also those who want to maintain or improve their physical and mental health. In addition to being concerned with helping patients return to work after an injury, for instance, physical therapists are also concerned with developing wellness programs in businesses and industries. Sports medical personnel not only oversee therapeutic activities to quicken the rate of healing among injured athletes, but also recommend specific programs focusing on diet and exercise for those who hope to maintain or increase their level of fitness. To perform these important tasks in society, health professionals are particularly adept at techniques of observation and interview, but many are also trained as researchers who experiment with various treatments and as educators who promote certain health care policies and procedures.

Health science professionals are not only interested in how to treat various illnesses, but are also interested in how to interact with their patients. In fact, an increasingly important area of concern in the health sciences focuses on ethical decisions made by health professionals. As a result, many courses that have traditionally provided instruction in diagnosing health problems also focus on ethical issues confronted by professionals on the job.

Students in courses in the health sciences can expect to be given the usual library research paper and observation paper, which will require them to employ skills that will enable them to write assessments such as the ones in Figures 10.1–10.3. Students also can expect to be asked to write personal responses to questions that require the making of ethical judgments.

In the health sciences, then, you can expect to perform the following kinds of writing tasks discussed more fully in this chapter:

1. review of current literature
2. observational analysis
3. personal response to ethical issues

Exercises

1. Look at a recent edition of your local newspaper. On a separate sheet of paper, make a list of news items you believe a health professional would be interested in. Select one issue and, in a paragraph, describe how you as a health professional would respond to it.

2. If you are interested in studying health sciences, make an appointment with a health professional in the field you are most interested in and ask that person the following questions in preparation for writing a brief report.
   a. How long has that person been a health professional?
   b. When did he/she decide to enter that field?
   c. Is the current field the one he/she wanted to enter? Does he/she have any regrets?
   d. Where did he/she attend school to receive training as a health professional? What is the single best professional experience he/she had during college? Since college?
   e. Does he/she plan on staying in the health professions?
   f. Would he/she have done anything differently?

   Now write a brief, informal report to share with a classmate or with your teacher. In addition to summarizing what you have found out from the person interviewed about his/her field, write a reaction to the individual interviewed (for example, was the person helpful, patient, interested in you as a prospective health professional, and so forth) and state your opinion of the health profession as it was presented to you.

3. *If you have access to a computer network and e-mail,* locate and subscribe to an on-line discussion or newsgroup that involves individuals working in a field of the health profession you are most interested in. For help in locating an appropriate on-line discussion, go to the library or a local bookstore and find a book on the Internet that provides a subject-focused index of on-line discussions and newsgroups. Seek help from your campus computing experts, knowledgeable friends, the technology consultant in the lab you use, or your teacher in subscribing to the list.

   Monitor the conversation within this discussion or newsgroup for at least three days. At the end of this period, *using a word-processing package,* identify the issues that have been covered in this conversation, providing a one- or two-paragraph summary description of each.

4. *If you have access to the World Wide Web,* use a browser (for example, Netscape, Mosaic, Lynx) to locate on-line copies of a newspaper published in a large city—either in this country or in another country of interest to you. Read five issues of this newspaper (either current issues or issues in the recent past), making notes on the health sciences articles contained in each issue.

   Using a word-processing program, list each issue you have come across, summarizing in two or three sentences the stories written about it.

Writing in the Undergraduate Health Sciences

Unlike courses in the natural sciences, social sciences, or humanities, courses in the health sciences are seldom used to fulfill electives. Nevertheless, an increasing number of students have decided to major in the health sciences because the number of positions in health professions has increased in recent years to include sports medical personnel, exercise physiologists, occupational therapists, recreational therapists, health educators, and coaches, in addition to more traditional careers such as nursing and physical therapy.

Writing and communicating are important in these fields because the records health professionals make serve as both historical and legal documents. The documents are historical because they are records of an individual's health. If you have read your own medical records, you know how interesting they can be. No doubt, you are interested because of the kind of history such records provide, a history that cannot be told in any other way. However, these are legal documents as well and are often used in court to make legal judgments where, for instance, malpractice is at issue. Health science documents such as health care plans indicate, on the one hand, why decisions concerning a treatment were made. Laboratory notebooks, on the other hand, trace experimental procedures and results required by the Food and Drug Administration in their determination of whether a new drug should be made available to those who need it.

To perform writing tasks that meet the high demands of the health sciences, you will need to be well-informed about the field. As a result, teachers in health science classes often require that you write a review of current literature.

Review of Current Literature

The review of current literature assignment in the health sciences serves much the same purpose as library research does in other introductory courses across the disciplines. You can expect to be asked to read an article and summarize it or, more often, to read several articles on the same subject and synthesize and/or critique those articles.

The first assignment asks you to review an article or a book, as in the following assignment given in an introductory course in nursing.

> Read "When Your Patient Can't Read" in the May 1994 issue of *The American Journal of Nursing*. Using both sides of a 5×8 notecard, summarize the article and then react to the potential usefulness of the strategy it offers to you as a prospective nurse.

This assignment requires that you employ summarizing skills as they are discussed in Chapter Two, but also to determine on the basis of what you already know about the nursing profession if the strategies offered in the article will be useful to you on the job.

The second kind of assignment is ultimately more difficult and more useful in its transference to other courses than is the first. Here is a typical assignment taken from an exercise physiology course asking students to critique and synthesize sources they have read.

Select a relevant subject that interests you from the following list:

- selecting personal trainers
- developing quickness in high-school football players
- using games to develop strength among preschool children
- preventing overtraining among college athletes
- training soccer players year-round
- preventing and rehabilitating rotator cuff injuries

Check through a database such as *Medline* for six articles on your subject. Write an essay, after I have approved your thesis statement, in which you inform your reader about what you have learned. Synthesize and/or critique your six articles with the intention of supporting your thesis statement.

As in most disciplines, the review of literature assignment enables you to obtain information using pertinent sources and provides you with a starting point in conducting your own research.

The following article, "Guidelines for Proper Stretching" by Joel Ninos, published in the February 1995 issue of *Strength and Conditioning,* is a professionally written and published piece that satisfies the requirements of the previous assignment.

GUIDELINES FOR PROPER STRETCHING

Joel Ninos, MS, PT, CSCS

A frequently overlooked component of strength and conditioning programs is the implementation of flexibility exercises. Flexibility or stretching exercises are directed at elongating soft tissue structures within the body. Many benefits such as injury prevention, enhanced athletic performance, improved joint range of motion, and decreased muscle soreness after strenuous activity may be derived from stretching exercises (5).

When stretching a relaxed muscle, it is the extensive connective tissue framework and sheathing within and around the muscle, not the myofibrils, that offers the greatest amount of resistance to stretch (1). This framework and sheathing is known as the parallel elastic component (PEC) and includes the epimysium, perimysium, endomysium, and sarcolemma (2). In a healthy individual, stretching exercises should not be directed at lengthening tendons, ligaments, or joint capsules. Excessive lengthening of these tissues can cause joint instability and could lead to injury.

The body's connective tissues, including those within and around the muscles, are viscoelastic structures composed mainly of a fibrous protein known as collagen (2). Their viscoelastic nature gives these tissues both elastic and viscous properties. The elastic property implies that changes in tissue length are proportional to the amount of the applied load, while the viscous property causes deformation to occur in proportion to the rate the force is applied (6). The more rapidly an elongating force is applied to a viscoelastic tissue, the greater the tissue's resistance to stretch. This resistance to stretch is referred to as the tissue's stiffness. Increasing the tissue's stiffness makes the tissue less likely to elongate. That is why ballistic movements are discouraged during stretching exercises.

Two stretching techniques are frequently used for elongating musculotendinous units. Static stretching is performed by passively placing the muscle in its maximally lengthened position and holding it there for a sustained period of time (30–60 sec). Proprioceptive neuromuscular facilitation, or PNF, involves using combinations of alternating contraction and relaxation of the agonist and antagonist muscle groups in order to create an elongation of tissue structures.

It is important to remember that flexibility is specific to each sport, each athlete, and each joint or muscle group. Before beginning a flexibility program, several steps should be taken to assure that maximum benefits will be obtained. Each athlete should be examined by a medically trained professional (e.g., athletic trainer, physical therapist) for excesses or deficiencies in muscular flexibility. The information gathered from a preseason screening can reveal which muscle groups need attention during the flexibility program.

The completion of a thorough, full-body warm-up before stretching is also important. A general warm-up may consist of 5 to 10 min of easy, low-level aerobic activity, for example jogging or cycling. A good indication that the body's core temperature has risen is the onset of perspiration (4). An *in vitro* study by Safran et al. (3) found that warming a muscle prior to applying an elongating force allowed the muscle to reach a greater length and require greater force to cause failure. These increases in length-to-failure and force-to-failure were compared to muscles that were not warmed up prior to stretching. A warm-up will not only increase tissue temperature but will also stimulate the circulatory system, enhance coordination, and promote easier movement through a more compliant musculoskeletal system (5).

Finally, just as with any strength training program, all stretching exercises should be taught by a trained professional. Improper technique while stretching can lead to injury. . . . It is critical that all of the athlete's previous injuries be considered so that a recurrence or exacerbation of the injury does not occur (e.g., subluxated/dislocated shoulder). Also, given the individual differences between athletes, each athlete may require a slightly different area of concentration in his or her program.

The following guidelines should be applied to flexibility programs:

- Screen all athletes before beginning the program.
- Undergo proper exercise instruction by a trained professional.
- Be specific about proper stretching technique and positioning.
- Stretching should be performed before and after a practice or competition.

- A thorough warm-up should be completed before stretching.
- Apply each stretch slowly, and only to the point of gentle discomfort, *not pain.*
- Maintain the stretch for 30 to 60 sec and then release it slowly.
- Repeat each stretch three to five times.
- Stretching in the off-season and preseason is vital for maintaining muscular flexibility.

A solid, well-prepared, and well-taught flexibility program can greatly enhance a strength training program. Future issues of this journal will feature more articles on flexibility exercises to help educate strength coaches as to proper stretching exercises and techniques.

REFERENCES

1. Cornelius, W. L., and M. R. Hands. The effects of a warm-up on acute hip joint range of motion using modified PNF stretching techniques. *J. Natl. Athl. Trainers Assoc.* 27:112–114, 1992.
2. Nordin, M., and V. H. Frankel. *Basic Biomechanics of the Musculoskeletal System.* Philadelphia: Lea & Febiger, 1989.
3. Safran, M. R., W. E. Garrett Jr., A. V. Seaber, R. R. Glisson, and B. M. Ribbeck. The role of warm-up in musculoskeletal injury prevention. *Am. J. Sports Med.* 16:123–129, 1988.
4. Sapega, A. A., T. C. Quendenfeld, R. A. Moyer, and R. A. Butler, Biophysical factors in range of motion exercise. *Phys. Sportsmed.* 9(12):57–65, 106, 1981.
5. Smith, C. The warm up procedure: To stretch or not to stretch. A brief review. *J. Sport Phys. Ther.* 27(2):12–17, 1994.
6. Taylor, D. C., J. D. Dalton, A. V. Seaber, and W. E. Garrett, Viscoelastic properties of muscle-tendon units. The biomechanical effects of stretching, *Am J. Sports Med.* 18:300–309, 1990.

Ninos draws on six published works for use in expanding on the statement that "Flexibility or stretching exercises are directed at elongating soft tissue structures within the body." As the above assignment requires, Ninos begins with a thesis statement and then proves his point by referring to six pieces of published literature. His goal is not to argue a point; rather, he sets out to provide information, since the dissemination of information is the goal of the journal in which the essay appears. The audience of the journal, mostly other exercise physiologists and sports medicine personnel, read the journal to obtain that kind of information.

Note that Ninos offers documentation of sources whenever what he has written satisfies the following criteria:

1. the assertion is debatable,
2. the information does not constitute common knowledge, or
3. the information is the product of a specific research study.

Notice as well that Ninos offers a very objective treatment of the subject; for instance, he does not cite *his* experience as an exerciser. He also writes in a formal style, no doubt a style required not only by the magazine for which he has written, but by the discipline as well. He avoids excessive jargon, relies on the formal names of muscle groups and bones, and does not use contractions or the word "I." These features are characteristic of writing in exercise physiology (as well as other health sciences areas). This style is also evident in the following student review of literature on performance-enhancing substances.

A Review of Current Literature on Ergogenic Aids to Athletes

Athletics is a competitive field. After the fun and excitement of little league, athletics turns into a job. To be a professional athlete, excellence and practice are prerequisites. But, how do you exceed the level of fitness that you currently possess? What if you are only a few hundredths of a millisecond off of a world record, like Ben Johnson a few years ago, but you just can't seem to break it? For many athletes, ergogenic aids are the answer.

Ergogenic aids are substances purported to enhance athletic performance or improve exercise capacity (Beltz & Doering, 1993). These substances are not a new trend in athletics. According to Wagner (1990), ancient Greeks in the third century consumed herbs and mushrooms in an attempt to improve athletic performance. European cyclists took caffeine-based sugar cubes dipped in nitroglycerine and used a mixture of coca leaves and wine to reduce fatigue. By the 1950s, drugs replaced the natural "enhancers." Amphetamines and steroids were first suspected to be used by athletes at both the summer and winter Olympics in 1952.

Throughout the 1960s, the International Olympic Committee (IOC) addressed the seriousness of the situation after the deaths and injuries of numerous athletes. By the 1968 Olympics, drug testing was instituted, and the misuse of these drugs started to decline, but did not cease entirely (Wagner, 1990).

By 1980, athletes themselves began to notice side effects resulting from the misuse of these drugs, especially steroids. As a result, some athletes began looking for other agents that could promote their needs. "Natural" ergogenics (or nutritional supplements) started to appear. Their advocates proclaimed that athletes could make incredible gains with no side effects, since the substances were "natural." Even today many argue that ergogenic nutritional supplements "increase performance either by renewing or increasing energy stores in the body, facilitating the biochemical reactions that yield energy, modifying the biochemical changes contributing to fatigue, or maintaining optimal body weight" (Beltz & Doering, 1993).

continued

Supplement manufacturers have received an elevated status on the nutrition market. Virtually any substance that works in the body, that can be produced in large quantities, and that can be argued to improve lean muscle mass and promote lipid catabolism has been advertised endlessly. These substances include everything from carbohydrate supplements, protein powders, liquids, and vitamins to minerals, enzyme complexes, and plant and herb extracts.

But there are those who believe manufacturers are making millions of dollars by misguiding consumers: "These products are marketed as nutritional supplements, not drugs, so the Food and Drug Administration does not require that they be proved safe and effective" (Beltz & Doering, 1993). Dosage guidelines are inadequate, and sometimes the quality of the products is not good. The fact is that not many scientific studies have been conducted to determine the quality and effectiveness of these supplements, and the studies that have been conducted usually contain some flaw so the results are inconclusive. Another problem with researching these supplements is ascertaining whether the gains observed are due to the supplement or due to changes in training techniques and methods.

Amino acids, along with chromium, are among the most popular ergogenic aids available today. According to Kreider et al. (1993), amino acids are most commonly known as the building blocks of protein; but they are also essential for synthesis of tissue, specific proteins, hormones, enzymes, and neurotransmitters. Amino acids are also used in energy metabolism through gluconeogenesis and in regulation of many metabolic pathways.

Reasons for taking amino acid supplements vary. Since the decline of steroid use, many bodybuilders have turned to amino acids due to the idea that they are "protein synthesizing" agents, and all athletes need to do is to lift, create the building site, so to speak, flood the system with amino acids, and wait for muscles to develop. Other beliefs are that they promote efficient utilization of energy and stimulate the release of growth hormone (Kreider et al., 1993).

A modern alternative to the use of amino acids is chromium supplementation. Chromium is an essential trace mineral which serves as a cofactor to insulin action. It has been identified as the active component of the glucose tolerance factor (Hunt & Groff, 1990; Stoecker, 1990). Currently there is no RDA for chromium, but the National Research Counsel has established a range of 50–200 mg for adults as an estimated safe and adequate daily dietary intake.

In body building and athletic magazines, chromium is advertised to be an insulin enhancer and an anabolic hormone. Advertisements promote chromium as a safe alternative to steroids. But chromium has been known to affect insulin, which functions in glucose transport into the muscle but also helps with amino acid uptake into the muscle as well (Clarkson, 1991). These properties have led those in search of increasing muscle mass to try supplementing chromium in the search for an anabolic enhancer.

As with other minerals, supplementation is probably only necessary when a deficiency is present. According to Anderson and Kozlovsky (1985), in one U.S. city they found the average daily chromium intake to be 25 and 33 mg, respectively, for men and women. The researchers suggested that up to 90% of the general population may have a deficiency. If these results were generalized to the rest of the United States, it would seem advisable to increase chromium intake or supplementation.

In conclusion, amino acid supplementation is new enough to merit further research, especially in regard to increasing carbohydrates in an athlete's diet. But, because chromium intake for the general population is considered suboptimal and since it is known that chromium loss during exercise can be a major inhibitor for athletes, athletes may very well feel confident in increasing their intake of chromium. In any event, athletes today, as in the past, should be cautious about any supplementation aimed at increasing their performance.

References

Anderson, R. A., & Kozlovsky, A. S. (1985). Chromium intake, absorption and excretion of subjects consuming self-selected diets. *American Journal of Clinical Nutrition, 41,* 1177–1183.

Beltz, S. B., & Doering, P. L. (1993). Efficacy of nutritional supplements used by athletes. *Clinical Pharmacology, 12,* 900–908.

Clarkson, P. M. (1991). Nutritional ergogenic aids: chromium, exercise, and muscle mass. *International Journal of Sports Nutrition, 1,* 289–293.

Hunt, S. M., & Groff, J. L. (1990). Chromium. *Advanced Nutrition and Human Metabolism.* St. Paul, MN: West Publishing Company.

Kreider, R. B., Miriel, V., & Bertun, E. (1993). Amino acid supplementation and exercise performance. *Sports Medicine, 16(3),* 190–209.

Stoecker, B. J. (1990). Chromium. In M. L. Brown (Ed.), *Present Knowledge in Nutrition* (6th ed.) (pp. 287–293). Washington D.C.: International Life Sciences Institute Nutrition Foundation.

Wagner, J. C. (1990). Use of chromium and cobalamide by athletes. *Clinical Pharmacy, 8,* 832–834.

David's review of literature meets the requirements set up by his professor. He uses seven sources (six were required) to support his thesis statement, that "[f]or many athletes, ergogenic aids are the answer" to the question of how to "exceed the level of fitness that you currently possess." Note that David's introduction is an effort to interest and prepare his reader for the thesis statement; the questions he asks are the questions he answers. He goes on to provide a brief, but useful, history of the use of performance enhancers, leading up to his introduction of the notion that athletes currently rely on amino acids and chromium supplementation to improve their performances.

David employs summary throughout his essay, citing Wagner as an authority on the history of performance-enhancing substances used by athletes. He synthesizes Hunt and Groff's commentary with Stoecker's to reinforce the point that chromium "has been identified as the active component of the glucose tolerance factor."

David has organized his review systematically, focusing first on a statement of his purpose, then on a general history of his subject, and finally on an analysis of amino acid and chromium supplementation. He concludes that, unless it is absolutely necessary, an athlete should avoid such supplementation altogether.

Guidelines for writing a review of literature
1. Consult a database such as *Medline.*
2. Write a thesis statement.
3. Set out to provide information, not to argue.
4. Document sources as necessary.
5. Treat the sources objectively.
6. Write in a formal style.
7. Avoid excessive jargon.
8. Rely on the formal names of muscle groups, bones, and other parts of the body, since your audience will know them and will expect you to use the language of the profession.
9. Write an introduction that both interests the reader and prepares the reader for what follows.
10. Employ summary, synthesis, and critique.
11. Organize your review systematically, that is, so a reader will be able to easily follow what you have written.

Exercises

1. Interview an athlete you know or someone you know who was an athlete in high school or college. The goal of your interview should be to find a subject, such as the one David writes about, that you might study further in a review of current literature. (Consider as well the topics listed in Exercise 2.)

   You might begin by searching *Medline* to find a minimum of six articles or books on the topic. Then write an introduction that both interests your reader and prepares your reader for your thesis statement. Make your thesis statement a sentence that you can actually support by reference to the works you have discovered. Then plan an organizational pattern that a reader will be able to follow. You might decide to use topic sentences as first sentences of each of your paragraphs (see Chapter One).

Break your task into the following manageable steps:

a. Interview an athlete. (Or, in the absence of an athlete to interview, call upon your own experience as an athlete or as someone interested in athletics or in staying healthy.) On the basis of this exchange, decide on a topic.

b. Have your teacher approve your topic.

c. Go to the library and consult *Medline*. Make certain to find a minimum of six articles or books for use in your report. You can help yourself here by making sure the articles and books are directly related to your subject. You might have to browse through more than six articles to find six relevant to your subject (see Chapter Two); not all of the authors whose articles you read will agree about your topic.

d. Read your articles and books, making notes as needed (see Chapter Two).

e. Write a thesis statement you can support using the essays and books you have read. Show your thesis statement to your teacher for approval before writing the first draft of your review essay.

f. Write a draft of your essay, making certain your introduction interests and prepares your reader. Be sure that your organizational pattern for your essay will be clear to a reader. To make sure your essay is clearly organized, show an outline to a classmate or to your instructor before writing. Remember that your goal is to inform, not to argue or persuade.

g. Revise your essay to make certain you have said everything you want to say about the subject. Remember that your readers probably have not read every article you cite in your review.

h. Edit to make certain you have used correct grammar, spelling, and punctuation and that you have documented your sources appropriately using APA style (see the Appendix).

2. Choose a topic of interest to you that is related to one of the health professions. Be sure to choose a topic you know something about and one that is controversial and that might be of interest to other students you know. Consider the following examples of topics as a starting place:

- the use of steroids to enhance sport's performance
- the health effects of caffeine consumption
- the efficacy of fat pills in controlling obesity
- the efficacy of condoms in preventing pregnancy
- the benefits of encouraging organ donation
- the patient's role in preventing mistakes in hospitals
- the dangers of weight training
- the pursuit of wellness versus athletic performance

If you have difficulty coming up with a topic, sit down with your writing group around a common computer. *Using a word-processing package*, conduct a group brainstorming session, spending five minutes creating a list of possible topics in each group member's area of interest. Save this file and print it out. From this list, choose the topic that seems most interesting to you and that is the most likely to interest other students you know. The topic you choose should be both controversial and timely. Have your teacher approve your topic.

Next, *if you have access to the Internet,* use a browser (for example, Netscape, Mosaic, Lynx) to locate six sources written by health professions (for example, documents, articles, reports, and so forth) that deal with this topic. Make a copy of these sources. *If you do not have access to the Internet,* go to the library to find these sources—*try to use on-line resources* (such as *Medline*) *only in this task.* Make a copy of the sources you find.

Then, using a word-processing package, follow steps *e–h* on page 365 to write an informative article on your topic that is suitable for publication in your student newspaper. In this article, you will have to synthesize the material from your six sources in a way that will interest a general group of student readers who are nonspecialists in the health professions. Check several back copies of your student newspaper—or visit the newspaper office and ask for a journalist's style sheet—to find out how it treats the documentation of information from sources. The format your newspaper uses for this purpose will differ from the format you have been taught to use in the typical research paper, but it provides readers, nonetheless, with a clear understanding of what material is quoted, summarized, or paraphrased from a source, and what material is written in a reporter's own words.

Writing an Observational Analysis

As you can see in the three sample pieces of writing from the health sciences, Figures 10.1–10.3, health professionals rely heavily on their observations.

What are they trained to see? In the therapeutic recreation assessment, Figure 10.1, a "therapist observation/patient interview" section is written so that the certified recreational therapist/author can record judgments about her patients and the details that lead her to those judgments. In fact, to be certain she is correct in her judgments, the therapist observes her patient in two different environments: with her during an interview and among others during therapeutic recreation sessions.

She notes his attention span, willingness to cooperate, ability to communicate, and various other patterns of behavior that reinforce her judgment about him. As you can see, the author is not satisfied with telling what she has observed. In fact, the author attempts to tie generalizations to the details that cause her to reach conclusions. She generalizes, for instance, that "his communication skills are poor." Then she provides evidence for her generalization: "He has a low monotonous voice and often speaks in a rapid manner. Therapist has noted patient mumbling to himself at times." She later provides details to support her observation that "Mr. X appears to lack appropriate socialization skills."

Note that the ability to observe behavior, interpret what has been observed, record clearly a generalization about a patient, and support that generalization with details is critical to the success of the following database summary, a writing activity nurses usually record on a patient's chart.

Mrs. Lamonda is a 79 yr. old white female admitted to DeGraff Hospital on 4 April 1992 c̄ a med. dx of COPD and Bronchiectasis. She's allergic to Augmentin. She has had a series of bronchoscopies, the last one being performed on 2 February 1992 due to thick secretions mostly in her Rt. lung. She is unable to expel them due to the thickness and her weakness. Pt. shows facial grimace and moans upon insertion of the tube. She weighs 67 lb. and is on Reg. diet to 1 intake. Upon introducing myself she says, "I don't really want you here. This is the 5th time that tube's going down my throat." She has IV in Lt. arm. She is receiving 02 at 2L via NC. RT checked on 02, no [triangle] made. I heard rales over Rt. lung field. Mrs. Lamonda says she wakes up round 4:00 A.M. and can't get back to sleep. She won't eat much, says she's "not hungry." VS are BP 149/82, P112, R8, T97. Chem panel concerns are . . . Mrs. Lamonda was NPD until 10:15 due to bronchoscopy. She was given Humabid L.A., Diflucan, cardizem at 10:30. She refused Trental and Oscal. Pt. said "They'll make me sick on my stomach." Pt. usually takes them c̄ a meal. Due to bronchoscopy she couldn't take her 8:30 dose until 10:30.

The database summary is usually done on a patient's chart and left at the foot of the patient's bed for other hospital personnel to periodically check and update. As you can see, this summary is a combination of patient history and nurse observation. A reader can find the patient's gender, race, age, date of admittance to the hospital, diagnosed illness, allergies to relevant drugs, and other prior efforts to treat her illness.

Note that the shift from history to observation is signaled in this document by a shift in tense: from "She has had . . ." to "Pt. shows. . . ." A reader finds more current information in the nurse's observations, including facial expressions, breathing difficulties, various treatments, and even conversations right down to the exact words spoken.

Nurses, then, like other health professionals, must learn to observe closely, interpret observed behaviors by filtering out behaviors that are random or just idiosyncratic to the patient, and record those observations clearly.

Now that you can see the need for making accurate and reliable observations, you are probably interested in learning how teachers in introductory courses in the health sciences will prepare you for such complex and sophisticated writing as the above summary. Let us look at an assignment from an introductory course in health education that is designed to teach skills of observation translatable in advanced courses to the writing of more demanding documents.

The following assignment is taken from an introductory course in personal health.

Check through this month's *Personal Health Register* and select a Health Education program or presentation to attend and report on. To be certain you can complete this assignment by the April 28 due date, your observation should take place before April 21. Take notes, pick up handouts, and draft a 1½-page summary of what you have observed. Be certain to keep in mind as you draft that your reader has not attended the program. As a result, you must select the most pertinent and revealing details of what you have observed for inclusion in your report. Remember: Revise, proofread, and edit! Go to the Writing Center if you need help.

Note that the above assignment requires students to observe a health educator in action during a program or presentation, pick out the highlights of what the students have observed, and, in 1½ typed pages, report on what they have observed. The instructor expects her students to select a relevant program, observe it, take notes on it, and present the experience in such a way that a reader who has not attended will know what transpired. She also expects the observational report to be revised, proofread, and edited.

The following essay was written in response to this assignment by a second-year student.

I observed health educator Dana White. She gives an hour-long class on contraceptives at the Student Health Clinic on campus. This is a class that all females must go to before being put on birth control. The most common form of birth control used by women on campus is the pill.

Dr. White teaches the class with some lecturing but mostly with demonstrations. She informs students what they can expect when they go in for their pap exam by letting them know what the doctor will do and how the exam is performed. The students are also shown different methods of birth control. One such method is called the barrier method. This method includes the male condom, the female condom, and diaphragms. The students are told how each method works and how to use each method. Hormone methods of birth control are also discussed. These include the pill, Depo shots, and norplant. Dr. White states the benefits of each and the side effects.

Dr. White describes what emergency contraceptives are. Many students do not know that the Student Health Clinic provides this service. Emergency contraceptives are used when a woman has sex without birth control and is concerned that she may become pregnant. The doctor will give the female an overload of hormones. Dr. White points out that it is important that women leave the decision to take such precautions up to the doctors because the doctors know which hormones to give and how much.

The students were told about different S.T.D.'s that are most common on campus. These diseases include chlamydia, gonorrhea, and syphilis. One out of four students on campus has contracted one of these S.T.D.'s.

The class seemed very interested in what Dr. White said. Having so many demonstrations helped to make the class interesting. Dr. White showed that she is well-informed on birth control methods and on how things are done at the Student Health Clinic. To do the job that Dr. White has, you would have to be comfortable talking about sex in front of a group. You would also have to have a lot of sex education and knowledge of birth control and S.T.D.'s.

This assignment was useful in showing me what some health educators do. It was interesting to hear what Dr. White had to say. I did not know that there is so much to know about birth control.

Guidelines for writing an observational analysis

1. Choose a topic that interests you. (Note the list of possible topics in exercise 2 on page 365.)
2. Arrange a time, far enough in advance of your due date, to make your observations.
3. Take notes and collect handouts, including programs or game plans.
4. Decide on a pattern of organization—note that the database summary is organized in two parts (history and current observations), while the student observational analysis is arranged by topic, perhaps in the order the topics were presented by the health educator observed.
5. Write a sentence that summarizes what you have observed, a general statement that you can support by reference to what you have seen.
6. Write a draft, including specific support of any general observations.
7. Revise, proofread, and edit.

Exercises

1. Divide a sheet of paper in half from top to bottom, making two columns. Now compare the database summary (p. 367), written by a senior nursing major, with the observational report (pp. 368–369), written by a sophomore in an introductory health education course. To do so, consider the following.
   a. To whom are these documents written? Characterize these audiences in terms of education, expertise in the field, seriousness of purpose, and understanding of professional jargon. Which document is easier for you to understand? Why?

b. Characterize the authors in terms of their education, expertise in the field, attitude toward their topic, and their use of professional shorthand. Which document are you currently best prepared to write? Why?

c. Compare the subjects of these two documents. Which goes into greater detail? Which does a better job of using language to show rather than tell? Why is detail necessary in these two reports? Why is it important to show and not just tell in these two writings? Find two places where the authors show rather than tell.

d. What are the purposes for writing these documents, as far as you can tell? How do you think the writing of the observational analysis serves as preparation for the writing of the database summary and other similarly sophisticated documents?

2. Write an observational report on one of the following:
   - Observe and report on a talk, lecture, or class run by a health professional.
   - Observe sports medical personnel as they prepare for a sporting event and report on their activities.
   - Observe a weightlifting class and report what you see there.
   - Observe a gym class and report what you observe.
   - Attend a sporting event and watch the head coach and his/her assistant coaches and report on what you observe.
   - Attend a wellness program session at a local business or industry and report what you see there.

3. *If you have access to the Internet,* use a browser (for example, Netscape, Mosaic, Lynx) to locate a Gopher site or a home page for a major hospital, a public health clinic, or a national health organization at the local, state, or national level. Choose a site that is designed for specialists in health care fields rather than one designed for the general public.

   Conduct an observational report of this site, taking notes on the following items. Include quotes if you feel it is advisable:
   - What is the purpose of the site?
   - What information is presented in the site?
   - What features of the site are designed specifically for the target audience?
   - How is the information arranged and organized? What are the major sections?
   - What are the design features of the site (for example, links, graphics, video, fonts, presentation, and so forth)?
   - How successful is the site in fulfilling its purpose? Why?
   - How would you change this site to improve it?

   In writing this report, follow the guidelines for writing observational reports, as listed on page 369.

Writing about Ethical Issues

So much has been written in recent years about ethics and the health professions that many introductory courses in the health sciences have taken up the study of ethical issues. AIDS testing and anonymity, smoking in public, assisted suicide, United Nations involvement in inoculation programs in Third World countries, and many other issues are just some of the controversial matters in which health professionals are closely involved.

Ethics is closely tied to morality and, in fact, can be viewed as a systematic study of moral behavior. The goal of moral behavior is to protect cherished values. We may value quality of life over prolonged and painful living, or the freedom to make decisions involving our personal well-being over enforced hospitalization. Morality is very personal. While one person may believe abortion to be immoral, another may believe requiring a woman to have a baby she cannot afford and does not want is immoral. While one person may believe Dr. Jack Kevorkian's notion of assisted suicide is immoral, another may believe that requiring people to endure pain without any hope of relief or cure is immoral.

Ethics is a systematic reflection on and analysis of morality. Most people reflect on the behavior of a friend or neighbor or classmate. No doubt you and your friends have thought quite seriously about the morality of one or more of your friends.

Reflections on the morality of certain health-related matters have made excellent reading in newspapers and magazines. For instance, should the 180,000 HIV positive patients who do not have AIDS be prescribed doses of AZT if the only benefit AZT brings them is a feeling that they will not contract AIDS? Should a company that stands to make substantial profit from their drug advocate its use even if they cannot prove it prevents the illness it purports to prevent?

As an example of such issues, the following short essay explores the ethics of using AZT to prevent the onset of AIDS in HIV-infected people.

HOW TO COPE WITH THE BURDEN

Many of the 180,000 people taking Wellcome's AZT do not have AIDS. What benefits does the drug bring them?

In August 1989, results from an American clinical trial showed that AZT, a drug then used against the human immunodeficiency virus (HIV) in people with AIDS, could help healthy people infected with HIV forestall the onset of AIDS. Since there are more infected people than there are people with AIDS and since, if they take a drug, they are likely to take it for longer than would those with AIDS, the potential market for the drug was greatly increased. Sales of the drug, made by Britain's Wellcome, were $384m in 1992, up from $159m in 1988; more people are taking it now than ever before. But the drug has side-effects which can be severe. It also costs a lot. And there are still doubts about the benefits it offers.

This week's issue of the *Lancet* contains the results of a clinical trial that addressed those doubts. The Anglo-French trial, Concorde, run by the British

Medical Research Council and its French counterpart, INSERM, is the largest to have looked at the effect of putting people infected with HIV on to AZT before they have the symptoms of AIDS. Its results offer no evidence that people who take AZT before they get AIDS live any longer than people who do not. This may come as a blow to Wellcome, to people pinning their hopes on AZT, and to those trying to find quick ways of testing drugs.

The Concorde trial recruited 1,749 subjects, divided into two groups. The drug was to be given to 877, while 872 were to receive a placebo. Over the three years of the trial, there were 79 AIDS-related deaths in the AZT group, 67 in the placebo group. That does not mean AZT did any harm. The difference is not statistically significant and could easily have been due to chance. But it certainly does not show a benefit to those taking the drug. The groups were also evenly matched in the rate at which they developed AIDS.

This cannot be taken to mean that AZT has no effect. When people became ill they were offered AZT, whichever group they had been assigned to; so everyone who had AIDS, wanted to take AZT, and could tolerate the drug was on it. The survival figures from the trial are a test of AZT taken early on against AZT taken after AIDS had been diagnosed—immediate treatment against deferred treatment—not a test of AZT against no treatment. But the fact that people in the group prescribed AZT developed AIDS at the same rate as those who did not certainly casts doubts on the efficacy of early therapy.

Though the two groups were evenly matched in survival and progression to disease, there were differences. The people in the AZT group suffered more side-effects. They also had consistently higher levels of CD4 cells in their blood. The CD4 cells are singled out for attack by HIV, and the number of them in the blood drops as infected people succumb to the disease. At the beginning of the Concorde trial, the average CD4 count in both groups was the same; after treatment, the people in the AZT group had more CD4 cells than their untreated peers.

The CD4 level has come to take an ever more prominent role in AIDS trials. Taking an improvement in CD4 level as a sign that the drug is doing some good speeds things up—CD4 effects can be measured quite quickly, while progression to disease is a slow process. Data on CD4 levels has aided the approval of a number of treatments. In the Concorde trial, though, CD4 counts proved misleading, in that they showed a "benefit" that did not correspond to any measurable clinical benefits. In the end it is the progress of the disease that matters to the patient, not the CD4 level itself.

This discrepancy is not extraordinary; it probably stems from the fact that the correlation between CD4 level and state of health, though real, is not as close as it might be. However, the discrepancy does make things awkward: it may well raise doubts in the minds of people who want to use CD4 levels to test the efficacy of a treatment.

Trials, especially of drugs with effects that are not dramatic, often give conflicting results, and Concorde was one trial among many. But it was large and long. More people got AIDS and died on Concorde than on all the other trials of the early use of AZT put together, which gives the trial some weight. And though a fair number of trials, including the original American one, have shown a benefit to early AZT use in terms of the rate of progression to AIDS, there have been very few data on the rate of survival. One study that did look at the matter, a recent trial in veterans' hospitals in America, also found that people using AZT early on did not live longer than people who started using the drug only when they got the disease, though unlike Concorde it did find that early use slowed the onset of illness.

There may well be a way of understanding these results in terms of the way the disease works. In test tubes the virus will develop resistance to AZT. Resistant strains crop up in people who are being treated, too, and it seems likely that the development of resistance means the AZT loses its effect—though this has not been proved conclusively. So AZT may only ever be able to provide a limited respite in the progression of the disease, whenever it is taken: If that respite is taken before symptoms develop, then it cannot be taken again later. That would fit the fact that the early and late AZT groups have the same survival rate, though it would not explain the fact that, in Concorde, they developed AIDS at the same rate, too.

Even if there is no overall survival benefit to early AZT use, it may still make sense. David Cooper, an Australian researcher who has worked on a number of trials, paid for by Wellcome, that have shown benefits to early AZT use, points out that there are new drugs coming along every year. If you think healthy people are more likely to benefit from a drug than sick ones, it makes sense to "cash in" potential AZT benefits early, rather than later, so as to be better placed to make use of new drugs and combinations of drugs.

However, Dr. Cooper gives warning that the effects of AZT are not, in biological terms, spectacular. Penicillin can reduce a population of bacteria a trillionfold: AZT may reduce the viral burden by a factor of ten. Statistics make correspondingly small clinical effects hard to measure—which may be why nothing turned up in the Concorde results. Dr. Cooper is a firm believer in using trials that measure disease progression and CD4 level to sort out which of the new drugs and combinations of drugs are best. To be sure of their true clinical effectiveness, though, large trials will be needed—far larger, even, than Concorde. Others feel that large trials are still needed for AZT, let alone any other drugs, to lay to rest for good the question of what help it gives to people who take the drug before they develop AIDS.

Note that the author of this short essay reflects upon a moral problem, "Since there are more infected people than there are people with AIDS and since, if they take a drug, they are likely to take it for longer than would those with AIDS, the potential market for the drug was greatly increased." The very thing that makes this article an ethical study is the author's reflection on the moral dilemma, whether to sell the drug to this large population of HIV positive people for large profits even if, as the author says, ". . . the drug has side-effects which can be severe. It costs a lot. And there are still doubts about the benefits it offers."

You might reflect upon this issue from several vantage points: the perspective of the manufacturer who stands to make a gigantic profit, the perspective of the healthy but HIV-positive population, and the perspective of the health professional who simply wants to make certain the right thing is done. The author of this article focuses specifically on AZT because, though the drug has undergone scrutiny as the first effective method for helping people with AIDS, there is "no evidence that people who take AZT before they get AIDS live any longer than people who do not." Yet, healthy HIV-positive people are routinely treated with AZT as a method for preventing development of AIDS.

Exercises

1. Whom does the author of the AZT article address? What assumptions does he make about his readers? Do you think the audience addressed by this article is apt to agree with the author or disagree?

2. Characterize this author. Do you believe he is a health professional? Why do you think so? What is his point of view about the use of AZT with HIV-positive patients? Do you agree with him or disagree?

3. What is the author's purpose in this essay? Does he succeed? Does he present information that is new to you? What information is presented most clearly? What proof is the most convincing to you?

4. If you believe the author should take a stronger stand than he does here, what more do you think he should say?

5. Write a paragraph in which you deal with the issue of whether to treat HIV-positive patients with AZT to prevent onset of AIDS. Use information provided in the essay as a basis for reflecting upon this moral dilemma.

6. Write a paragraph from the manufacturer's point of view. For example, you might argue that one study is inconclusive and until more research is done the prudent thing to do is to continue treating patients with AZT while they are HIV positive.

7. *Using a word-processing package,* write a document that compares the two Web sites you have analyzed for previous exercises (one targeted at health specialists and one targeted at nonspecialists). In this analysis, address differences in the following factors:
   • purpose
   • information presented
   • organization
   • design features
   • success
   In addition, discuss which site most interested you and why.

Similar to "How to Cope with the Burden," the following topic is from an assignment for an introductory course in health education:

> Read through several sources including recent editions of student and local newspapers until you have found at least three possible topics that give rise to ethical issues in the health profession. Select the one you feel most strongly about and use a minimum of four sources to support your view on the issue. Write a paper of approximately four pages in which you argue one side of an ethical issue.

The paper that resulted, "Smoking Should Not Be Allowed in Public," takes issue with smokers who believe they have a right to smoke in public.

Smoking Should Not Be Allowed in Public

Prior to the 1920s, smoking began to establish itself in the American culture. The image of a smoker was portrayed by advertisers as a symbol of fashion and sophistication. By 1964, 40 percent of the adult population smoked; yet, in that same year Surgeon General Luther L. Terry reported that there was a direct link between smoking and lung cancer. Due to continuing reports and strong warnings on cigarette packs, smoking steadily declined but continued to cause controversy. One major complaint derives from more recent evidence that environmental tobacco smoke harms nonsmokers (Daniel, 1993). Due to this evidence, the right to smoke has become an issue of both health and personal rights. Smokers and nonsmokers alike have formed arguments to protect their rights as individuals, but research studies clearly substantiate that the effects of second-hand smoke are so threatening to nonsmokers that the problems cannot be solved by simply restricting smokers to designated areas. In fact, many believe that smokers should not be allowed to smoke in public.

Those against a ban on smoking, like Walter Merryman (1992), vice-president of the Tobacco Institute, insist that a ban on smoking will be unfair to smokers. Support for his opinion derives from various informal polls that claim that American people agree with Merryman's views. To justify his issue of unfairness, Merryman uses the research from the Gallup Organization's December 1991 poll, reported in Merryman's essay, "Are Smoking Bans Justified?" Merryman states that polls in the last year show overwhelming evidence that people support equal treatment for smokers and nonsmokers. The poll establishes that most American people prefer separate smoking areas.

continued

There are several discrepancies in Merryman's argument which concern the American people and their willingness to permit restricted smoking areas. First, a study conducted two years prior to the Gallup poll clearly indicated that implementing separate smoking sections was not an adequate solution to the problem of secondary smoke. This study, published in the February 1989 issue of the *Journal of the American Medical Association (JAMA),* indicated that "providing separate nonsmoking sections in airplanes was not effective in keeping the air healthy for nonsmokers." The *JAMA's* basis for this statement comes from their research showing ALL passengers on the plane showed traces of nicotine in their bodies up to three days after flying, and ALL people suffered from dry burning eyes, coughing, sneezing, and scratchy throats (Heath, 1993). New evidence, such as the study by *JAMA,* on the ill effects of environmental tobacco smoke continues to surface every year. This evidence is causing a growing concern among nonsmokers. If it were clear in 1989 that separate sections did not suffice, then Merryman demonstrates his bias in insisting otherwise two years later.

Another problem Merryman encounters when trying to validate his argument also concerns his use of the Gallup poll. When stating that the American people are ready for a compromise concerning the ban on smoking, he fails to establish any real statistical data. He uses neither numbers nor reference to support his opinion. Therefore, one cannot know if his conclusions are substantiated. Because Merryman writes an emotional essay, rather than one that presents empirical findings, his readers may assume that the poll is inadequate altogether.

Merryman, along with the majority of the smoking population, believes that research on the effects of second-hand smoke is inconclusive. In the latter part of his essay, Merryman uses an October 1992 *JAMA* study of subjects who died of diseases related to cancer. He quotes researchers who claim that when performing autopsies on lung tissue samples, they observed cell changes. Researchers noted that these changes could either be "lung cancer risk indicators" or "possibly cancerous lesions" (1992). It is ironic that Merryman quotes words such as "maybe" or "possibly." He does not take into consideration that these words are common to scientific vernacular. Scientists never make the mistake of declaring something as an absolute fact.

A second point Merryman makes is that individuals used in the study were not interviewed prior to their deaths. He feels the interviews would have determined if the subjects had been exposed to smoking or what other environmental influences they may have encountered during their lifetimes. This point totally destroys Merryman's whole argument. Merryman's argument points out the various extraneous variables scientists did not take into consideration when conducting the study. He does not realize the scientists were completely aware of these errors; therefore, their vague terminology only left room for continued research.

B. Bruce-Briggs is also an advocate of smoking in public. Like Merryman, he also believes research declaring passive smoke dangerous is based on inaccurate data. In "The Health Police Are Blowing Smoke" (1993), Bruce-Briggs claims the war on passive smoke is turning into a war on smokers. He refers to the research as "scam science." To reiterate his opinion, Bruce-Briggs counteracts the statement by the Surgeon General declaring cigarette smoke toxic. He believes that the statement is invalid because it doesn't specify a dosage. According to Bruce-Briggs, too much of anything can be considered toxic. He says, "This magazine is toxic—eat too much of it and you will get sick." This kind of logic is common among those who support the right to smoke in public. Like most, Bruce-Briggs doesn't consider all of the evidence that has directly stated that second-hand smoke is poisonous. In 1992, the U.S. Environmental Protection Agency classified environmental tobacco smoke as a class A ("Known" human) carcinogen (Heath, 1993). How much more concrete evidence is needed to convince those who champion the right to smoke in public that they are wrong?

Smokers should not be allowed to smoke in public. Supporters for smoking in public base their opinions on the belief that research is inconclusive. They write a lot of words that are not based on concrete evidence. Neither the Tobacco Institute nor any of the other groups agreeing with the right to smoke in public have conducted studies that have provided a reason to take their side on the issue. Those against smoking in public have adequate research to validate their opinion. Nonsmokers like Clark W. Heath, Jr. (1993) believe the evidence should be enough to promote immediate action. He asks, "How quickly will the report's findings be translated into effective community action?" This is a question all nonsmokers would like to have answered.

References

Bruce-Briggs, B. (1993). The health police are blowing smoke. In Eileen Daniel (Ed.), *Taking Sides: Clashing Views on Controversial Issues in Health and Society,* 231–34. Hartford: Dushkin.

Daniel, Eileen L., Ed. (1993). *Taking Sides: Clashing Views on Controversial Issues in Health and Society.* Hartford: Dushkin.

Heath Clark W., Jr. (1993). Environmental tobacco smoke and lung cancer. *The Lancet, 341,* 526.

Merryman, W. (1992). Are smoking bans justified? *C Q Researcher, 23,* 1065.

Guidelines for writing about ethical issues

1. Choose a topic that can be written about convincingly from at least two perspectives.
2. Select the side of the issue you feel strongly to be the best for you to argue based on your personal values and on what you know about the issue.
3. Support your view of the issue in one of the following three ways: by showing the weaknesses of arguments to the contrary of your view, by gaining support from reliable sources for your point of view, or by a combination of the above.
4. Write with the intention of persuading your reader to agree with you.
5. Take notes on sources to be used in number 3 above.
6. Decide on a pattern of organization that begins by stating the problem. Then take a stand on the issue and systematically convince your reader to agree with your view of it.
7. Draft, revise, proofread, and edit.

Exercises

1. Divide a sheet of paper in half from top to bottom, making two columns. Now compare "How to Cope with the Burden" with the student essay, "Smoking Should Not Be Allowed in Public." To do so, consider the following.
   a. To whom are these documents written? Characterize these audiences in terms of education, expertise in the field, seriousness of purpose, and understanding of professional jargon. Which document is easier for you to understand? Why?
   b. Characterize the authors in terms of education, expertise in the field, attitude toward their topic, and their understanding of the issue. Are you inclined to agree with the authors? Why or why not?
   c. Compare the subjects of these two documents. Which author does a better job of using detail? Why is detail necessary in these two reports? Why is it important to consult secondary sources and cite them in these two writings? Find two places where the authors summarize secondary sources.
   d. What are the purposes for writing these documents, as far as you can tell? Under what circumstances do you imagine the authors deciding to write their ethical perspectives on their chosen topics?
2. Write a three-to-four page paper on one of the following ethical issues by following the above guidelines.
   • smoking in public buildings
   • engaging in assisted suicide
   • using life-support systems with terminally ill patients
   • violating patient confidentiality
   • dispensing condoms in high schools
   • using controlled substances to ease the pain of terminally ill patients

3. Read the following short article from *People* Magazine about Hall of Fame baseball player Mickey Mantle. Identify ethical issues confronted in the decision to perform a liver transplant on Mantle. Choose one side of one of those issues and write a paper focusing on it. Follow the guidelines on page 378.

4. *If you have access to the Internet,* use a browser (for example, Netscape, Mosaic, Lynx) to locate five Gopher sites or Web sites containing information about ethical issues in a particular area of the health professions. Explore each of these sites and take notes. Look specifically for a set of sites that explore similar or related ethical issues.

Choose one of these sites on which to concentrate. Pick the site that contains the richest possible set of information in an area that interests you. *Using a word-processing program,* answer the following questions about the site in writing:

a. What is the purpose of the site? (Quote from the text introducing the site if appropriate.)

b. Who is the audience for the documents or the information contained within the site?

c. Who wrote the documents in this site? Characterize them in terms of their education, experience, and understanding of the issue.

d. What are the differences between these documents on ethical issues and the other documents you have studied in the health professions? What are the similarities?

SECOND STRIKE

Mickey Mantle battled cancer in his liver—now it's in his lungs

The news hit just as hard the second time. Mickey Mantle, one of baseball's all-time greatest hitters, was suffering from cancer—again. Just two months after a lifesaving liver transplant, Mantle disclosed on ABC's *Good Morning America* on Aug. 1 that the disease had spread to his lungs. "I was doing fine," said the frail-looking Mantle. Now his recovery prospects look dim indeed. In fact, Mantle's doctors say that had they known about the lung cancer, they would never have done the transplant. "Absolutely not," said Dr. Robert Goldstein of Baylor University Medical Center in Dallas.

Mantle's trials began May 28, when he was hospitalized with stomach cramps. A week later doctors concluded that his liver was so damaged by cancer, hepatitis C, and decades of alcohol abuse that only a transplant could save his life. On June 8, after a seemingly short wait, Mantle received a new liver. There were complaints that his celebrity had moved him to the head of the waiting list, but doctors say his extreme illness gave him priority.

One of the nation's best-loved sports heroes, Mantle, 63, has also been one of its most dissolute. A Yankee Hall-of-Famer, he lost his health to drinking. In 1994 he confessed there were some mornings he began the day with the "breakfast of champions"—a drink of brandy, Kahlua and cream. Earlier that year, he put a cap on that, enrolling in the Betty Ford Center, where he eventually dried out.

This time it may be too late for a comeback. Despite a new regimen of chemotherapy, his life expectancy may be only 6 to 18 months. Dr. J. Richard Thistlethwaite, chief of transplant surgery at the University of Chicago Medical Center, says, "His chance of a cure is quite small." Still, Mantle refuses to give up. Told of the lung cancer, he reportedly said, "Let's take care of it. Let's get it out of there."

---

5. Using the same five Gopher or Web sites you identified for the last activity, choose one ethical issue that is represented in at least three of the five sites you locate. If necessary, explore more sites until you find an appropriate issue. Download and print out at least three sources on this issue.

   Using a word-processing package, write a three- to five-page essay that focuses on the ethical issue you have chosen. For the first half of this paper, using both summary and synthesis skills, identify the important ethical aspects of this issue, and describe the controversies surrounding it.

   For the second half of the paper, identify a thesis that represents your particular perspective or position on the issue you have chosen. Using material from your own life, from your personal experience, and from the sources you have identified, support your view on this issue, as identified in the thesis, with the intent of persuading a reader to agree with you.

   When you have completed a draft of your essay, attach the three source articles to it and find a group member with whom to exchange these materials. Make sure that you provide your partner with a disk copy of your essay.

   Using the disk copy of your partner's essay, complete the following tasks:

   a. Read the three articles your partner has summarized and synthesized.

   b. In the first half of the article italicize one sentence in every paragraph that you think contains the main idea of that paragraph.

   c. At the end of the first half of the article, using the all caps key, identify any key aspects of this issue that were mentioned in the source articles, but not mentioned in the summary and synthesis your partner has written.

   d. In the second half of the essay, using the underline feature, identify the thesis your partner has identified to organize his or her argument.

   e. At the end of the second half of the essay, provide your partner with a list of counterarguments (arguments on the other side of the issue) that he or she has not considered—and should consider—in supporting the thesis.

   When you are done with these tasks, provide your partner with the disk (on which you have annotated his or her draft essay file) and the source articles you have read.

Use the materials you are given by your own writing partner to revise your essay.

URLs for the Health Sciences

Health Sciences Resources
http://lib2.med.cornell.edu/SubjResources.html

Internet Resources—Medical Resources
http://www.nurs.utah.edu/internet_resources.html

MedWeb: Medical Libraries
http://www.emory.edu/WHSCL/medweb.medlibs.html

The World-Health Agencies
http://www.hslib.washington.edu/world.html

National Academy of Sciences—Institute of Medicine
http://www.nas.aas.org/

CHAPTER ELEVEN

Writing in Engineering and Technology

Responsibilities of Engineers and Technical Professionals

Importance of Communications to the Engineering
and Technical Professional

Writing from the Professional's Viewpoint

Writing in Undergraduate Technical Curricula and Preparing
to Write in Engineering and Technology

Think about our everyday activities that use technology. Microwave ovens allow us to cook foods in a few moments, rather than the hours previously required. We can board a plane in the middle of the United States and arrive in Europe, South America, or Africa less than half a day later. Satellite technology allows us to view events from thousands of miles away at the very moment they happen. We communicate with people around the world by sending electronic messages delivered over fiber optic networks. We conduct real-time computer conversations with friends at other colleges, perhaps hundreds or thousands of miles away. Indeed, as the songwriter Paul Simon says, "These are the days of miracles and wonders / This is the long distance call." As commonplace as these events and actions may seem to us, they would have been considered extraordinary or impossible little more than a decade ago. The truth is that we have become remarkably accustomed to such modern conveniences for we have integrated them into our daily lives. Thus, some would argue also that we have become very dependent on these features of contemporary life, and, one might argue, we have therefore become very dependent on the people who design and produce these conveniences of modern society.

Responsibilities of Engineers and Technical Professionals

There is a reasonable likelihood that some of you in this class may some day play a major role in developing such technologies as those described above. If you are planning to become an engineer or technician, you may very well help create, design, and maintain the devices and machines society uses. People who work in these fields design, test, and often supervise the construction of the vehicles we drive, the roads we drive on, the bridges we cross, and the household appliances, televisions, VCR's, and sound systems we use each day. It is easy to see how much we depend on these members of society. It is also easy to understand that because of their work, engineers and technicians become members of highly specialized communities that possess a storehouse of technical knowledge. Importantly, they are also directly responsible for using their technical knowledge for the best interests of the general society, as well as the advancement of their companies. Note that the following definition of the engineering profession (from the *Engineer's Council on Professional Development*) stresses far more than just the accumulation of technical knowledge:

> Engineering is the profession in which a knowledge of mathematics and natural sciences gained by study, experience, and practice is applied with judgment to develop ways to benefit mankind.

This definition clearly states that engineering is developmental; that is, it continues throughout the lifetime of an engineer. Notice that it focuses on the engineer's responsibility to society as a whole, not to just the organization or company that employs the engineer. Further, the definition indicates emphatically the importance of judgment in the job of an engineer. Remember that in Chapters One and Two—Writing in the Disciplines and Reading in the Disciplines—we emphasized the range of cognitive skills needed by college-educated people. Certainly, an engineer must be able to gather information, to report on work done, and to analyze data. However, as we see in the definition from the Engineer's Council, engineers are also expected to exercise critical judgment, the highest of the range of cognitive tasks. In this chapter, we shall present a range of writing activities from a variety of engineering and technical courses. While these activities do not exhaust the writing assignments from engineering and technology programs, they do provide important examples of assignments from such programs. Additionally, some of the examples demonstrate connections to writing required of professionals in technical fields.

Importance of Communications to the Engineering and Technical Professional

Part of an engineer's responsibility is met by the wise use of technical knowledge and, in part, that responsibility is carried out by communicating ideas, issues, beliefs, and policies to both customers and to the public. In fact, those of you who become businesspeople, government employees, or scientists will probably work very closely with engineers and technicians. The interdependence of those working in these fields and the increasing emphasis on team approaches to problem solving create specific demands on the communication skills of today's and tomorrow's professionals. As we have shown throughout this text and as we shall show in this chapter, the writing of professional people demands an awareness of a complex set of requirements, among which are the following:

- the ability to understand the needs of diverse audiences and to write for these audiences
- the ability to read and understand documents written by people from both inside and outside your own company
- the ability to communicate orally in both formal and informal meetings and gatherings with coworkers, customers, and the general public.

These requirements offer only a glimpse at the abilities needed by college-educated people who enter technical fields. As well, such professionals must function efficiently, and often creatively, within organizations that require employees to understand their own jobs as well as the interaction of various jobs within and outside the company. Such requirements demand that employees understand organizational culture, appreciate a diverse work force, and work in teams to solve problems. The writing activities we present in this chapter often provide practice in these areas, for writing provides a rich ground to develop communication and problem-solving skills.

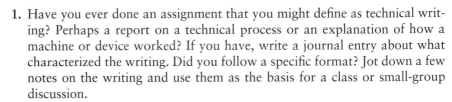

Exercises

1. Have you ever done an assignment that you might define as technical writing? Perhaps a report on a technical process or an explanation of how a machine or device worked? If you have, write a journal entry about what characterized the writing. Did you follow a specific format? Jot down a few notes on the writing and use them as the basis for a class or small-group discussion.

2. *If you have access to a word-processing program,* use it to write a short paragraph that explains part of a technical process. One of the most important aspects of technical writing is the format of the document, such features as arrangement of text on the page and the use of visual and mathematical material. How does the word-processing program enable you to customize the writing to accomplish such formatting? What other advantages do you see for using a computer to do such writing?

3. Interview someone (either in person or by e-mail) who works in the career area you hope to enter on graduation. Ask whether each of the following requirements holds true for that profession:

   • the ability to understand the needs of diverse audiences and to write for those audiences

   • the ability to read and understand documents written by people from both inside and outside your own company

   • the ability to communicate orally in both formal and informal meetings and gatherings with coworkers, customers, and the general public

   Use the information you gather in the interview as a springboard for a group discussion, either on disk or on-line.

   If you have access to a computer network and synchronous (real-time) conferencing software—for example, access to Internet Relay Chat or to software like the Daedalus Integrated Writing environment—hold a ten-minute, in-class, on-line discussion about the information you have gathered from your interview source and from your own firsthand experiences. At the conclusion of the synchronous discussion, jot down what you consider to be the three most important points that were made. Use these points to continue the discussion in a traditional face-to-face format with the class.

4. Go to the library and ask the reference librarian to help you locate a popular style manual for members of your chosen profession. If you cannot find a style manual that is focused on your profession, find a journal, technical journal, or trade magazine for the profession—a publication written by people in your chosen career for people in your chosen career.

   Using a word-processing program, individually describe some of the elements that seem to characterize the writing style valued in your discipline.

Look at the following kinds of things to start, then add some of your own items:
- length of sentences and paragraphs
- use of specialized vocabulary
- conventions of formatting
- conventions of organization
- use of headings and subheadings
- use of graphs and figures
- bibliographic style

Discuss with your writing group or class members what you have found. Speculate about why various professions seem to value different things or similar kinds of writing styles.

5. *If you have access to a computer network and synchronous (real-time) conferencing software*—for example, access to Internet Relay Chat or to software like the Daedalus Integrated Writing environment—hold a ten-minute, in-class, on-line discussion about the information you have gathered from your review of writing styles within your profession.

Writing from the Professional's Viewpoint

Before we present writing assignments from college courses in engineering and technology, we would like you to consider the perspectives of some experienced professionals in technical fields. Frequently, after working a few years in their chosen fields, college graduates see their undergraduate preparation far differently than they did when they were students. As undergraduate students in technical majors, students often believe their most important learning will be based on memorizing and amassing large quantities of information. In fact, some students actually talk about absorbing information, as though their minds were sponges. After graduating and working as professionals, however, these same people realize that other aspects of their learning should have been emphasized. Here are some examples of what practicing engineers have to say about the importance of writing in their professional work.

A recent, unpublished survey, authored by Steven Youra and Christine McGuinness, of nearly 1,500 Cornell University engineering graduates from the years 1950–1992 revealed some very interesting information. First, engineers spend virtually the same percentage of their time writing as do teachers, about *25% to 30%* of their time, or about *ten to twelve hours per week*. Counting the time required to prepare and deliver oral presentations, engineers spend close to half of their work time in formal writing and speaking activities. Second, on a scale of one to five, indicating unimportant to essential, engineers scored the importance of writing in their careers as *4.4*. And, third, when asked to state the "attributes that an undergraduate engineering education could enable students to develop," these engineers ranked effective oral and written communication skills as second only to the "ability to evaluate problems and design solutions." This ranking placed these skills well ahead of such under-graduate emphases as "understanding mathematics and physical sciences" and "breadth/depth of technical knowledge."

What do engineers learn after a few years in the profession that so changes their perspective and causes them to place such importance on writing and speaking? Many say the answer is quite simple: They learn that their success at work depends directly on their abilities to communicate what they know, what they have done, and what they propose to do. And they learn that pos-sessing masses of technical information amounts to very little if they can't con-vey that knowledge accurately and convincingly to others. In short, they understand that individuals and organizations must communicate well in order to succeed. Preparing for those communication tasks while you are an under-graduate will serve you well.

As we move into the next section of this chapter, we shall continue to draw comparisons between certain writing tasks of professionals in engineering and technology and assignments from undergraduate courses. However, not all as-signments covered in this chapter are included for comparative purposes; some are included because professors have found them helpful to students who are learning the specific discipline.

Writing in Undergraduate Technical Curricula and Preparing to Write in Engineering and Technology

In order to prepare for communications requirements, undergraduate engi-neering and technology majors should engage in activities both that help them learn their discipline and that prepare them to be effective communicators in their professions. Fortunately, most engineering and technology faculty rec-ognize the value of solid communication skills, acknowledge the importance of those skills to the development of successful professionals, and include in their courses various kinds of writing and speaking assignments. In order to gain a better understanding of these communications requirements, we will examine a few representative assignments from courses that reflect the basic conditions and problems encountered in responding to writing assignments in engineering and technology curricula. These assignments will range from very brief re-sponses to very complex ones and have their counterparts in writing done after college.

First, in order to get an idea of what will be expected of upper-division students in technical fields, let's look at a representative statement from one engineering professor in an interdisciplinary engineering curriculum. Here's a portion of what this professor writes about the requirements in a senior-level design course, a course that, according to most professors, provides students with an opportunity to demonstrate their fullest understanding of their aca-demic major. As well, it represents the type of requirements you will encounter as you move toward upper-division courses in an engineering or technology major.

Here is the professor's description of the requirements in the course:

> The primary assignment is a semester-long design project. To achieve this, students complete multiple written assignments, including proposals, funding requests, progress reports, and a final technical report. Students are required to make at least four oral presentations during the semester. In addition, there are three written quizzes during the semester, contributing 27% of the final grade. The project is based on reports and presentations at midterm and end-of-term; this accounts for 49% of the final grade. The remaining 24% of the final grade is made up of homework and notebook assignments.

Exercises

1. List your responses to the following questions: What would you say are this professor's assumptions about the students' preparation, emphases in the course, and connection of the course to professional work?
2. What does the distribution of credit across a variety of assignments indicate to you? Write down and share your answers with a partner.
3. *If your class has access to stand-alone computers or an asynchronous (not occuring in real-time) on-line conference,* complete this assignment (describing the professor's assumptions about students' preparation) on a disk conference. Compare your answers with those of other students.
4. From several courses within your major, collect a series of writing assignments—try to get at least three. In a word-processing file, start making a list of the assumptions about students' knowledge that underlie these assignments. Try to imagine yourself as an archeologist looking at some artifacts of a culture—try to imagine the kind of educated professional that the assignments are aimed at creating. Among the questions that you might want to ask yourself about these assignments are the following:
   - What professional *knowledge or understanding* (for example, in science, engineering, computer science, biology, medicine) do the assignments assume?
   - What professional *skills* do the assignments assume?
   - What writing *skills* do the assignments assume?
   - What other communication *skills* (for example, in listening, speaking, and reading) do the assignments assume?
   - What *knowledge or understanding* about communication do the assignments assume?

   In the reading-response conference (on disk or on-line), share what you have found out with other members of your class.

If you have access to a computer network and synchronous (real-time) conferencing software hold a ten-minute, in-class, on-line discussion about your findings. At the conclusion of the synchronous discussion, jot down what you consider to be the three most important points that were made. Use these points to continue the discussion in a traditional face-to-face format with the class.

5. On a disk or using e-mail, write a letter to a friend in high school, to your parents, or to a friend at another school who is not in the same major as you are. In this letter, describe what you have learned about the expectations people have for professionals in your field. Which of these expectations are surprising to you? Which loom as the greatest challenges? Which seem easy? How far along the road of becoming a professional do you see yourself? How is your education preparing you for meeting these expectations? What things can you do to better prepare yourself? Send the letter by post or e-mail.

Now that you have responded to the questions above, consider these points:

• We can see that this professor expects that students will have already gained sufficient knowledge of science, mathematics, and engineering to grapple with the subject matter of the course. The emphases placed on communicating knowledge and expressing solutions to a design problem indicate very clearly that the professor assumes sound knowledge of the technical basis for the course. Much the same can be said of employers who hire these same graduates: Employers expect that employees will possess the basic knowledge required to solve problems encountered in their work.

• Further, we can tell that this professor wants to provide students with training and experiences in written and oral communication, for she has designated writing and communications skills as two of the major educational goals of the course. In part, this professor brings these requirements to the course because her work with manufacturing firms has informed her teaching. Elsewhere in the course syllabus, she quotes industry sources as believing that "engineering graduates lack skills in Computer-Aided Design (CAD) . . . manufacturing practices, and communications skills."

• Finally, note that the assignments and activities are ones that encourage *process*. There are several parts to the design report, culminating in a final technical report. Additionally, oral presentations figure prominently in the course, and are, most likely, related directly to the stages of the design report. An approach that links assignments throughout the term fosters a sense of connection, especially when the course is focused on a primary activity—the design report—that the students can develop and refine as the semester proceeds. In this particular course, writing is used as one of the primary means of demonstrating the student's developing knowledge and coherence.

The above course description represents, as we said, what many professors see as the culminating experience of an undergraduate engineer's experience in the major field of study. It includes some homework and problems, but it also places an emphasis on a complex report, complemented by other written as- signments and oral presentations. This kind of course is often called a **capstone course,** one that showcases the student's ability to bring together knowledge of science, mathematics, engineering methods and solutions, and effective oral and written communication skills.

A bit later in this chapter we shall focus on a formal report and shall use that report to examine in detail the key elements of writing in engineering courses. First, however, let us prepare for that activity by looking at a few assignments from engineering courses that prepare for writing in capstone courses and by connecting those activities with a summary of information from research about the writing required of professional engineers. We believe a knowledge of these requirements will present a solid case for principles we are advocating in this book: the significance of writing and reading as processes; the benefits of addressing various audiences; and the importance of disciplinary culture in both the academic and professional worlds.

The Diversity of Engineering Writing

Throughout this book we have encouraged you to regard writing as both an intellectual and a social act, one that is accomplished through understanding the type of writing (for example, reporting, analyzing, evaluating), the form of the writing (for example, memo, essay, proposal), and the cultural context (for example, the discipline, organization, social group, industry) of the writing. Examples from the writing of professional engineers clearly demonstrate the need for students to prepare themselves for such a writing environment. Here is a list of typical writing tasks, gathered from interviewing engineers:

Letters and Memos	Reports and Proposals
responses to requests	status reports
inquiries	test reports
test report cover letters	proposal for original research
thank you's	inspection reports
proposing improvements	equipment reports
information on procedures	

While these lists are not exhaustive, they are representative of the range of writing for which engineers are responsible. Also, note that several of these forms have appeared earlier as writing assignments and tasks in other disci- plines. Study the lists and answer the following questions.

Exercises

1. While you are probably not familiar with such specialized engineering documents as status and inspection reports, you have gained valuable

knowledge about reports from other chapters in the book. Using your knowledge of the reports covered in other chapters, write a paragraph in which you explain which of the above reports would prove most difficult to write.

2. Make an appointment to interview a practicing engineer or a person who has practiced engineering in the last five to ten years. Ask this person to look at the list of writing tasks on page 391. Ask the individual to customize this list—adding or removing items—for their particular situation. Ask the person to answer the following questions: How much of your time each week do you spend in writing? Which of the kinds of writing seem most difficult or challenging for you? Record these answers as fully as possible.

   When you return from the interview, post on the *reading-response conference* (on disk or on-line) the information you have found and compare your findings with those of other individuals in the class.

3. *If you have access to the Internet,* find a discussion list or a newsgroup for engineers in the specific area you hope to enter (for example, biomechanical engineering, civil engineering, industrial engineering). Join the list or new group, but do not participate yourself. Observe the kinds of messages that are included in this forum for a period of five days.

   At the end of this time, report back to your writing group or to your class on the following questions:

   • What *professional knowledge or understanding* does the list/newsgroup assume or mention?
   • What *professional skills* does the list/newsgroup assume or mention?
   • What *writing skills* does the list/newsgroup assume or mention?
   • What other *communication skills* does the list/newsgroup assume or mention?
   • What *knowledge or understanding about communication* does the list/ newsgroup assume or mention?

Did you notice that in these examples of what is sometimes called "real-world" writing there is a wide variety of tasks? A proposal for original research is probably more intellectually challenging than a report on equipment, which might be a simple listing of equipment on hand. As well, did you note that the letters and memos were ones for which there are diverse audiences? Responses to requests, for example, might be written to a project member, a supervisor, a member of a town council, or any other of a vast potential audience. In fact, surveys show that a considerable amount of engineering writing is written for audiences who know less about the subject matter than the engineer writing the document.

With respect to audiences for writing, then, engineers, scientists, business-people, and most other professionals must develop the skills to write to nonexpert audiences. An important goal, then, of an undergraduate engineering education should be to acquire practice in writing in different forms for different audiences. Returning to our capstone course example, if we consider only the final report from the course, it represents just one possible type of assignment; however, if we look carefully at the description of writing activities in the course, we see additional possibilities, ranging from progress reports to funding requests. It is the kind of assignment that prepares students to develop a range of writing options and skills, especially in a variety of different formats.

Now, let's look at some writing assignments which engineering professors regard as helpful to students as they learn engineering, develop their communications skills, and prepare for writing beyond college. All of these assignments are regularly assigned by professors in undergraduate classes.

The following list of assignments, from a professor of mechanical engineering, represents the wide range of potential assignments for engineering majors.

- keeping a journal or academic notebook.
- using written annotations to explain solved mathematical problems
- rewriting a document to balance visual, mathematical, and written components
- writing a short research paper on the course's relevance to the real world
- speculating on original solutions to mathematical problems
- redesigning lab report formats
- emphasizing synthesis and evaluation sections of lab reports

Exercises

1. In an earlier exercise we asked you to consider the relationship between types of engineering and levels of cognitive skills. Working with a partner, discuss what kinds of thinking would be involved in speculating on original solutions to mathematical problems. You might want to use the work you did in Chapter Eight on annotating mathematics problems as a way of approaching this execise. Write a brief statement summarizing your discussion.

2. Using the previous exercise, connect the listed assignments to the cognitive skills listed in Chapter One. Complete this assignment on a disk conference, in an asynchronous on-line conference, or in an e-mail message to a friend or classmate. Compare the connections you identify with those of your classmates.

3. Engineering problems almost always contain mathematical solutions to problems. Find a partner and choose a simple mathematical problem to solve. Each of you should individually annotate the problem using the annotation feature of a word-processing program. In your annotations, describe the hints/strategies required to solve this kind of problem at each stage of the process. Exchange files and compare the annotations you have made with those your partner made. Combine the best aspects of both annotations. When you are done, give the problem and the annotations to someone who may be experiencing difficulty in solving this kind of problem in a math class that they are taking.

The assignments on page 393 are not only typical of ones assigned across the engineering curriculum, but they are being assigned more frequently in engineering courses. Because there are often large numbers of students in engineering classes, particularly 100- to 300-level courses, brief writing assignments are preferred frequently by engineering professors. Notice that several of the examples could easily fit that criterion: journal entries, written annotations, short speculations on original solutions, and redesigning laboratory report formats. The following outline of course requirements from a 200-level electrical engineering laboratory course reveals a similar range of writing assignments.

Preliminary Lab Schedule for EE 232

	Week	Technical Topic	Prelab	Written Output	Technical Output	Due Date	Follow Up
Critique and Summary	1	Writing Skills		*Critique* of a short discussion of accuracy, precision, and significant digits	None	Two days after lab	*Summarize* discussion in week 2
Explanation and Revision	2	Thevenin's Theorem		*Explanation* of Thevenin's Theorem in a format similar to the discussion from the first week	Determine the value of $R_{Thevenin}$	Two days after lab	Return discussion for *resubmission*
Discussion and Revision	3	Voltmeter and Ohmmeter Design	Solve parameters	*Discussion* of the design and operation of ohmmeters	Determine the value of $R_{unknown}$	Two days after lab	Return discussion for *resubmission*
Revision and Summary	4	Oscilloscopes		*Discussion* of the use of oscilloscopes and critique of a sample lab report		Two days after lab	Return discussion for *resubmission* and *summarize* sample lab report
Report and Revision	5	RL and RC Circuits		*Report* on how the RC time constant can be used to obtain the value of C	Determine the value of $C_{unknown}$	Two days after lab	Return report for *resubmission*
Report and Revision	6	Phasors		*Report* on how phasors can be used to determine Z_L	Determine the value of $L_{Lunknown}$	Two days after lab	Return report for *resubmission*
Report and Revision	7	Power Factor (PF)		*Report* on how to obtain and correct PF's	Determine the PF and the necessary value of C to correct the PF to within a certain tolerance	Two days after lab	Return report for *resubmission*

	Week	Technical Topic	Prelab	Written Output	Technical Output	Due Date	Follow Up
Report and Revision	8	RLC Circuits	First Draft of Final Report	None		End of Lab	Return first draft of Final Report for *resubmission*
	9	Resonance		None		End of Lab	
	10	Lab Exam	Final Report	None			

This course is taught on the ten-week quarter schedule, and the instructors for the course are all teaching assistants, graduate students working on a master's or doctorate degree. The course director and the university writing program director designed assignments that would provide a variety of writing experiences while fitting into the once-per-week meeting schedule of the lab. The assignments during weeks one through four are all short, about one typescript page, and ask for analysis, explanation and general discussion. The major report is staged from weeks five through ten, with sections being turned in weekly from weeks five through seven, a preliminary draft turned in during week eight, and the final draft turned in during week ten. Remember, we have emphasized the benefits of efficiently managing writing assignments. This method enables students and instructors to do just that. Students get practice in important forms of learning and communication in engineering, and are given the opportunity to do their best work. Another important feature of the learning in this class is the follow-up activities, which provide opportunities for students to revise and resubmit their writing and reconsider initial responses to assignments. Such a schedule, of course, acknowledges the process of writing, an important feature in determining the best way to learn material, approach solving a problem, or learn to do any new task.

The Memo: A Critical Writing Activity

One of the most frequent writing tasks faced by professional engineers is the **memo,** or memorandum; it is also assigned frequently as part of undergraduate engineering reports. Like the business memos you studied in Chapter Nine, engineering memos range from one or two lines to several pages; and like all memos, the ones written by engineers are one of the primary means of transmitting important technical and business information throughout companies. In this section we will review and apply within an engineerng context the memo activities in Chapter Nine, "Writing in Business and Mangement," and you should consult that chapter for detailed information on writing memos. In engineering, the memo serves such purposes as the following:

- proposing work to be done
- reporting progress on work underway
- responding to a request for information

- offering a solution to a problem
- requesting assistance with a problem
- submitting a request for funding
- following up on a contact

The major point to remember about memos is this: they are *functional* pieces of writing. The readers of memos, whether they are professors or coworkers, are interested in getting the precise material they need, usually in the most compact form. Designed to transmit important information, initiate action, pose solutions to problems, or respond to people's concerns, these documents emphasize the following:

- Audience
- Clarity
- Precision
- Organization
- Format

The following memo is an adaptation of an actual document from a major international firm. We have changed the name of the company and other identifying features in order to ensure anonymity; however, we have maintained the format and major purpose of the memo. We will use the memo in subsequent exercises, so refer to it frequently as we move through this section.

CACTUS PLANT

SUBJECT: FAULTY THERMO COUPLING INVESTIGATION

Mail Drop   1234
Telephone   600-543-3040

COPIES: B. Blue   J55
           L. Hampton M23
           F. Fillmore   M29
           R. Moore   P25

Identifying Heading

October 11, 1995

R. Dunn, Manager
Quality Control Technology

Intro & Compliment

Just a quick note to let you know our appreciation of the excellent support we have received from your Structural Imaging group over the past few months.

The most recent example of the quick turnaround time possible with the Image Modeling facility is last week's investigation of two faulty Thermo Coupling components, which were returned by Federated Enterprises (see attached Directive DL-8).

Problem & Solution

In this particular case, the possibility of a field quality problem was an immediate concern. The couplings were screened using image modeling equipment, and potential quality problems were mapped. The faulty couplings were then tested using the ZAP facilities to assist the Materials Group in their failure investigation. This combined effort enabled our team to respond quickly to a serious customer concern.

Future Applications

Other uses for the imaging data that have proven useful are definition of component boundaries and fluid element regeneration. Currently we are investigating the possibility of implementing quality control plans utilizing IM on the production process of seals. We see a great potential for IM in a production quality role and look forward to continuing to work with your people to make full use of this powerful tool.

Close & Applause

Carla and Eric, in particular, deserve special mention for their expertise and patience during the numerous tours and investigations that have been in support of these efforts.

Again, we appreciate the work that is being performed with the Image Modeling facility, and we see great potential for IM as a production quality-control tool.

Walter J. Bowen, Engineer
A133 YYB Systems

F. W. Bailey, Manager
A134 YYB Systems

Exercise

Form groups of four or five and discuss the features of the memo. You might want to consider the following points: What is the primary purpose of the memo? What other purposes do you find? What can you say about the style of the memo? Considering your work on the memo in Chapter Nine, would you agree that there is a "business" tone in this memo? Discuss the implications of the tone of the memo with regard to undergraduate engineering study.

As illustrated in the Cactus Plant example, the basic format of a memo contains two main sections: **heading** and **body.** The heading section usually contains:

- the writer's name and initials
- the company (and sometimes unit or department) logo
- the recipient's name
- the names of those receiving a copy of the memo
- the subject addressed in the memo

Other information is sometimes included in the heading, given the special needs and preferences of the specific company. As we said, in this example the identifying names have been deleted, but you can determine the places where such information would appear. The other main part, the **body**, usually contains the following:

- a short statement of purpose
- a brief discussion of issues, problems, solutions
- a recommendations and/or conclusions section

We can identify a number of features and issues from just one reading of the memo. For example, the ostensible purpose of this memo is stated in the "subject" section in the upper right of the memo: "Faulty Thermo Coupling Investigation." Also, we know that this is an **internal memo**, one directed to an employee who works in another department of the same company as the writer, and we find that a problem has been the cause of a "serious customer complaint." We can sense, too, that the issues here are probably very serious ones because the defective part was returned by "Federated Enterprises" after the part had "failed." What might we imagine the results of such a failure to be? Of course, not all memos address problems of this magnitude; some involve much less serious implications. For example, the memo on pages 415–416 ("Study on landfill and leachate control") provides an example of a communication that prepares readers for the detailed information contained in the report, which we discuss later in this chapter. Still, memos very often concern matters of major scope to the companies involved. Let's return to the memo concerning the faulty couplings to illustrate what a careful reading will reveal.

This memo provides an excellent example of the way writing may sometimes serve more than one purpose. Read paragraph four of the memo. Is the purpose of this paragraph the same as the stated purpose of the memo? In this paragraph, the writer signals a departure from the memo's stated purpose by opening with the words "Other uses" and goes on to indicate further applications of the technology used to analyze the faulty coupling problem. Would you agree that such phrases as "great potential" and "full use" clearly move the purpose of the memo beyond its original one? Additionally, of course, the writer applauds the work of the reader's group and specifically names two individuals who were particularly valuable in so seeking a solution to the problems. Thus, we might say that this memo has at least three purposes: to address the stated purpose of the memo, to suggest further applications of the technology, and to thank the group and specific employees for their contributions.

The versatility of the memo form is demonstrated by yet another function of the memo we are considering. This memo fulfills most of the characteristics of another type of technical document, the **progress report.** In fact, the progress of many projects is reported through memos. In relating the status of work on the faulty part, the author of this memo, in effect, provides information about the progress of the work which was done to analyze the problem. Progress reports are among the most important that engineers write; they are also very important documents in upper-division engineering classes which stress project work and team-oriented activities. Please note that exercise 2, following, asks you to write such a report.

Exercises

1. Imagine that you are the lead engineer on a major project and that a critical stage of the project is being delayed because a supplier, Technology Innovators, never delivers parts on schedule. Although you are very concerned that these delays will seriously affect timely completion of the project, there is a major issue related to your filing a complaint with your supervisor: Your supervisor is the sister of Technology Innovators' president. Write a memo to your supervisor which explains the problems caused by late deliveries but which will not cause difficulties for you!

2. Progress reports, also known as status reports, help keep colleagues up to date on both long-term and short-term projects. Usually, the report is divided into the following sections: 1) work done prior to the report, 2) work being reported on, and 3) future plans and recommendations. Using this format, choose a current project of yours and write a progress report to an interested audience. We suggest that you organize your report chronologically, although there are other choices. The subject need not be an academic one.

A last note about memos. As we said earlier in this section, Chapter Nine, Writing in Business and Management, develops the importance of the memo as a communication medium in the world of business. We suggest that it is just as important to the work of engineers. Most engineers, in fact, will say that although they have undergraduate degrees in a field of engineering, they really function as much as businesspeople as they do as engineers. It is not surprising, then, that a large percentage of those with undergraduate degrees in engineering go on to obtain graduate degrees in business and related areas. The memo is, then, a critical writing activity in many professions. It is used to address problems on both a profound and minor scale; it keeps a company's employees aware of what's developing on specific projects; it provides opportunities for employees to propose projects and to suggest new approaches to troublesome practices. It is so important, in fact, that business and industry spend millions of dollars a year on seminars, workshops, and training programs, all in an attempt to foster superior memo-writing skills among their employees.

Exercises

1. *If you have access to the Internet,* identify and join a discussion list or a newsgroup in a specific engineering field. When you have observed the exchanges of this group for a few days, post the following note to it:

> Hello. I am a student in a _____ class (or engineering program) at _____ (university, college, community college). In an assignment for my class, I am required to ask a group of professional engineers to tell the story of a difficult memorandum they had to write in connection with their professional business. Are any of you willing to post your stories, removing names and necessary details to protect identities and proprietary information? Thank you in advance for your help.
>
> Signature

Summarize the responses you get to your writing group or to your classmates in the reading-response conference (on disk or on-line).

2. Using the word-processing package on your computer, write one of the following four memorandums:
   - a memorandum to the president or leader of a student organization to which you belong describing a problem facing student members of this organization and describing possible solutions to this problem
   - a memorandum to one of your teachers about a problem or a success you are experiencing in the class
   - a memorandum to the chair of the department in which you are a major, describing a problem facing students who major in this area (for example, in advising, in curricular offerings, in getting internships or co-ops) and possible solutions to this problem
   - a memorandum to your boss in the job you currently hold describing a problem facing employees in the business and possible solutions to this problem

   Consider elements of audience, clarity, precision, organization, format. Share this memo with your writing group or other members of the class. Get their input on how such a memo might be perceived by the reader and ask for feedback on improving the memo.

The Formal Engineering Report

The remainder of this chapter will consider what many believe is the most important document engineers write: the **formal report.** The listing of types of reports we provided earlier (page 391) should give you a basic idea of the range of this type of technical document. It can provide extensive factual information on test results which are vital to the day-to-day operation of engineering firms, can document a student's work on laboratory experiments in the sciences and engineering, can provide a brief overview of an inspection, or it can elaborately detail the process and results of many years of original research. Many engineering students, in fact, think that everything they write, regardless of the discipline concerned, is a report!

This presentation will focus on a longer, formal report which was written for a 400-level class in civil engineering. We chose this report for several reasons. First, the general topic of the report, a Municipal Solid Waste (MSW) program, is important to society. We have all heard, and most likely you have read, about the difficulties of disposing of our communities' waste products. Indeed, disposing of domestic and industrial waste in safe ways is a worldwide problem. Second, because this report does not include numerous calculations and specialized mathematical information, the topic is more accessible to a general audience than many engineering reports would be, even though it was written for a 400-level class. In fact, this report was written as a response to a request from a municipal government to a university professor. Thus, because a primary audience for the report was city officials, most of whom were not engineers, much of the report is written to a nonexpert audience. Finally, this lengthy, detailed report covers virtually all areas encountered in college-level engineering reports. We have integrated enough material from this report into this section to give you an idea of its components. (See additionally pages 415–419.)

Notes on using the report material

As we discuss the application of the MSW report to an understanding of report writing in general, we shall move between the material in the examples to the discussion and explanation in the body of this chapter. During this process, we will refer directly to specific parts of the document and focus on specific principles of report writing. In order for this method to succeed, you must approach the points discussed very critically; that is, we encourage you to play an active role in this process, not a passive one. The more you question, the more engaged you will be and the better you will understand the presentation. The additional pages from the report should also provide you with interesting possibilities to connect this type of technical writing to writing in previous chapters. As part of your preparation for this section, we also suggest that you review the material on researching in science and technology in Chapter 3, Researching in the Disciplines, and the sections on writing reports in the other discipline-specific chapters. While there are differences in how disciplines approach report writing, there are many similarities, as well.

The fundamentals of a formal report: An overview

Regardless of the type of report you are writing, all reports must address the following questions:

- Who is the audience for this report? Is it experts or novices?
- How much information do they need to understand the report?
- Is my plan for executing the report clear to my audience?
- Have I written an organized, clear statement of the problem?
- Is the language—written, mathematical, visual—appropriate?

Before we address these questions in more detail, take a moment to examine the project assignment provided below.

Midwestern Technical University
Department of Civil and Environmental Engineering

CE 455—Solid Waste Management   Fall 1993

Design Project

Objective: To evaluate the city of Woodvale solid waste management system.

The class has been asked by the city of Woodvale to study its solid waste collection system. The attached letter from Rhonda Jack, City Manager, poses a number of questions that the city would like us to consider as a class. Because there are a number of issues and problems that need to be studied objectively, the class will be divided into two-person design teams, each of which will work on one or more tasks. Interim results will be presented in class during the design session. Each group should be prepared to give a brief oral report of its weekly progress. The final report will consist of a written and an oral component. In addition, each student is to write an executive summary of his/her specific project.

Each team is relatively free to pick a topic of special interest to it, but as a class we will try to coordinate activities to cover as many topics as possible. Some of the following tasks have been done for us or will be done by the class as a whole. For example, also attached is a data sheet summarizing some information about Hancock's solid waste system and generation rates.

Tasks	Information Needed
1. Define Service Area	City map
2. Predict Waste Generation	Population data
	Waste generation data
3. Component Analysis	Waste survey or
	Literature review

4. Evaluate Type of Service	User survey or Engineering judgment
5. Allocation of Service Demand	Population density Housing density

6. Select Collection Equipment	Equipment specifications from
	    manufacturers
	Crew size
	Distance to processing or disposal
	    point
	Compressibility of refuse

7. Layout Collection Routes	Housing locations Routing guidelines
8. Consider Transfer Stations	Distance to disposal site(s)

In this case, the professor has provided the students with clear requirements and procedures. For example, the audience for this report is clearly established in the instructions to the students. Most of the writing done by college students is written for the professor who teaches the class. In this case, one of the most important parts of this report, the executive summary, was presented directly to the city officials who requested the study. As we said earlier, much of the writing done by professional people—engineers as well as other occupations— is directed to audiences who know considerably less about the subject than the writer. Note that all of the fundamentals relate directly to audience. Perhaps this is an indication why some say that in technical writing, there are three critical issues: audience, audience, and audience. This is a point well worth committing to: Without strict attention to the audience for your writing, you stand little chance of succeeding, regardless of how knowledgeable you are about the subject.

Other aspects of the design project description prepare the writer to understand the task at hand. For example, the description includes a clearly stated objective: "To evaluate the city of Woodvale solid waste collection system." A key term, then, is *evaluate,* for that term demands that decisions be reached concerning many issues, that judgments be made. Evaluation requires the writer not only to analyze the problem, but also to reach conclusions, to propose solutions, and to make recommendations. Indeed, an executive summary section presents an overview of conclusions and results. We know from our work in earlier chapters that evaluation processes form the highest order of the cognitive processes. It is at that level where one judges the worth, value, and applicability of, in this case, methods, materials, and procedures.

A close look at the table of contents for the design report we selected (provided on page 405) reveals that the writers, for the most part, have followed the professor's guidelines and suggestions concerning necessary sections and arrangement of those sections. Note, however, that the professor supplies an "example final report format," (below) not a required format. Thus, students were free to adapt this format to some degree, depending on the exact nature of the topic they covered. For example, some topics require more of a literature review than others; while, in fact, some topics might not require a literature review at all.

Midwestern Technical University
Department of Civil and Environmental Engineering

CE455—Solid Waste Management
Example Final Report Format

1. Letter of Transmittal attached to cover of report.
2. Title Page, List of Tables and Figures
3. Project Summary—Conclusions and Recommendations (one by each student)
4. Main Body of Report
    a. Introduction—project description, objectives and scope of study
    b. Review of literature
    c. Approach—methods of analysis, data collections, etc.
    d. Results and Discussion—summary tables and figures, etc.
5. Appendixes
    a. Maps or drawings, if appropriate
    b. Details of analysis, as necessary
    c. Example calculations

Report will be graded on the basis of completeness, organization, clarity, and correctness.

Remember, it is not so important as to how long the report is in terms of pages or words, but how long it takes to read. If it only takes 10 minutes to read, it probably doesn't have enough detail. If it takes more than 30 minutes, it is too detailed or not very well-written.

Still, if we compare the table of contents to the suggested format, which fulfills the assignment's basic requirements, we see that they are similar. Having estabished that the writers follow the basic format, and that they have presented what appears to be a document, what else can we say about the success of this document? In order to answer this question, let's spend the remainder of the chapter addressing two key questions:

• Is the writers' use of language appropriate for the intended audience?
• Are the visuals (graphs, charts, figures) and visual cues (headings, bullets, and so forth) used effectively?

Table of Contents

I.   INTRODUCTION
     A. Definition of problem .... p. 3
     B. Method of Analysis .... p. 3

II. DETAIL OF CURRENT LANDFILL
     A. State design requirements .... p. 4
     B. Specifications .... p. 5
     C. Current leachate disposal practices .... p. 7

III. TECHNICAL DEFINITIONS
     A. Leachate .... p. 7
     B. Leachate collection systems .... p. 9
     C. Leachate treatment systems .... p. 12
         1. Biological processes .... p. 12
         2. Chemical processes .... p. 14
         3. Physical operations .... p. 14

IV. RECOMMENDATIONS
     A. City Landfill .... p. 17
     B. Long-term .... p. 18

V.   SUMMARY .... p. 19

VI. REFERENCES .... p. 20

                        List of Figures
Figure 1   Plan view of city landfill .... p. 6
Figure 2   Landfill liner—single composite barrier .... p. 10
Figure 3   Cross-sectional view of leachate collection system
           in place .... p. 11
Figure 4   Activated sludge or trickling filter process .... p. 13
Figure 5   Chemical treatment for heavy metals and organics .... p. 13
Figure 6   Baffled reactor process .... p. 16

                         List of Tables
Table 1   Typical leachate compositions .... p. 8

Since this is an introductory text, we offer these questions as a guide to thinking about writing reports. As with other features of writing we have covered, these questions will not answer all questions about the example we are studying; they will, however, provide a frame within which we can explore writing.

Using appropriate language in reports

One of the major reasons why some reports fail is that the very language used in the report is inappropriate for the intended audience. For example, consider the meaning of the following sentence: *A singular rapidly rotating mass of consolidated mineral matter agglomerates no bryophytic substance.* Did you know right away that this rather strained sentence can be translated as, *A rolling stone gathers no moss?* Although most of us know many, if not all, of the words which comprise the first sentence, many of us probably experienced some pause in understanding the sentence. It is, therefore, a good example of inappropriate use of language . . . for most audiences. We might even ask under what circumstances a geologist or a biologist would use this language to convey this particular idea. This type of language is known as **jargon,** language which is particular to a specific discipline or specialization. Certainly, as we have discussed elsewhere (see Chapter Two, for example), jargon has its place. If one engineer is speaking to another, the use of engineering jargon is far more likely to be appropriate than it would be if an engineer is speaking to an accountant.

Since the following executive summary from the city of Woodvale evaluation report is written to a nonexpert audience, let's examine it to determine whether the language used is appropriate to that audience. As you study the executive summary, keep in mind the following description: The executive summary is very important because it gives one or more of your primary readers an overview of the report. Further, in industry this may be the only section of the report that is read by the people who decide whether your project is approved or rejected: Writing a clear, concise summary is critical to the success of any report. Because the summary is condensed from the larger body of the report, write it after completing the revisions of the main body. The following four parts should always be included in the executive summary:

- synopsis of objectives
- procedures and methods used
- conclusions
- recommendations

Options for Dealing with a Leachate in an Integrated Solid Waste Management System

Executive Summary by A. McDermott and C. Shant

Report Objective

The initial focus in this report was to examine the current conditions at the Woodvale landfill in (Home County), and determine if it is competent enough to handle the composition and quantity of solid waste delivered there. The landfill service area is not only the City of Woodvale but the entire western regional area.

Analysis of Procedures and Methods

The current design requirements for leachate collection systems and landfills in general, from the type of soil to the quality control procedures are covered first. The next aspects we focus on are the details involved with the size and location of the landfill, along with specifications for the liner. We also looked at the current leachate collection system as well as the in place method for dealing with the leachate that is collected now.

The current system in place is based on the sloped-terrace principle. It collects approximately 150,000 gallons of leachate per month with a BOD_5 ranging from 100 mg/l to 12,000 mg/l. The leachate is collected in a 10,000 gallon storage tank until disposed of at the local wastewater treatment plant at a cost between 1.0 - 3.5 cents per gallon. The variable rate is based upon the BOD_5 concentration of the leachate.

Findings and Definitions

Technical definitions including leachate, leachate collection systems and leachate treatment systems are then discussed. The landfill currently has 1 completed section (Phase I) and has started to deposit wastes into Phase II. Both sections of the landfill are considered to be immature landfills since Phase I has not yet met the definition of a landfill (>10 years old) and Phase II has not had its final cover. We cover some of the biological, chemical and physical processes that occur in the landfill and also those processes that are used to clean up the wastes.

Suggestions and Recommendations

Some suggestions are made that should help the landfill become a more proficient and economically feasible operation now and in the future: combining leachate collection systems, using foam as a daily cover, and using evaporation as a means to help reduce the volume of leachate produced. These are some of the possible recommendations that will help the system continue to work efficiently.

Exercises

1. Find an example of writing that presents an idea or issue in a complex manner. Rewrite it, or a brief section of it, so that the ideas in it are accessible to your classmates.

2. Carefully reread the executive summary and answer the following questions: Is the language used in the summary appropriate to a general audience? Are there words, terms, and constructions used that are difficult to understand or that make ideas difficult to understand fully?

3. Suggest some revisions to the executive summary to increase its effectiveness. Have one person record these suggestions in a word-processing file and print out a copy for everyone in the group.

Individually, use the revision suggestions to rewrite and improve the executive summary. Bring your revision in to share with your writing group. In your group, have all the members explain how they revised the summary and what decisions they made in doing so.

4. *If you have access to a computer network and synchronous (real-time) conferencing software* hold a ten-minute, in-class, on-line discussion to identify the characteristics a good executive summary should have in a formal report. Assign one person the job of summarizing these characteristics in a list form as the conversation proceeds. At the end of the ten minutes, print out one copy of these criteria for each member of the class.

5. Next, in your smaller writing groups, read the executive summary and use the criteria list that the class just generated to suggest improvements to it. At the end of your discussion, identify what you consider to be the three most important revision suggestions you would like to pass along to the authors of this report should you be able to meet and talk with them.

The need for precise and concise technical language

While you want to avoid using language that is inappropriately complex or esoteric, remember that most specialized terms are very functional within specific contexts. We would not say that the word *nostrils* should be replaced by *nose holes,* unless, perhaps, we were speaking to a very young child. Engineers, depending on their discipline, are very accustomed to using such words as *iteration, oscilloscope, thermo-coupling,* and *capacitor.* When you consider the use of language in any piece of analytical, argumentative, or descriptive writing, remember that using precise technical terms is extremely important. In engineering writing, as with writing in any other specialized field, the need for precision, coupled with an emphasis on conciseness, means that word choices must be both *precise* and *concise.* Finally, remember that audience is the key here. Therefore, one way of determining the success of language used in this document would be to pick any section and study that section for both precise and concise language which is appropriate for the audience.

For example, in order to critically read the city of Woodvale evaluation report, one would have to understand a key term, *leachate.* Study the following definition the writers offered in their report under a section entitled, "Technical Definitions," then turn to the exercises that follow it.

Leachate: Any particular leachate may be interpreted as liquid that has percolated through solid waste and has extracted dissolved or suspended materials. In most landfills leachate is composed of the liquid that has entered the landfill from external sources, such as surface drainage, rainfall, ground water, and water from underground springs and the liquid produced from the decomposition of the wastes.

When water percolates through solid wastes that are undergoing decomposition, both biological materials and chemical constituents are leached into solution.

How well do you understand this definition? Indicate any part of the definition that might confuse a nonexpert. Then rewrite the definition for a nonexpert, say, an interested ninth-grade student.

Using visual language in technical documents

The last question we will work with in this chapter is a very important one, for it regards the use of visual language in technical documents. Engineers and other professionals who write technical documents convey messages, argue issues, and propose solutions through the use of four distinct but complementary means of communication: *written, spoken, visual,* and *mathematical languages.* In Chapter Eight we introduced mathematical language, which is recognized generally as a system of thought that conveys meaning through a set of shared symbols. Using the term "language" to describe visual structures is clearly assigning a specialized definition to the word *language.* Yet it is an aspect most engineers would be comfortable working with.

There are many different types of visuals, but among the most commonly used in engineering writing are:

bar charts: useful for comparing different sizes and quantities
pie charts: useful for showing proportions
flow diagrams: useful for explaining a process
graphs: useful for showing changes in at least two values

When you use visuals in a report or presentation, there are several basic guidelines you should follow:

• Number visuals in order of presentation.
• Give each one a title.
• Place each visual as close as possible to its first reference.
• Provide headings for columns in tables, and for areas in charts.
• Don't refer to a visual before you present it.
• Maintain consistency in formatting visuals.

Throughout the city-evaluation section of the report, the writers used such visuals as drawings, tables, and charts to convey information about their study of leachates in this MSW system. In deciding whether visuals are needed, we must answer one question before all others: Will this visual present information better than words can? Keeping this question in mind, let's consider the use of the following two visuals from the report.

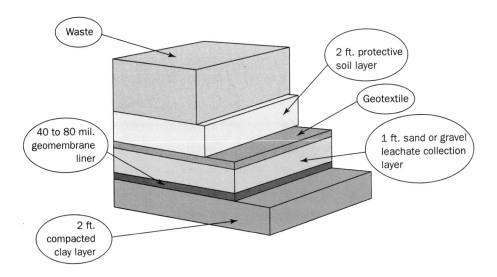

Typical Landfill Liners—Single-composite Barrier Type I

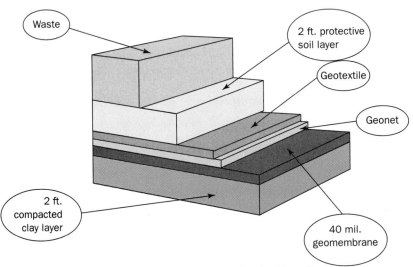

Single-composite Barrier Type II
FIGURE 2

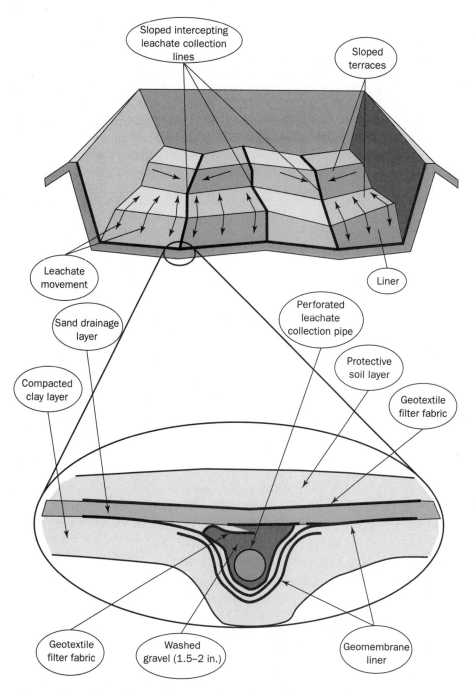

FIGURE 3 Cross-sectional View of Leachate Collection System in Place

Exercises

1. Do you agree that the visuals should be as large as they are? Why have the writers chosen to size them as they do?
2. Could you suggest changes in the positioning of any of the visuals? *If you have access to a graphics package,* you might work with a partner to reformat the flow of text and one of the visuals. For example, you might wrap the text around one of the visuals. What might be the effect of such a change? Would it change the way one reads and understands the report?
3. Find a written presentation of information that might be more meaningful if changed to a visual.
4. *If you have access to a computer network and synchronous (real-time) conferencing software* hold a ten-minute, in-class, on-line discussion in which the members of your class discuss the effectiveness of the visuals in the sample report using the specific information provided on page 409.
5. Individually, go out and find at least two graphics (for example, tables, charts, flowcharts) and the text that accompanies these graphics—choose only those graphics you think are effective in presenting information. Be sure to get at least one graphic from a technical source within the field of engineering; the second graphic can come from a less technical source. As possible sources for the technical graphic in the field of engineering, look in your engineering textbooks or in engineering trade magazines in your school library. As possible sources for the less technical graphic, look in popular magazines, your local newspaper, or the annual reports of companies, government agencies, or organizations.

   Meet in your writing group to examine the graphics each member has chosen. Working with a word-processing package, create a group list of the characteristics that can be used to identify an effective technical graphic in engineering fields. Also create a separate list of the characteristics that can be used to identify an effective graphic in a less technical field. Compare the criteria on the two lists. What is similar? What is different?

Benefits of visual text

The benefit of visuals in a technical document is very simple: Appropriate visuals allow the reader of the document to *see* information, rather than *read* the information. For example, in the previous sentence, we italicized several words, hoping that this visual technique would emphasize the main point of the sentence. Oftentimes, the choice between using words to describe a cross-section or proportions or using a visual that allows readers to view the information is a simple one. The visual on page 410 allows readers a view of the multilayered, single-composite barrier. How would you go about putting what this visual displays into written language? What does the visual allow you to see about the barriers? Despite these obvious benefits, don't assume that all one needs to produce an accurate technical document is a collection of attractive visuals. As you decide whether to use visuals or words, here is a good rule to keep in mind: Rarely does a visual completely replace the author's words in a technical document; rather, text and visuals join together with mathematical and verbal language to more fully present technical information and ideas than any one could do alone.

Exercises

1. In your *on-line reading log,* identify the most important points within this chapter. You can do this either as or after you read the material. Save the file each time you add material. By now you should have a useful set of notes/guidelines to consult about writing.

2. *If you have access to a computer network* (for example, a campus network or the Internet), join a network discussion group or subscribe to an on-line news group related to your engineering career interest (ask the central campus computing folks for help). Introduce yourself as a student taking a writing class and ask one or more of the following questions: What writing strategies have worked particularly well for you when you are writing a formal report? Have you ever had a particularly difficult time writing a formal report? Does your company or organization have specific guidelines for formal reports (for example, organizational, stylistic), and can you provide me a copy?

   Make a list of all the responses people offer, or print some of them out, and bring them to class to contribute to face-to-face discussions.

3. Go out and find a formal engineering report in your area of expertise that you can photocopy and use for purposes of analysis in your class. As sources for such a report, try public records collections (for example, collections of government documents, city and county records), family members who are engineers, friends who have had co-op experiences in engineering, teachers in engineering, technical writing textbooks that may include samples of formal reports, or WWW or Gopher sites on the Internet. Photocopy (or print out) this report and bring it in to a meeting of your writing group.

   Compare the report to the sample report we have included in this chapter. Sitting around a computer as a group, make a list of the similarities and differences between the two reports in terms of the standard conventions of a formal report as a genre, or type, of professional writing in engineering.

   Take the material from this list and publish it in your class's *reading-response discussion* (on disk or on-line).

4. *If you have access to the Internet,* spend an hour cruising the nets to locate resources in engineering that may interest you. Look for Gopher or WWW sites that specialize in engineering materials, newsgroups for engineers, discussion groups for engineering students, colleges (other than your own) that offer excellent engineering education. Choose one document (one artifact) from your cruise and print it out. Bring this to class and share it with the other students in the course or with the students in your writing group.

In preparation for your final writing assignment in this chapter, we have included several pages from the student report we have been considering. These selections come from different sections of the report, so you should get a sound idea of the information included in such sections, as well as how the students developed these sections. Combined with the material covered earlier in the chapter, this information should provide a solid basis from which to write the final assignment. Read these sections carefully before you go on to the final assignment.

Client's Confirmation of Interest Letter

STUDY OF THE CITY OF WOODVALE SOLID WASTE COLLECTION SYSTEM

Dear Al:

This letter is to confirm the city of Woodvale's interest in being a project for the Fall term of CE 455.

The city has been discussing rate structure, recycling, and collection methods for the past three years and would welcome the independent analysis of your 100-student class.

Some of the goals of our discussions have focused on a) reducing the amount of tonnage generated by the Citizens through recycling or higher fees, b) increasing the role of recycling in the community though we don't seem to see any real markets for the recycled materials, c) revising the rate structure so small-volume users of the system are rewarded by reduced rates.

The city accepts that our wastes will continue to go to a landfill in the foreseeable future and that landfill costs will rise per ton at least by the rate of inflation each year. It is not possible for the city to build its own landfill, thus we must use the existing facility(s).

Some other questions we hope to resolve are 1) Can we use incineration to dispose of paper and cardboard products using existing local incinerators, or should we build a small one operated by the city? 2) We expect to receive a proposal to contract out the collection and disposal process. Is that advisable at this time? 3) We currently subsidize the system. What would the rates have to be to remove the subsidy yet reduce costs for the low-volume user? 4) Exactly what type of materials make up our waste stream and how much of it is comprised of cardboard and paper? 5) Who exactly generates the most garbage in our community? Is it residential or commercial? 6) Dumpsters have been used to consolidate garbage collection. What rate should they pay?

From the introduction to the project

The city of Woodvale has posed a serious task for our class. The City Manager, R. Jacques, would like some answers to the growing problem of municipal solid waste (MSW) in her community. There are many different areas to be considered when you are looking at updating local collection and disposal systems. Everything from predicting future waste generation estimates to assessing resource recovery possibilities will have to be studied. One of the important areas to be studied is the current landfill design to see if any improvements can be made to reduce the overall cost of municipal solid waste disposal. Specifically, we will focus on leachate collection and treatment improvements at the landfill.

Definition of problem

This report will focus on several questions: What is a leachate and why should we be concerned about it? What are the options (processes) for dealing with the treatment and/or recycling of the leachate? Finally, what other specific improvements can be made at the landfill to make it more efficient and less costly in the future? Although these are not specific questions asked by Ms. Jacques, we hope to show that she should be concerned with their answers.

Method of Analysis

Our methods for contemplating this particular problem will be both qualitative and quantitative. We will first look at the existing design of the operating landfill (Local Landfill—Northern County) and then we will focus on the leachate disposal practices that are currently being used there. In both areas we will evaluate what is being done now and offer some suggestions to both improve the operation of the landfill and reduce its daily operational cost. (All information on the local landfill was provided by Mr. Dean, Landfill Operations Manager. . . .)

MEMORANDUM TO CLIENT

TO: City MSW Committee
FROM: MSW Consultants, Inc.
DATE: November 5, 1993
RE: Study on landfill and leachate control

Here is the report on the Woodvale landfill and its current leachate collection and disposal methods. As you can see, our report initially presents general information

continued

on the state design requirements for landfills, and then describes the specifications of the Woodvale landfill. (All of the information on the old landfill was provided by Mr. Simpson, the Landfill Operations Manager for APF). Next, we present some common types of landfill construction, focusing on the leachate collection system design. Finally, a general description of some common practices for leachate treatment are offered, along with their corresponding advantages and disadvantages.

The recommendations which are offered in this report are, for the most part, echoes of what has been requested by Mr. Dean. From the discussions with him, it became apparent that the landfill is essentially a profitable business currently, and it will appear to remain so in the future with no appreciable increase in charge for disposal of MSW. For the western geographical area that it serves, the MSW landfill is entirely adequate and the suggestions for improvement will only serve to make it a more efficient operation.

From the technical definitions biological processes section

Leachate collection systems

Before we attempt to analyze the possibilities for leachate treatment, disposal, and the revenues possibly generated from these, we must first describe the type of system used to collect the leachate at the landfill. The three main concerns in the design of a leachate collection system are the type of liner used, the slope and grading of the landfill bottom and the placement of the drainage channels and collection pipelines underneath; and the layout of the leachate removal, collection, and holding facilities.

To prevent the contamination of groundwater, nearly all landfills currently constructed in the United States use a liner system consisting of a type of plastic geomembrane placed over a compacted clay liner. The thickness and number of liners depend upon the local geology and other factors. In two-liner systems, the primary liner is used to collect leachate, and the secondary liner is intended as a backup should the first one leak. (Leakage detection probes are placed just below the first layer.) A sand or gravel layer 1.5 to 2 feet thick on top of the geomembrane is intended to serve as a collection and drainage layer for leachate. The leachate collection pipes are placed in this layer, usually enclosed in a gravel envelope, on top of the geomembrane. Two typical landfill liner systems are shown in Figure 2.

In order to collect the leachate as it filters through the sand or gravel layer, the landfill bottom usually is graded to form a series of "sloped terraces." Perforated pipe is installed along the edge of these terraces. These collection pipes usually have a slope of 0.5 to 1.0 percent.

An alternative to sloped bottom terraces are piped bottom layers. In this system, the entire bottom area is divided into sections separated by clay barriers, and several slotted leachate collection pipes are run through these sections to a larger collection pipe. A two-foot layer of sand is used to cover the pipes. Both sloped terraces and piped bottom layers are shown in Figure 3.

Once leachate is collected from the landfill, it must be stored in a holding tank. In order to reach the tank, either the main collection pipe must be passed through the side of the landfill, or the leachate must be pumped from an inclined collection pipe within the landfill. The holding tank itself will be large enough to hold between one to three days' worth of leachate during peak times of leachate production.

Now that the leachate collection system has been considered, what is done with the collected leachate? There are many management options, and the most appropriate one can be found by considering many factors, including leachate composition, leachate quantity, and landfill proximity to treatment facilities.

Leachate treatment systems

There are three basic types of processes used for the treatment of leachate generated by various types of industrial and landfill processes: (1) biological processes, (2) chemical processes, and (3) physical operations. We will look at each of these basic types as well as the individual components that make up the processes respectively.

Biological processes

The different types of proficiency processes that make up a biological treatment are generally used for the removal of organics. The first of these is activated sludge (refer to Figure 4). This process may require the augmentation of a defoaming additive. Also, a separate clarifier will be needed to reduce the volume of effluent produced. Sequencing batch reactors are similar to activated sludge. They are only applicable to relatively negligible flow rates, but no separate clarifier is needed to decrease the volume of the effluent; therefore, it can be a cost-efficient alternative. Aerated stabilization basins are a very good long-term approach and an immeasurably cost-effective alternative to areas that have access to a large territory of land.

continued

Fixed film processes such as trickling filters and rotating biological contactors (refer to Figure 4) are known to work exceedingly well for the removal of organics. These are commonly used on industrial effluents that are similar in composition to landfill leachates, but so far they have not been utilized for actual landfill leachate. Anaerobic lagoons and contactors have lower animation requirements and lower residual sludge production than aerobic systems, but they . . .

From the recommendations section

Overall, the current system in place at the landfill is entirely adequate for the quantity and composition of the waste that it now receives. Phase I is currently in place and has received the preliminary stages of its final cover.

Landfill
    Our first recommendation would be to connect the future leachate collection system with the system currently in place beneath Phase I. With the two systems being joined, along with the addition of a leachate collection and transmission vault, the practice of leachate recycling could be introduced to the operations agenda. The recycling of leachate will help reduce the volume and biological composition of the leachate being produced at the landfill. (The components of a recycled leachate are attenuated by the biological, chemical, and physical processes occurring in the landfill itself. Simple organic acids will be converted into CH_4 and CO_2. Combined with the rising pH, this will help facilitate the precipitation of metals within the landfill. This helps to contain possible contaminants within the landfill.)
    Section 1 of Phase II has been started using a single composite barrier liner. We recommend that with this second phase, a few procedural changes be made at the landfill which will reduce costs. First, the local landfill's location is such that the spraying of leachate back onto the waste for the purpose of evaporation may be useful, at least during the late spring to early fall months. The volume of leachate would be greatly reduced, and therefore some of the hauling costs would be eliminated.
    Another recommendation is to start using foam as a daily cover treatment for the MSW. This would greatly reduce the wasted volume in the landfill. The initial cost of purchasing the foam spraying equipment,

although considerable for a landfill of this size, would be made up with saved space in the landfill. The sprayer could also serve a dual role as foam layer applicator and as a leachate sprayer for the evaporation process. This multipurpose use will help save landfill volume and will also conserve the amount of money being spent on equipment.

Exercise

For this final assignment suggestion we ask that you select an actual college situation you would like to improve or a problem you would like to solve. While this document may bear a strong resemblance to the recommendation report we suggested in Chapter Eight, there will be some major differences.

This report should involve an engineering problem. For example, you might want to see major changes made to a campus building, the addition of a new parking structure, the removal of an unsightly structure from a central place on the campus. The topic you choose should involve building, removing, renovating, realigning, or some other structural, construction-based, design change. The major requirement is that the topic be a real situation or problem.

Here are some possible points to guide you in the assignment:

a. Do some research on campus. Contact student and faculty members and groups, interview faculty department administrators and deans, talk with building maintenance staff, search through back issues of the student newspaper. There must be long-standing as well as recent issues on the campus.

b. The audience for the report should be whoever would decide whether your recommendation would be approved. This might be the college president, the director of facilities or physical plant, the board of control. Find out. One of the tasks here is to do the investigating that figures prominently into writing a convincing report. You must know who will decide on your recommendation in order for you to be convincing. Additionally, understand that many people might read such a report, so you can't write it to only one level.

c. Remember, a report such as this must be persuasive as well as factually accurate. Collecting large bodies of numbers and charts will not get most projects approved. Projects cost money, and decision-makers must establish priorities. It is critical for you to establish your project as one worth funding.

d. Include in the report a number of the types of writing we have presented. Summaries, letters, memos, background information, problem statements, analyses, recommendations, tables, charts, graphs—select from among the many available.

e. As with the other major assignments in scientific and technical areas (natural sciences and decision sciences for example), we suggest a team approach to this assignment. If you plan well, divide responsibilities appropriately, and manage your work, you should be able to construct a solid and interesting report.

URLs for Engineering and Technology

National Academy of Sciences—National Academy of Engineering
http://www.nas.aas.org/

Engineering and Technology
http://www.einet.net/galaxy/Engineering-and-Technology.html

Engineering and Technology
http://www.acm.uiuc.edu/signet/JHSI/tech.html

Civil and Construction Engineering (Engineering and Technology)
http://www.einet.net/galaxy/Engineering-and-Technology/Civil-and-Construction-Engineering.html

Manufacturing Engineering Resources
http://marg.ntu.ac.uk/resources.html

Good Starting Points for Exploring the Internet—Engineering Resources
http://www.commscope.com/StartingPoints.html

Civil Engineering Resources
http://www.civl.port.ac.uk/resource/resource.html

Engineering Resources
http://www.lib.umich.edu/chouse/inter/630.html

A Brief Guide to Documentation Style

An important part of doing research and of writing a paper is properly documenting the sources you consult and those you use in the paper. Whether the paper is a term-ending major project or merely a minor part of the course requirements, accurate documentation is critical to the overall success of the assignment. Just as there are stylistic writing preferences among disciplines, there are also preferences regarding documenting sources in those disciplines. Therefore, while the variations among the forms for, say, documenting a book for a biology assignment, a literature paper, and a sociology essay may seem slight to you, your professors will expect you to follow the guidelines preferred in their disciplines. In short, adhering to the preferred documentation style of a discipline is usually a requirement, not an option.

In this appendix, we cover the four most often used style guides and provide you with a basic foundation for documenting sources. It is, however, very likely that you will need information on documenting a source that we do not include. For example, one of the current style guides devotes about 150 pages to documenting sources, so we strongly advise that you consult the four style guides when you encounter a question not covered in this section. Additionally, a complete style guide will assist you with important information on such subjects as quoting and paraphrasing material, constructing cover pages and tables of contents, and writing extended documentary notes. The examples we offer illustrate traditional sources and, as well, provide an overview of documenting electronic sources, a dynamic and rich source of material for writers at all levels. Finally, we include a bibliography of the style manuals and valuable on-line sources for using APA and MLA styles.

The style guides covered are the *Publication Manual of the American Psychological Association* (APA), *The Chicago Manual of Style* (Chicago), *Scientific Style and Format: The CBE Manual for Authors, Editors, and Publishers* (CBE), and the *MLA Handbook for Writers of Research Papers* (MLA). While some disciplines authorize specific guides to writing in their fields, these four style guides are accepted throughout higher education. As you can determine from the broad list of disciplines in the following section, understanding these guides will be helpful to those majoring in these fields. Even if you do not major in one of these areas, you will take required courses in these disciplines, so all students will benefit from learning about these style guides.

Use of Style Guides by Disciplines

The following lists provide a general idea of which style guides are preferred by specific disciplines. Remember, these are only general guidelines; always consult your professor before choosing a style guide. Additionally, as you can tell from this listing, some disciplines allow more than one style guide.

APA
Anthropology
Business
Communication Studies
Composition
Nursing
Political Science
Psychology
Sociology

CBE
Computer Sciences
Engineering and Technology
Health Sciences
Mathematics
Natural and Applied Sciences

Chicago
Anthropology
Art
Business
Communication Studies
History
Mathematics
Philosophy
Political Science
Sociology

MLA
Art
Communication Studies
Composition

English
Foreign Languages
Literature

American Psychological Association (APA) Documentation Style

Like all organizations that authorize a style guide, the APA's guide enables writers to provide an accurate record of the use of others' materials and work. Because there are similarities between the APA and the MLA (which we begin on page 429) and because these two style guides are the ones you will probably use most often during your first two years of college, we compare some features of the APA and the MLA styles. We think this approach will help you understand some of the key features of both, while establishing a sound basis for your use of the two systems.

The APA guide, like all style guides, requires that an author who uses another writer's material identify the source in two ways. First, *in-text citations* (which include the author's name and the date of publication) provide the reader with a quick reference to the source of the material. The *references* section, a list of all works referred to in the text placed at the end of the paper, provides full information on sources. Like MLA style, APA style relies upon correspondences—citations and references which are linked by key features. In APA, the author's name and the date of publication in the in-text citations correspond to the alphabetically arranged list of references at the end of the paper.

However, the APA documentation format differs from the MLA format in two major ways. First, the APA format requires that the date of publication appear in in-text citations. Second, the APA style emphasizes different information in the references section. Unlike the MLA works-cited section that is designed to highlight each author's name, APA references emphasize the date of publication, as indicated in the examples. The reason for these differences is that disciplines that employ APA style are especially concerned about the relevance of publications as reflected by their dates of publication.

Because style guides present a large amount of highly detailed information, please note the following three usages in APA style:

- In-text citations do not include page numbers when information is paraphrased or summarized. However, when a direct quotation occurs, in-text citations must identify the page (p.) or pages (pp.).
- Regarding written notes, on occasion, an author may want to write an explanation of an idea or provide a bit more information about a point covered in the body of the paper. APA style calls these "content" notes, and they are placed on a separate page and numbered consecutively with superscript numbers. APA cautions, however, that writers should avoid numerous content notes as they are often disruptive; instead, APA suggests that writers consider

integrating such information into the text or including it in an appendix, whichever is more appropriate.

• Concerning whether to indent the first line of items in your reference list, most teachers who require APA style will prefer that you indent the first line of the reference items five spaces. However, if you see an article published in a journal that requires APA style, you may notice that first lines of references items begin with a "hanging indent"—a practice that extends the first line to the left of all other lines in the entry. Don't be confused by this difference. The APA guide specifies that reference pages in manuscripts submitted for publication should follow the first-line indent practice. Journals then change those first lines to hanging indents to highlight the names of the authors. To be sure about this issue, ask your teacher.

Examples Following the *APA Style Guide*

First examples are reference form; second examples are in-text citation forms.

Book by one author

Bizzaro, P. (1993). *Responding to student poems: Applications of critical theory.* Urbana, IL: National Council of Teachers of English.

As Bizzaro (1993) notes, "Adaptations of the New Criticism to the evaluation of student poems are limited by the dispassionate nature of the method" (p. 226).

Book by two authors

Best, S., & Kellner, D. (1991). *Postmodern theory: Critical interrogations.* New York: Guilford.

Postmodern theories abandon the rational in favor of the decentralized and fragmented (Best & Kellner, 1991).

Edited book

Anson, C. M. (Ed.). (1989). *Writing and response: Theory, practice, and research.* Urbana, IL: National Council of Teachers of English.

Selection from an edited book

Goulston, W. (1987). Women writing. In C. L. Caywood & G. R. Overing (Eds.), *Teaching writing: Pedagogy, gender, and equity* (pp. 19–30). Albany: State University of New York Press.

Article in an encyclopedia or dictionary

Curti, M. (1973). Psychological theories in American thought. In *Dictionary of the history of ideas* (Vol. 4, pp. 16–30). New York: Charles Scribner's Sons.

Article in a journal

Bizzell, P. (1987). What can we know, what must we do, what may we hope: Writing assessment. *College English, 49* (5), 575–584.

Article in a magazine

Greenfield, M. (1986, June 30). The land of hospitals. *Newsweek,* 74.

Daily newspaper article

Smith, P. (1989, June 20). Stopping leaks in Washington. *The Washington Post,* pp. 1, 14.

Film or video

Weber, C. (Producer/Director). (1992). *Workplace stress* [Video recording]. Chatsworth, CA: AIMS Media.

Scientific Style and Format: The Council of Biology Editors (CBE) Documentation Style

In 1994, the CBE revised their style manual in the hope of offering one uniform way of documenting sources for all scientific and science-related disciplines. The CBE now offers two ways to cite sources in the revised CBE style. One is the *citation-sequence* (c-s) system (similar in some ways to Chicago style); the other is the *name-year* (n-y) system (similar in some ways to APA style). The format for references depends on which of these you choose. All of the following examples are references formatted for a paper written in the name-year system since it tends to be the more widely used. For formatting citation-sequence references, see the *CBE Manual for Authors, Editors, and Publishers* (6th ed.).

When you use the name-year system, citations are given in the body of the paper ("in-text" citations), rather than in footnotes or endnotes. Citations are made in the text within parentheses that contain the name of the reference's author(s) and the year in which the work was published. Then, at the end of the paper, full bibliographic references are given for all the sources that were cited in the body of the paper. This section is called *cited references* in the CBE style.

Book by one author

Harborne JB. 1977. Introduction to ecological biochemistry. London: Academic Press. 278 p.

As Harborne (1977) has long maintained . . .

Book with an editor

Boucher DH, editor. 1985. The biology of mutualism. New York: Oxford U. 388 p.

Selection from an edited book

Dean AM. 1985. The dynamics of microbial commensalisms and mutualisms. In: Boucher DH, editor. The biology of mutualism. New York: Oxford U. p 270–304.

Article in a journal

Sredl MJ, Collins JP. 1991. The effect of ontogeny on interspecific interactions in larval amphibians. Ecology 72: 2232–2239.

A recent study has found that initial tadpole density had little effect on mass and mean growth rate (Sredl and Collins 1991).

Article in a journal, organization as author

[CSA] Council on Scientific Affairs, American Medical Association. 1993 Jan 11. Report of the council on scientific affairs: diet and cancer: where do matters stand? Archives of Internal Medicine 153 (1): 50–6.

Article in a newspaper or magazine

Chalmers DJ. 1995 Dec. The puzzle of conscious experience. Scientific American: 80–6.

Conference proceedings

Sangwan RS, Sangwan-Norreel BS, editors. 1990. The impact of biotechnology in agriculture. Proceedings of the International Conference: The Meeting Point Between Fundamental and Applied In Vitro Culture Research; 1989 July 10–12; Amiens, France. Boston: Kluwer. 485 p.

Paper presented at a professional meeting

Schuett GW. 1992. Fighting dynamics of male copperheads *(agkistrodon contortrix)*: body size and prior agonistic experience as predictors of dominance. Annual meeting of the Society for the Study of Amphibians and Reptiles; 1992 Aug 2–6; El Paso, TX.

Scientific or technical report

Bonting SL. 1993. Space biology research development: final technical report. Washington, DC: National Aeronautics and Space Administration. Contract nr NASA CR-192830. 1 volume. Available from: NTIS, Springfield, VA: 93-1028-M.

Film or video

Tourmen F, Moutlin E, editors. 1991. The development of the human brain [video recording]. La Sept, Films of the Levant, Guigoz, CSI La Villette, coproducers. [Princeton]: Films for the Humanities. 1 videocassette (VHS): 40 min, sound, color, 1/2 in.

The *Chicago Manual of Style* (Chicago) Documentation System

The *Chicago Manual* strongly recommends two forms for citing and referencing sources. The form we explain here is one generally preferred by professors in the humanities, history, and art, as well as many social scientists. The other recommended version of Chicago style of documentation allows you to use in-text citations and a list of references or works cited (similar to the MLA or APA style).

The specific version of Chicago style preferred by most professors is characterized by the following:

- A *superscript number* placed at the conclusion of the cited material, typed above the line, and numbered consecutively throughout the text. Chicago recommends that these numbers be placed at the ends of sentences or clauses and that they should follow all punctuation marks except dashes, which they precede. Finally, numbers are not placed within parentheses or brackets.
- *Footnotes* (at the bottom of the page) or *endnotes* (at the end of the paper on a separate page). These are generally known as reference notes and are numbered, usually on the line, in correspondence to the note numbers in the text. Our examples show that most teachers prefer different forms for first references and subsequent references. This practice requires that the first time you make reference to a source, the footnote or endnote must be what is referred to as a full reference, one which provides complete bibliographic information. All second or subsequent references to that work are made in a special shortened form. In disciplines, authors write explanatory notes which present short discussions, using such introductory phrases as "See particularly . . ." or "A detailed discussion can be found in. . . ." So that you can become familiar with the placement and use of notes in Chicago style, we suggest that you look at two or three articles which employ the style. While citing sources can be time consuming and confusing, you should also note that most current word-processing programs contain features that allow you to use footnotes or endnotes easily by taking care of the time-consuming tasks they involve, such as renumbering notes, should you decide to add or delete any, and figuring the amount of space needed at the bottom of a page to contain the footnotes.
- A *bibliography* is usually included at the end of the paper and contains complete bibliographic references for all sources cited in the paper in an alphabetically arranged section called the "bibliography" or "selected bibliography."

Examples from Chicago Style

Book by one author
Bibliographic Citation
Crunden, Robert M. *Ministers of Reform: The Progressives' Achievement in American Civilization, 1889–1920.* Urbana, IL: U of Illinois Press, 1984.

First or Full Reference (the style of the footnote or endnote)

2. Robert M. Crunden, *Ministers of Reform: The Progressives' Achievement in American Civilization, 1889–1920* (Urbana, IL: U of Illinois Press, 1984), 135.

Subsequent References (the style of footnote or endnote)

3. Crunden, *Ministers of Reform*, 223.

Selection from an edited book

Dawley, Alan. "Workers, Capital, and the State in the Twentieth Century." In *Perspectives on American Labor History,* ed. J. Carroll Moody and Alice Kessler-Harris, 152–200. Dekalb, IL: Northern Illinois U Press, 1989.

Article in an encyclopedia or dictionary

Benson, Eugene, and L.W. Connolly, eds. *Encyclopedia of Post-Colonial Literatures in English.* New York: Routledge, 1994. Vol. 1. "Ricardo De Ungria," by Rosario Cruz Lucero.

Article in a journal
Bibliographic Citation

Rose, Ellen Cronan. "Custody Battles: Reproducing Knowledge about *Frankenstein.*" *New Literary History* 26 (autumn 1995): 809–32.

First or Full Reference (the style of the footnote or endnote)

38. Ellen Cronan Rose, "Custody Battles: Reproducing Knowledge about *Frankenstein,*" *New Literary History* 26 (autumn 1995): 811.

Subsequent References (the style of footnote or endnote)

39. Rose, "Custody Battles," 826.

Article in a magazine

O'Toole, Patricia. "The Old Square Dance, It Ain't What It Used to Be. . . ," *Smithsonian,* February 1996, 92–9.

Article in a newspaper

Bowditch, Gillian. "Breakthrough in Meningitis Treatment." *The London Times,* 19 January 1996, A1.

Unpublished interview

Gruber, Charlotte. Interview by author, 24 February 1996, Linden, New Jersey. Tape recording.

Film or video

Burns, Ken. "The National Pastime, 1940–1950: Bottom of the Sixth Inning." *Baseball.* Produced by Ken Burns and Lynn Novick. 83 min. Florentine Films and WETA-TV, 1994. Videocassette.

The *MLA Handbook for Writers of Research Papers* Documentation Style

Over the past ten years, the Modern Language Association (MLA) has shifted its emphasis from citing sources in footnotes or endnotes to documenting them within parentheses within the body of the paper itself. These parenthetical references, commonly called in-text citations, are used to refer readers to a list of sources known as works cited which appears at the end of a paper. This method has proved simpler for readers to follow and easier for writers to employ and for students to learn than the old methods.

Like APA style, sources are documented in MLA style by a system of *correspondences:* A source cited within parentheses in the text corresponds to a work listed alphabetically in the works cited section, which includes all works used in the paper. Each parenthetical source in the text includes the *author's name* and the *page* from which the information being cited has been obtained.

Here are a few points to note carefully about using MLA style:

- Abbreviations used for sources cited within the text: These should briefly and clearly guide the reader to the source. For example, if you have only one source by an author, use only the author's last name. If you use the author's name in the text, give only the page numbers cited. If you have two sources from the same author, use the author's name, followed by a comma, and an abbreviation of the titles in the citation, and begin the abbreviation with the first word of the title. If a source has two or three authors, give the last name of each author. In short, provide readers with concise, specific information to guide them as they use your material.
- Citing indirect sources: MLA recommends citing original courses whenever possible. First, this practice enables you to get the full context of someone's ideas, instead of those ideas being filtered through a second party. If on occasion it's necessary to quote indirectly, document this source by the abbreviation *qtd. in (quoted in)* placed before the indirect source in parentheses.
- Citing more than one source in a single in-text citation: At times you might want to use more than one source in a citation. In that event, cite each source as you normally would, and use semicolons to separate items.

Book by one author

Graff, Gerald. *Beyond the Culture Wars: How Teaching the Conflicts Can Revitalize American Education.* New York: Norton, 1992.

They have no strategy for dealing with cultural and educational conflict except to deny its legitimacy (Graff 43).

Book by two authors

Best, Steven, and Douglas Kellner. *Postmodern Theory: Critical Interrogations.* New York: Guilford, 1991.

According to Best and Kellner, "Foucault rarely analyzes the important role of macropowers such as the state or capital" (71).

Book with an editor
Williams, Jeffrey, ed. *PC Wars: Politics and Theory in the Academy.* New York: Routledge, 1995.

Selection from an edited book
St. John, David. "Teaching Poetry Writing Workshops for Undergraduates." *Creative Writing in America: Theory and Pedagogy.* Ed. Joseph M. Moxley. Urbana: NCTE, 1989. 189–93.

Article in an encyclopedia or dictionary
"Constantinople." *Encyclopedia Britannica.* 1989.

Article in a journal
Anastas, Benjamin. "Three Ways of Being Modern: The Lost Generation Trilogy by James R. Mellow." *The Iowa Review* 23.1 (1993): 161–81.

Article in a magazine
Crane, Theresa. "Stress Management and Weight-lifting." *University of California at Berkeley Wellness Letter: The Newsletter of Nutrition, Fitness, and Stress Management* Feb. 1996: 4.

Article in a newspaper
Gibson, Lynn. "Residents Issue Plea for Fire Station." *The Daily Reflector* 9 Feb. 1996: A1.

Unpublished interview
Kirkland, James W. Personal Interview. 10 Feb. 1996.

Film or video
Carolyn Forché. Videocassette. Lannon Foundation, 1991.

Television or radio program
"Black Mountain College: Interview with Fielding Dawson." Exec. Prod. Kris Hoffler. *The Spoken Word.* WZMB, Greenville. 12 Mar. 1995.

Lecture or live performance
Jones, Robert. "Disciplinary Culture and Written Communication." Presented to the students in Management 502: Introduction to Global Management. Arizona State University West, 7 Feb. 1996.

Documenting Electronic Sources

Like almost every aspect of electronic communications, the rules and protocols governing the documenting of electronic sources are very dynamic. For example, as we prepared this list, our search of just one "search engine" turned up almost 1,600 guides to writing style! Therefore, you may well find that the forms recommended for citing electronic sources have changed considerably since this section was written.

For that reason, rather than attempting the impossible task of providing examples of all the various forms and accounting for the dynamic nature of documentation guides, we have instead included examples of three of the primary types of sources you are most likely to consult and then document.

- CD-ROM databases. Transportable databases that are published periodically and contain a wide range of materials including books, articles, newspapers, and conference proceedings.
- Subscription-based computer search services. Usually accessible through your library's electronic network and include such databases as ERIC, BA on CD, and DISCLOSURE/SEC.
- Computer network search engines (accessed through the World Wide Web). Contain such services as *infoseek, Lycos, Megellan, Yahoo,* and *Excite.*

If the style guides have authorized a form for the type of entry, we have used one example from each of these three categories and constructed them using the forms recommended by the four major authorities—APA, Chicago, CBE, and MLA. These examples and forms should provide you with a sense of how the various style guides document sources.

APA

Material accessed from a database on CD-ROM

Philo, T. (1995, May 16). Billions at issue in for-profit conversion of health plans. *Sacramento Bee,* p. A1 [CD-ROM]. Business NewsBank: Record Number: 00850-19950516-00173

Material accessed through a computer service

Calder, William M. (1992). Was Aristotle a Myth? *Mnemosyne,* v. 45, fasc2, p.225. [On-line serial]. Available: EPIC, Doc. No. BHUM92013068

Material accessed through a computer network

Weiss, D. H. (1993). Biblical history and medieval historiography: Rationalizing strategies in crusader art. *MLN: Modern Language Notes 108* (4), 710-737 [On-line]. Available http:muse.jhu.edu/journals/mln/v108/ 108.4weiss.html

Chicago

Material accessed through a computer service

Calder, William M. 1992. "Was Aristotle a Myth?" In Mnemosyne [database on-line]. Netherlands: H.W. Wilson Company, 1984. Accession no. BHUM92013068. Available from EPIC database.

Material accessed through a computer network

Weiss, Daniel H. "Biblical history and medieval historiography: Rationalizing strategies in crusader art." *MLN: Modern Language Notes* 108, no.4 (1993): 710–737. [http:muse.jhu.edu/journals/mln/v108/108.4weiss.html]

CBE

Material accessed through a computer network

Valenti, Michael. October 1996. Putting power on ice. Mechanical Engineering. Available:HTTP:www.memagazine.org/contents/ current/ features/ powerice/powerice.html. Accessed 1996 October 20.

MLA

Material accessed from a database on CD-ROM

Philo, T. "Billions at Issue in For-profit Conversion of Health Plans." *Sacramento Bee* 16 May 1995: A1. *Business NewsBank.* CD-ROM. Dec. 1995.

Material accessed through a computer service

Calder, William M. "Was Aristotle a Myth?" *Mnemosyne* v. 45, fasc2, p.225, accession no. BHUM92013068. (1992) : n. pag. Online. EPIC database. 21 October 1996.

Material accessed through a computer network

Weiss, Daniel H. "Biblical History and Medieval Historiography: Rationalizing Strategies in Crusader Art." *MLN: Modern Language Notes* 108:4 (1993):710–37. Online. Internet 9 May 1994. Available HTTP: muse.jhu.edu/journals/mln/v108/ 108.4weiss.html

Citation Manuals and Electronic Guides to Documentation

We conclude this appendix with a list of sources you should consult for more extensive guidance in documenting papers for various disciplines. As you will discover when you consult these guides, the APA, CBE, Chicago, and MLA guides offer a wealth of information on using the documentation styles your professors will specify in your writing assignments. Additionally, we have included several electronically accessed sources, ones that offer the possibility of providing up-to-date documentation guides to this expanding field. These electronically accessed sources are particularly valuable for forms governing the use of Gopher sites, E-mail messages, the World Wide Web, listservs, and the many other types of electronic sources.

The Chicago Manual of Style. 14th ed. Chicago: U of Chicago P, 1993.

Gibaldi, Joseph. *MLA Handbook for Writers of Research Papers.* New York: Modern Language Association of America, 1995.

Li, Xia, and Nancy Crane. Electronic Style: A Guide to Citing Electronic Information. Westport: Meckler, 1993. Available: [http://www.uvm.edu/~xli/reference/estyles.html].

Page, Melvin E. pagem @ etsuaarts.east-tenn-st.edu. "A Brief Citation Guide for Internet Sources in History and the Humanities." October 1995.

Publication Manual of the American Psychological Association. 4th ed. Washington, DC, 1994.

Purdue University's Online Writing Lab Guide. Based upon the fourth edition of *The Publication Manual of the American Psychological Association.* Available: http://owl.trc.purdue.edu/files/34.html

Scientific Style and Format: The CBE Manual for Authors, Editors, and Publishers. 6th ed. Cambridge, UK: Cambridge UP, 1994.

Style Manuals in Brief: APA and MLA from the University of Illinois Writer's Workshop. Available: gopher://gopher.uiuc.edu/11/Libraries/writers

Turabian, Kate L. *A Manual for Writers of Term Papers, Theses, and Dissertations.* 6th ed. Chicago: U of Chicago P, 1996.

Walker, Janice R. "MLA-Style Citations of Electronic Sources." [http://www.cas.usf.edu/english/walker/mla.html].

CREDITS

Literary Credits

Angelo, Susan. "Critique: Causes of divorce in the monogamous willow tit, *Parus montanus,* and consequences for reproductive success." Reprinted by permission of the author.

Bean, John C., et al. Excerpt from "Microtheme Strategies for Developing Cognitive Skills." From *Teaching Writing in All Disciplines,* edited by C. Williams Griffin. Copyright © 1982 by Jossey-Bass Inc., Publishers. Reprinted by permission of the publisher.

Blakey, Paula. "We All Want Life to Make Sense." Copyright © 1966. From *Good Writing,* 1. By Simon. Reprinted with permission of St. Martin's Press, Inc.

Boyce, Ernest, and Maria Greene. "Essay Exam: MIS strategy set." Reprinted by permission of the authors.

Brown, Richard. "Preliminary Lab Schedule for Electric Engineering Course." Reprinted by permission of the author.

Capps, Susan. "Description of Senior-Level Design Course." Reprinted by permission of the author.

Carby, Hazel V. "Ideologies of Black Folk." Copyright © 1989. From *Slavery and the Literary Imagination* by Carby, pp. 125–126. Reprinted by permission of the Johns Hopkins University Press.

Carey, Thomas M. "What Variables Affect the Rate of Photosynthesis?" Reprinted by permission of the author.

Catton, Bruce. "Grant and Lee: A Study in Contrasts." Copyright U.S. Capitol Historical Society. All rights reserved.

Chappell, Fred. "Birthday 35: Diary Entry." Reprinted by permission of Louisiana State University Press from *Midquest: A Poem by Fred Chappell.* Copyright © 1981 by Fred Chappell.

Collins, James P., and Michael J. Sredl. "The Interaction of Predation, Competition, and Habitat Complexity in Structuring an Amphibian Community." From *Copia* 1992, No. 3. Copyright © 1992 by the American Society of Ichthyologists and Herpetologists, Allen Press. Reprinted by permission of the publisher.

Constable, John. "The Hay-wain." By permission of the National Gallery—London.

Curtis, Jim, Brian Kincaid, Brian Taylor, and James Wilde. "User's Manual: Big State University's Career Placement Database." Reprinted by permission of the authors.

Deglow, Carrie. "Health Education Review." Reprinted by permission of the author.

Easterbrook, Craig. "The Sincerest Flattery." From *Newsweek,* July 29, 1991, and Copyright © 1991, Newsweek, Inc. All rights reserved. Reprinted by permission of the publisher.

Fields, Kayse. "Smoking Should Not Be Allowed in Public." Reprinted by permission of the author.

Harrison, Jim. "Looking Forward to Age." Reprinted with the permission of Clark City Press from *The Theory and Practice of Rivers and New Poems.* Copyright ©1989 by Jim Harrison.

Hauser, Richard. "Course Description: Decision Sciences Syllabus." Reprinted by permission of the author.

Hauser, Richard. "DSCI 4133—Exam 2." Reprinted by permission of the author.

Hirsch, E. D., Jr. "Preface," *Cultural Literacy* by E. D. Hirsch, Jr. Copyright © 1987 by Houghton Mifflin Company. Reprinted by permission of Houghton Mifflin Company. All rights reserved.

Hoffmann, Roald. Excerpt from "Under the Surface of the Chemical Article." From *Angewandte Chemie: International Edition in English,* Vol. 27, No. 12. Copyright © 1988 by Angewandte Chemie. Reprinted by permission of the publisher.

Hopper, Donald J., and Robert Stryker. "Leachate Options Materials." Reprinted by permission of the authors.

Howard, Jay. "Contemporary Christian Music: Where Rock Meets Religion." From *Journal of Popular Culture,* Vol. 26, No. 1, Summer 1992. Copyright © 1992 by Popular Culture Association. Reprinted by permission of the publisher.

"How to Cope with the Burden." From *The Economist.* © 1993. The Economist Newspaper Group, Inc. Reprinted with permission. Further reproduction prohibited.

Photo Credits

Chapter Four © 1996 Marin Moutain Bikes, WebRangers.
Chapter Five © *Homage à Louis/David* by F. Les Loisire. Giraudon/Art Resource, New York.
Chapter Six © 1995, Comstock.
Chapter Eleven © Michael Rosenfield/Tony Stone Images.

INDEX

ABI Inform, 93, 94
Abstracts, 90
Accuracy of letters, 317–319
Acknowledgments section, of
   scientific writing, 231–232
Agricola, 113
AIDA method of organization,
   214–215
Alfoxden Journal (Wordsworth),
   158–161
Alfred, Randall, 185–186
Allen, Woody, 99
Analysis of text, 59–67
Angoff, William H., 186
Annotation
   for critical reading, 60–61
   definition of, 56
   for understanding and recall,
     56–57
Annotation feature, of word-
   processing packages, 129,
   131
Application of theory report,
   103–104, 199–211
Art Index, 101

Bad news letters, 313, 316–318
Bar charts, 409
Bibliographies, 90
Biographies, 90
Blakey, Paula, 44–45
Bloom, Benjamin, 11–13
Bloom's Taxonomy, 11–13
Body
   of letter, 314
   of memo, 398
   of progress reports in business,
     321
Book Review Index, 90, 101
Brown, LaVonne, 142
Buffer, in bad news letters, 317
Business and management
   collaborative writing in,
     122–123, 301–302
   E-mail, 305–312
   group collaboration systems
     and presentation facilities,
     122–123

importance of communications
   in, 305
letter writing, 301, 313–319
memos, 300–301, 303–312
progress report in, 321–322
recommendation reports,
   322–339
report writing in, 321–339
responsibilities in, 298–299
sample assignments in, 13–14,
   322
sample technical report,
   325–338
Universal Resource Locators
   (URLs) for, 340–341
writing in, 305–339

Carby, Hazel V., 164–165
Case study, 103, 104
Catalogs
   Internet access to, 123
   on-line library catalogs,
     91–92
Catton, Bruce, 154–157
CD-ROMs, 93, 101, 106
Chappell, Fred, 174–176
Chemical Abstracts, 113
Clipper Chip, 126
Clues in writing, 48–49, 150
Coherence, definition of, 25
Collaborative writing, in business
   and management, 122–123,
   301–302
Collaborative writing
   communities, 121–123
Collins, James P., 222–229
"Column" feature of word-
   processing packages, 129,
   130
Compact disk technology, 93
Complimentary close of letter,
   314
Comprehension in reading,
   43–57
Computer science. *See also*
   Mathematics and
   information technology
   definition of, 258

informal learning logs,
   273–275
programming and
   documenting, 275–280
writing in, 272–280
Computer searching. *See also*
   Internet
   CD-ROMs, 93, 101, 106
   humanities databases, 101
   in library research, 91–94,
     101, 106, 113
   locating books and articles
     using, 91–93, 101, 106, 113
   natural sciences databases,
     113
   on-line computer catalogs,
     91–92
   Proquest, 93–94, 101
   social sciences databases, 106
Computer-supported writing
   access and distribution,
     128–129
   benefits of, 120–124
   collaboration and group
     exchanges, 121–123
   E-mail, 122, 132–133
   flaming, 124–125
   fluency, organization, and
     invention, 121
   Gopher, 136
   hypertext and hypermedia
     environments, 130–133
   information and research aids,
     123–124
   Internet, 121–123, 135–137
   listservs, 122, 132–133
   Mosaic, 136
   newsgroups, 122, 132–134
   problems and challenges
     associated with, 124–129
   revision aids, 121
   surveillance, 125–126
   synchronous conferencing
     software, 133–135
   Wide Area Information Service
     (WAIS), 135–136
   word-processing packages,
     129–131
   World Wide Web (WWW),
     136–137

Computer-supported writing
(*continued*)
writers' tools for, 129–137,
139
writing and reading on-line,
126–128
Conclusion
of progress reports in business,
321
reading of, 50
Conferencing software, 133–135
Congressional Quarterly, The,
106
Constable, John, 158–161
Context clues, in reading, 49
Cowley, Malcolm, 15
Creative texts, in humanities, 96
Critical inquiry. *See* Report
writing
Critical interpretation essays,
162–178
Critical reading, 44, 59–79
Critical thinking, 10–14, 59
Critique. *See also* Report writing
definition of, 71
steps in writing, 71–74
Critiquing stage, of writing
process, 26, 30–31
Cues in writing, 48–49, 150
Cultural Literacy (Hirsch), 64–67
Cultural values
definition of disciplinary
culture, 6–7
in different disciplines, 3–5
Current Periodicals Index, 92

Databases. *See also* Computer
searching
CD-ROMs, 93
in humanities, 101
for locating books and articles,
92–93, 101
in natural sciences, 113
Proquest, 93–94, 101
in social sciences, 106, 190,
192
Date in letter, 314

Decision sciences. *See also*
Computer science;
Mathematics and
information technology
end-of-term project, 286–294
essay examination, 283–286
sample assignments in,
281–284
writing in, 280–295
Digital signature devices, 126
Disciplines. *See also* Reading in
the disciplines; Researching
in the disciplines; Writing in
the disciplines; *and specific
disciplines*
cultural values of, 3–5
definition of disciplinary
culture, 6–7
report writing in different
disciplines, 5–6
Discovery techniques. *See*
Planning stage
Distance-learning courses, 124
Documentation of sources, 85, 151
Double-entry journal, for
analyzing text, 62–63
Drafting stage
goals of, 31
in humanities writing, 151–154
of writing process, 24–25, 26,
29–30, 31

Earth sciences, 109. *See also*
Natural sciences
Easterbrook, Gregg, 77–79
Editing stage
guidelines for, 31
of writing process, 26, 31
E-mail, 122, 132–133, 305–312
Encryption devices, 126
Encyclopedias, 90
End-of-term project, in decision
sciences, 286–294
Engineering Index Annual, 113
Engineering and technology
course requirements in,
389–391, 394–395

definition of engineering
profession, 384–385
diversity of engineering
writing, 391–395
formal engineering report, 391,
400–419
importance of communications
in, 385–386
letter writing, 391
memos, 391, 395–399
progress report, 398–399
proposals in, 391
responsibilities in, 384–385
sample assignments in,
393–395, 402–403
Universal Resource Locators
(URLs) for, 420
writing from professional's
viewpoint, 387–388
writing in undergraduate
technical curricula, 388–419
Engineer's Council on
Professional Development,
384
Essay examination, 283–286
Ethical issues in health sciences,
370–380
Ethnographic information, 103
Evaluating a text, in reading,
67–68
Evidence
in humanities, 94–96
in natural sciences, 111–112
in social sciences, 103–104
Explanation
in bad news letters, 317
in good news letters, 317
Exploration
through journal writing, 19–21
planning through, 18
External clues, in reading, 48–49

Field, in social sciences, 103, 185
Field report, 103
Field research, 103, 185–186
Flaming, 124–125
Flow diagrams, 409

Formal engineering report, 391, 400–419
Format
    of formal engineering report, 404
    of letters, 314
    of memos, 311, 397–398
    of recommendation report, 322–323
    of scientific writing, 229–232
Frankenstein (Shelley), 144–146
Frazer, June M., 147
Frazer, Timothy C., 147

Georef, 113
Goldstein, Warren, 147
Good news letters, 313, 317–319
Goodwill
    in bad news letters, 317
    in good news letters, 317
Gopher, 136
Grant, Ulysses S., 154–157
Graphs, 409
Guided inquiry writing, in mathematics, 268–270
Gulliver's Travels (Swift), 99

Haight, Frank A., 186
Harris, Ian, 69–70
Harrison, Jim, 176–177
Heading
    of letter, 314
    of memo, 397–398
Health sciences
    ethical issues in, 370–380
    importance of communications in, 344–345, 355
    literature review in, 357–364
    observational analysis, 366–370
    patient records, 345–353
    responsibilities in, 345–353
    sample assignments in, 357, 358, 368, 375

sample literature reviews, 358–364
sample observational analysis, 368–369
sample writing on ethical issues, 371–380
Universal Resource Locators (URLs) for, 381
writing in, 356–380
Hearing before the Subcommittee on Asian and Pacific Affairs, 71–74
Hirsch, E. D., 64–67
History and culture studies, 100–101
Hoffmann, Roald, 218
Home pages, 136
Howard, Jay R., 166–172
Humanities
    critical interpretation essays, 162–178
    databases in, 101
    disciplines within, 142
    division between natural sciences and, 214–215
    drafting stage in writing, 151–154
    evidence in, 94–96
    example of major writing assignment in, 25–38
    history and culture studies, 100–101
    importance of communications in, 146–148
    personal interpretation in, 97–99, 142–146, 148, 154–161
    planning stage of writing, 149–151
    questions asked in, 96–101
    reading skills in, 148
    reconstructing and interpreting in, 148
    reflective and reconstructive writing, 97–100, 142–144, 148, 154–161
    research in, 83–85, 94–101
    responsibilities in, 144–146
    revision in writing, 153

sample assignments in, 84–85, 98, 158, 173
sample critical interpretation essays by professionals, 164–172
sample critical interpretation essay by student, 177–178
sample reflective and reconstructive essay by professional, 154–157
sample reflective and reconstructive essay by student, 158–161
Universal Resource Locators (URLs) for, 179
writing in, 149–179
Humanities Index, 101
Hypercard, 130
Hypermedia environment, 130–133
Hypertext, 130–133

Incidents in the Life of a Slave Girl (Jacobs), 95, 96
Indexes, 90
Industrial technology, definition of, 259
Informal learning logs, 273–275
Information technology. *See* Mathematics and information technology
Infotrack, 92
Inside address of letter, 314
Internal clues, in reading, 49
Internal memo, 398
Internet
    business and management, 340–341
    computer-supported writing, 121–124, 135–137, 139
    costs associated with, 128
    engineering and technology, 420
    health sciences, 381
    humanities, 179
    mathematics and information technology, 295

Internet (*continued*)
  natural sciences, 255
  researching, 91, 116–118, 122, 123
  social sciences, 212
Interoffice memo, 232–234
Interpretive writing in humanities, 97–99, 142–144, 148, 162–178
Introduction
  of progress reports in business, 321
  reading of, 50

Jacobs, Harriet, 95, 96
Journal critique paper, 242–249
Journal writing
  double-entry journal for analyzing text, 62–63
  exploration through, 19–21
  informal learning logs in computer science, 273–275
  in mathematics, 268–270

Laboratory, 103
Laboratory notebooks, 110, 238–240
Laboratory reports
  example of, 251–254
  in natural sciences, 87–88, 114–115, 249–255
  in social sciences, 103–104
Laboratory summary assignment, 236–238
Learning logs, 273–275
Lee, Robert E., 154–157
Letter writing
  in business and management, 301, 313–319
  client's confirmation of interest letter, 414
  in engineering and technology, 391
  in natural sciences to school class, 220–221

Library of Congress Subject Headings, The, 92
Library research
  computer searching and databases, 91–94, 101, 106, 113
  Internet, 91, 116–118, 123
  locating books and articles using computers, 91–92, 101, 106, 113
  Proquest, 93–94, 101
  reference area, 89–91
Library research reports, 104, 106, 188–195
Liebow, Elliot, 186
Life sciences, 109. *See also* Natural sciences
Lindsay, R. C. L., 186, 190–192
Ling, Amy, 142
Listing and branching, 18–19
Listservs, 122, 132–133
Literature review
  guidelines for, 364
  in health sciences, 357–364
  in natural sciences, 113–114
  in social sciences, 190–192

Magazine Index, 92, 93
Management. *See* Business and management
Mathematical Association of America, 20, 268
Mathematics and information technology
  definition of, 258–259
  disciplines within, 260
  importance of communications in, 261–262
  journals and guided inquiry writing in mathematics courses, 268–270
  responsibilities in, 258–261
  short written responses in mathematics courses, 264–268
  Universal Resource Locators (URLs) for, 295
  writing in, 263–272

McGuinness, Christine, 387–388
Medline, 364–365
Memos
  in business and management, 300–301, 303–312
  engineering and technology, 391, 395–399
  internal memo, 398
  in natural sciences, 232–234
Message encryption devices, 126
Microbiological Abstracts, 113
MLA. *See* Modern Language Association (MLA)
MLA International Bibliography, 101
Modern Language Association (MLA), 145, 153
Moral problems in health sciences, 370–380
Mosaic, 136

National Newspaper Index, 92, 93
National Security Agency (NSA), 126
Natural sciences
  databases in, 113
  disciplines within, 109
  division between humanities and, 214–215
  evidence in, 111–112
  formatting scientific writing, 229–232
  group collaboration systems and presentation facilities, 123
  Hoffmann's definition of science, 218
  importance of communications in, 217–218
  journal critique paper, 242–249
  laboratory notebooks, 110, 238–240
  laboratory reports, 114–115, 249–255
  laboratory summary assignment, 236–238

letter writing to school class, 220–221

literature review, 113–114

microtheme, 240–242

occupations entered by persons with majors in, 215–216

personal involvement minimized in, 111

precise measurements in, 111

questions asked in, 112–115

research in, 87–88, 109–115

responsibilities in, 215–216

sample assignments in, 87–88, 240–244

sample journal critique paper, 245–249

sample laboratory report, 251–254

Universal Resource Locators (URLs) for, 255

workplace memo, 232–234

writing to expert audiences, 222–229

writing of professional scientists, 219–234

writing in undergraduate natural sciences, 235–254

New York Times Index, 93, 101

Newsgroups, 122, 132–134

Ninos, Joel, 358–361

NSA. *See* National Security Agency (NSA)

Observational analysis, in health sciences, 366–370

Observational report, in social sciences, 103, 195–198

One from None (Rollins), 166, 173, 177–178

On-line computer catalogs, 91–92

Organization

AIDA method, 214–215

definition of, 24

of formal engineering report, 404

in humanities writing, 152

of letters, 314

of memos, 311, 397–398

of recommendation report, 322–323

of scientific writing, 229–232

Outliners, 129–130, 132

Outlining, in humanities writing, 152

PAIS, 106

Paraphrase

definition of, 70

documentation of, 85

example of, 70

Participant/observer method, in social sciences, 182, 184

Patient records, 345–353

Personal interpretation, in humanities, 97–99, 142–46, 148, 154–161

Personal observation report, 103, 195–198

Philosophical ideas, 99–100, 142–144

Physical sciences, 109. *See also* Natural sciences

Physics Abstracts, 113

Pie charts, 409

Plagiarism, 85

Planning stage

in humanities writing, 149–151

of writing process, 17–24, 25–29

Planning through exploration, 18

Political scientists, 182. *See also* Social sciences

Pollitt, Katha, 50–53, 68

Polsky, Ned, 196, 201–211

Postreading, 42

Prereading, 42

Previewing, in reading, 48–49

Privacy issues, and computer-supported writing, 125–126

Programming and documenting, 275–280

Progress reports, 321–322, 398–399

Proposals

in engineering and technology, 391

Request for Proposals, 315–317

Proquest, 93–94, 101

Psychlit, 106, 190, 192

Psychologists, 182. *See also* Social sciences

Public Affairs Information Service (PAIS), 106

Public writing. *See* Writing in the disciplines; Writing process

Qualitative research, 102, 185–187

Quantitative research, 102, 185–187

Quantitative research reports, 107–108

Questions

in humanities, 96–101

in natural sciences, 112–115

in social sciences, 105–108

Quotations, documentation of, 85

Radio Days, 99

Readers' Guide to Periodical Literature, 92, 93

Reading in the disciplines

analysis of text, 59–67

annotating for critical reading, 60–61

annotating for understanding and recall, 56–57

broad definition of, 41

for comprehension, 43–57

context clues in, 49

critical reading, 44, 59–79

critique of, 71

double-entry journal for analyzing text, 62–63

evaluating a text, 67–68

external clues in, 48–49

humanities, 148

internal clues in, 49

introduction and conclusion for main points and purpose, 50

on-line reading, 126–128

Reading in the disciplines (*continued*)
overview of reading process, 9, 40–41
paraphrase of, 70
postreading, 42
prereading, 42
as process, 42–44
purposes of, 42–44
responding to a text, 69–79
skimming, 48–49
summary of, 69–70
synthesis of, 75–76
textual features and, 50, 54–56
topic sentences, 54–55
underlying assumptions for, 40
understanding what is read, 45–57
World Wide Web reading strategies, 136–137
Recommendation reports in business, 322–339
Reconstructive and reflective writing in humanities, 148, 154–161
Reference area/room, 89–91
Reflective writing in humanities, 99–100, 142–144, 148, 154–61
Rejection letters, 313, 316–318
Report writing
application of theory report, 103–104, 199–211
business and management reports, 321–339
in different disciplines, 5–6, 12–13
field report, 103
formal engineering report, 391, 400–419
laboratory reports, 14–15, 87–88, 103–104, 249–255
language usage in, 406–409
library research reports, 104, 106, 188–195
observational report, 103, 195–198
personal observation report, 103, 195–198

progress reports, 321–322, 398–399
quantitative research reports, 107–108
recommendation reports in business, 322–339
visuals in, 230, 409–413
Request for Proposals
cover letter for, 315–316
rejection letters concerning, 316–317
Research report. *See* Report writing
Researching in the disciplines
assumptions underlying, 82
humanities, 83–85, 94–101
Internet, 91, 116–118, 123
library research, 89–94
natural sciences, 87–88, 109–115
plagiarism and, 85
qualitative research, 102
quantitative research, 102
skills required to perform, 83–88
social sciences, 85–87, 101–108
as stage of writing process, 26, 82–117
Universal Resource Locators (URLs), 116–118
Responding to a text, 69–79
Review of current literature. *See* Literature review
Reviews, 90
Revising stage
in computer-supported writing, 121
guidelines for, 31
in humanities writing, 153
of writing process, 26, 31
Rheingold, Howard, 122
Rollins, Henry, 166, 173, 177–178
Ruoff, A., 142

Salutation of letter, 314
Science Abstracts, 113

Sciences. *See* Natural sciences; Social sciences
Serials, 90–93
Shelley, Mary, 144–146
Signals in writing, 48–49, 150
Simon, Paul, 384
"Sincerest Flattery, The" (Easterbrook), 77–79
Skimming, in reading, 48–49
"Smurfette Principle" (Pollitt), 50–53, 68
Snow, C. P., 214
Social sciences
application of theory report, 199–211
disciplines in, 101–102, 182
evidence in, 103–104
field research in, 103, 185–186
importance of communications in, 188
library research reports, 104, 106, 188–195
literature review, 190–192
methods used in, 182–184
participant/observer method in, 182, 184
personal observation report, 103, 195–198
qualitative research in, 185–187
quantitative research in, 185–187
quantitative research reports, 107–108
questions asked in, 105–108
research in, 85–87, 101–108
responsibilities in, 185–187
sample assignments in, 85–87, 189–190, 196
sample library research report, 192–193
sample personal observation report, 196–198
statistical method in, 183–187
survey/interview method in, 182–186
Universal Resource Locators (URLs) for, 212
writing in, 188–212
Sociofile, 106

Sociological theories, application of, 103–104, 199–211
Sociologists, 182. *See also* Social sciences
Spelling checkers, 121, 127
Sredl, Michael J., 222–229
Statistical method, in social sciences, 183–187
Storyspace, 130, 131, 133
Streetcar Named Desire (Williams), 199–200
Style, definition of, 25
Style analyzers, 121, 127–128
Summary
　definition of, 69
　documentation of, 85
　examples of, 69–70, 189–190
　executive summary in formal engineering reports, 406–407
Supreme Court Reporter, The, 106
Surveillance, 125–126
Survey/interview method, in social sciences, 182–186
Swift, Jonathan, 99
Synchronous conferencing software, 133–135
Synthesis
　definition of, 75
　steps in writing, 75–76

Technology. *See* Engineering and technology
Text analysis, 59–67
Textual features, and reading, 50, 54–56
Theoretical text, in humanities, 97
Thesis, definition of, 24
Thesis statement, 151
Thoreau, Henry David, writing assignment on, 27–38
Time-stamping devices, 126
Toolbook, 130
Topic sentences, reading of, 54–55
Two Cultures, The (Snow), 214

Understanding, reading for, 45–57
Unity, definition of, 24
Universal Resource Locators (URLs)
　business and management, 340–341
　computer-supported writing, 139
　definition of, 116, 136
　engineering and technology, 420
　health sciences, 381
　humanities, 179
　mathematics and information technology, 295
　natural sciences, 255
　research sources, 116–118
　social sciences, 212
University classes, computer access to, 124
URLs. *See* Universal Resource Locators (URLs)
Using Writing to Teach Mathematics, 20, 268

Values
　cultural values, 3–5
　of writing after college, 5
Vindication of the Rights of Woman, A (Wollstonecraft), 98
Virtual communities, 122
Visuals
　in formal engineering report, 409–413
　in scientific writing, 230

WAIS, 135–136
Walden (Thoreau), writing assignment on, 27–38
Wall Street Journal Index, 93
Ward, Jerry W., Jr., 142
West's Law Review, 106
Wide Area Information Service (WAIS), 135–136

Williams, Tennessee, 199–200
Wishart, Ronald, 71–74
Wollstonecraft, Mary, 98
Word-processing packages, 129–132. *See also* Computer-supported writing
Wordsworth, Dorothy, 158–161
Workplace memo, 232–234
Worland, Rick, 142
World Wide Web (WWW), 116–118, 136–137, 139
Writing in the disciplines. *See also* Computer-supported writing; Writing process; *and specific disciplines*
　business and management, 305–339
　characteristics of, 8
　as collaborative endeavor, 10
　computer sciences and decision science, 272–295
　critical thinking and, 10–14, 59
　cultural values in different culture, 3–7
　definition of disciplinary culture, 6–7
　engineering and technology, 387–419
　fundamentals of writing process, 16–32
　goals of, 7
　guiding assumptions for, 2–3
　health sciences, 356–380
　humanities, 149–179
　mathematics and information technology, 263–272
　natural sciences, 219–255
　report writing in different disciplines, 5–6, 12–13
　social sciences, 188–212
　typical writing assignments in college, 15
　value of writing after college, 5
　writing as process, 8–10
　writing process applied to, 15–16
Writing process. *See also* Computer-supported writing; Writing in the

Writing process (*continued*)
disciplines; *and specific disciplines*
applied to writing in the disciplines, 15–16
critiquing stage of, 26, 30–31
and development of knowledge and understanding, 17
drafting stage of, 24–25, 26, 29–30, 31, 151–154

editing stage of, 26, 31
example of major writing assignment, 25–38
fundamentals of, 16–32
guidelines on, 16–17
as manageable, 16–17
overview of, 8–10
planning stage of, 17–24, 25–29, 149–151
as recursive process, 17

researching stage of, 26, 82–117
revising stage of, 26, 31, 153
stages of, 16–32
WWW. *See* World Wide Web (WWW)

Youra, Steven, 387–388